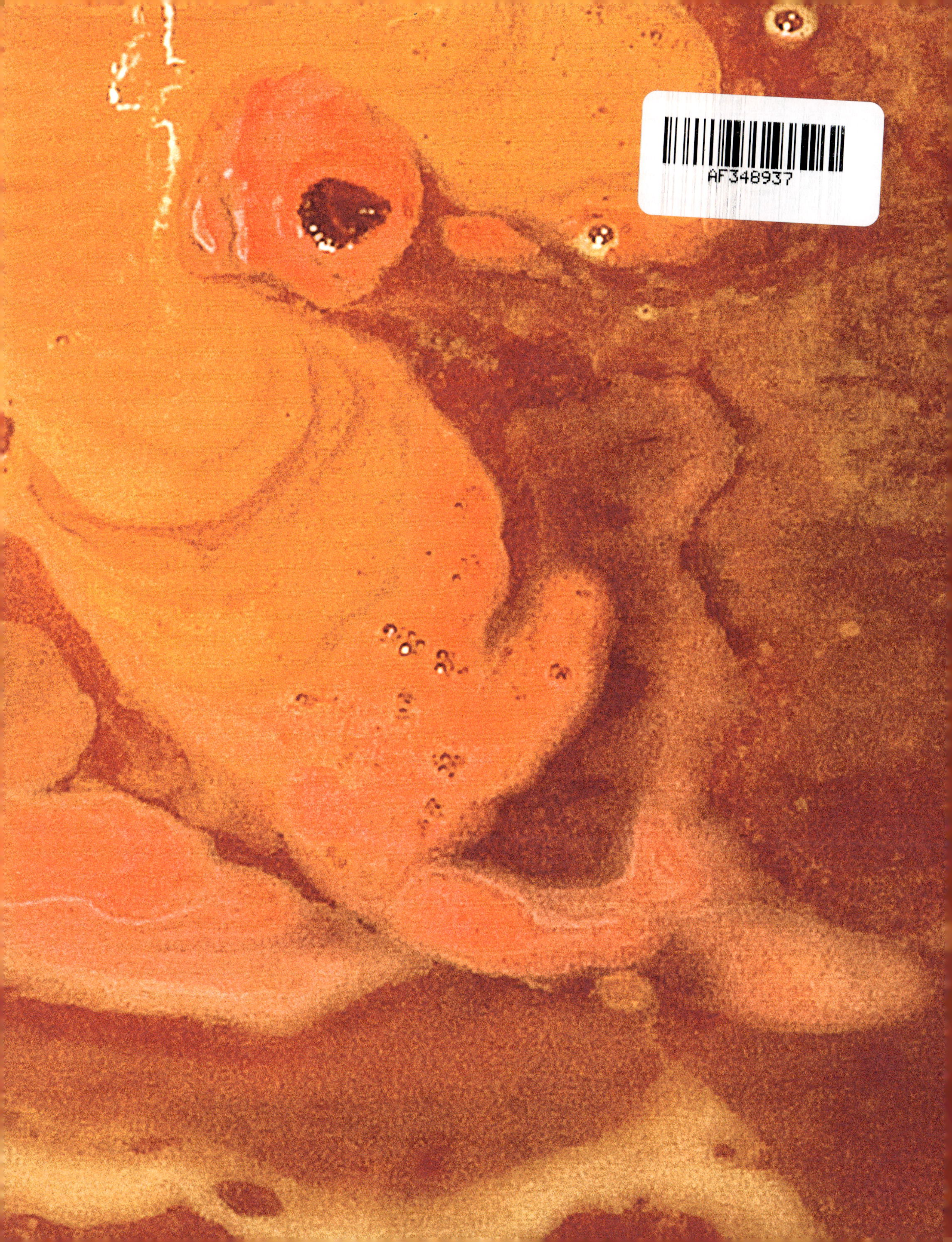
AF348937

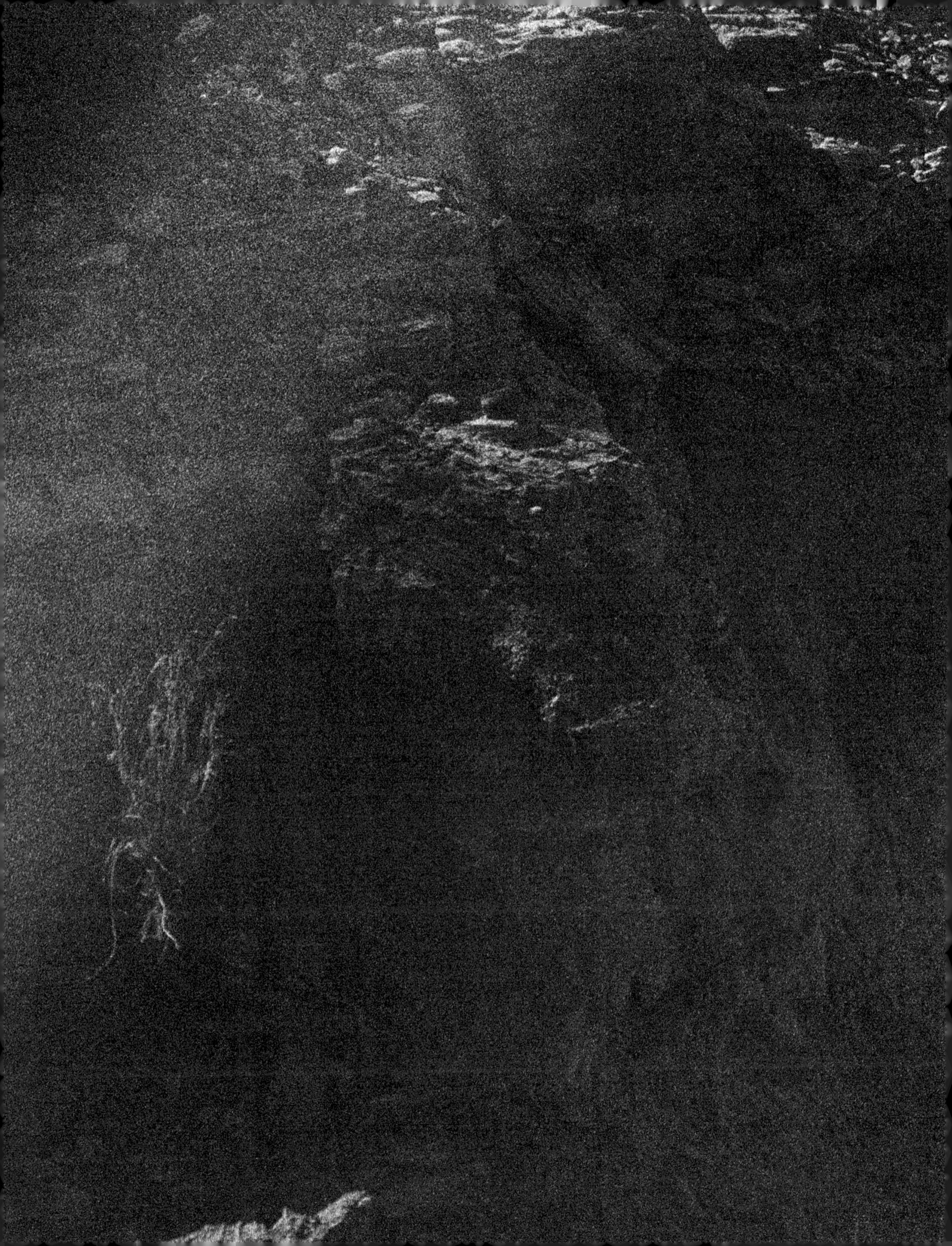

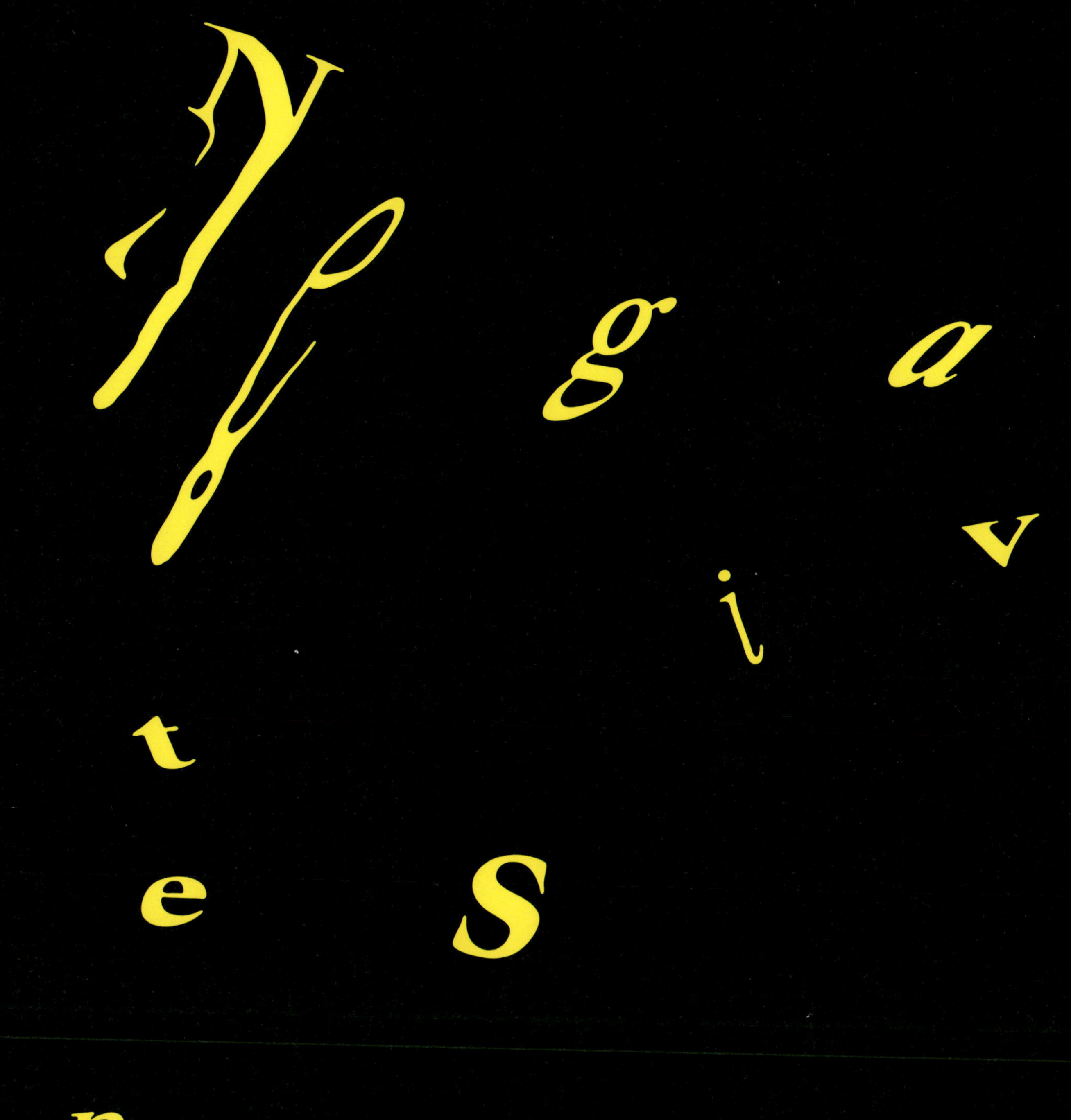

Negative Space
a.k. burns

A.K. BURNS

NEGATIVE SPACE

EDITED BY KAREN KELLY
& BARBARA SCHROEDER

CONTRIBUTIONS BY
MEL Y. CHEN, CACONRAD,
ARUNA D'SOUZA,
MEGAN HICKS, &
SIMONE WHITE

CONVERSATION
WITH KAREN ARCHEY

DANCING FOXES PRESS
BROOKLYN, NEW YORK
IN ASSOCIATION WITH
WEXNER CENTER FOR THE ARTS

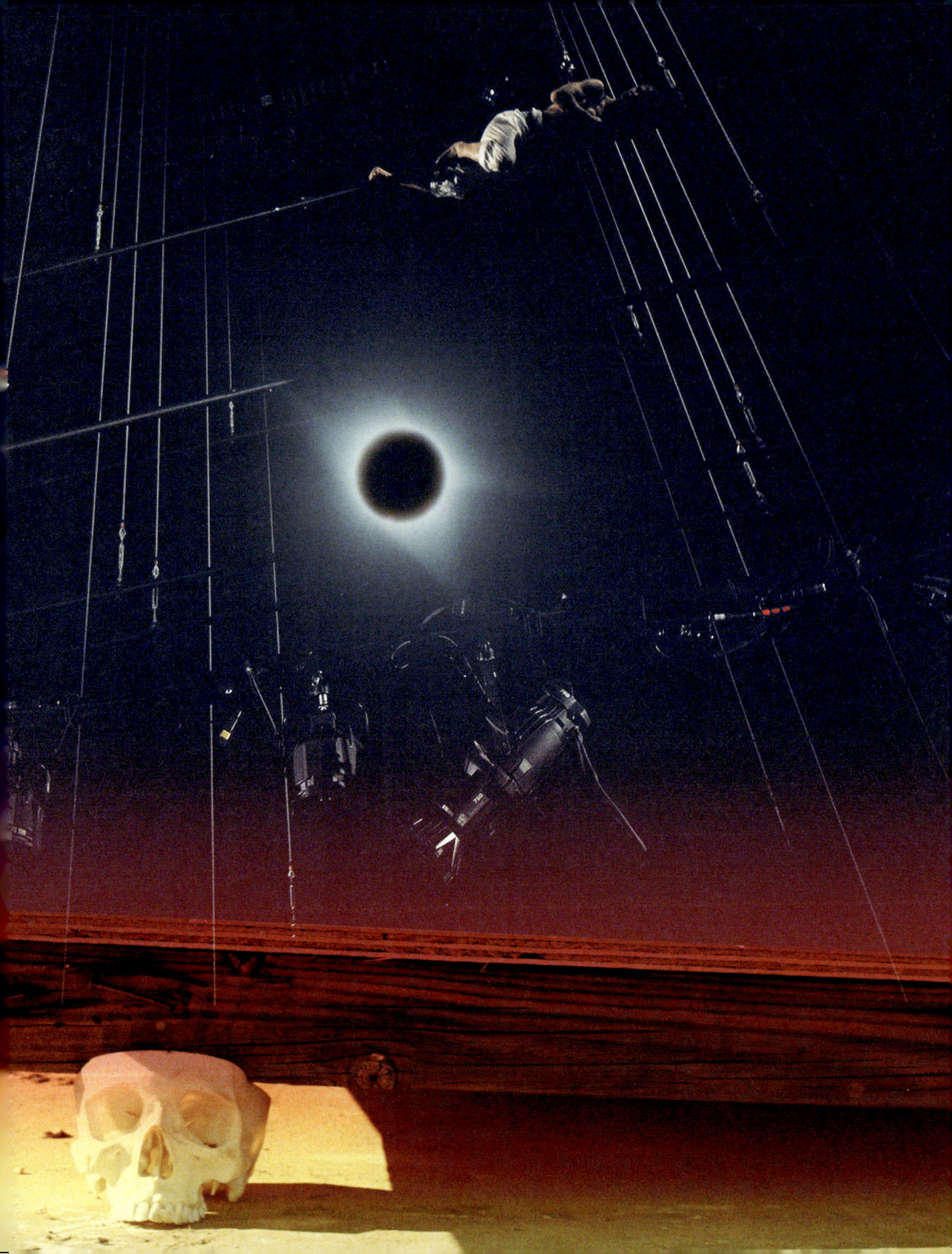

Raised in Northern California during the drought of the late 1980s, A.K. Burns has long been engaged with questions of ecological crisis and materiality and the interrogation of value systems. Burns's interest is further enhanced by her examination of bodies—in all their multiplicity—in relation to technology, capitalism, and the extraction of resources.

This publication brings together all parts of Burns's science-fiction epic *Negative Space*. Encompassing allegory, art history, philosophy, and current events, *Negative Space* comprises a cycle of four interrelated multimedia installations. Presented together for the first time in 2023 at the Wexner Center for the Arts, each installation examines an essential physical system: void, body, land, and water. *A Smeary Spot (NSO) (2015),* the opening to the cycle, counters the common misconception that the void is an empty space to be occupied and instead privileges the vital metaphor as undefinable and limitless. The second work, *Living Room (NSOO) (2017),* examines various conceptions of the body and humanity's challenge to maintain sanity and subsistence, while *Leave No Trace (NSOOO) (2019)* studies land use with a series of vignettes in which performers resist containment and categorization. The fourth work, *What is Perverse is Liquid (NSOOOO) (2023),* commissioned by the Wexner Center, explores the subjects of water and death, highlighting themes of transmission and transition. *Negative Space* places the viewer in what the artist calls a "speculative present," an imagined moment where boundaries are permeable and hierarchies are thrown into question. Poetic in nature, *Negative Space* presents a layered, surreal narrative in which the environment is the protagonist and performers act as concepts.

Anchoring the publication, Aruna D'Souza's essay introduces us to Burns's focus on queer world-building in *Negative Space* through investigations of history, gender, language, and borders. Next, and led by Burns's interest in collective thinking, the artist invited four writers to reflect on the physical system that structures each work. Poet Simone White addresses the sensations, perceptions, and shifting qualities of the void; scholar Mel Y. Chen considers philosophies of the body across the spectrums of absence and presence, the material and immaterial; scholar Megan Hicks explores her personal relationship with the land as an archaeologist by excavating the cultural memories of Black earths; and poet CAConrad contemplates the necessity and fragility of our water sources through a series of short poems. Interwoven throughout is a sequential interview with Burns by curator Karen Archey that focuses on the four works that compose *Negative Space* while collectively exploring the making of the multiyear project. This compilation of texts and images highlights how Burns's practice aims to resist fixity and instead advocate for a continuous state of becoming. In a political moment where the expression of boundaries and the fate of bodies are in question, this publication offers a contrasting vision of affinity and coexistence.

Kelly Kivland, Head of Exhibitions, Wexner Center for the Arts
Gaëtane Verna, Executive Director, Wexner Center for the Arts

← *Negative Space Poster* (recto), 2019. Offset-printed poster, edition of 500, 23⅜ × 33⅛ inches (59.4 × 84.1 cm)

...ETE INDEX OF 'INTRA-ACTION'S

PROTAGONISTS

LAND/SCAPE

THE 'FUTURE' IS LIGHTWEIGHT + FAST
ACCELERATIONISM

WATER

BODY

ABILITY

DEPENDANT

...IAL/SOCIETY

BEING
ONTOLOGY
PRESENCE
SELF DETERMINATION

TERESTRIAL
GRAVITY
MASS
ROCK/DIRT/SAND
SOIL/EARTH
FOUNDATION

POSES
CONTROL

ISOLATIONISM?

PROPERTY
(MONEY/ECONOMY)

ANTI GRAVITY
FLUID
(CONTINUOUS) MOVEMENT
AMORPHOUS

STATES: GAS/LIQU...

BOTTLED → CONTAC...

LEAKY — ATTEMPT TO F... AT...

...DER
X → BIO
...RODUCTION
...BOR
...ATER"

SEPRATISM

INTENTIONAL
COMMUNITY

DAM

GENERATORS

BIRTH
DEATH (VULNERABILITY)

BORDERS
TERRITORY
FENCE/WALLS
TRESSPASS → PASSING

POLITICAL AGENCY THRU SMALLER SOCIAL UNIT
PARTICULATE

GENDER

FAIL
AT CONVINCING (PERFORMANCE)
TO MEET SOCIAL IDEALS

SHIFTING LIFE (DEPE...
CONDI...
ARI...
DESE...
DROU...

CONDITIONAL / TRANSITION / OPERATION

...VE

...TIVE
(PHYTOSAPIEN)
POSTHUMANISM

ACCESS

PASS (OPERATION)

IDENTIFICATION

CLOUD
SEEDING

RAW
MATERIAL

FLOO...
TSU...
MON...
TYP...

DR...

SEEDS
(EGGS?)
POLLIN

POSTHUMAN

CONSTRUCTION → COMPOSITION

PLANTS
(INTER SEXED
INTER SPECIES)

SI...
F...

C...

DECAY / ROT / DECOMPOSE / COMPOST

TEMPORALITY
(CHANGE) → CONSTANT CHANGE

DECAY

ICONIC /
...CENTRIC

To Think and Feel a Then and There: A.K. Burns's *Negative Space*

Aruna D'Souza

Queerness is not yet here. Queerness is an ideality. Put another way, we are not yet queer, but we can feel it as the warm illumination of a horizon imbued with potentiality. We have never been queer, yet queerness exists for us as an ideality that can be distilled from the past and used to imagine a future. The future is queerness's domain. Queerness is a structuring and educated mode of desiring that allows us to see and feel beyond the quagmire of the present. The here and now is a prison house. We must strive, in the face of the here and now's totalizing rendering of reality, to think and feel a then and there.

—José Esteban Muñoz, *Cruising Utopia*

← *Untitled (Negative Space mind map)*, 2013 (detail). Permanent marker on paper; 36 × 102 inches (91.4 × 259.1 cm)

After a year of Zoom calls with A.K. Burns, reading about her work, delving into the writings she draws on in her art, and watching her films, I sat down to put my thoughts into essay form. It was November 20, 2022, Transgender Day of Remembrance—and, in a devastating reminder of what needs to be remembered, the day of the mass murder at Club Q, an LGBTQIA+ venue in Colorado Springs. I want to thank A.K. for giving me the opportunity that day and in the days following to think about queer futurity—a possibility and potential that exists beyond the limits of our terrible world, if only we would find a way to understand our place in that world differently.

1 José Esteban Muñoz, *Cruising Utopia: The Then and There of Queer Futurity* (New York: New York University Press, 2009), 1.

2 A.K. Burns, "Scripting *A Smeary Spot*," interview by Melissa Ragain, *Art Journal*, December 8, 2017, https://artjournal.collegeart.org/?p=9381.

José Esteban Muñoz's words could well be understood as the conceptual program for A.K. Burns's *Negative Space,* a series of four video installations created between 2015 and 2023—*A Smeary Spot (NS0), Living Room (NS00), Leave No Trace (NS000),* and *What is Perverse is Liquid (NS0000)*—combining moving image, sculpture, and built environment. Muñoz describes queerness not as an identity but as a potentiality that exists when the limits of the present—the horizon—are legible in all their mundanity, mendacity, and violence. It is a utopian hope for what lies beyond that horizon. "Queerness is that thing," Muñoz writes, "that lets us feel that this world is not enough, that indeed something is missing."[1]

Like Muñoz, Burns proposes thinking otherwise about time, matter, and our imbrication in both. Each of the four works stands alone yet links in myriad ways to its companions. Together, they trace a world in which normative hierarchies are fully jettisoned, a world that seems to be hovering in the future at the same time as being fully enfolded in the present and drawing upon the past. They are strange enough to be science fiction and familiar enough to be its sibling, speculative fiction—they take place in a future present, a present that could be. "My vision for an alternative future is created through this space, of what I call 'the speculative present,'" says Burns, "in which we perceive, create, perform, and are completely different."[2]

Boundlessness

The title of the cycle is *Negative Space,* a term used by art historians to denote the area around a depicted figure (animate or inanimate), whether in painting or sculpture—the emptiness or void against which the object of our attention stands in relief. It is the space beyond—where there are no aesthetics, where nothing happens, where there is no meaning. It is the Other of the material world. There is no end to negative space; no border defines it. Yes, in a painting, negative space is delimited by the edges of the canvas, but make the canvas bigger and negative space expands, even as the figure remains the same.

But what if that emptiness were not an absence of meaning but its very possibility—the space of potential; a generative space, akin to Muñoz's "warm illumination" at (or beyond) the horizon, in which new worlds can be created? In other words, what if the void were our collective queer future? And what if we didn't stand apart from our environment but were made from it? What if we were not agents who acted on our environment but existed as its condition or by-product?[3] What if entities (including us humans) were constituted out of infinite intrarelationships, inseparable from everything else—what would negative space even mean in such a conception, where thingness falls away, where materiality has no Other? It is an antihumanist, or at least posthumanist, idea, to be sure, that we are woven into the surface of the world (or the surface of meaning) rather than distinct from it—that the world is not simply a backdrop to our performances of gender, politics, and relations. Burns asks us to imagine such a boundless realm of existence.

The subtitles of the *Negative Space* installations underline the idea of the void: they are not called *NS01, NS02, NS03, NS04,* but *NSO, NSOO, NSOOO, NSOOOO.* This naming strategy suggests that one work does not build on the last to create an accumulation or a structure, but rather that together they expand outward, endlessly, the succession of zeroes signifying an ever-increasing lack (nothingness) and infinitude (the endlessness of the loop).

The mind map for *Negative Space,* which hangs on the wall of Burns's studio, lays out that seeming contradiction—negative space or nothingness as a space of infinite possibility. Across the top, BODY, LAND/SCAPE, WATER, POWER/SUN, VOID, and again BODY: the overarching themes of the video cycle. Each of these is the summa and the limit of our existence, each is a horizon. The body is the signifier of our being and our eventual mortality. The landscape extends ever outward in a manner that seems beyond comprehension, at least in relation to the scale of our body; it also offers us the means to survive. Water is a condition of being, a foundational necessity for human existence. The sun is that star that makes life on Earth possible—and potentially impossible; the latter is on our collective mind now as we face the disastrous effects of the warming of our planet. The void is that space that allows us, or perhaps coerces us, to distinguish self from nonself.

In her drawing, Burns literally maps connections between these terms, considering the body and the landscape together to

3 Karen Barad's posthumanist notion of "agential realism" is central to Burns's thinking in *Negative Space.* Barad introduces the idea as follows: "To be entangled is not simply to be intertwined with another, as in the joining of separate entities, but to lack an independent, self-contained existence. Existence is not an individual affair. Individuals do not preexist their interactions; rather, individuals emerge through and as part of their entangled intra-relating. Which is not to say that emergence happens once and for all, as an event or as a process that takes place according to some external measure of space and of time, but rather that time and space, like matter and meaning, come into existence, are iteratively reconfigured through each intra-action, thereby making it impossible to differentiate in any absolute sense between creation and renewal, beginning and returning, continuity and discontinuity, here and there, past and future." Karen Barad, preface to *Meeting the Universe Halfway: Quantum Physics and the Entanglement of Matter and Meaning* (Durham, NC: Duke University Press, 2007), ix. The ontological condition Barad describes is, at root, a refusal of the humanist, art historical idea of negative space, because it rejects the idea of a thing that is bounded and separate from what is around it.

contemplate the concept of being. Linking landscape to water leads Burns to property—an unsurprising connection to draw in a country where land has obsessively been privatized, in which water rights are bought and sold out from under us, in which people are unhoused (deprived of land) and lack drinkable water. Water and power together prompt "resources"—a thing as elemental as water becomes a resource when someone or something controls it. "Consumption→construction→composition" reads one vector in the diagram. "Decay/rot/decompose/compost" reads another. Borders and dams, leaks and criminals show up in Burns's chart, which is larger than the photograph I have of it. It extends past the frame.

Such boundlessness is intrinsic to the world of *Negative Space*, a vast work that resists narrativity and whose seemingly banal motifs only gradually reveal their interconnectedness and meanings. Each video is a loop; there is neither beginning nor end—indicators that are keys to conventional storytelling—and the human actors are not characters but agents, catalysts, concepts, no more or less important than the props or environments in which they play their roles.

Another sense of boundlessness (a refusal of borders) emerges in the rejection of the distinction of medium. Burns insists that she is not a filmmaker but a sculptor, as evidenced by the care with which the works are presented in the gallery. Each setup is keyed carefully to the body of the viewer and their movements as they perambulate through the space or sit for a while and incorporates objects that appear in the films in a way that extends the projected space into our own, meshing the imaginative there and then and here and now. It would be wrong to think of these installations simply as tricked-out theaters, as screens that are embellished with sculptural set decorations. Rather, in every case, what we are seeing is sculpture to which Burns has added the element of time via the moving image, which unmoors the punctuality of the three-dimensional object.

All of this makes synopsizing the works difficult, but perhaps this will suffice at the outset:

• *A Smeary Spot* is set in a barren landscape (in southern Utah) and a black-box theater. Near-nude hikers squeeze life out of the desert (foraging, collecting water); we see the same figures in the black box wearing black shirts and jeans; Burns calls them Free Radicals, referring to the highly reactive particles that can attach themselves to and change the function of cells in the body—catalytic agents as likely to be destructive as productive. Another figure, Aunt Be/e, covered in bee pollen, busies themself with making and doing things with elements they salvage from a garbage heap on the floor. Mother Flawless, also known as Flawless Sabrina, the iconic drag persona of performer and activist Jack Doroshow, functions as a seer, a prognosticator who speaks of folding time so that we are not trapped in the dystopian present.[4] The script borrows words from different writers (Karen Barad, Simone de Beauvoir, T. S. Eliot, Guy Hocquenghem, and Ursula K. Le Guin among them), words Burns has edited, shaped, reused, refashioned, and repurposed. The script, that is, is a tissue of citations. Radio announcers (found audio clips, mostly from NPR) discussing survival

4 Jack Doroshow passed away on November 18, 2017; see https://www.nytimes.com/2017/11/30/obituaries/jack-doroshow-drag-pageant-impresario-dies-at-78.html.

strategies in the aftermath of Hurricane Sandy, disastrous news from the Supreme Court, and the refugee crisis can be heard in the background. The three channels of this video are projected onto seven-by-twelve-foot freestanding screens arranged in a row, forming a wall and a horizon line; a fourth, smaller screen positioned alongside and overlapping the others shows a continuous loop of credits. Rolling office chairs, artifacts of the work's filmic world, are arrayed in the room to serve as seating.

• *Living Room* maps the body onto a building, turning the structure into an organism, blurring the lines between animate and inanimate: the living room is the psyche, the stairwell the digestive tract, the bathroom the kidneys, the basement the uterus. (Note that the psyche is assigned as material a space as the baser parts of the corpus.) Three children per-forming as celestial bodies—Makemake, Pluto, and Eris, dwarf planets in our solar system—are dressed in jumpsuits to match the upholstery of the couch on which they clamber in the living room, gazing at a fish tank, sometimes scavenging pennies from inside. Two figures—the Pregnant Backpacker and Mx. Manning, the latter dressed in high heels and a military jacket with the name tag MANNING[5]—carry garbage down the stairs. A pair of figures—one in a bathtub and the other sitting alongside it—discuss the vagaries of language. In the basement, figures dance. Their black T-shirts are printed with large white letters: HER, AGAIN, OR BUST, NO—telegraphic but unmistakable references to the toxic rhetoric of the 2016 presidential election. The two channels of *Living Room* are projected on screens propped against the exposed studs of a not fully built wall, suggesting that the space itself is in the process of becoming; against another wall leans a piece of plasterboard. Nearby, the frame of a gutted couch, like the one the children sit on, glows with LED lights and is propped up by sculptures that look like sandbags.

• *Leave No Trace* follows a group of figures through a scrubby desert. They come across an abandoned trailer and scavenge for things—all the cupboards in the trailer are filled with skulls. They push a fish tank and a couch (echoes of *Living Room*) across the sand. They take apart the couch and with its components build a platform on which Go-Go Boi—oiled and wearing silver lamé hot pants and a jockstrap repurposed as a half-bra— dances. In another black-box theater, a performer clambers across scaf-folding and sings a song about technologically altered beings; someone vacuums in a smoky room. Mx. Manning appears again wandering through the landscape, trespassing on a military base at one point and finding ref-uge at another under the wheel well of a trailer while reciting a text about borderless sensation. The video is projected on the five exposed sides of a cube that sits on the floor, held up on one side by a human skull; an arch-way of stacked speakers stands nearby, casting its shadow like a sundial.

• *What is Perverse is Liquid* moves between three sites: a marshland, in which two figures in waders (the Swamp Sisters) call to each other in a birdlike language; an abandoned office building, in which three other figures (the children who represented dwarf planets in *Living Room*,

0   1   2

5 The jacket is suggestive of the former US soldier Chelsea Manning, who was convicted of leaking sensitive military information that confirmed reports of US drone strikes on civilians and journalists and who was imprisoned from 2010 until 2017, during which time she came out as trans. When *A Smeary Spot* was first shown, in 2015, Manning was still incarcerated. A replica of the military jacket appears in each of the *Negative Space* works and metaphorically represents the concept of "leaks." Sometimes it is worn by a performer, who, in these instances, represents Mx. Manning.

dressed similarly but markedly older, now teenagers) sit at desks in vast, nearly empty spaces, deliver full bottles of water and collect empty ones, answer phones, and type on obsolete computers; and a forest, in which the Pregnant Backpacker (we've seen her before) hikes, wearing little more than a T-shirt emblazoned with the words WITNESS PROTECTION PROGRAM. An owl flies through the office building; a skeleton twitches, dances, bangs at equipment it doesn't know how to use, and peers through mail slots. One figure tends to a plant growing in a plastic bag of soil by pouring water from a plastic bottle; another pulls wiring from the ceiling and strips it of copper. In a grotto-like space demarcated by concrete piers, a performer climbs out of the water and begins to play a piano and sing. Everywhere and at every point, water flows, falls from rock ledges, drips, and tinkles. Two channels of *What is Perverse is Liquid* are projected on seven-by-twelve-foot screens abutting each other in the corner of a room. In the center, a smaller, third screen shows the third channel (with the footage of the Swamp Sisters hooting in the marsh). A circular arrangement of sandbags functions as seating, half of it surrounding a "dry pool" and the other half a "wet pool" constructed from a reflective acrylic sheet on the floor, evoking the water repeatedly appearing in the film.

Waste Lands

Here is no water but only rock
Rock and no water and the sandy road
The road winding above among the mountains
Which are mountains of rock without water
If there were water we should stop and drink
Amongst the rock one cannot stop or think
Sweat is dry and feet are in the sand
If there were only water amongst the rock
Dead mountain mouth of carious teeth that cannot spit
Here one can neither stand nor lie nor sit

—T. S. Eliot, "The Waste Land"

The form and structure of *Negative Space*—via its multipart organization, refusal of narrative, and polyvocality—along with its themes evoke T. S. Eliot's "The Waste Land," a poem written in the aftermath of the Great War by someone who saw around him only death, decay, privation, and violence. A lamentation for the present and humanity's afflicted state, it understands dystopia not in the future but in the now. Eliot repeatedly invokes the name Tiresias, the blind prophet whose inner eye allows him to penetrate modernity's chimera to the graveyard beyond.

Negative Space is filled with wastelands and waste—but we must understand waste as defined only by its usefulness to capitalism, to production and reproduction, a specious standard. The spot in southern Utah where much of *A Smeary Spot* was filmed is public land. Historically tied up with settler colonialism in the United States, such lands were seized in the process of westward expansion. Over time, much of that territory has been reprivatized; what remains public is largely understood to be unproductive—useless for agriculture and other profit-based enterprises. *Leave No Trace* was made on private land in Joshua Tree that borders Little Baghdad, a military war-games base. *What is Perverse is Liquid* was shot in two sites that no longer serve their industrial purposes: a former IBM building in Kingston, New York, and a grotto-like cave in the abandoned Widow Jane Mine in Rosedale, New York, from which the raw materials for the cement used in the construction of the Statue of Liberty and the Brooklyn Bridge were excavated. Garbage—piled in the center of the black-box theater in *A Smeary Spot* and carried down the stairs in bags in *Living Room*—is everywhere.

In Eliot's "The Waste Land," the human condition is reflected in and understood via barren earth, expanses of rock and sand where there is no water to sustain life: "Dead mountain mouth of carious teeth that cannot spit/Here one can neither stand nor lie nor spit." But there are other ways to regard wasteland and to comprehend the continuity of body and landscape. There is Karen Barad's concept of "agential realism," in which all entities in the material world are seen to be interpenetrating. Consider the scene in *A Smeary Spot* in which an actor covers their face in mud: Burns has described the image as a moment where the face becomes a mountainous terrain, where the thinness of the line between animate and inanimate is revealed. "Rather than being in a place, she *is* the place."[6]

Natalie Diaz begins her poem "The First Water Is the Body" with a sentence whose pathos sneaks up on you: "The Colorado River is the most endangered river in the United States—also, it is part of my body."[7] The piece sets the Mojave idea of the continuity of all matter against the violence of settler colonialism; destructive damming of the river directly corresponds with the genocide of Native Americans over centuries. (Lake Powell, a site in *A Smeary Spot,* was created by one of those dams.) To kill the river is to kill the people: "If I say, *My river is disappearing,* do I also mean, *My people are disappearing?*"[8] And then, later, a line quoted, barely recognizably, emerging from the miasma of the Swamp Sisters' hoots in *What is Perverse is Liquid:* "Unsoothable thirst is one type of haunting."[9] We lay waste to landscapes and, in doing so lay waste to ourselves: "If the river is a ghost, am I?"[10] We turn ourselves into ghosts, like the skeleton that twitches around the office building or the figures who intently type away on technological relics in *What is Perverse is Liquid.*

But Diaz's poem signals something more urgent: that this land is not a void, it is replete. It is a place where life has happened, still happens, and—if we begin to honor our material continuity with it—will happen. Plants grow in even the most arid of Burns's filmic panoramas, bugs crawl and eat each other, and an owl inhabits a desolate building. In *Negative Space,* creatures—human and non—exist in inhospitable

6 Burns, interview by Ragain. The entanglement, here and elsewhere in the series, of body and environment, echoes in words uttered in *A Smeary Spot*: "As if knowing comes from an exterior point. I am not [an] outside observer of the world. Nor am I simply located at particular places *in* the world; rather, I am part *of* the world." The lines are an edited version of a passage in Barad's "Posthuman Performativity: Toward an Understanding of How Matter Comes to Matter," *Signs* 28, no. 3 (Spring 2003): 828, doi.org/10.1086/345321.

7 Natalie Diaz, "The First Water Is the Body," in *Postcolonial Love Poem* (Minneapolis, MN: Graywolf Press, 2020), 46.

8 Ibid., 48.

9 Ibid., 50.

10 Ibid.

environments. To see wastelands as a life source is to reject the capitalist idea of productivity or unproductivity, profitability or unprofitability. It is perhaps, for many who live outside the norms of mainstream society, the only place of survival. "What I love about the 'natural' world," says Burns, "is its insistence on persisting against all odds."[11] The wasteland, that is, can be a refuge, a place to build alternative worlds—worlds that, precisely and urgently, reject the ways in which this one operates.

In a 1978 interview, the queer filmmaker Jack Smith—who has been described as an "anarcho-nihilist, and a fetishist," and whose anti-institutional, anticultural, and antiauthoritarian work was rooted in a profound anticapitalism, offered his vision for how space could be organized to exceed the stultifying cubic regularity of American cities:

> I can think of other types of societies.... Like in the middle of the city should be a repository of objects that people don't want anymore, which they would take to this giant junkyard. That would form an organization, a way that the city would be organized ... the city organized around that. I think this center of unused objects and unwanted objects would become a center of intellectual activity. Things would grow up around it.... There could be exchange, that would start to develop. You take anything that you don't want and don't want to throw up [*sic*] and just take it to this giant place, and just leaving it and looking for something that you need.... Then things would form the way they always do around that.[12]

The image finds its way into Burns's video cycle: waste piles accrue and dissipate, as agents add and remove items to make things or do things. Making and doing, accumulation and consumption, don't follow a logic of capital here—what is done or created is often nonsense, the performance of productivity. Trash doesn't turn into treasure, the product is not greater than the sum of its parts. While surveying land—measuring, plotting, and dividing—is the prerequisite for turning it into property, the Obsurveyor in *A Smeary* Spot observes the land without actually appraising it. Another figure, Aunt Be/e, who represents "Re/productive Labor," stands covered in yellow dust (pollen?) at a table that seems to emerge from the pile of trash in the center of the black-box theater; they are a busy bee, photocopying discarded tennis shoes and putting all manner of things (organic and inorganic) into a juicer. Everything retrieved and used in this space goes back to that trash pile; it is at once origin and destination. One of the agents in *What is Perverse is Liquid* strings plastic bottles into a useless chain, while others type ineffectually on keyboards, pick up unplugged phones, and bang on or fiddle with equipment to produce nothing but racket. The Pregnant Backpacker never gives birth. Free Radicals in the basement (the uterus) of *Living Room* dance with headlamps on, the words on their T-shirts never coalescing into sense.

11 A.K. Burns, note to the author, December 10, 2022.

12 Jack Smith, "Uncle Fishhook and the Sacred Baby Poo-Poo of Art," *Semiotext(e)* 3, no. 2 (1978): 199.

None of this is a waste of time, of course; time is only wasted if measured and assigned monetary value, like a wage. *Negative Space* conjures immeasurable kinds of time—geological, cosmological. Forms of time that are vast, beyond our ability to count.

Scavenging

What seems to stand in opposition to productivity, in Burns's work, is survival. The Free Radicals in *A Smeary Spot* employ survivalist tactics to glean drinking water; the dwarf planets in *Living Room* fish pennies out of a fish tank; one of the figures in *What is Perverse is Liquid* strips wires for copper. Scavenging, a widespread activity in the world of *Negative Space*, points to a common trope in postapocalyptic science fiction and speculative fiction: people find themselves without the ordinary tools and resources they need to survive, so must use their wits and instincts to find alternatives. They are forced to come to terms with their codependency and coexistence with their environment, however bleak.

It's impossible not to think here of Lauren Oya Olamina, the protagonist of Octavia E. Butler's 1993 novel, *Parable of the Sower,* who both revives ancestral and Indigenous knowledge (turning acorns into bread, for example) and learns contemporary skills to navigate a world plagued by drought, violence, a destructive pharmaceutical industry, and the privatization of everything—the collapse of the world in late-stage capitalism, in short. (Though Butler insisted the book was not prophetic, it's nearly impossible not to see our current world in hers, sketched thirty years ago.)[13] Lauren lives in a reality rife with racism and misogyny; she and a band of co-travelers, all of whom have left increasingly precarious situations, recognize that to survive they must create a reality with new forms of sociality and relationships. To envision this new approach to being (Lauren calls it a religion), they scavenge from a variety of sources, including the Bible and various other forms of lore and myth, reinterpreting and reimagining their lessons. *Parable of the Sower* haunts *Negative Space*—especially with respect to its world-building out of the detritus of the past. The terms *construction*, *deconstruction*, and *reconstruction* often operate literally in Burns's opus—for example, with the partially built walls and stripped couch of the *Living Room* installation and the fabrication of a dance platform out of the remains of the couch in *Leave No Trace*.

Leakage

In *Negative Space*, Burns uses art history to present history not as a given, a substrate, or background to the present, but as material from which to concoct new ways of being through reorganization. In each work, Burns recasts a canonical artwork to undermine the original's idea of power and difference. The Shapeshifter in *A Smeary Spot* appears as Édouard Manet's *Olympia* (1863), the controversial sensation of the Paris Salon of 1865. Manet's transgression was that he refused to honor the politesse surrounding the nineteenth-century Parisian courtesan, whose airs and elegances were meant to obscure the fact that she

13 Abby Aguirre, "Octavia Butler's Prescient Vision of a Zealot Elected to 'Make America Great Again,'" *New Yorker,* July 26, 2017.

was a woman and commodity in one; he pictured a prostitute fully and frankly in control of her own body and price. Burns's Olympia—who lies on a pile of air mattresses instead of white linens and whose sexual characteristics are supplied (or perhaps reiterated, as the wearer's body is not in question) by a flesh-colored suit—takes further command of her body. Channeling Guy Hocquenghem, she speaks of herself as a "future woman" who refuses to fulfill the reproductive role offered to her: "Oh! To be a woman, to be fertile, to be cunt-ile, rather than feeling the capitalist desire to impregnate! I know I am ranting."

In *Living Room*, a turbaned character in a bathtub who puzzles over the postsemantic condition of language is Marat, the French revolutionary martyr whose death was famously depicted by Jacques-Louis David. In Burns's revision, Marat dies not at the hands of the historical assassin Charlotte Corday but from, according to the artist, "economic toxicity."[14]

In *What is Perverse is Liquid,* it is Marcel Duchamp's ghost who appears when the Pregnant Backpacker stops during a hike in the woods and lies down with legs splayed. With his installation *Étant donnés: 1. La chute d'eau, 2. Le gaz d'éclairage (Given: 1. The Waterfall, 2. The Illuminating Gas)* (1946–66), Duchamp invited the viewer to look through a peephole at an inert (dead, sleeping, animate or inanimate?) body in a diorama-like space; she is female, though her genitals are not clearly so. In Burns's film, the dancing skeleton likewise peeks through empty mail slots and other peepholes, but when the camera offers up the spread-legged view of the naked backpacker, the skeleton's (and our) gaze is obliterated by eye-piercing reflections from a mirror wielded by the backpacker.

In *Leave No Trace*, the figure dancing on the platform in the desert directly references Felix Gonzalez-Torres's *Untitled (Go-Go Dancing Platform)* (1991), a wooden stage on which a man dressed in a silver lamé bikini and running shoes dances for five minutes on each day the work is on view (no one knows which five minutes—his performance is unscheduled and unannounced). The dancer wears a Sony Walkman, so the rhythms that propel his body are known only to him. He is on display but retains a kind of opacity, dancing to his own tune. Unlike the dancer in *Untitled*, who is legibly cisgendered, the dancer in *Leave No Trace* is gender nonconforming, an intentional rejection of Gonzalez-Torres's binary conception. This is not the only recollection of a work by Gonzalez-Torres in *Negative Space*: a stack of posters, reminiscent of many Gonzalez-Torres's sculptures, with the script for Burns's film is offered to viewers in the installation of *A Smeary Spot*; in the film itself, a headless figure drops wrapped sweets—the kind that Gonzalez-Torres spilled into his iconic piles of candy—into a blue military helmet. The same confections are embedded in the bags of topsoil that prop up the neon-lit couch in the installation of *Living Room* and sit at the foot of the half-constructed walls that surround it.

Burns understands gender, too—perhaps above all—as a form of bricolage. The Shapeshifter in *A Smeary Spot* is constantly at their toilette, intoning lines from Hocquenghem's *The Screwball Asses,* a treatise on polymorphic desire that eschews all labels and categorizations

14 A.K. Burns, conversation with the author, February 11, 2023.

and seems to suggest that what heteronormative capitalist patriarchy has crystallized as identities are simply endlessly occupiable positions that have the potential to make revolution possible. When the Shapeshifter pins the MANNING name tag on a jacket, they imply that gender identity is as provisional as the addition or removal of a lapel pin. Makeup and mud are applied in equal measure to fashion and conceal identity. In *Leave No Trace*, jockstraps are repurposed as bras.

And language: Burns conceives it as another slippery thing—as slippery as "Manning"/"manning" and just as arbitrary. A performer in *Living Room* asks, "Who's making words these days?," suggesting that the assignment of meaning itself is a patriarchal and colonialist assertion of power, and then wonders if we're in a "postsemantic age," where words no longer have to "perform the way that it's described anymore." (This, too, is a discussion about gender and its performativity, as well as the burden of reproduction that some bodies bear and the possibility of no longer having to bear that burden—bodies, like words, don't have to perform the way they're described.)

In the imaginative world of *Negative Space*, borders are oppressive and flimsy at once: in *Leave No Trace*, Mx. Manning dismisses tiny demarcating signs with threatening language and easily transgresses the almost comically ineffectual barbed-wire barriers they find in the vast expanses of the desert. The image is foreshadowed in *A Smeary Spot,* whose script includes an edited quotation from Ursula K. Le Guin's 1974 novel *The Dispossessed*: "There was a wall. It did not look important. It was built of uncut rocks roughly mortared. Where it crossed the roadway, instead of having a gate it degenerated into mere geometry, a line, an idea of boundary. But the idea was real. It was important. Like all walls, it was ambiguous, two-faced. What was inside it and what was outside it depended upon which side of it you were on." A decidedly androgynous Free Radical—with bright-red lipstick, buzzed hair, black T-shirt, and jeans—recites the line.

History, gender, language, borders—they're all leaky. Mx. Manning shows us that every time they appear on the screen. They are the sign of the leak—not just of state secrets but of everything. Water leaks, too, and water is everywhere (or, as alarmingly, not where it should be) in *Negative Space.* When it is contained—as in Lake Powell and the plastic bottles handed out by Makemake in *What is Perverse is Liquid*—it is transformed into a commodity, valuable according to the logic of capitalism. But when it leaks, it exceeds, defies, or undermines its monetary status—it is waste. (Whether leaking water is valued or wasted depends on which side of the wall—or dam—you're on.)

History, gender, language, borders—they're all part of the same waste pile as that which appears in the black-box theater in *A Smeary Spot* and the garbage dump at the center of Jack Smith's imaginary city: full of the obsolete, outmoded, compromised, and tainted. This is Muñoz's "quagmire of the present," a slag heap of history that becomes, in Burns's vision, available to whoever wants to make out of it what they will—even, if we are willing, a queer future, an ideal *there and then.*

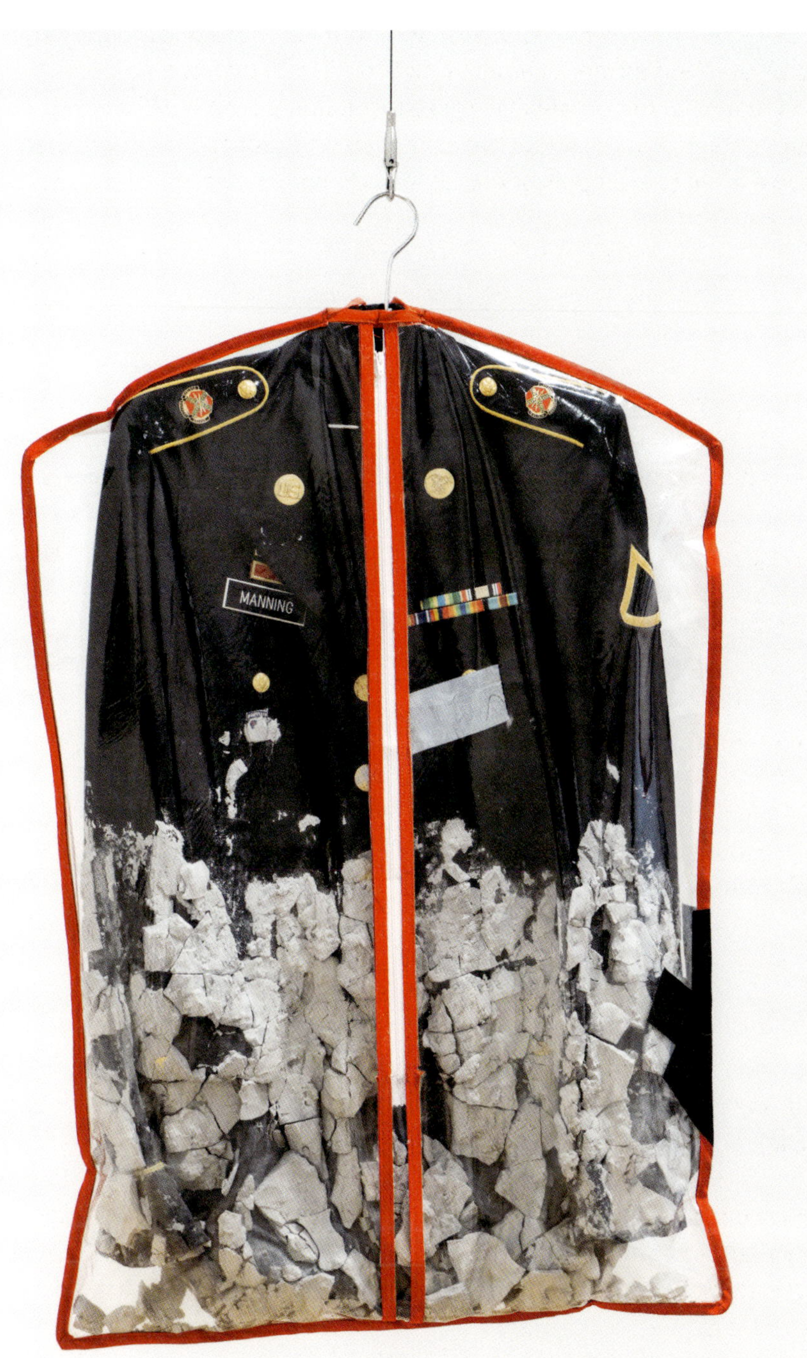

↗ *The Leak*, 2022. Replica of
Chelsea Manning's military
jacket, concrete, garment bag,
and metal hanger; 62 × 24 ×
18 inches (157.5 × 60.9 ×
45.8 cm)

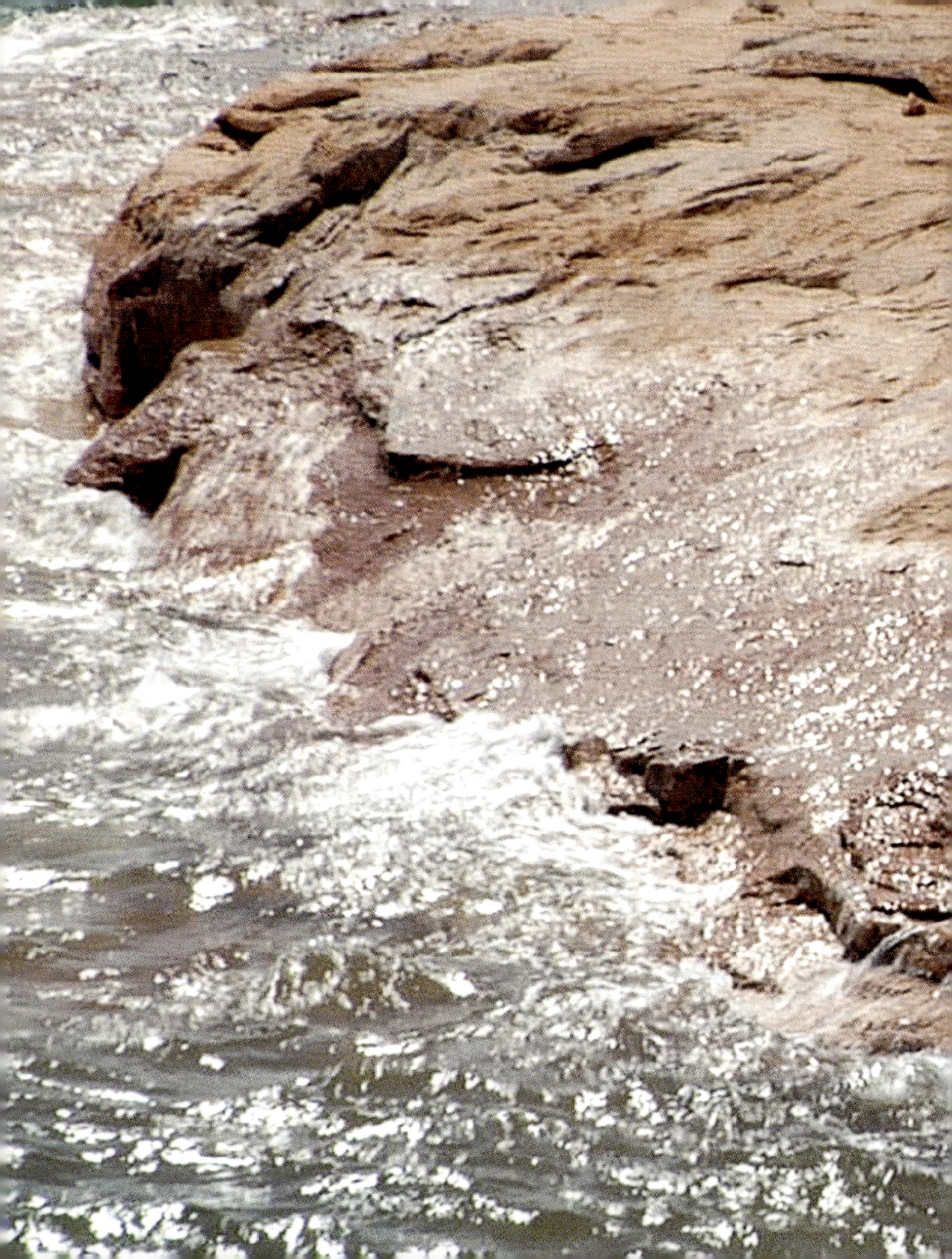

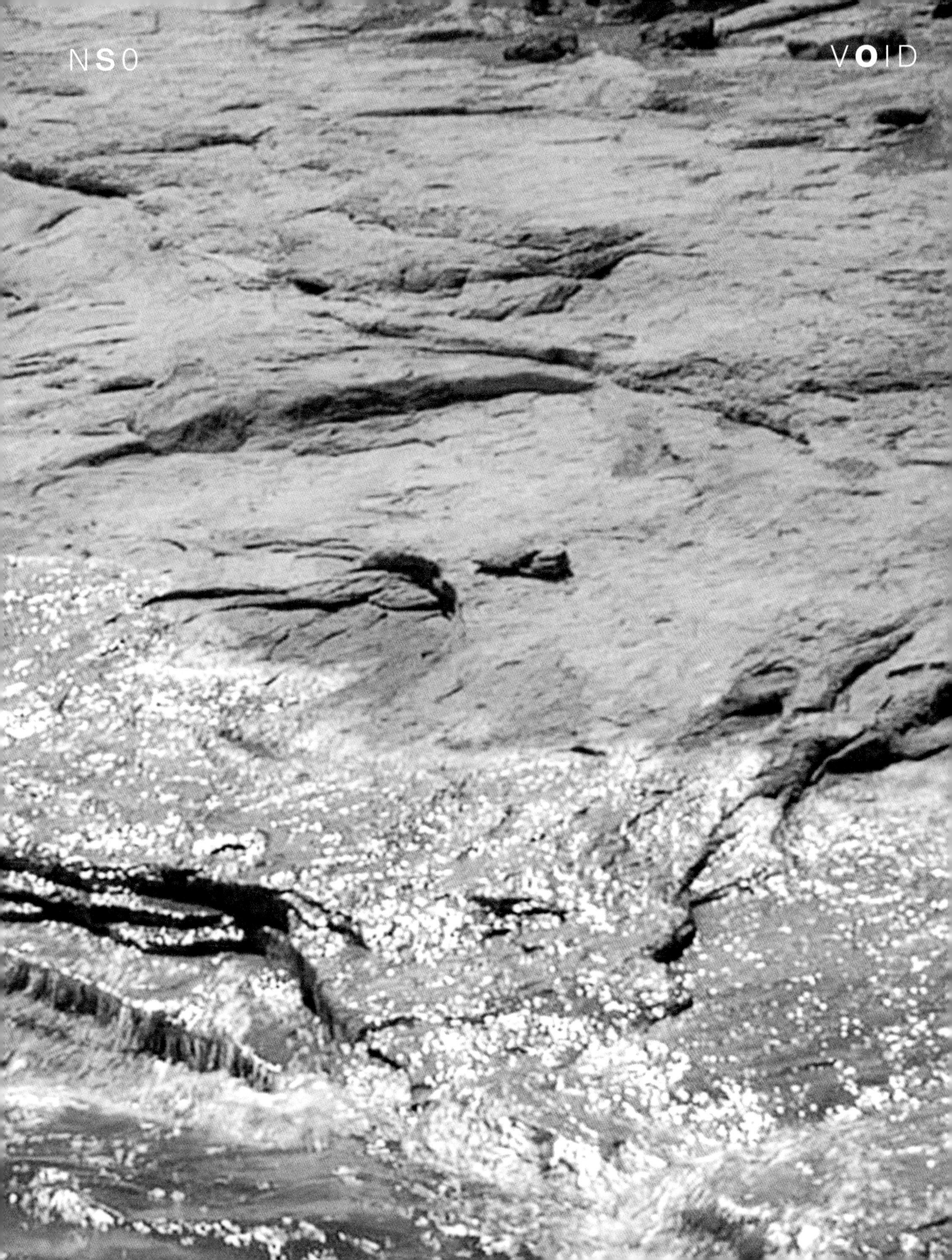
NS0
VOID

What is preserved—the thing or the work of art—is a *bloc of sensations,*
that is to say, a compound of percepts and affects. . . . However, blocs
need pockets of air and emptiness, because even the void is sensation.
All sensation is composed with the void in composing itself with itself,
and everything holds together on earth and in the air, and preserves the
void, is preserved in the void by preserving itself.
—Gilles Deleuze and Félix Guattari, *What Is Philosophy?*

rent and rent
things cleave
separate from what is composed
what was within
the property
of a body
then no longer
and a new space
so to speak
opens as what absolutely was
not previously
present

precisely division is not this
hesitant emergence of new borders
loosely healing

in october the darkest month
or november
it is dark so dark
the stoop always in darkness
Fanny reads and
I know why I do this work
or why
a figure
hunched in a series of dark hoods
eternally passing by
must stumble along the rim of a coverture
that binds it to darkness
skin of darkness

to inhabit
an abyss
a simple line between figures
is stumbling between
the house across the street
come into the possession
of a very young man
who lives alone in a palatial house
a dwelling so improbably unfit
for a single human

Simone White

whose white skin is a false clue
all the backs of these Bedford-Stuyvesant houses
hunched up
against the brick of themselves
one whose roof is caving in
abutting the house where I am said to live
yet outdoors
holds that notion of living in utter contempt
don't one move life in the dark line
between garments and walls
indeed my illusory possession of the space inside
the house that also scrapes the nonpossession
of a house held by a corporation
occupied at this time by those who are unhoused who live
in pink sweaters
or single shoes spastically displayed
beside the chair where someone has gone on
to live without
this single shoe
stepping like ONE
because the covered foot is too terrible to accept

thus improperly exposed
to hold the body awkward
on one
not allow
what is called gesture to take place
continually remaining within the pressure of the void
surge before violence
one's habitus
a perpetual coil
of drink-bound impecunity
delirious heckled armor
wanting the aroma on the armpit of the void
what brushed the eyelids and cervical spine down
such a curve
but what soft

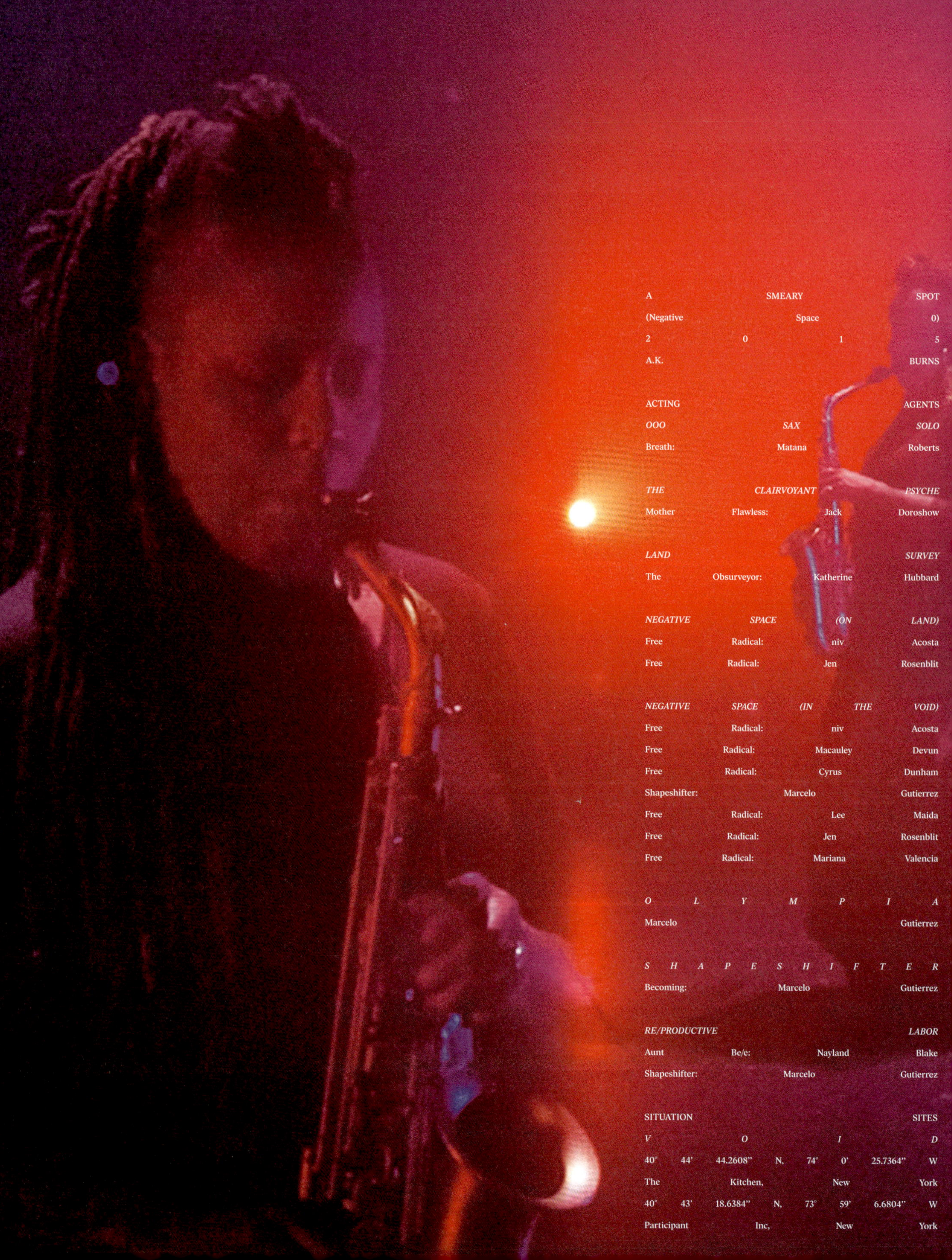

A SMEARY SPOT
(Negative Space 0)
2 0 1 5
A.K. BURNS

ACTING AGENTS
OOO SAX SOLO
Breath: Matana Roberts

THE CLAIRVOYANT PSYCHE
Mother Flawless: Jack Doroshow

LAND SURVEY
The Obsurveyor: Katherine Hubbard

NEGATIVE SPACE (ON LAND)
Free Radical: niv Acosta
Free Radical: Jen Rosenblit

NEGATIVE SPACE (IN THE VOID)
Free Radical: niv Acosta
Free Radical: Macauley Devun
Free Radical: Cyrus Dunham
Shapeshifter: Marcelo Gutierrez
Free Radical: Lee Maida
Free Radical: Jen Rosenblit
Free Radical: Mariana Valencia

O L Y M P I A
Marcelo Gutierrez

S H A P E S H I F T E R
Becoming: Marcelo Gutierrez

RE/PRODUCTIVE LABOR
Aunt Be/e: Nayland Blake
Shapeshifter: Marcelo Gutierrez

SITUATION SITES
V O I D
40° 44' 44.2608'' N, 74° 0' 25.7364'' W
The Kitchen, New York
40° 43' 18.6384'' N, 73° 59' 6.6804'' W
Participant Inc, New York

A Smeary Spot

BODY

36° 54' 13.5432" N, 111° 23' 26.8548" W
Salt River Project, Navajo Generating Station, Page, AZ

36° 56' 14.8776" N, 111° 29' 1.0464" W
Glen Canyon Dam, Page, AZ

LAND

38° 23' 23.751" N, 110° 53' 34.8102" W
off Coal Mine Road, Wayne County, UT

38° 20' 50.7222" N, 110° 59' 14.6394" W
38° 20' 44.0628" N, 110° 59' 8.7252" W
38° 22' 12.522" N, 110° 54' 43.1028" W
38° 22' 9.9006" N,
110° 47' 42.054" W
38° 22' 9.9006" N,
110° 47' 42.054" W
near State Route 24, Wayne County, UT

37° 44' 8.3292" N, 111° 26' 34.368" W
off Spencer Flat Road, Garfield County, UT

38° 1' 3.0894" N, 110° 31' 44.457" W
near State Route 95, Garfield County, UT

37° 15' 44.6286" N, 109° 50' 11.1372" W
Valley of the Gods, UT

WATER

37° 30' 20.1126" N, 110° 43' 27.2454" W
Bullfrog Bay, Lake Powell, UT

37° 2' 20.7774" N, 111° 19' 6.0312" W
Lake Powell, UT

PRODUCTIONS
A.K. Burns

PRODUCTION ASSISTANT
Sage Donahue

ASSISTANTS
RJ Messineo
Saar Shemesh

DIRECTOR OF PHOTOGRAPHY
A.K. Burns

ADDITIONAL CAMERA
Jaffa Aharonov
Sage Donahue
Glen Fogel
Lauryn Siegel

SET DESIGN
A.K. Burns

WARDROBE AND PROPS
A.K. Burns
Katherine Hubbard

PROPS AND WARDROBE COORDINATOR
Katherine Hubbard

ADDITIONAL PROP
Re-creation of "Boner Killer" T-shirt by permission of K8 Hardy

PROP RENTAL
Eclectic/Encore Props

HAIR AND MAKEUP
A.K. Burns
Leslie Allison

TECHNICAL COORDINATOR
Lauryn Siegel

TECH ASSISTANT
Lazar Bozic

LIGHTING (THE KITCHEN)
Brittany Spencer

AUDIO TECHNICIAN (THE KITCHEN)
Andrea Ambro

STILL PHOTOGRAPHY (THE KITCHEN)
Patrice Helmar

EDITOR
A.K. Burns

SCORE
Geo Wyeth

ADDITIONAL AUDIO
"Desert Migration": New Humans with A.K. Burns
Drums on "Desert March": Nickel van Duijvenboden
"Red Desert" samples: Colin Self
"Running H20" and "LRJAINE" samples: Matana Roberts
Saxophone: Matana Roberts
Trombone on "Airplane" and "Red Desert": Koen Doodeman

AUDIO MIX AND MASTERING
Quentin Chiappetta

POSTPRODUCTION
A.K. Burns

ADDITIONAL POSTPRODUCTION (OUTPOST RESIDENCY)
Matthew Hysell

SCRIPT
Excerpt from Karen Barad, *What Is the Measure of Nothingness: Infinity, Virtuality, Justice* (2012)
Excerpt from Ursula K. Le Guin, *The Dispossessed: An Ambiguous Utopia* (1974)
Excerpt from Karen Barad, "Posthumanist Performativity: Toward an Understanding of How Matter Comes to Matter" (2008)
Excerpt from Joanna Russ, *We Who Are About To . . .* (1977)
Excerpt from T. S. Eliot, *The Waste Land* (1922)
Excerpt from Guy Hocquenghem, *The Screwball Asses* (2010)
Excerpt from Friedrich Engels and Karl Marx, *The Communist Manifesto* (1848)
Excerpt from Georges Bataille, *The Accursed Share: An Essay on General Economy, vol. 1, Consumption* (1988)
Excerpt from Joanna Russ, *The Female Man* (1975)
Excerpt from Simone de Beauvoir, *The Ethics of Ambiguity* (1947)

SCRIPT COMPOSITION
A.K. Burns

REFERENCES
Édouard Manet, *Olympia*, 1863

SPECIAL THANKS
Malin Arnell
Fia Backström
Callicoon Fine Arts
Lauren Cornell
Anna Craycroft
Dean Daderko
Olga Dekalo
Sage Donahue
Glen Fogel
Lia Gangitano
Andrea Geyer
Katherine Hubbard
Jamie Hubbard
Andrew Kachel
Clara López
Matthew Lyons
John Panagis
Jordan Strafer

FUNDED WITH THE GENEROUS SUPPORT OF
Creative Capital Visual Arts Grant

ADDITIONAL FUNDING AND SUPPORT
Collective Address Artist in Practice Residency
The Kitchen
Participant Inc

Could you describe A Smeary Spot, *what it is and what led you to create it?*

A.K. BURNS   This project came on the heels of *Community Action Center* (2010), a single-channel video I made in collaboration with A.L. Steiner. As I was wrapping up that project, I realized I wanted to continue to explore cinematic genres. If *Community Action Center* was a rethinking of pornography, my next project would reconsider science fiction. Science fiction would give me an opportunity to reflect on sociopolitical concerns and fantasy.

In 2012, I traveled to pick up a family car from California, taking a southern route through Utah to drive back to New York. I was struck by how that landscape's otherworldly qualities evoked sci-fi clichés—the vastness, the scale, and the diversity of land formations—and it was easy to access, since so much of Utah is public land. Because the timing of my trip coincided with the early stages of developing this science-fiction-based project, my curiosity about this land quickly laid the groundwork for what would become the *Negative Space* tetralogy—a cycle of four video installations. *A Smeary Spot* is the first one I developed in the series and the central work, which the other three orbit and reflect upon.

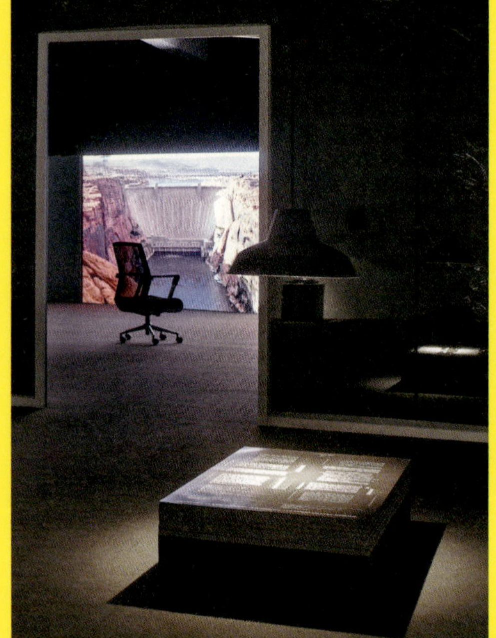

As a formal term in art, *negative space* denotes the matter between and around the subject(s). The subject is the focus of our attention, a definable or known entity. Negative space, however, is a compositional gap used to accentuate the primacy of the subject. What is compelling about negative space is that it is undefined, an open set of possibilities. This concept is not an empty space to be occupied or filled;

rather, I see it as a site of political agency that is full of potential because it remains changeable, amorphous, and unmeasurable. The larger premise of *Negative Space* is to explore agency within subjugated positions to interrogate hierarchical and hegemonic orientations.

Each of the works that make up the *Negative Space* series responds to a physical system—void, body, land, or water. *A Smeary Spot* explores the void, which I see as interchangeable with the concept of negative space. It is structured around a script made up of a series of quotes from research texts that lay out a political and conceptual framework for all four works.

KA   *A remarkable aspect of* A Smeary Spot *is that it's not only panoramic but also epic: it's long in duration, nearly an hour, and there are many different layers of production and various actors, both human and environmental. What specifically was the driving force in making the multipart series? Was it planned to be a series, or was it something that took shape during the process of creation over the course of months and years?*

AKB   I would say it developed slowly over three years, but the foundation of it came out of that trip. One of the premises of *Negative Space* is that I build each video work from sites I shoot in—exploring the

Nothingness. The void. An absence of matter. The blank page. Utter silence. No thing, no thought, no awareness. Complete ontological insensibility.

Shall we utter some words about nothingness? What is there to say? How to begin? How can anything be said about nothing without violating its very nature, perhaps even its conditions of possibility? Isn't any utterance about nothingness always already a performative breach of that which one means to address? Have we not already said too much simply in pronouncing its name?

Perhaps we should let the emptiness speak for itself. [1]

There was a wall. It did not look important. It was built of uncut rocks roughly mortared. An adult could look right over it, and even a child could climb it. Where it crossed the roadway, instead of having a gate it degenerated into mere geometry, a line, an idea of boundary. But the idea was real. It was important. For seven generations there had been nothing in the world more important than that wall.

Like all walls it was ambiguous, two-faced. What was inside it and what was outside it depended upon which side of it you were on. [2]

As if knowing comes from an exterior point

On any agential realist account of technoscientific practices, the "knower" does not stand in a relation of absolute externality to the natural world being investigated — there is no such exterior observational point. It is therefore not absolute exteriority that is the condition of possibility for objectivity but rather agential separability — exteriority within phenomena. *I am* not outside observer of the world. Nor *am I* simply located at particular places *in* the world; rather, *I am* part *of* the world [3]

This is space travel. Imagine a flat world, a piece of paper, say, with two spots on it but very far apart. If you were a two-dimensional triangle, how would you get from one spot to the other? Walk? Too far. But fold the paper through the third dimension (ours) so that the spots match exactly – if you were a triangle you couldn't see or feel this, of course – and you *are* at the proper place. We do this in the fourth. Don't ask me how. Only you must be very, very careful, when you fold spacetime, not to sloosh the paper around or let it slide; then you end up not on the spot you wanted but who knows where, maybe entirely out of our galaxy, which is that dust you see in the sky on clear nights when you're away from cities. The glittering breath of angels. Far, far from home. The light of our dying may not reach you for a thousand million years. That ordinary sun up there, a little hazy now at noon, that smeary spot. We do not know where we are. [4]

Which are mountains of rock without water
If there were water we should stop and drink
Amongst the rock one cannot stop or think
Sweat is dry and feet are in the sand
If there were only water amongst the rock
Dead mountain mouth of carious teeth that cannot spit
Here one can neither stand nor lie nor sit

Here is no water but only rock
Rock and no water and the sandy road
The road winding above among the mountains [5]

I now dream of lesbians who do not copy men, who live without the phallus and without the terror of the phallus. Even if one single lesbian exists, I wish to lie at her side, like someone on the point of fainting, like a future woman. For an instant, for the instant of the sexual revolution, I will think of myself as a lesbian.

Oh! Wanting to be woman, to be fertile, to be cunt-ile, rather than feeling the capitalist desire to impregnate! I know I am ranting. Long live snails! [6]

enemies of intra-activity. Agency is about the possibilities and accountability entailed in reconfiguring material-discursive apparatuses of bodily production, including the boundary articulations and exclusions that are marked by those practices in the enactment of a causal structure. Particular possibilities for acting exist at every moment, and these changing possibilities entail a responsibility to intervene in the world's becoming, to contest and rework what matters and what is excluded from mattering. [7]

I became

slaves for the workers. He becomes an appendage of the machine, and it is only the most simple, most monotonous, and most easily acquired knack that *was* is required of *me*. Hence, the cost of production.

At first sight it is easy to recognize in the economy – *in the production and use of wealth* – a particular aspect of terrestrial activity regarded as a cosmic phenomenon. A movement is produced on the surface of the globe resulting from the circulation of energy at this point of the universe. The economic activity of men appropriates this movement, making use of the resulting possibilities for certain ends. The living organism, in a situation determined by the play of energy on the surface of the globe, *planet* ordinarily receives more energy than is necessary for maintaining life; the excess energy (wealth) can be used for the growth of a system (e.g., an organism); if the system can no longer grow, or if the excess cannot be completely absorbed in its growth, it *will* must necessarily be lost without profit; it must be spent, willingly or not, gloriously or catastrophically.

In other words, the possibility of pursuing growth is itself subordinated to giving: The industrial development of the entire world demands of Americans that they lucidly grasp the [9]

25

crossing radicalism; then came the Polarization; then came the Split. The middle dropped out and we were left with the two ends, being, for when people began short on we shall act in accordance with truth and justice. To the idea of present war there is opposed that of a future peace when man will again find, along with a stable situation, the possibility of a morality. But the truth is that if division and violence define war, the world has always been at war and always will be; if man is waiting for universal peace in order to establish his existence validly, he will wait indefinitely: there will never be any other future. [11]

I hope I will be granted these phantasies and the utopia that goes with them. The fact remains that homosexuality can only escape heterosexuality by becoming a relation of weaknesses, of non-rivalry, or non-property, that is, by inverting male paranoia into schizophrenia. If reserve and human respect remain whole, as in transfixed, suffering and dignified lovers, if the purity of sentiments absorbs the shadows, then the homosexual is but half a rebel. Rigged with a mythical third sex, *I* continues to drone out virility, the tests of conquest, and an aching heart. [12]

1. Karen Barad, *What Is the Measure of Nothingness: Infinity, Virtuality, Justice*
2. Ursula K. Le Guin, *The Dispossessed*
3. Karen Barad, *Posthumanist Performativity: Toward an Understanding of How Matter Comes to Matter*
4. Joanna Russ, *We Who Are About To...*
5. T.S. Elliot, *The Waste Land*
6. Guy Hocquenghem, *The Screwball Asses*
7. Karen Barad, *Posthumanist Performativity: Toward an Understanding of How Matter Comes to Matter*
8. Karl Marx, *The Communist Manifesto*
9. Georges Bataille, *The Accursed Share: An Essay on General Economy*
10. Johanna Russ, *The Female Man*
11. Simone de Beauvoir, *The Ethics Of Ambiguity*
12. Guy Hocquenghem, *The Screwball Asses*

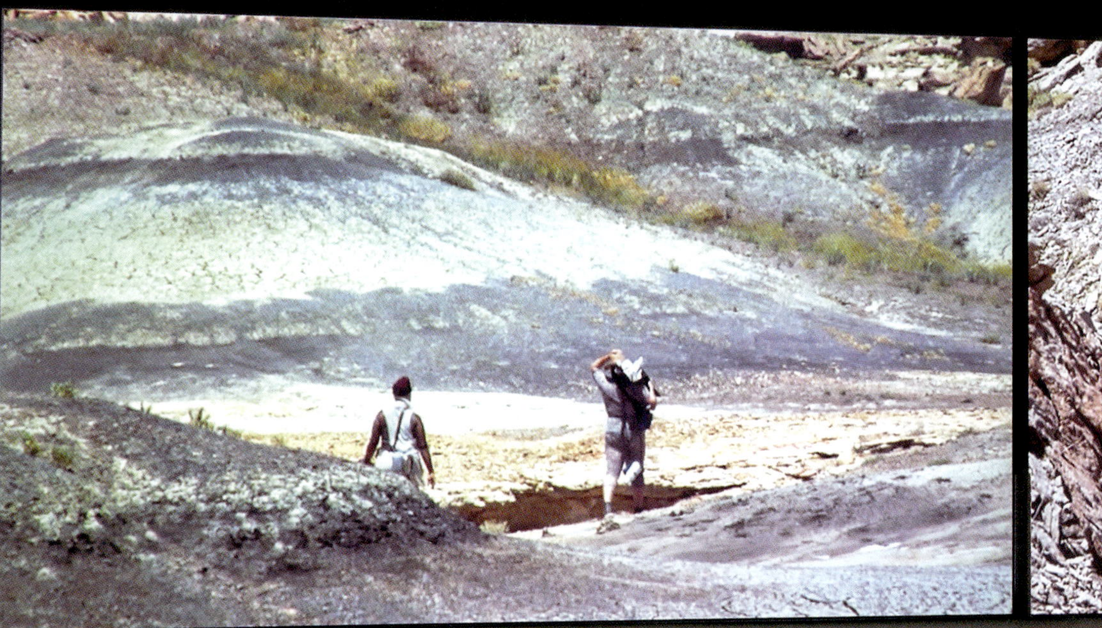

↳ Page 26: *A Smeary Spot (NSØ)*,
  2015. Installation view with
  takeaway poster (script) in
  foreground, *A.K. Burns: Negative
  Space*, Julia Stoschek Foundation,
  Düsseldorf, Germany, 2019

↳ Page 27: *Negative Space Poster
  (verso)*, 2015–23, with script
  for *A Smeary Spot*, 2015. Offset-
  printed poster, open edition,
  dimensions variable

↑ *A Smeary Spot (NSØ)*, 2015.
  Installation view, *A.K. Burns:
  Negative Space*, Julia Stoschek
  Foundation, Düsseldorf,

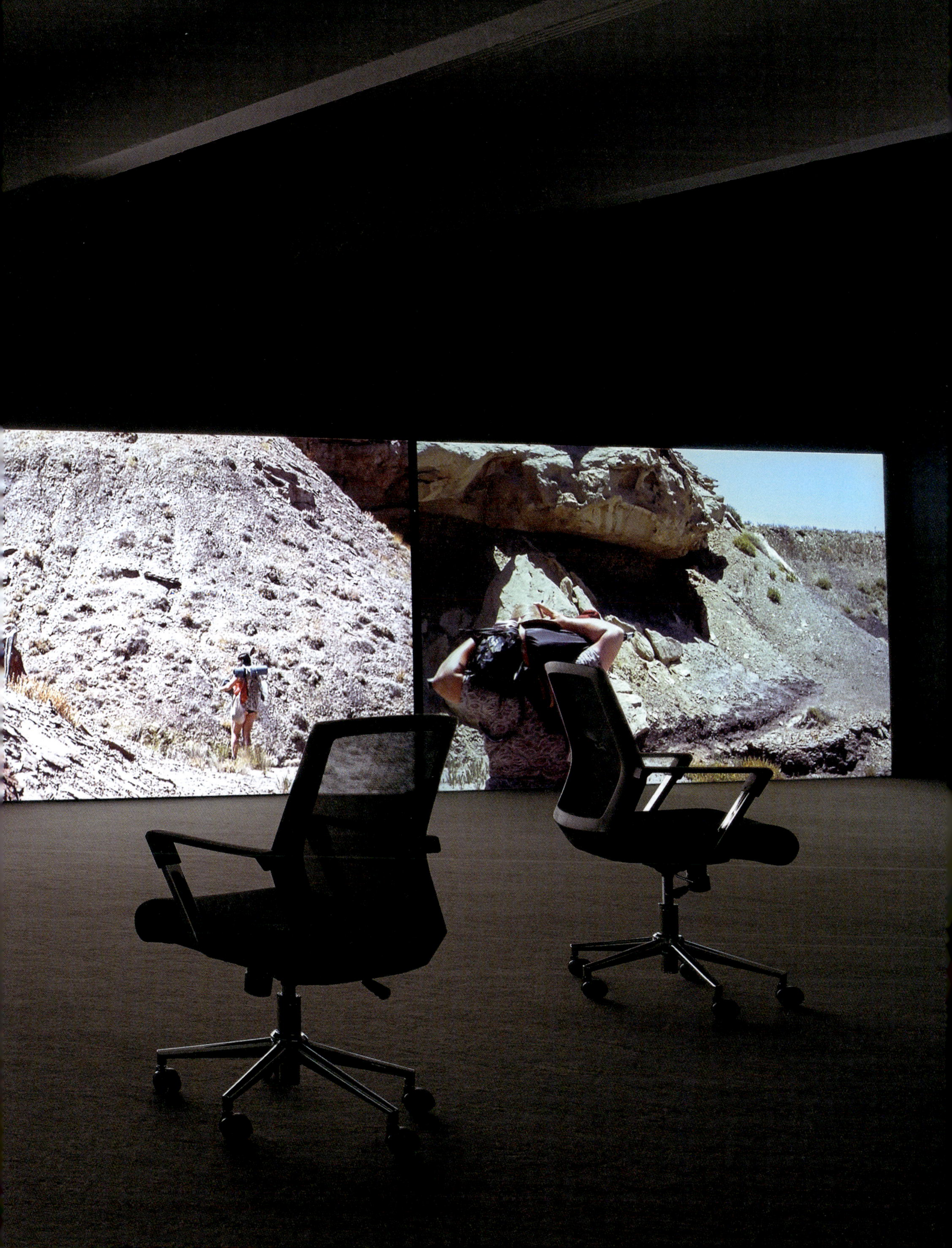

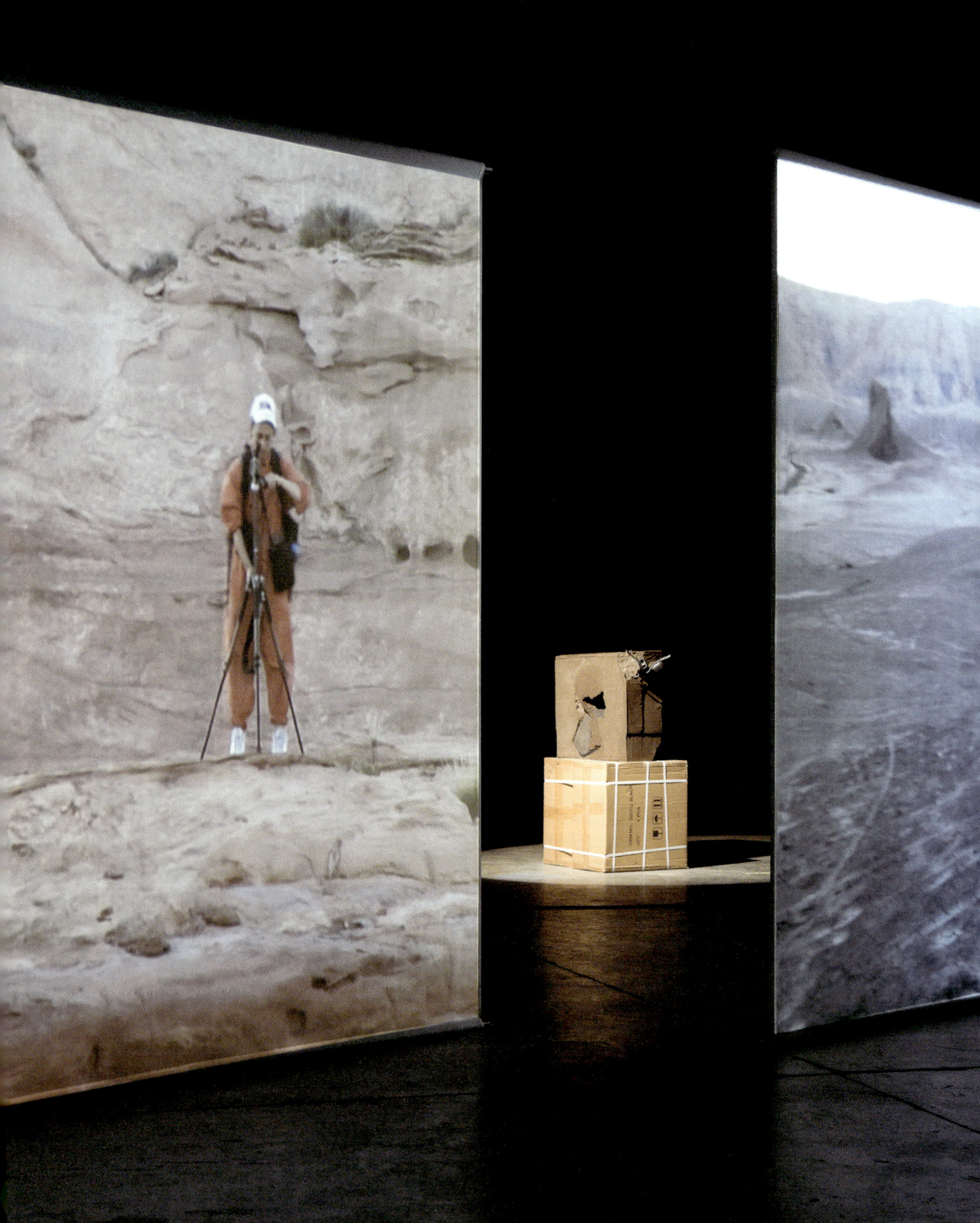

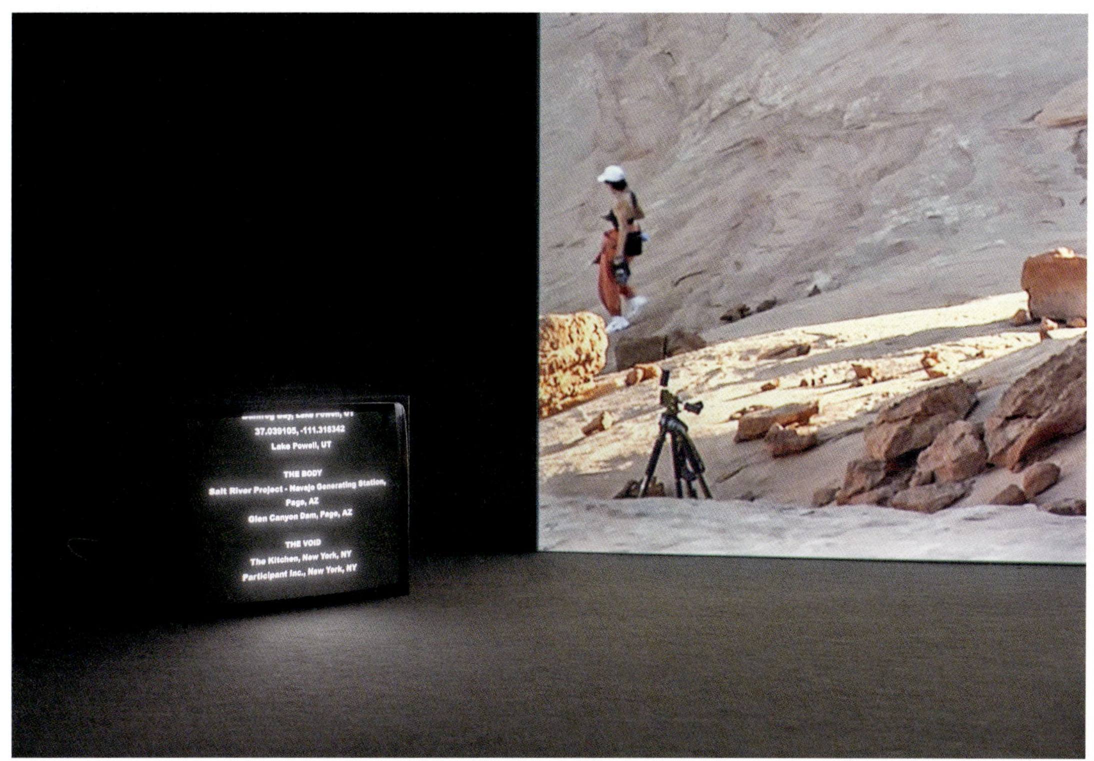

0 3 1

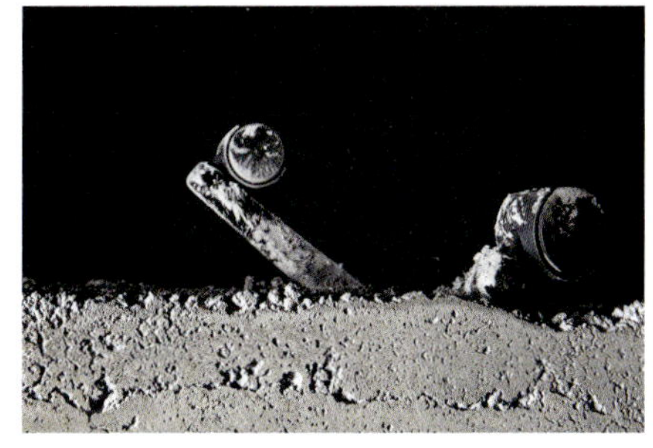

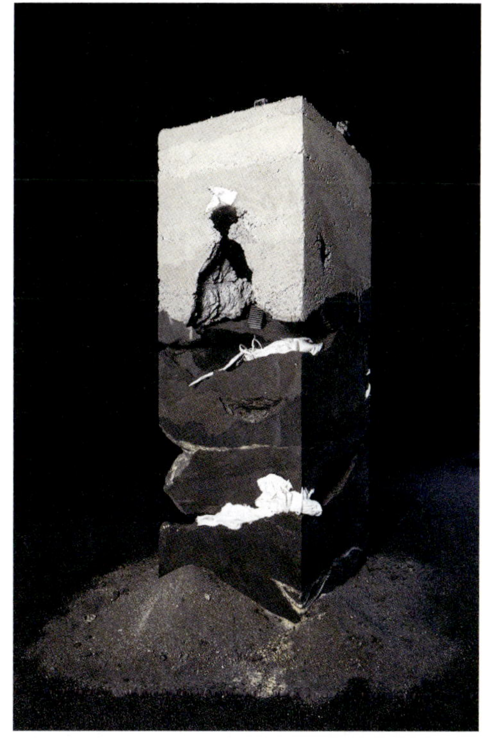

←↗ *A Smeary Spot (NSO)*, 2015.
Installation view, *A.K. Burns: A
Smeary Spot*, Portland Institute
of Contemporary Art, Portland,
Oregon, 2017.

↑→ *Untitled*, 2015. Sand, concrete,
office chair, woven polypropylene
sandbags, India ink, and epoxy
resin; 65 × 21¼ × 25 inches
(165.1 × 53.3 × 63.5 cm). Detail
and installation view, *A.K.
Burns: A Smeary Spot*, Participant
Inc, New York, 2015

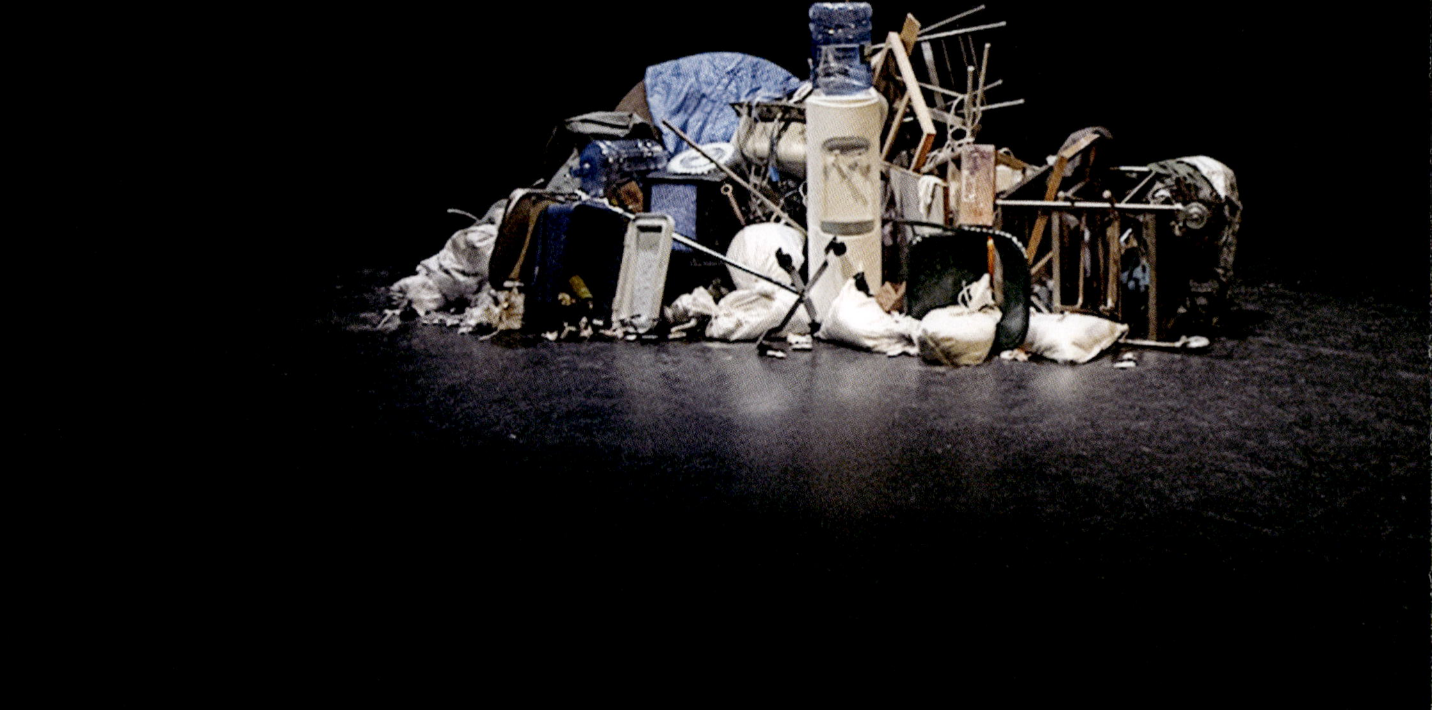

context and histories of locations as an entry point. In the desert, I experienced many strong sensations, like the feeling that our anthro-centered worldview is irrelevant. Standing in open landscapes where the strata of millennia have accumulated into giant mesas makes it clear that humans are a speck of dust in space and time. Because I was mostly shooting on public lands, there were often no fences or markers to indicate boundaries. The physical experience of being in a space without visible borders or property lines set into motion one of the most important questions for me: what are the social and political ramifications of living with space differently? I imagined that an entirely different ontology would materialize simply if our proprietary and nationalistic relationship with land radically transformed or ceased.

KA

There's obviously so much thought behind landscape and the relationship of the body to it in A Smeary Spot. *Regarding being a body on Earth, I was wondering what it means for you to cast a performer in your work and about how various roles in the work are played not just by humans but also by the landscape itself.*

AKB   Well, I think about the landscape or site as the protagonist. If there is a hierarchy in the work, the environment is the primary actor. But I'm not talking about a singular kind of protagonist; it's a spatialized, decentered redefinition of the term. The performers act as concepts or metaphors, so there is no character development in the way typical of cinema. Performers are there to activate language, props, and gestures in each scene.

So, you took multiple trips to Utah to shoot over the course of the years?

AKB   Yes. Three trips: the first, in 2012, was when I realized this landscape would be the initial building block for the work. A second trip was to location-scout and shoot the landscape alone. And on the third, in 2014, as I was beginning to understand the structure of the work, I wanted to explore what happens when performers interact with the landscape. After that trip, I realized that the black-box theater was going to be a crucial additional location.

KA

What made you want to work in the black box, which is such a drastically different background from the Utah landscape?

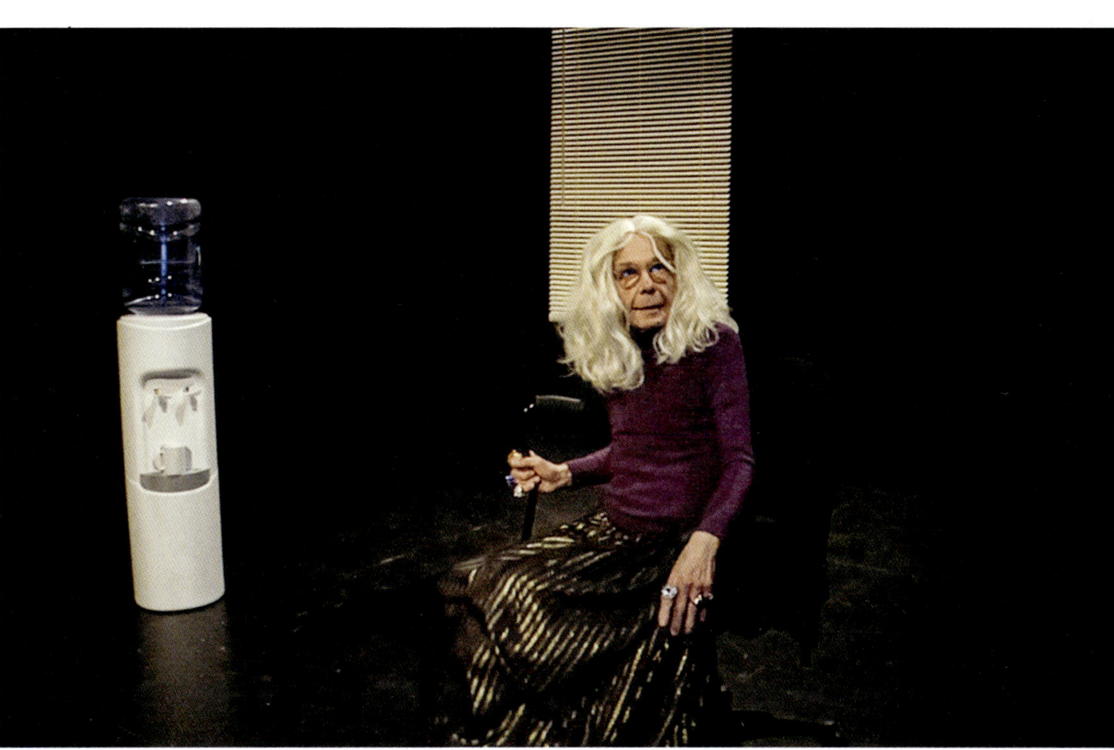

AKB   It began mostly as a practical decision because of the cost and how physically stressful it was to work in the desert, in remote places under a hot sun. Many locations were hours away from any gas, lodging, or food. By the time we had set up, it would already be midday and the heat would be at its peak. Often, there was no shade except for in the car, which was always full of equipment. I'm thankful for the people who were willing to work with me, as it was taxing. I felt I was having trouble developing the work much further in that environment.

Another thing that haunted me was an interview with the filmmaker Jack Smith in which he talks about his vision of a city whose economic, intellectual, and social exchange revolves around the garbage dump located at the center of town. Rather than being marginalized to the edge of town, where people can pretend waste doesn't exist, it becomes a vital resource central to societal formation. This helped inform my conception of *Negative Space*, which encourages a reorientation of our value systems through an embrace and incorporation of things that are overlooked (or lack visibility), are discarded, or are intentionally ignored. As it became clear that I needed to find a site that could be in conversation with the desert, the black-box theater offered the Illusion of infinite space on film, where performers and props could emerge from the darkness. Like the desert, this could act as a type of void or negative space. Additionally, the theater is a space that is built and unbuilt for each event—an active site of mutability, which is at the core of the politics of *Negative Space*. So I imagined the waste pile could live in the theater and be the source of all props, with every scene built from the pile and returned to it.

When it became clear that *A Smeary Spot* would be shot on these two sites—the desert and the black box—I started to think that one site might be reality (or external) and the other psychological (or interior), but we wouldn't know which one is which. The two sites are high contrast—one is a dark interior and the other a bright exterior. I had binary spaces that needed to appear as one world, but because we all experience a gap between our interior perceptions and the exterior world that contrasts with our perceptions of both, these two sites began to make a lot of sense together.

KA   *How long did it take for you to shoot the black-box scenes? I assume it was a theatrical studio?*

AKB   The black box was at the Kitchen in New York. Everything was shot in a day and a half at the Kitchen, except for some extra takes shot at Participant Inc, also in New York, a month before the work debuted there.

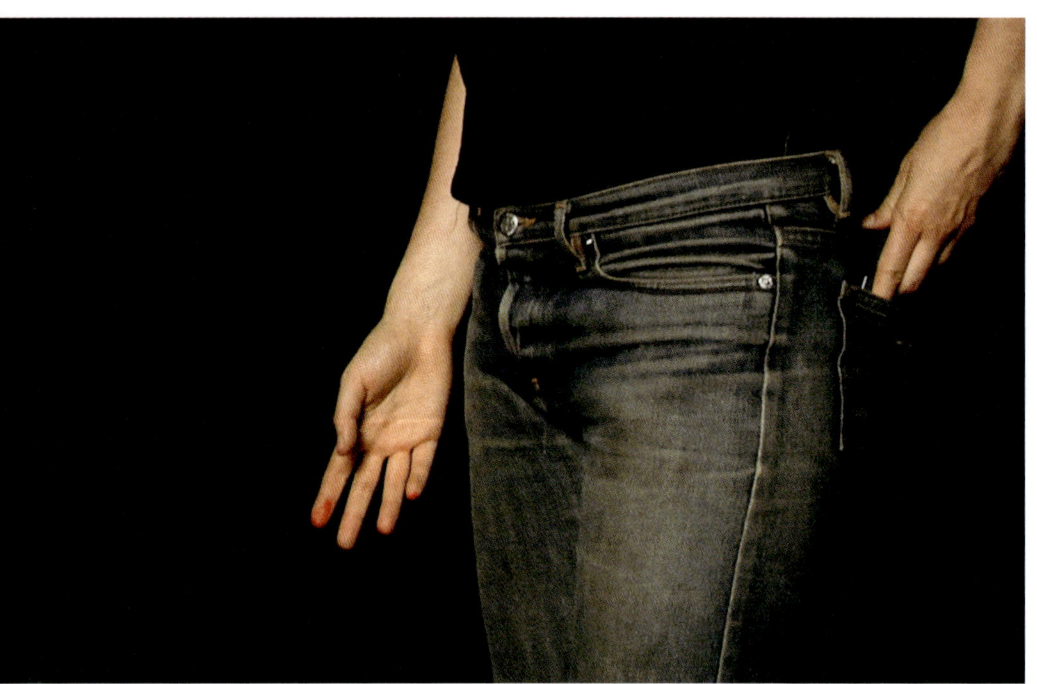

KA   *Could you talk about how you approached casting the performers in the work and character building?*

AKB   I work with what I call intimacy-based talent—people with whom I'm in proximity and whose practice feels akin to my own. It takes a certain kind of personality to be willing to experiment with me. Also, the performers are what I call acting agents rather than characters, since their role is to activate props and language, performing as concepts or metaphors.

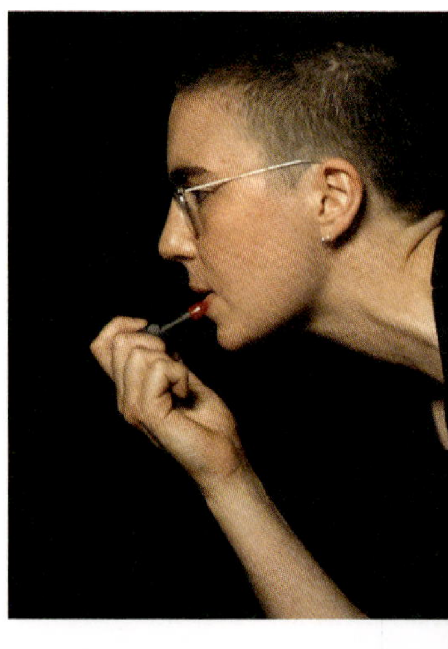

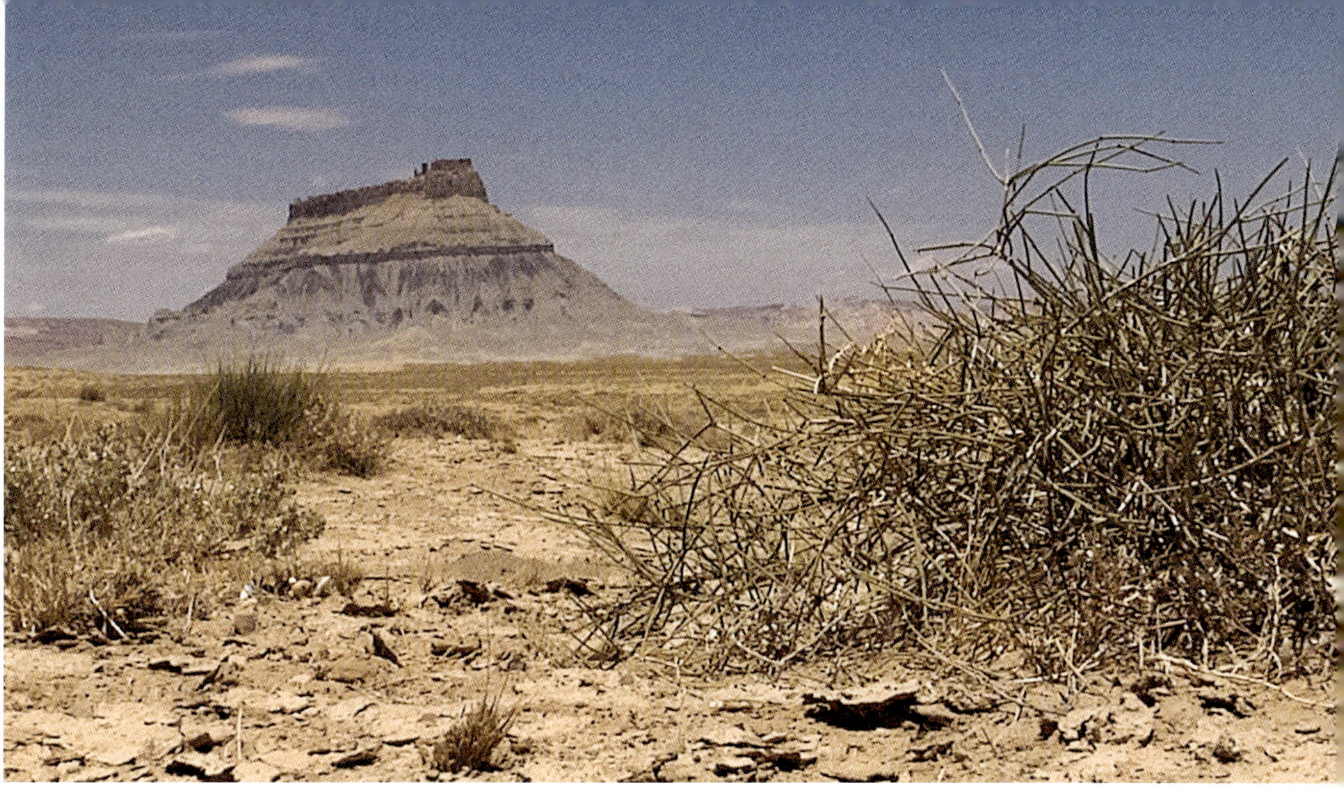

As for the casting, it came in stages. The first trip in the desert was just with my wife, Katherine Hubbard, also an artist and photographer. She was wearing an orange jumpsuit that she had picked

up at a thrift store. While I was out there shooting the landscape, she had her four-by-five camera and was working on her own work. So the first body in the landscape was me observing her observing the landscape. I called her the Obsurveyor, which came out of thinking about surveying land as an entry point into monetizing and claiming land. But she's not measuring or assessing the land; she's just looking. That was the first agent to develop.

The second shoot was more focused and explored the interaction among landscape, bodies, and movement. I brought niv Acosta and Jen Rosenblit with me because they are dancer-performers and their primary tool as artists is their bodies. They developed into the Free Radicals—dually representing unstable molecules that set off chain reactions and wandering activists/activators. Hence, when we see the Free Radicals in the black-box space, they all wear what I call activist drag—black combat boots, black shirts, and jeans.

Then, in 2014, I did a screen test for *A Smeary Spot* while at a residency. I invited members of a local artists' community to read and dramatize the texts I was starting to piece together into the script. That's how I met Marcelo Gutierrez, who plays the Shapeshifter and performs as my interpretation of Manet's *Olympia*, lounging on air mattresses. Because they are a shape-shifter, they become or mimic other agents in *A Smeary Spot*, taking on an ever-changing presence. I asked myself, "What does a shape-shifter look like prior to shape-shifting?" Hence the scenes with the robe and head towel, as if they've just emerged from a bath and are preparing to "become."

With Nayland Blake's performance as Re/productive Labor,
I was searching for symbols of labor, and the worker bee
came up. I found this gorgeous picture of a bee covered in
pollen—a close-up of bright-yellow dust caked in bee hair. I
decided to work with Nayland Blake because I wanted the
most hirsute person I could think of to coat in yellow dust.
Additionally, I wanted a performer who wouldn't be read as
cis female, since I was making a counterrepresentation of
the term *reproductive labor*, as coined by feminist scholar
Silvia Federici. Their primary task was to operate a photocopy
machine—to reproduce things. They are wearing a chemical
apron with a jockstrap, ass exposed. I modeled this agent
as a critique of "maid porn"—as a hybridization of blue-collar

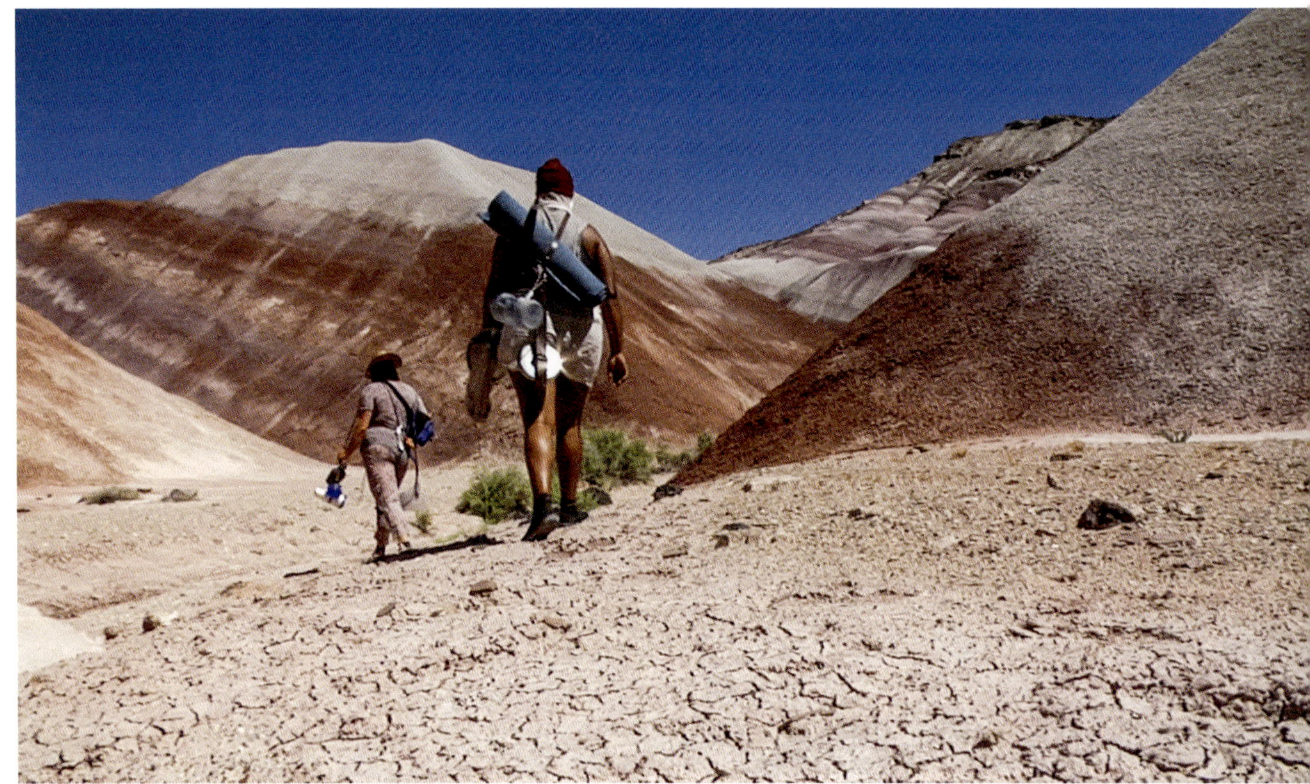

labor and the association of subservient sexuality with
domestic work.

KA
*I'm curious about the structure you bring to the piece at
each stage. After hearing about your casting and shooting
practices, I'd like to know more about how you transform
these elements into the work itself through editing. What
did that process look like?*

AKB   Every performer is based on a combination of who they actually are and what I need them to
symbolize, as are the locations, which are often represented as mythical spaces that are grounded
in the politics or problems of the real site. For example, a slow-moving shot of rocks emerging
out of the water: it looks quite surreal, sublime even. But the reason it looks surreal is because

it is not natural. It is man-made, owing to the Glen Canyon Dam, one of the many dams on the Colorado River, which is currently experiencing extraordinary water loss because of the damming and drought. We also see a power plant, one of the most toxic facilities in the United States, on the lands of the Navajo Nation, which contrast with the eerie beauty of Lake Powell. I don't directly address the politics of this but instead point to them through a combination of sound and image; each forbiddingly registers capitalism's exploitive relationship to the environment.

This cycle of works does not have a plot. It's more like a poetic structure—as in, it is a series of fragments that, when put in relation to one another, produce layered meaning. I do my own camerawork, because some parts are improvised on set, and I don't always know how to frame a scene until I see the action. I have a general logic or agenda when constructing and shooting each scene, but there is no overall storyboard since the relationship of each scene to the whole gets resolved through editing. I also do all my own editing, as this is how I learn about the sequential structure of the film, discovering

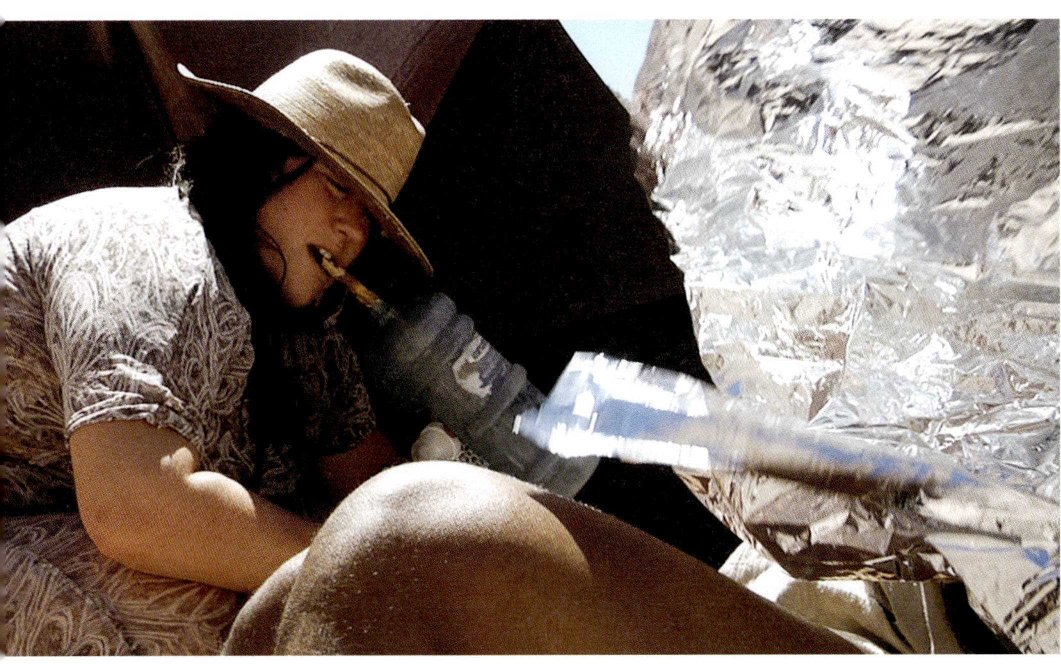

how it should flow from one event to the next. Soundtracking is essential to this form of storytelling as well.

KA

It is like writing in a way; editing is so integral to the shape of the piece.

AKB Yeah, it's very similar. *A Smeary Spot* took the longest to produce because I was developing a new form of nonnarrative multichannel science fiction, as well as building a framework for the whole *Negative Space* series. I also had to reshoot scenes late in the process. I realized I needed certain images that would bridge the binary qualities of the two sites. For example, in the scene with the mud mask, the mud is applied in excess until it consumes the face and begins to evoke a land-scape. And the juicer overflows—with red juice from beets and orange from carrots—to imagisti-cally recall the strata of the desertscapes. The other big component, of course, is the sound, which we began to conceive only after my first rough edit; it was built somewhat simultaneously with the final edit.

KA

Sound is a spatialized and structural element of the work, and Geo Wyex produced all the soundtracks in Negative

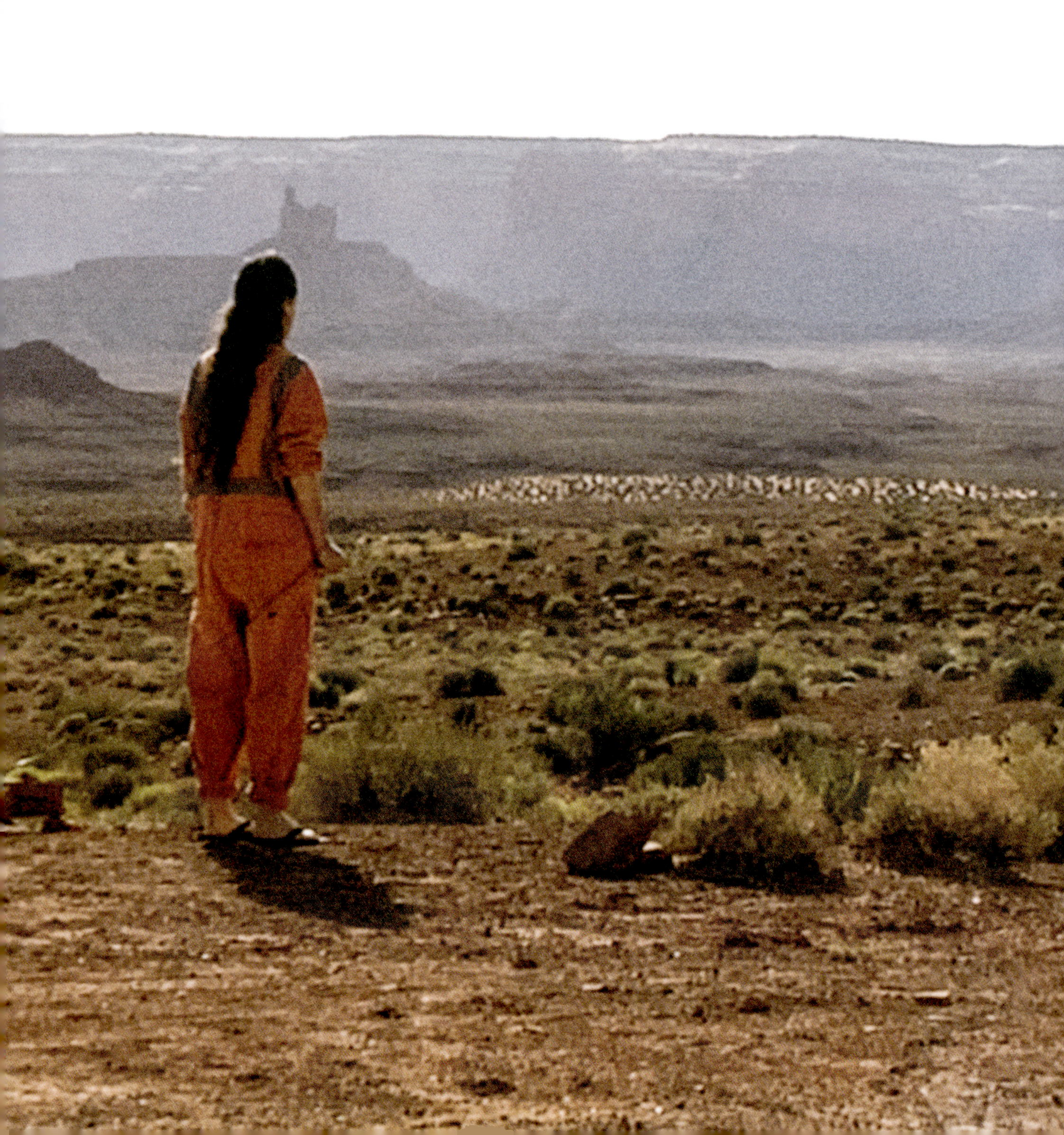

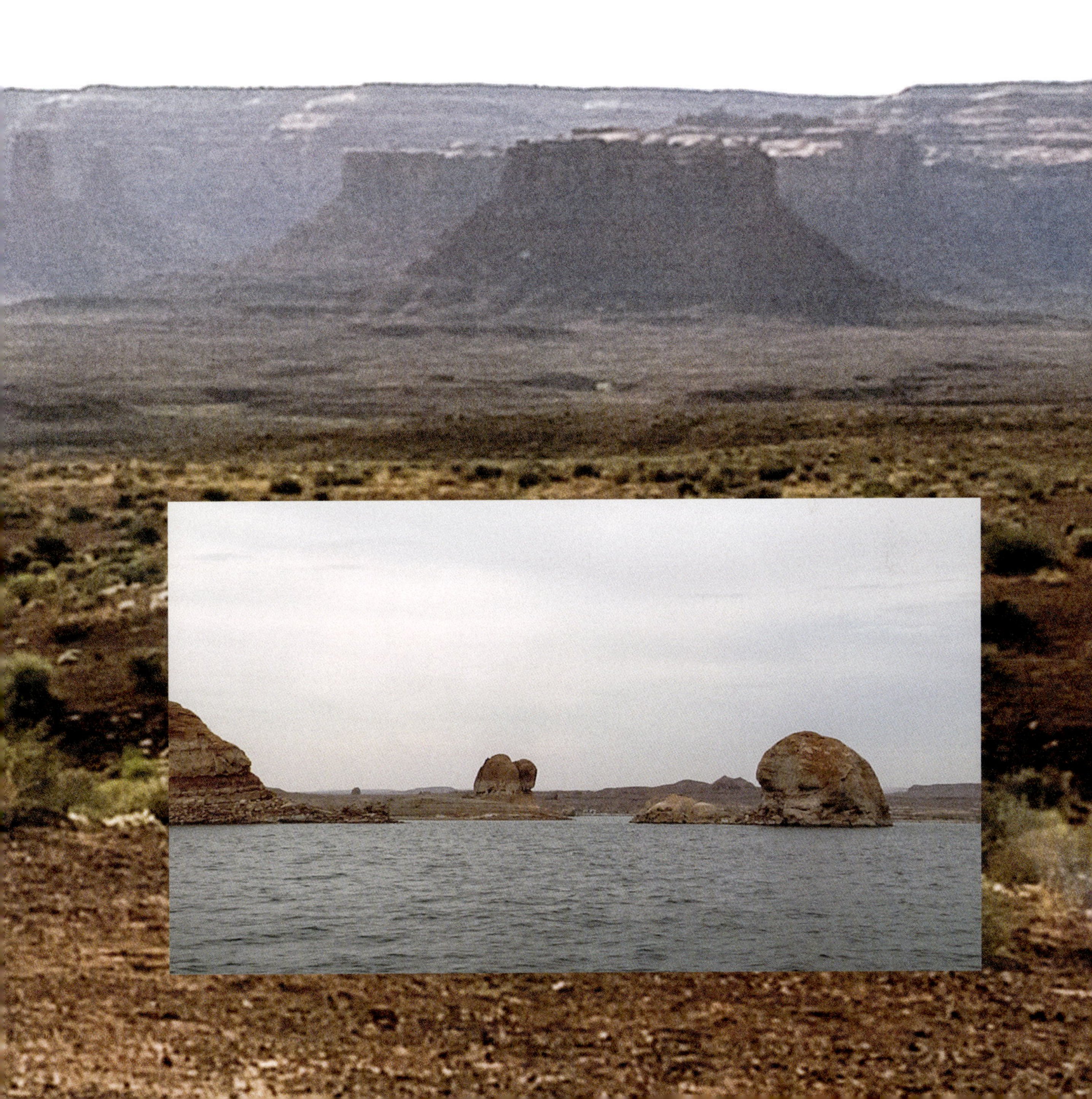

AKB   Geo has been amazing, because I can say something like, "I want the sun to sound synthetic," or "We're in a basement; I need it to feel heavy and low." We have these abstract sensory-centered conversations. There is a lot that I don't have to explain that he just gets, so we can move relatively quickly from idea to actualization. He translates our conversations into sound sketches, and then we go back and forth with edits. Because of this ease, he has been my primary collaborator on the *Negative Space* series. I may be dictating what I want from the sound, but Geo provides such a compelling articulation of my ideas. The work simply wouldn't function without him.

There's also a dance track in each of the four works in *Negative Space* because I think of dance as a liberatory form. In *A Smeary Spot*, we see a Free Radical dancing on the crest of a waterfront rock, flagging the sun with a space blanket. This scene is meant to play with the history of flagging (hanky codes) at gay bars, but in this case the prospective love interest is the sun.

Time-based, audiovisual content can be a consuming medium. Audio has a lot to do with that. I want my viewer to trust me enough to stick with me for fifty-three minutes, following a nonnarrative logic that may prove elusive. I think these seductive tools—cultivating audiovisual curiosity—are essential to communicating with the gut of my viewer.

KA   *You mentioned that in making the* Negative Space *tetralogy, you were exploring the cinematic genre of science fiction, which is fantasy driven and generally*

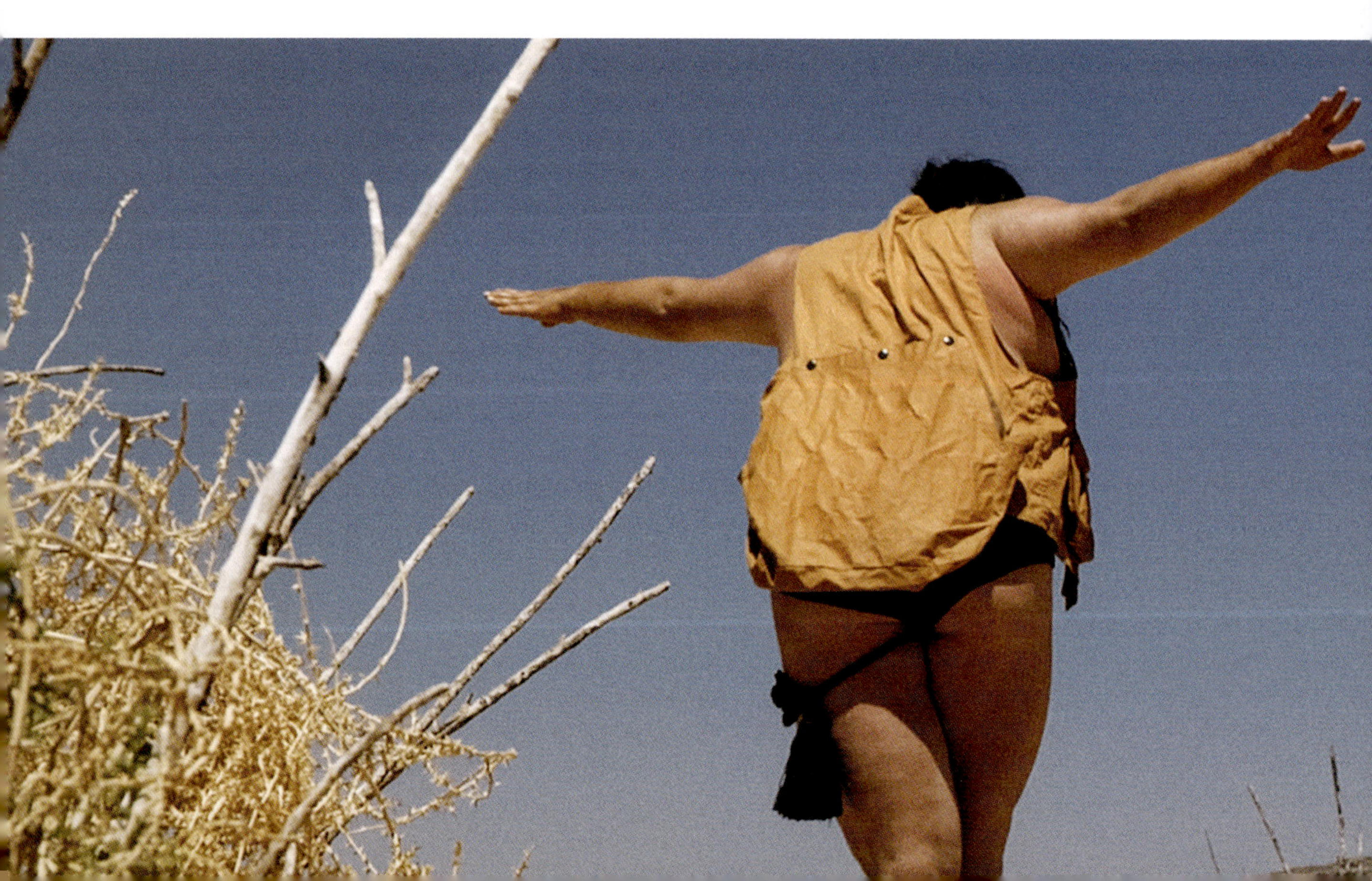

AKB   Well, yes, but not necessarily. I enjoy figuring out ways to imbue a scene with surreal or fantastical qualities through low-budget means. I achieve this quality mostly with sound, camera angle, and editing. The videos that *Negative Space* comprises are responding to the reality of the world they are shot in. This is where another of the premises for the work emerged: the idea of locating it in a speculative present. The present is the past ending and the future becoming simultaneously, so the present has the future within it. Therefore, I believe you can't have an alternative future without creating an alternative present. The speculative present came from the idea that if I wanted a different kind of future, I would have to approach the whole notion of futurity differently. The concept

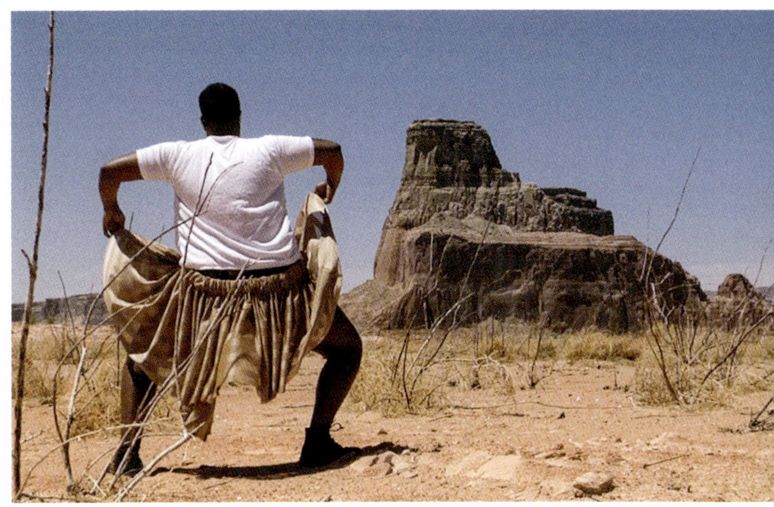

of the speculative present allowed me to draw on current or contextual events, related to the site and the time I was shooting in, and incorporate them into the work. I believe the future is terrestrial and ecological—embedded with all the problems of being a body on Earth (not on a spaceship or another planet). You'll notice technology is only lightly represented in the films, because I'm intentionally stepping away from the techno-romance typical of mainstream science fiction.

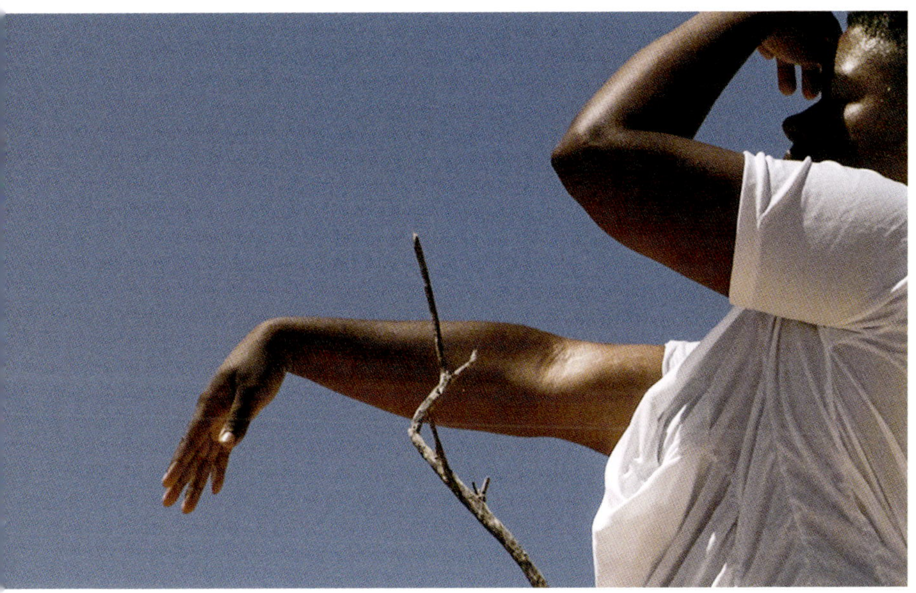

KA   *I have noticed that your works often celebrate and intimately depict queer life. And I'm wondering what you think* A Smeary Spot *does in terms of representation— whether thinking through queer representation was a goal for you in this work. You haven't spoken about that at all.*

AKB   Yes, I've been avoiding that, because I think the expectations of what constitutes queer representation are problematic. I'm anchoring this project in the writings of Karen Barad. Barad does a brilliant job reexamining, through a queer feminist lens, the work of physicist Niels Bohr, who proposed the

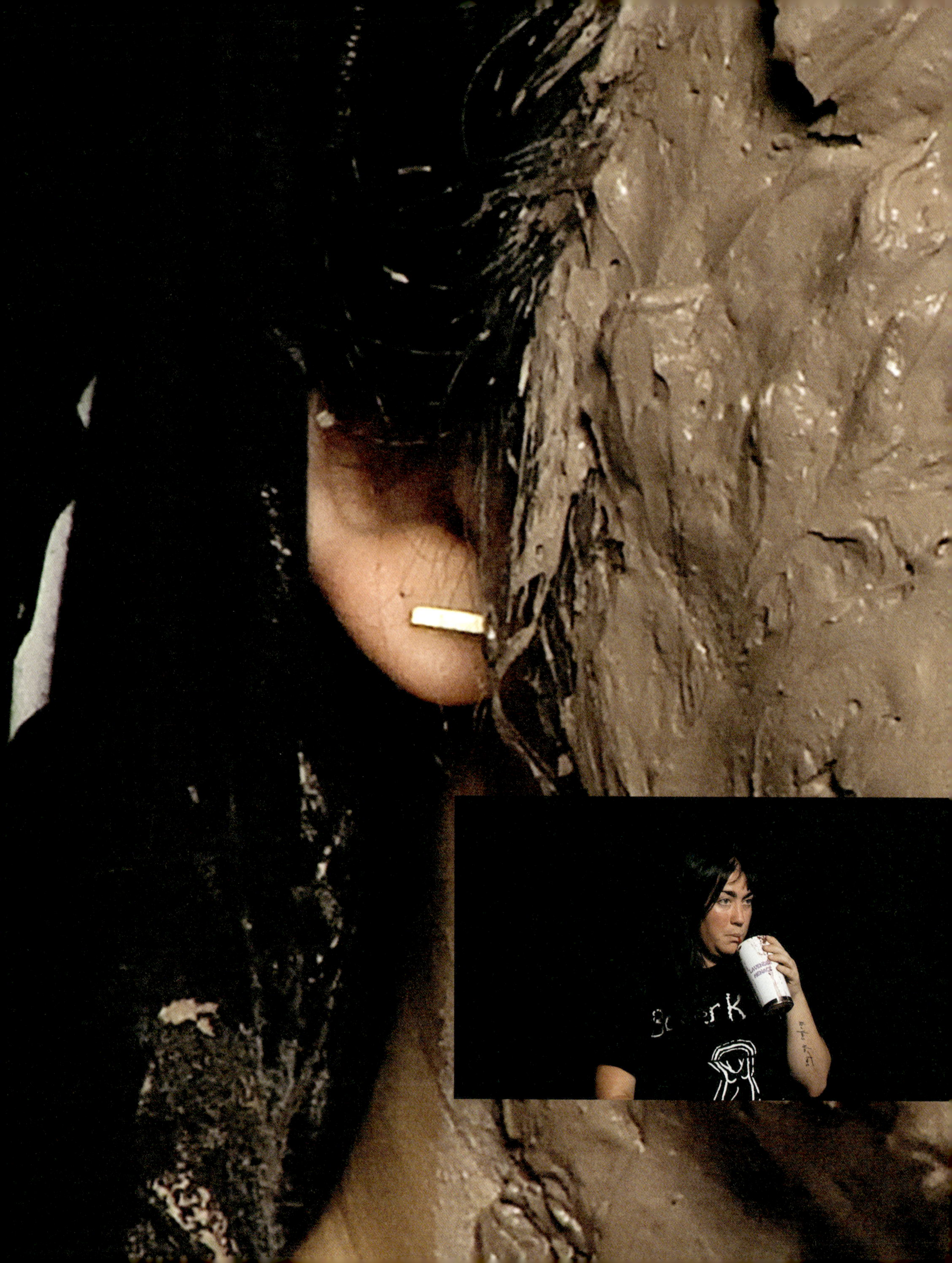

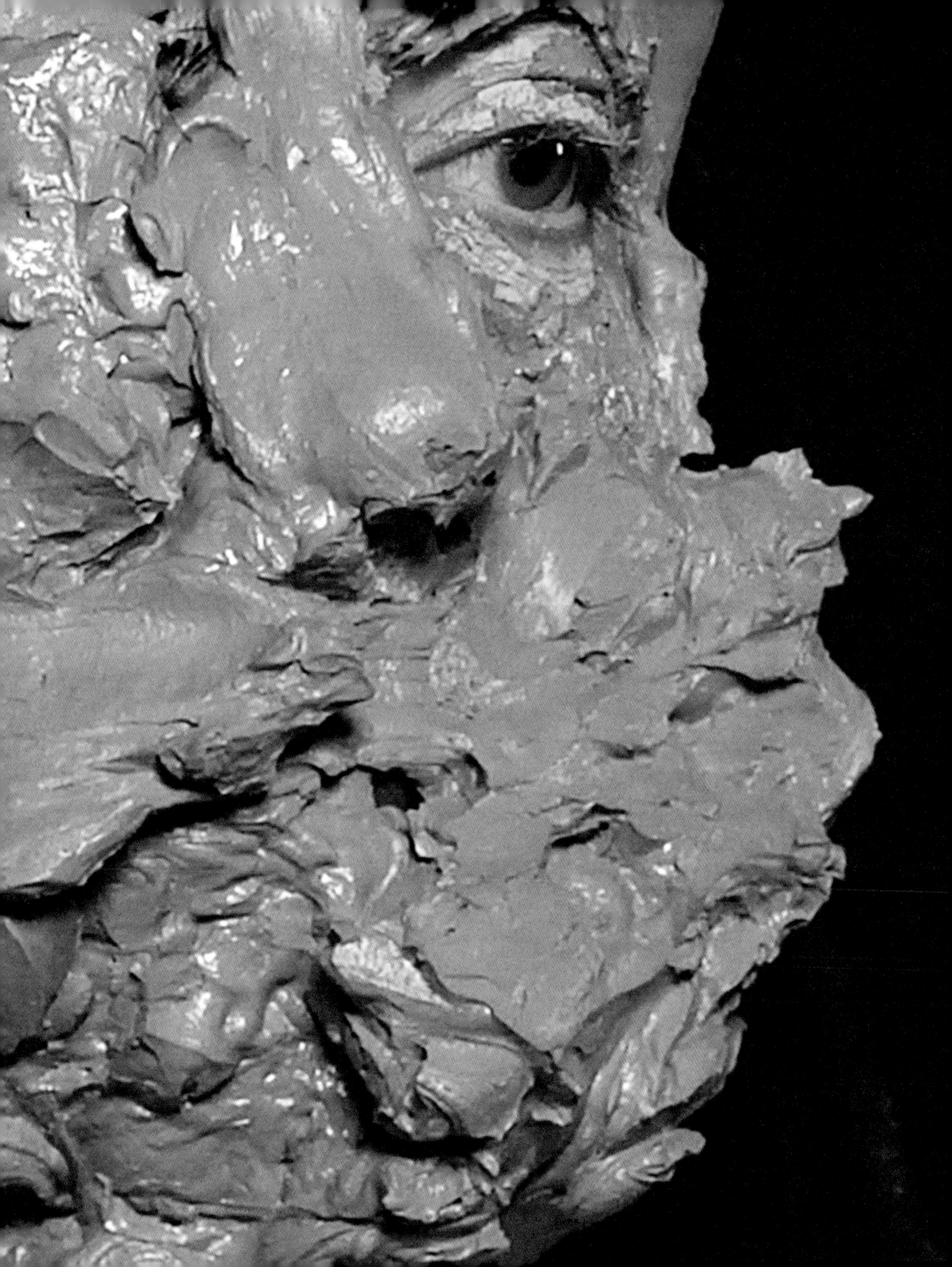

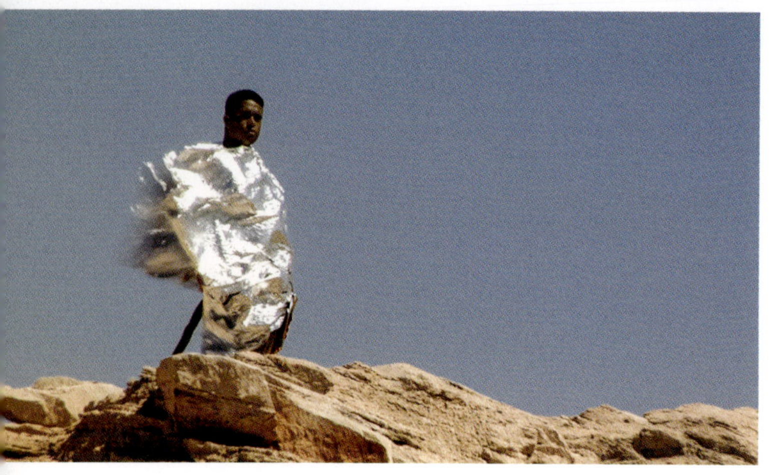

idea of wave-particle duality to explain the results of the double-slit experiment. This experiment exposes the ambiguity of matter and its potential to be multiple things—is it a particle, a wave, or both? What it reveals is that the nature of matter is determined by the tools we use to observe it. The tools of observation change the thingness of a thing. The thing remains open to possibility until the act of observation and translation intrude on the formation of meaning. This poses key questions about the responsibility we have to the tools we use (i.e., the technology we create) and the role technology plays in our (de)formation of the world. Barad is exploring meaning and representation on the quantum molecular (material) level rather than the rainbow-flag (symbolic) level. She goes even further by questioning how material perception changes symbolic representation. In embracing how "queer" matter is and acknowledging how difference takes shape on the smallest scale, I am more invested in queering representation than in representing queerness. Sure, the work is an ecofeminist, queer, utopian proposition. But it's not presented through common queer or sci-fi tropes, as I'm more concerned with reorienting your worldview than with telling you a story.

KA

You are critical of cinema for its propensity to manipulate, and this is uniquely bound up with the politics

of attention. There's a psychological element beyond sound in narrative cinema—for example, one that develops through character by way of professional actors—which you don't emulate in your work. You cast characters as widely as possible, even including landscapes as actors. Still, A Smeary Spot *functions as science fiction. What do you think that your play with and rejection of the tropes of cinema mean in terms of the viewer's experience?*

AKB

Tropes are one tool of many I use to produce affect or create new meaning (when I critique a trope) within the work. But it's important to note that I don't think about my work as cinema; I think about it as sculpture. I think about it as an animated, auditory, physical, time-based sculpture. A lot happens spatially in constructing the installation and mastering the sound.

It's important that viewers feel they are inside the work, so the screens are human scaled. *A Smeary Spot* is a four-channel video installation with three seven-by-twelve-foot screens aligned horizontally to create a panorama that cuts diagonally across a black-box-like space. The fourth channel is a box monitor that runs annotated credits on a loop. The seating evolved from a desire to engage the viewer as an active participant, so I replaced typical stationary seating with office chairs on wheels. There are also accompanying sculptures with office chairs embedded in cast sand, as well as office chairs used as props in the film. I use these chairs to reference white-collar or seated labor.

Through six channels of sound, the viewer's attention is guided across the wide arena of the installation. For example, you might be looking at the screen on the

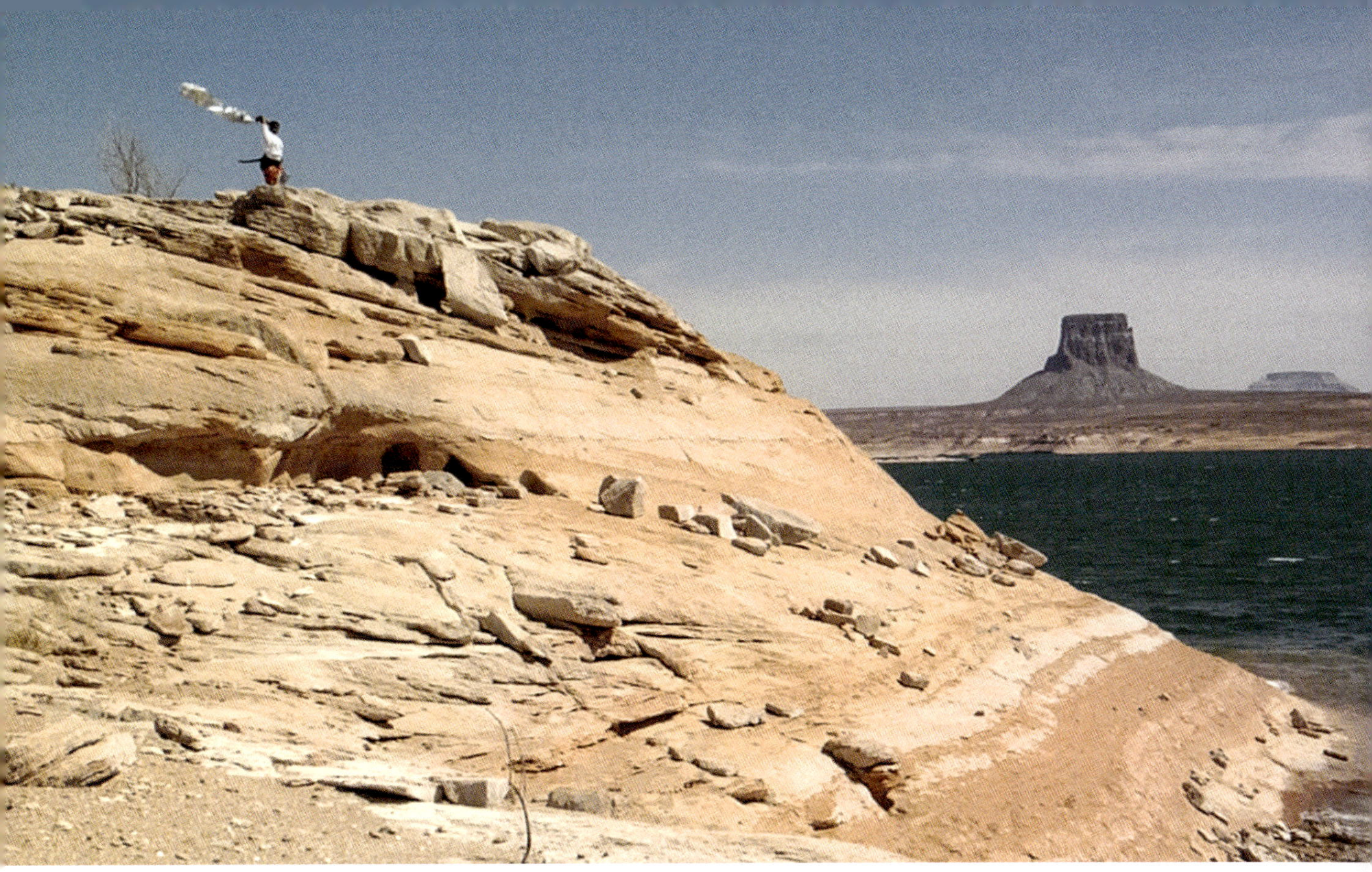

left because the other screens have gone black, but then you hear something from the right and move your attention toward the sound. At other times, you'll experience full surround sound. Ultimately, I'm concerned with creating a physically spatialized experience, not a typical narrative cinematic experience. This is because I want to speak to my viewer through their bodies to get to their mind, that is, through the gut—a felt, sensory, and aesthetic perception first.

KA *Can you tell me about the role of that little cube monitor in the installation setup?*

AKB That box monitor is cycling the credits so that the main three screens can run continuously with no obvious beginning or end. Time is cyclical in *Negative Space*. I've added atypical things to the credits, treating them more like footnotes. There is information about the script and the longitude and latitude of the shooting sites, and the performers are named in ways that give a viewer some language for how I think about organizing this world. So if you actually sit there and read the credits, there's information to orient you in the world-building. That's also why a poster of the script is available for viewers to take home with them. The poster makes explicit the sources of the quotes I borrowed to create the script, as well as my edits to them—edits I made to make theoretical texts feel less didactic or to remove gender. The pronouns *he/him* are often used in older texts to refer generally to humans, so I changed all those instances to the first-person *I*, enabling the performers to embody what they were saying. Also, making credits integral to the work exposes the way these installations require collective labor to come to fruition.

KA *The script must have helped to structure the piece. While reading it, I was wondering how you put it together. There are affinities, affiliations, and politics—from*

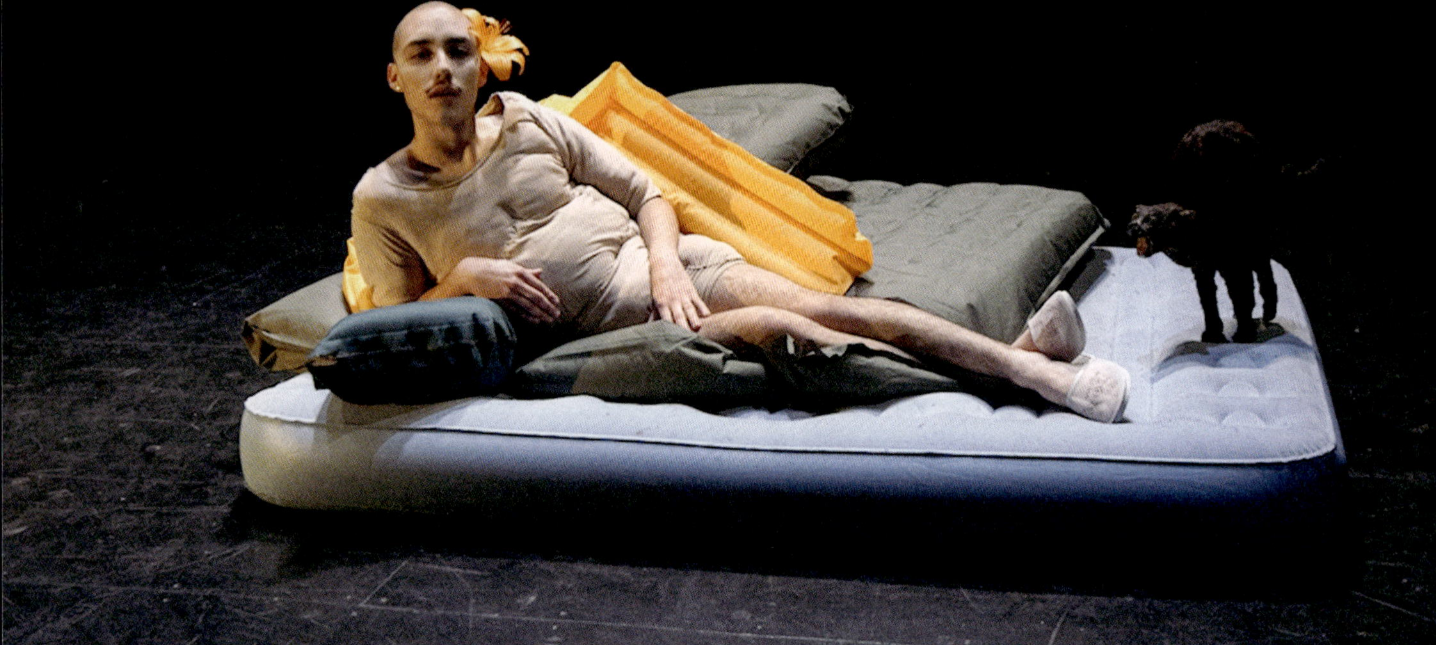

AKB   The script developed from all the initial research. At some point, I had extracted quotes that interested me. I had a pile of photocopied texts. I started to arrange them and think about them threading
together as a manifesto of sorts; much like the film, these fragments of language would coalesce
into a larger statement. Both the research and the arrangement of the quotes was rather intuitive, so
it structured itself in a way.

      Then I realized the script could structure the theatrical space of the black box, which led
me to think more about theater and the function of the script as the driver of narrative.
For me, the script addresses the way language is a material unto itself. In *A Smeary Spot*,
there is a trifecta of language, action, and props (matter) that is activated by the performers
to create new interpretations of the texts.

KA

AKB   They're not sketches. That is, they were not made prior to the videos. After I had finished the films
and knew what elements of my research had made it into the final video edit, I created them from
my collection of research images. I started with way more content than what made it into the final

works. And I made them not only to catalogue the source material that went into building each film but also to serve as annotations for the hybridized visual concepts I use to develop each scene. The titles are usually associated with qualities or elements of the scenes that they're representing.

KA — *Their titles point the viewer specifically toward things in the films, putting words to them.*

AKB — Yes. The titles together with the images that make up the collages offer a lot of clues to how to read scenes in the film. It's a big demand on the viewer to make the leaps necessary to decipher all the intellectual and conceptual components of the work; the collages are a way to provide visual footnotes. I want viewers to give in to thinking or perceiving things differently as they watch the videos—understanding land as a protagonist or the actors as metaphors, for example. For me, the collages are an additional tool, offering insight into how I build allegory through numerous visual and textual sources. These collage works function similarly to sharing the scripts as a takeaway poster and featuring the credits so prominently. Annotation is a part of the vocabulary of *Negative Space*; I'm often exposing the inner workings or process.

When I realized I wanted to add these collages to the project, I started thinking about the composition of a collage, and that the piece of paper, the support for the collage, would essentially be the negative space of the composition. For viewers who walk by them and observe them, the mirrors offer a surface that is active and a constantly shifting reflection of the environment. Thereby, the mirror both is the compositional negative space and signals the conceptual framework for *Negative Space* as a larger project.

KA — *This also makes me think of the title of the work,* A Smeary Spot. *How did you come up with that title, and how does it relate to its content?*

AKB — The title comes from an excerpt from Joanna Russ's novel *We Who Are About to . . .* that is recited in the middle of the film by the Clairvoyant Psyche, who is performed by drag legend Flawless Sabrina (rest in power). In the novel, "a smeary spot" is a reference to the visual trace or light blur that comes from looking directly into the sun. A smeary spot is the afterglow—the temporary imprint on your retina. Our relationship to the sun represents our most fundamental relationship to power; this centralized entity dictates so much for us—how we relate to time, our ability to eat, etc. It brings life and can take life away in its absence. The sun is luminous, enhancing our ability to see, yet looking into the sun can ruin your eyes. Like all forms of power, it has positive and negative potential. In a sense, a smeary spot is the blur that happens when we look away and reorient our relationship to power.

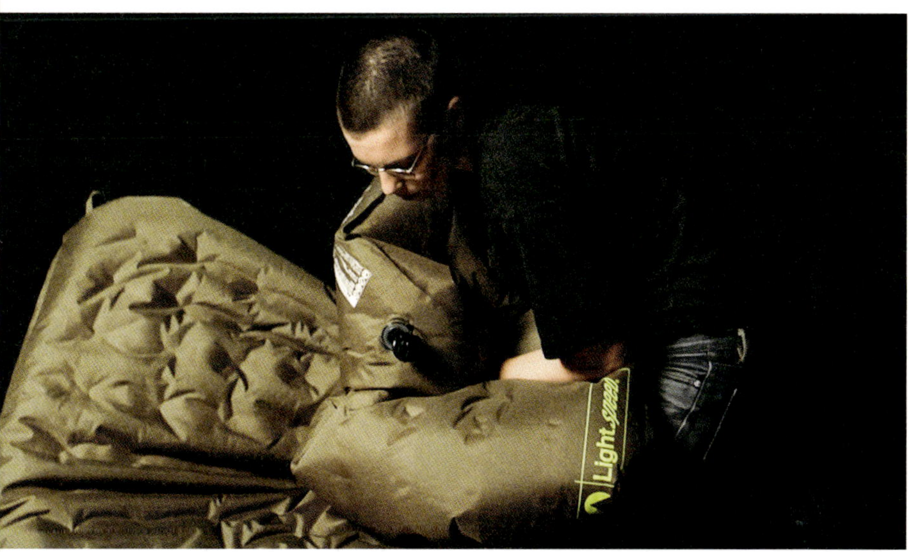

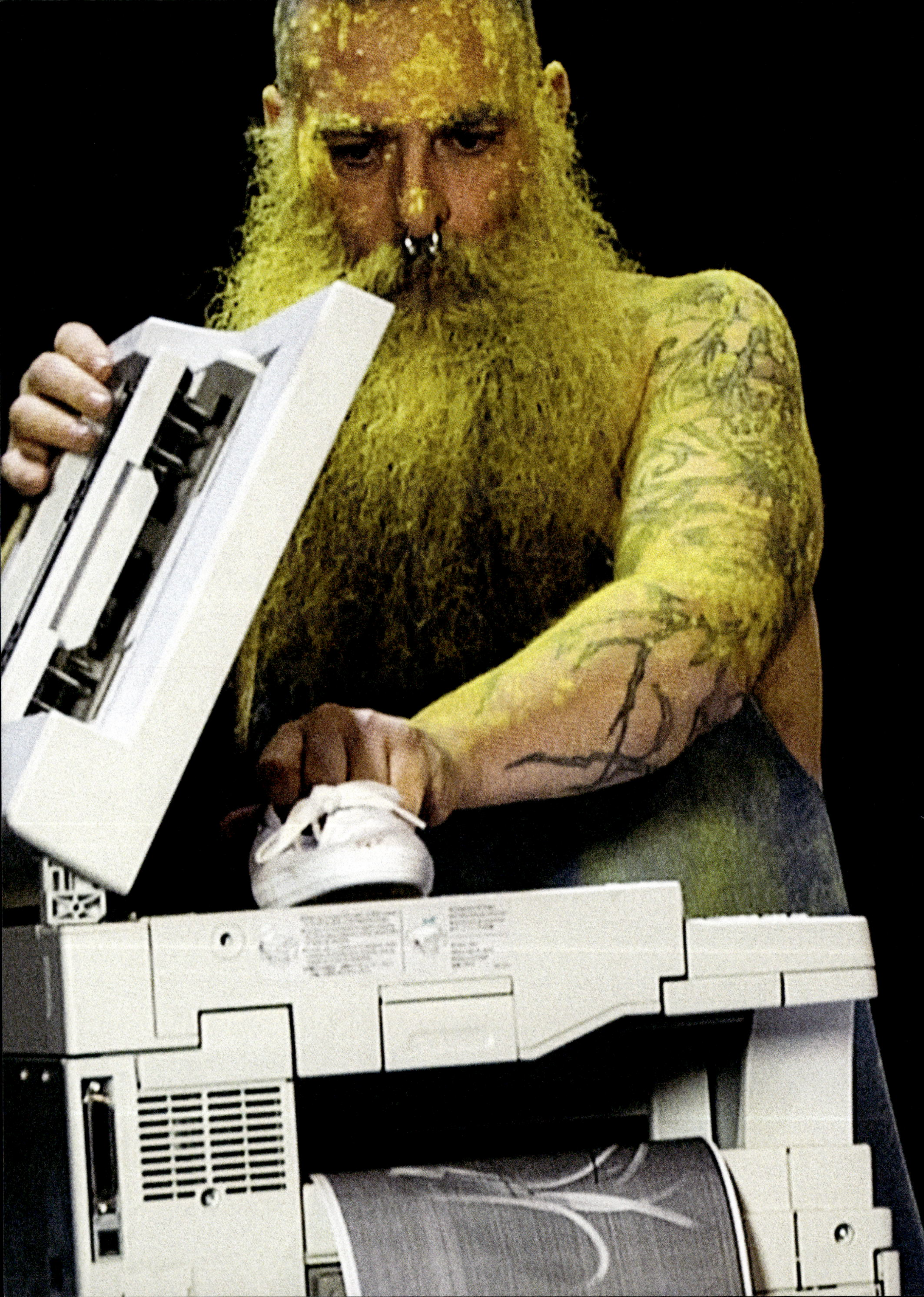

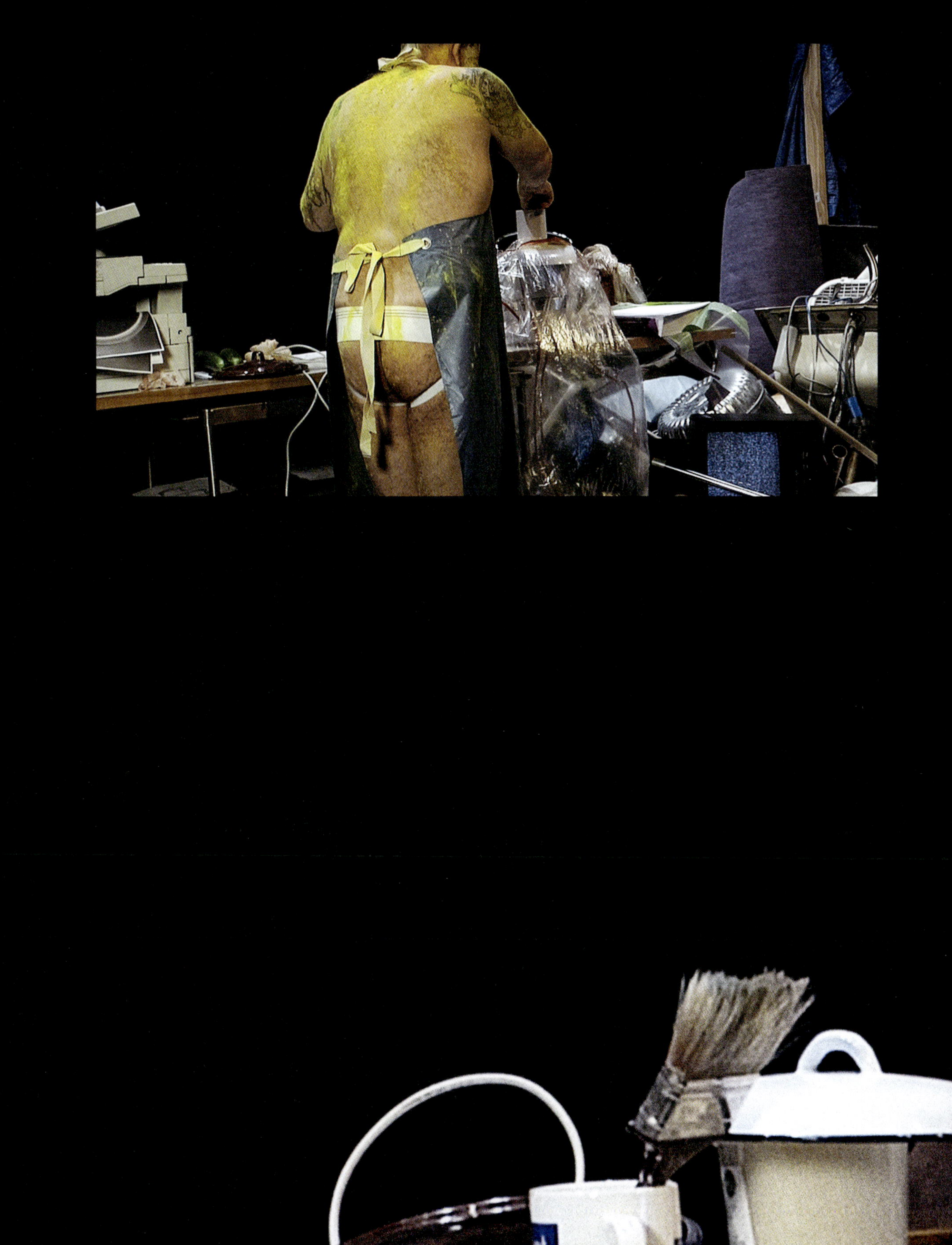

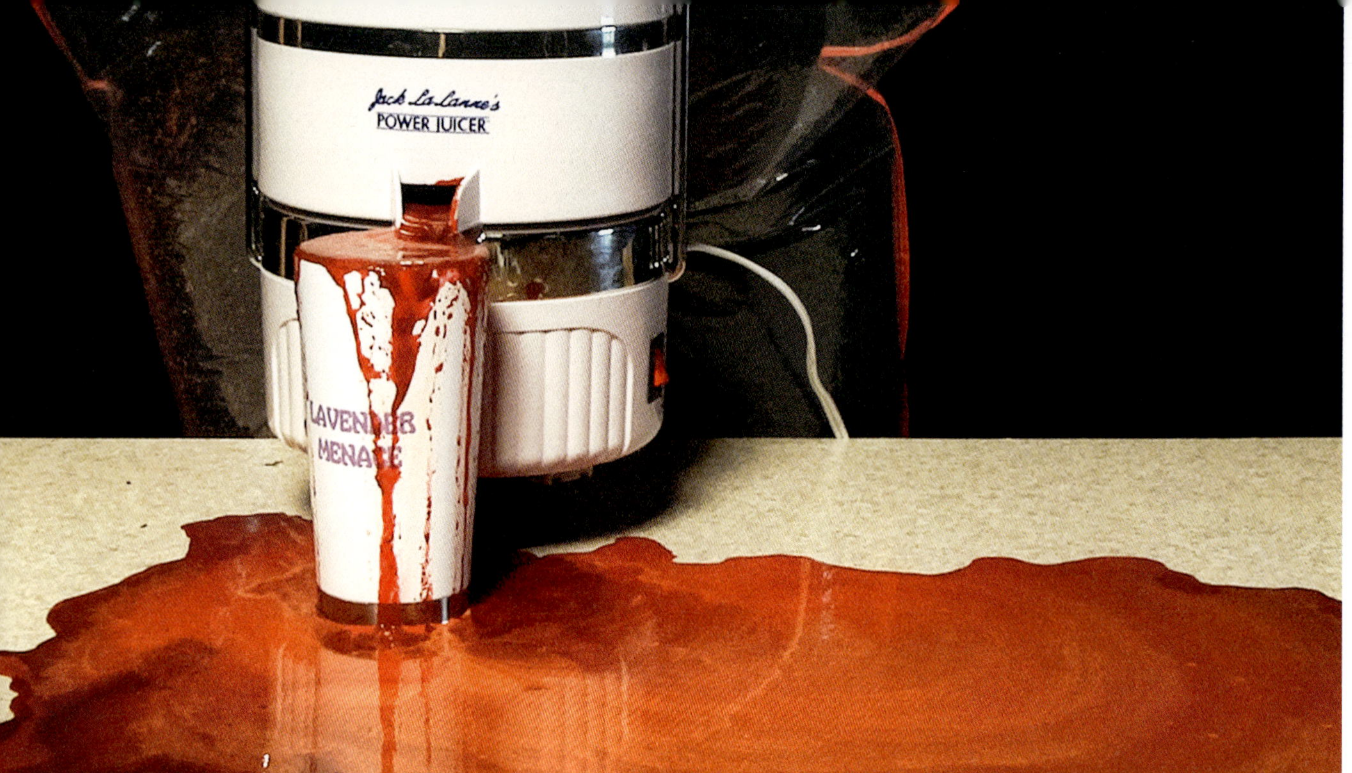

KA   *Let's zoom out a bit; you mentioned that you learned a lot by making* A Smeary Spot—*that it almost felt like*

0 5 0

you were relieving yourself of your research. Looking back on it now, seven years later, what do you think of it? What does the perspective of time give you with this work?

AKB   Well, it's interesting . . . sometimes, it surprises me how much it still resonates. Of the four works, *A Smeary Spot* is the longest in duration, and parts of it, especially some of its desert scenes, have a wandering quality. I think I was wandering through the process of its making, and that is partially what the viewer experiences. But it's also representative of the way that I work. Fia Backström and I joke that we're epic artists. For me, everything is so deeply interconnected. I don't have an interest in synthesizing things into discrete, easy-to-digest artworks. I've spent my lifetime as an artist gradually allowing the work to be more entangled because I want to express the complexity of the world as it is. *A Smeary Spot* is the first time I opened this can of worms, so to speak, for myself and told myself, "You have total freedom to wander, experiment, and explore." Through building this work, I feel like I have learned how to be expansive and pointed at the same time.

KA   A Smeary Spot *seems to be wandering for a purpose. You wanted to have the freedom to wander around your thoughts to get into the core of the work, not only because it was the first time you opened the can of worms but also because it reflects a naturally complex politics.*

AKB   The whole project of feminism and queer politics is not discrete or concise. I believe that the most antipatriarchal thing you can do is to not organize yourself in an easily digestible manner. The whole strategy of branding and creating an economy around your work as an artist is about having a "thing" that you do. The searching and learning are what is truly feminist and truly queer about the work.

KA *Your attention to not just the content of what you're making but also how it's made is meaningful. I sense the politics of making in your work—they are particularly palpable in this piece—as well as in your solidarity with other artists, in how you bring their practices into your work in a way that's respectful and consent based.*

AKB Not to sum things up too much, but for me the process is the product. It's through process that the work takes formation. And this is something I encourage in my teaching: an undoing of one's orientation toward the thesis or concept to be executed. I teach to stay inside the process of asking questions and pursuing a path of inquiry. This works against the time of the art world—nothing in our world is built for durational wandering, you know. But wandering doesn't mean that you don't know what you're doing. You have to know yourself well, and you have to know what politics or ideas matter to you. You have to know a lot of things in a way that is embodied and intuitive. Only then can you find out what the work will become.

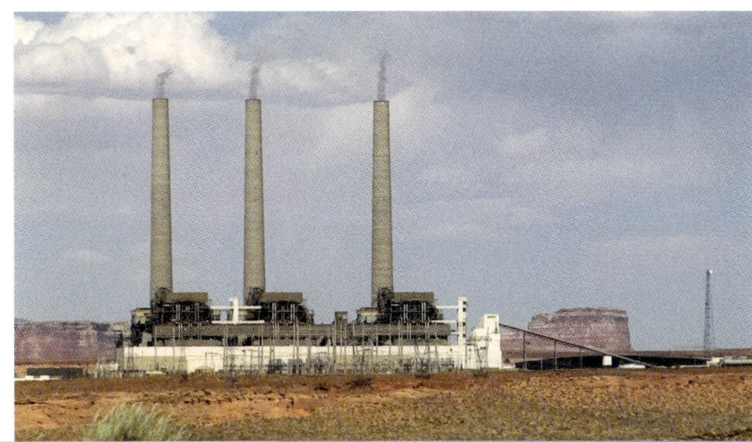

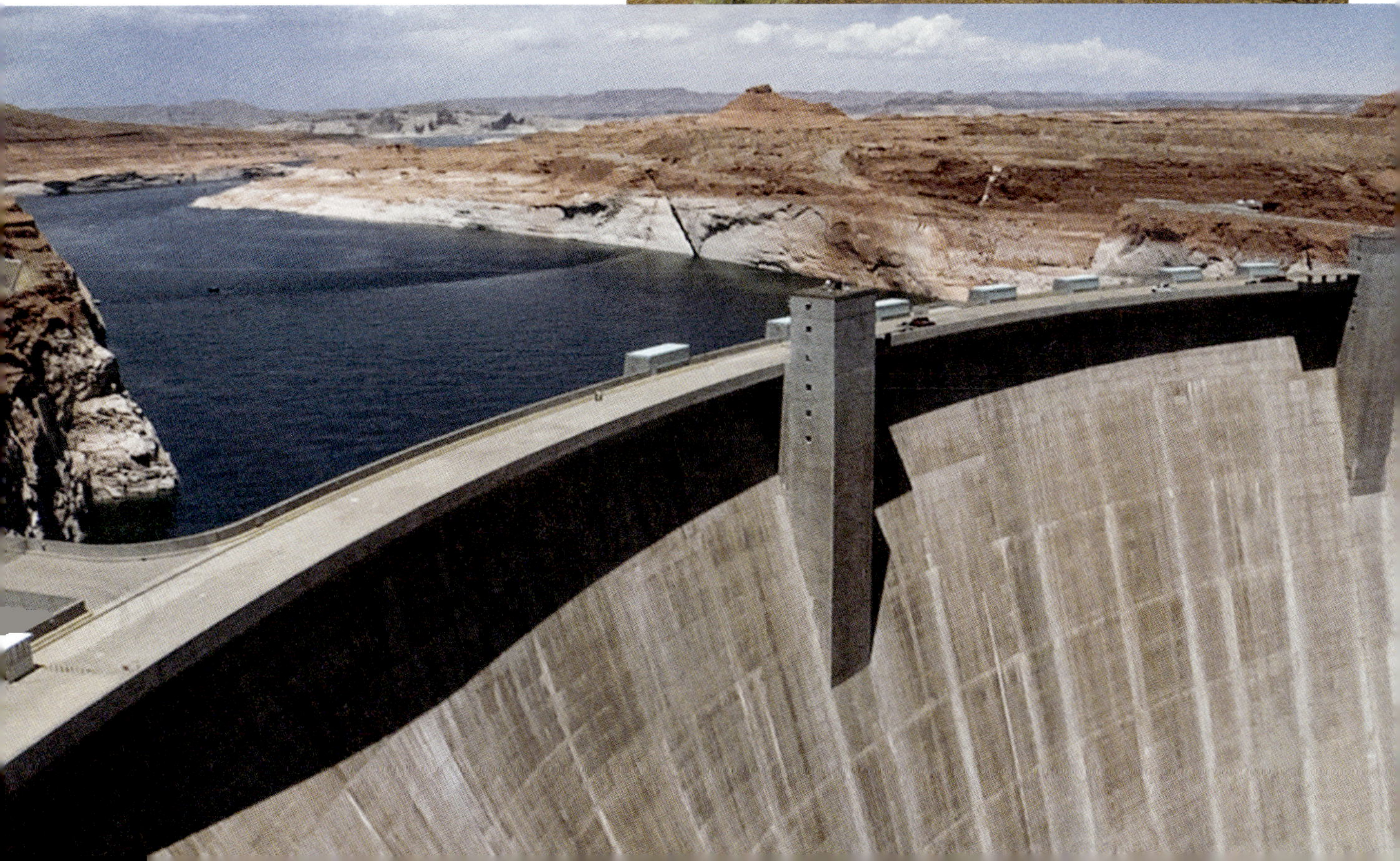

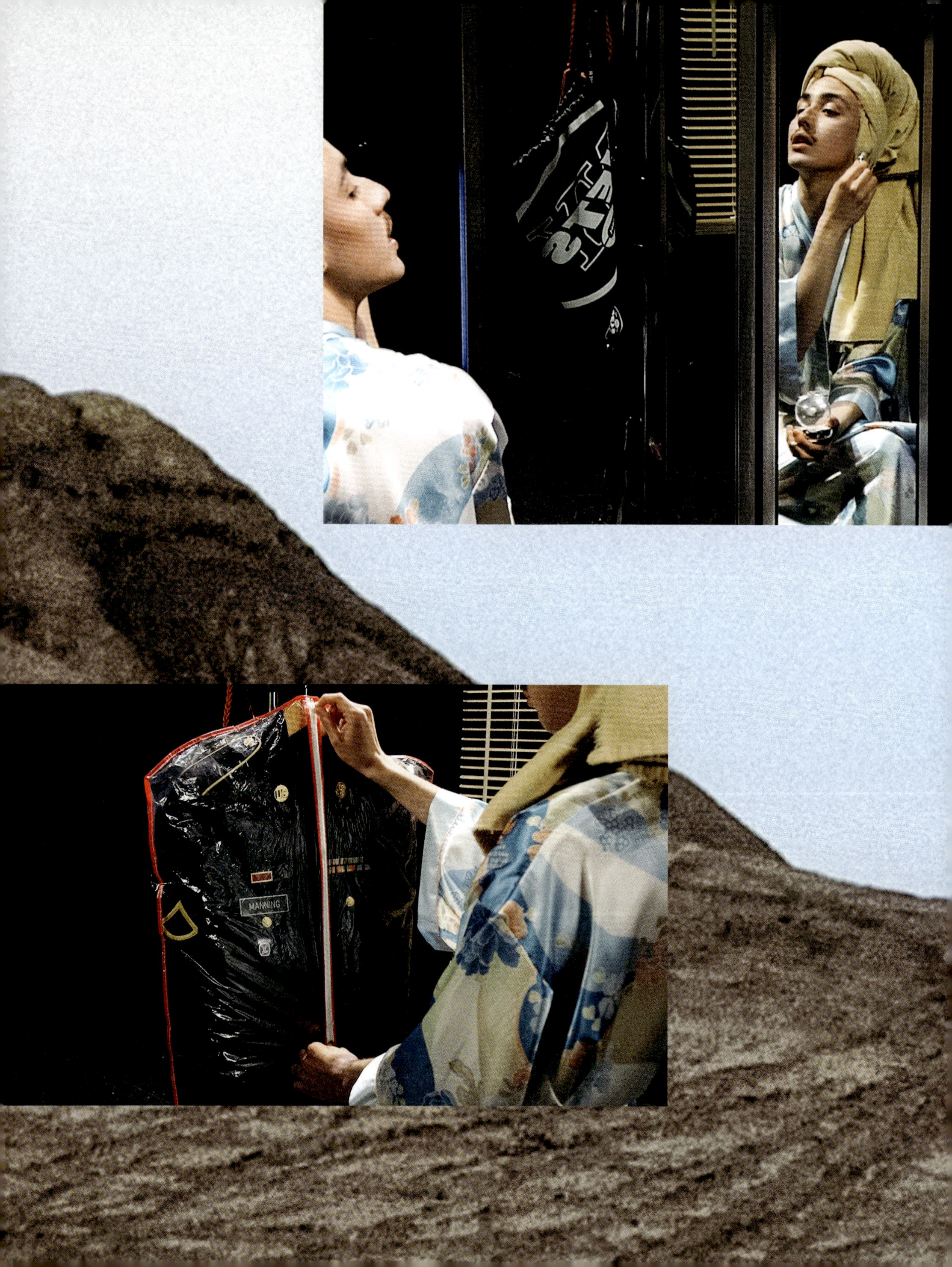

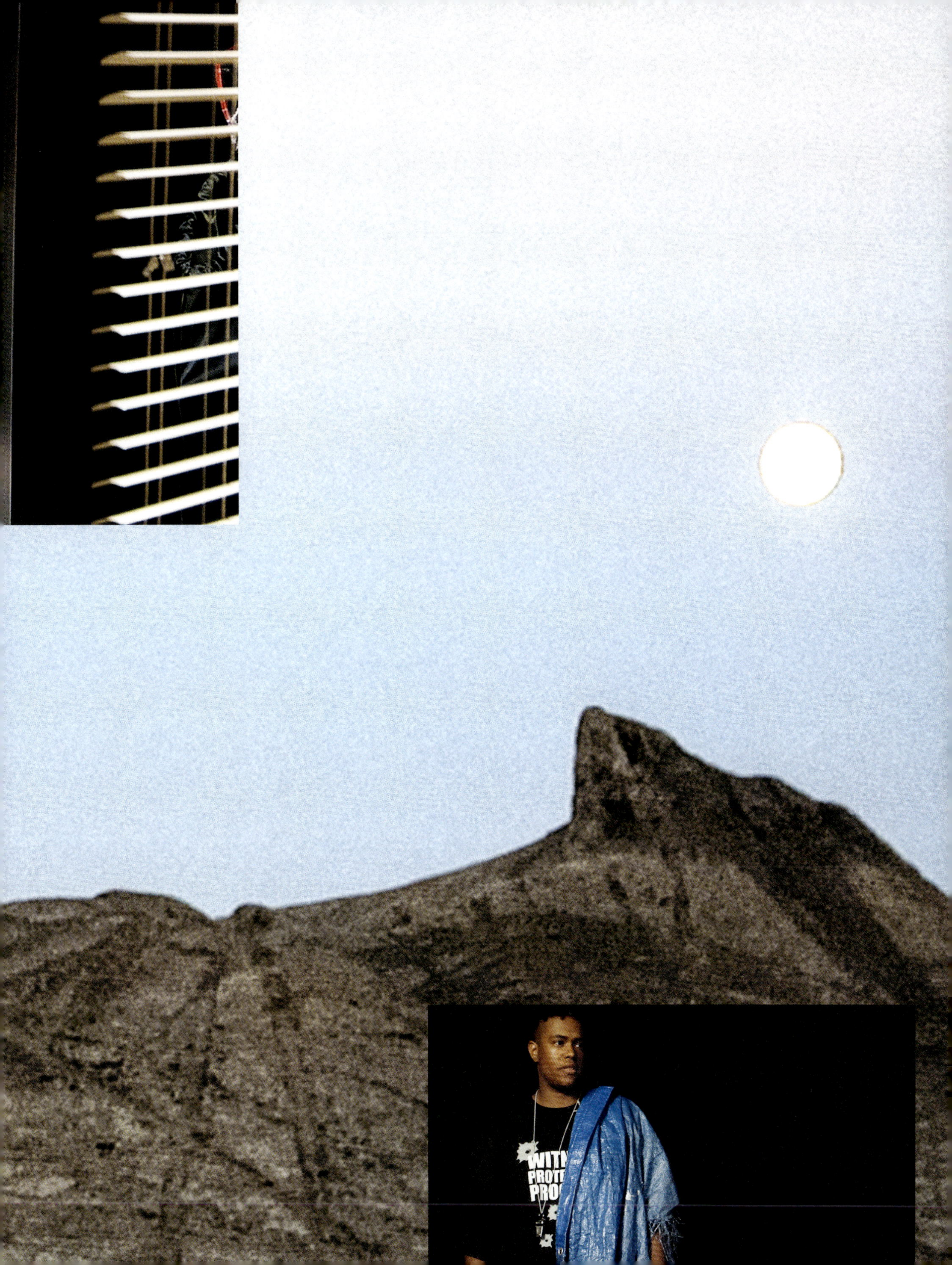

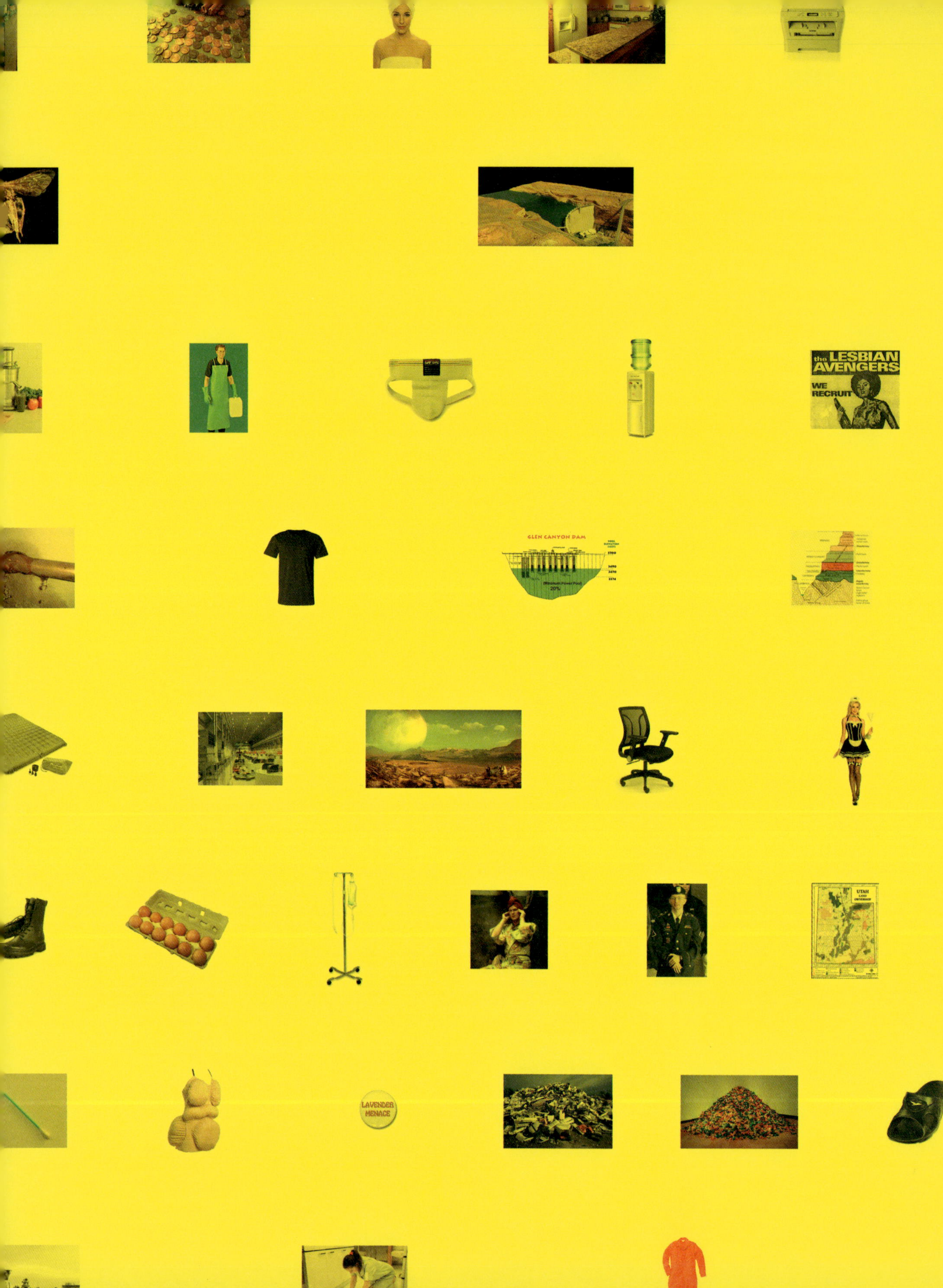
the LESBIAN AVENGERS
WE RECRUIT
GLEN CANYON DAM
LAVENDER MENACE
UTAH LAND OWNERSHIP

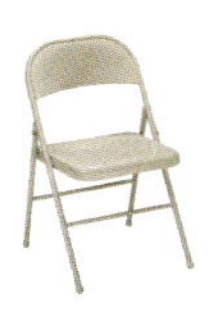

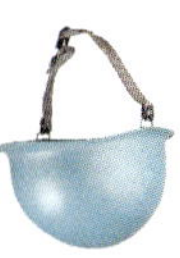

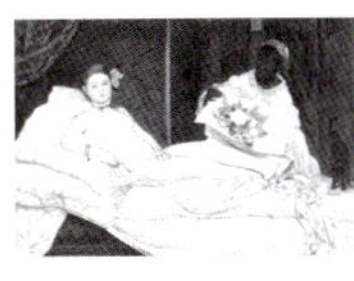

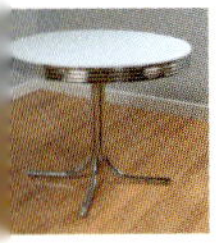

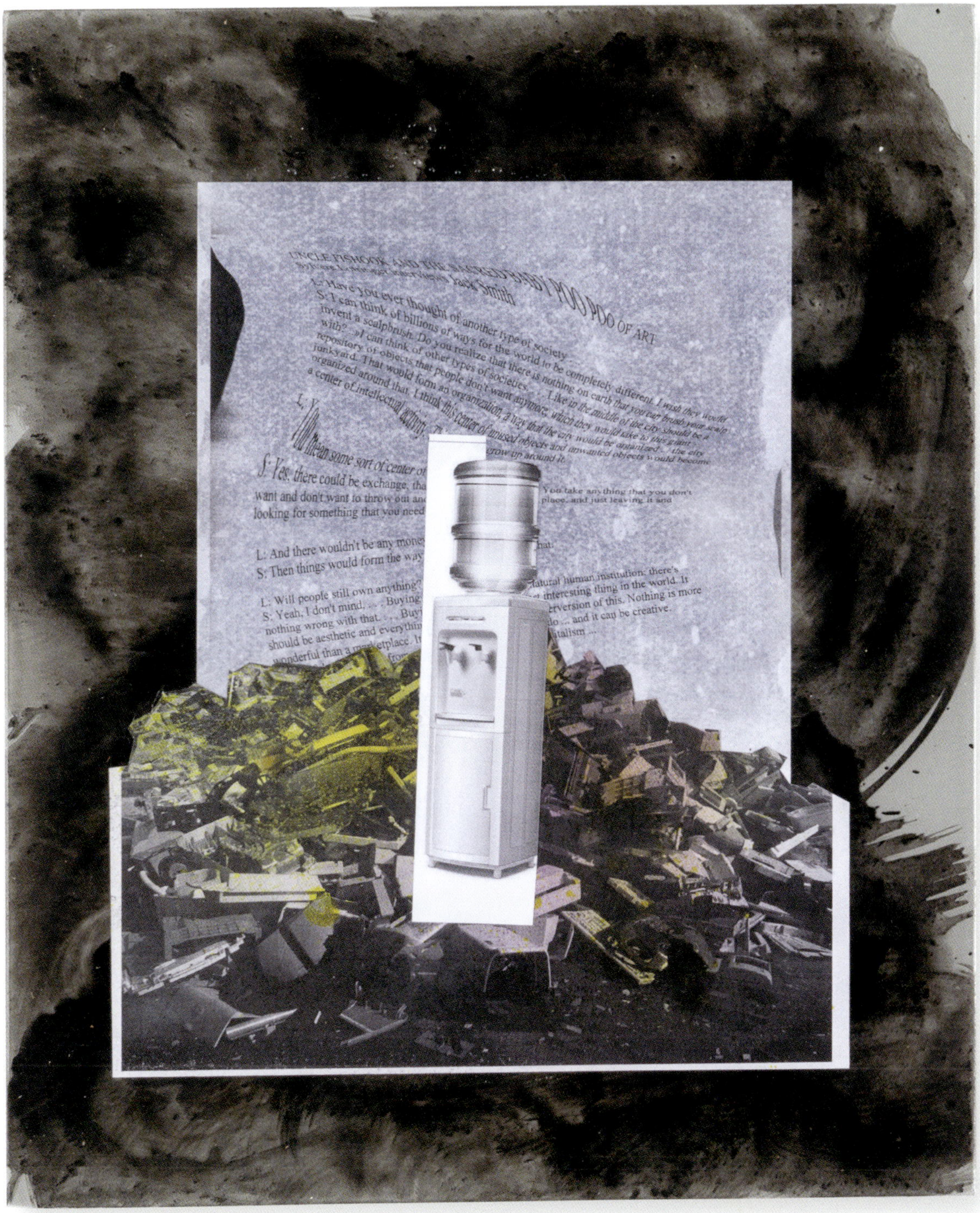

0 5 5

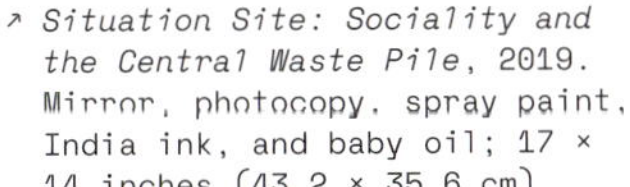

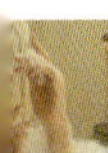

> *Situation Site: Sociality and the Central Waste Pile*, 2019. Mirror, photocopy, spray paint, India ink, and baby oil; 17 × 14 inches (43.2 × 35.6 cm)

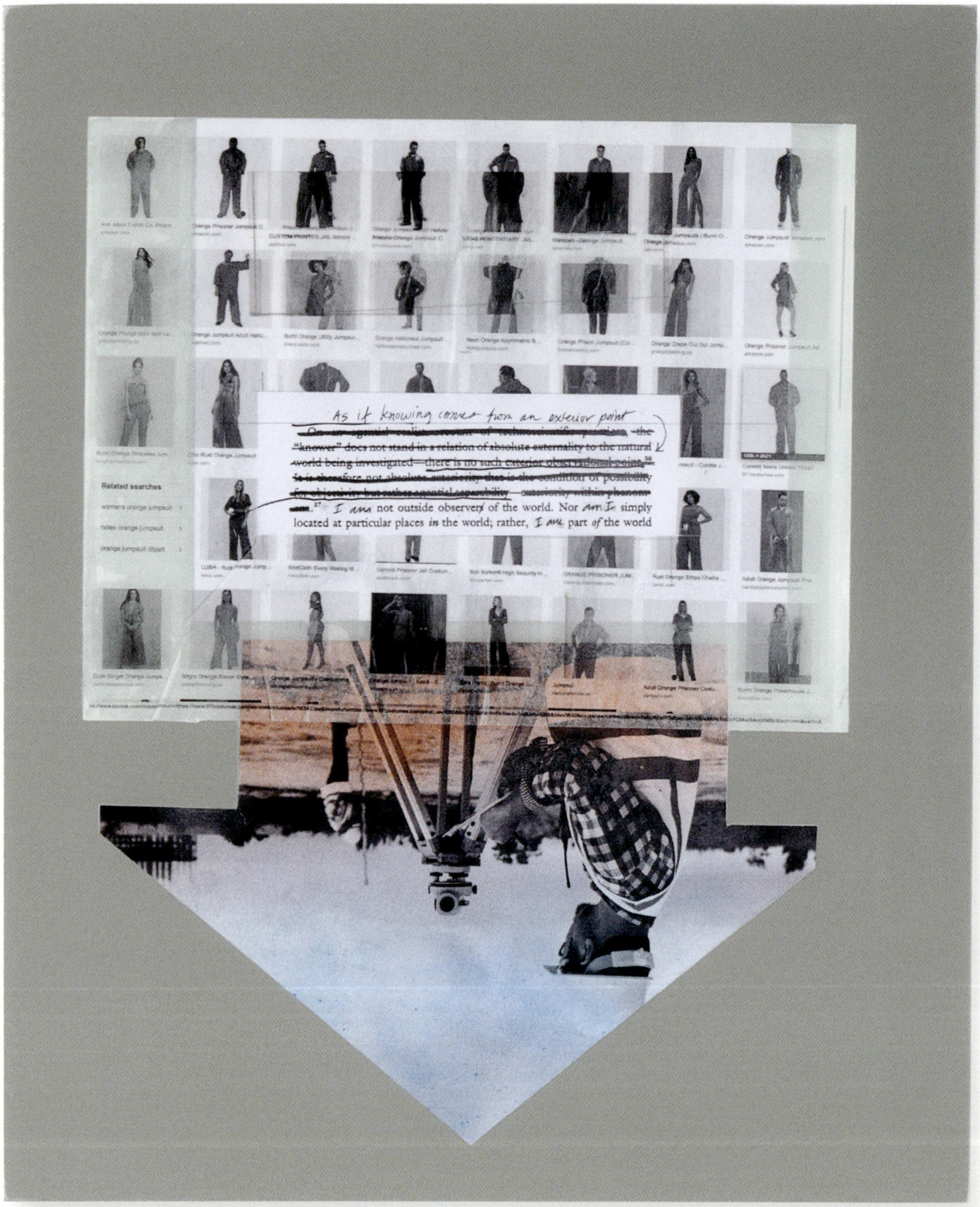

↑ *Obsurveyor*, 2019. Mirror, photocopy, and spray paint; 17 × 14 inches (43.2 × 35.6 cm)

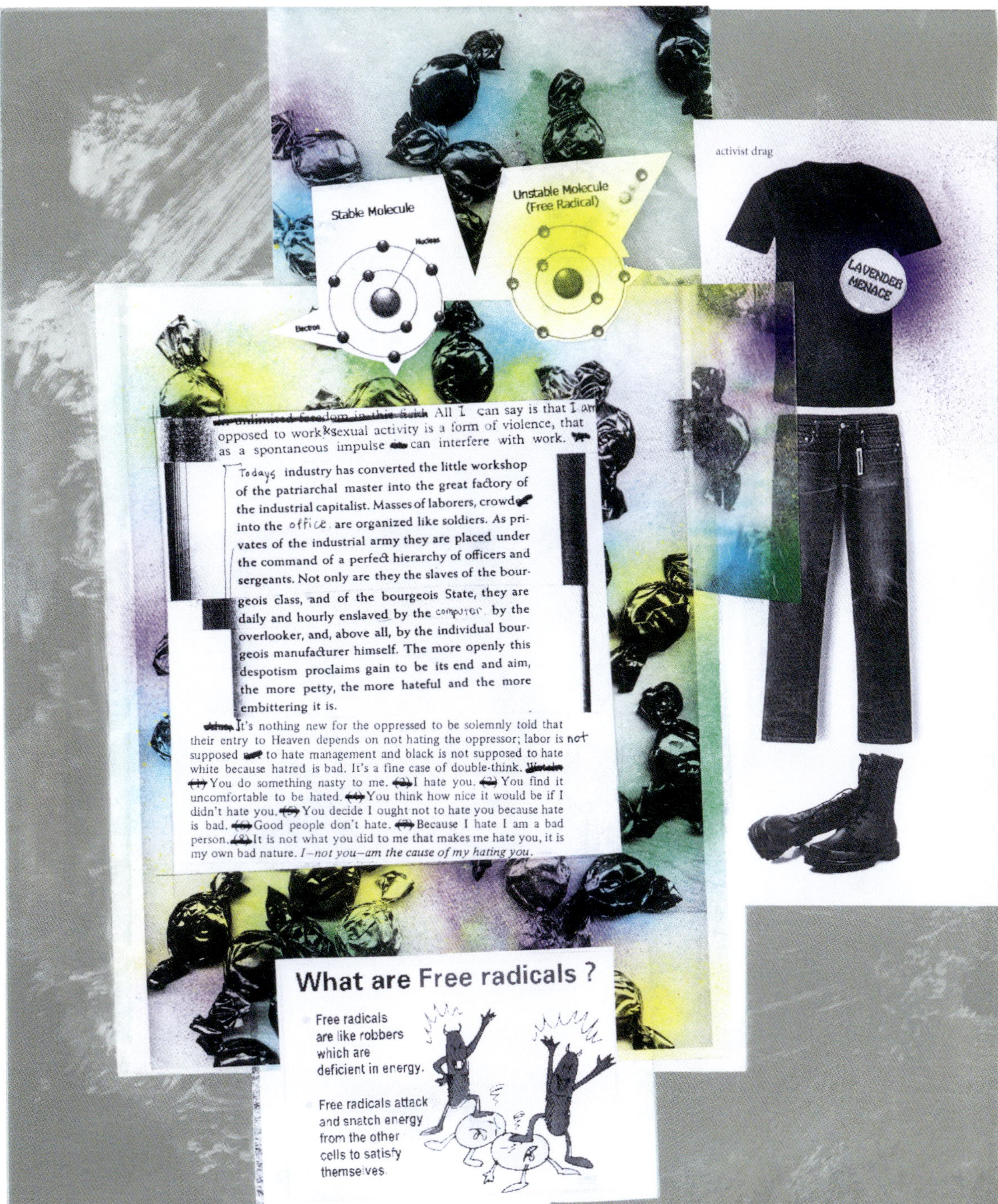

↗ *Free Radicals*, 2019. Etched mirror, photocopy, and spray paint; 17 × 14 inches (43.2 × 35.6 cm)

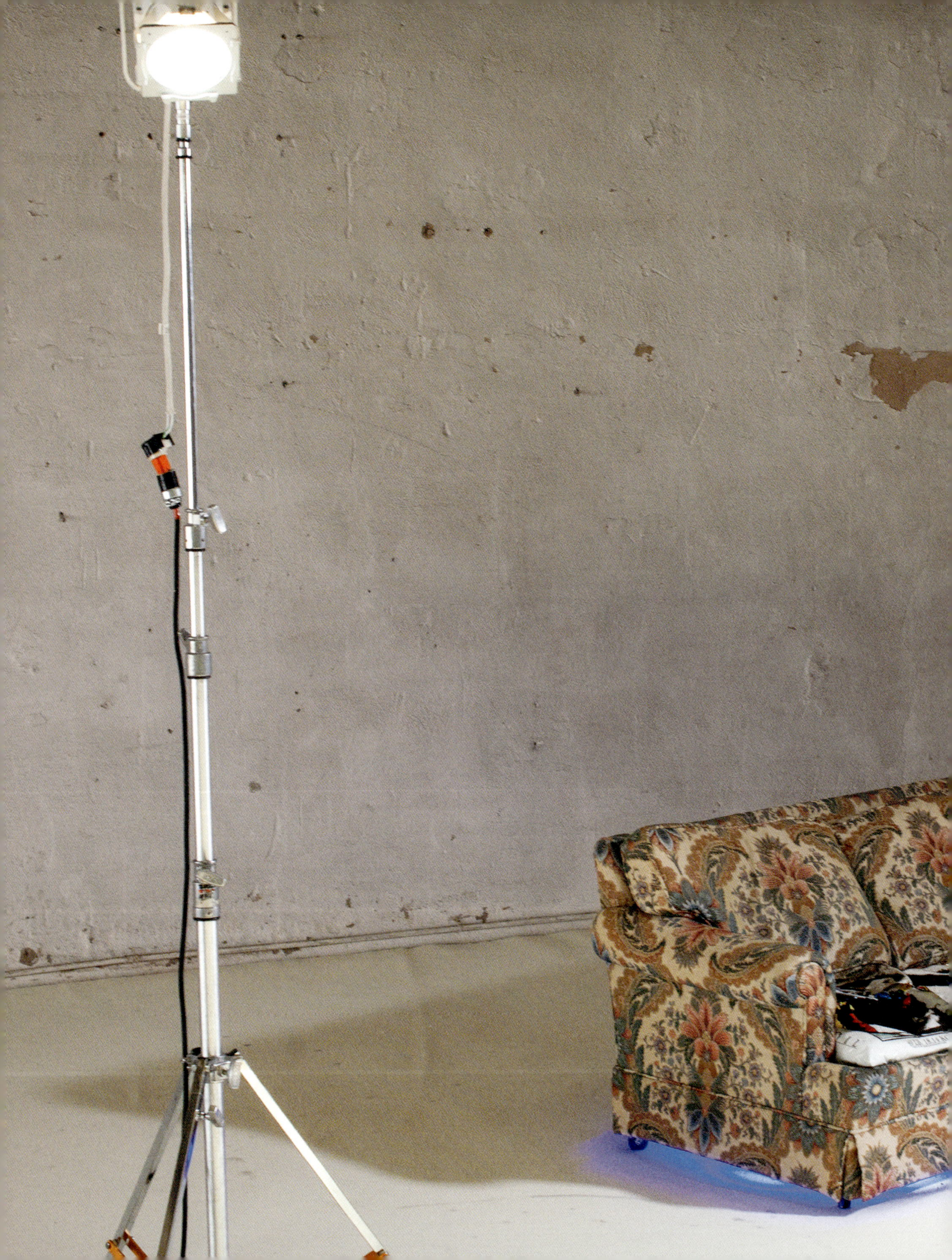

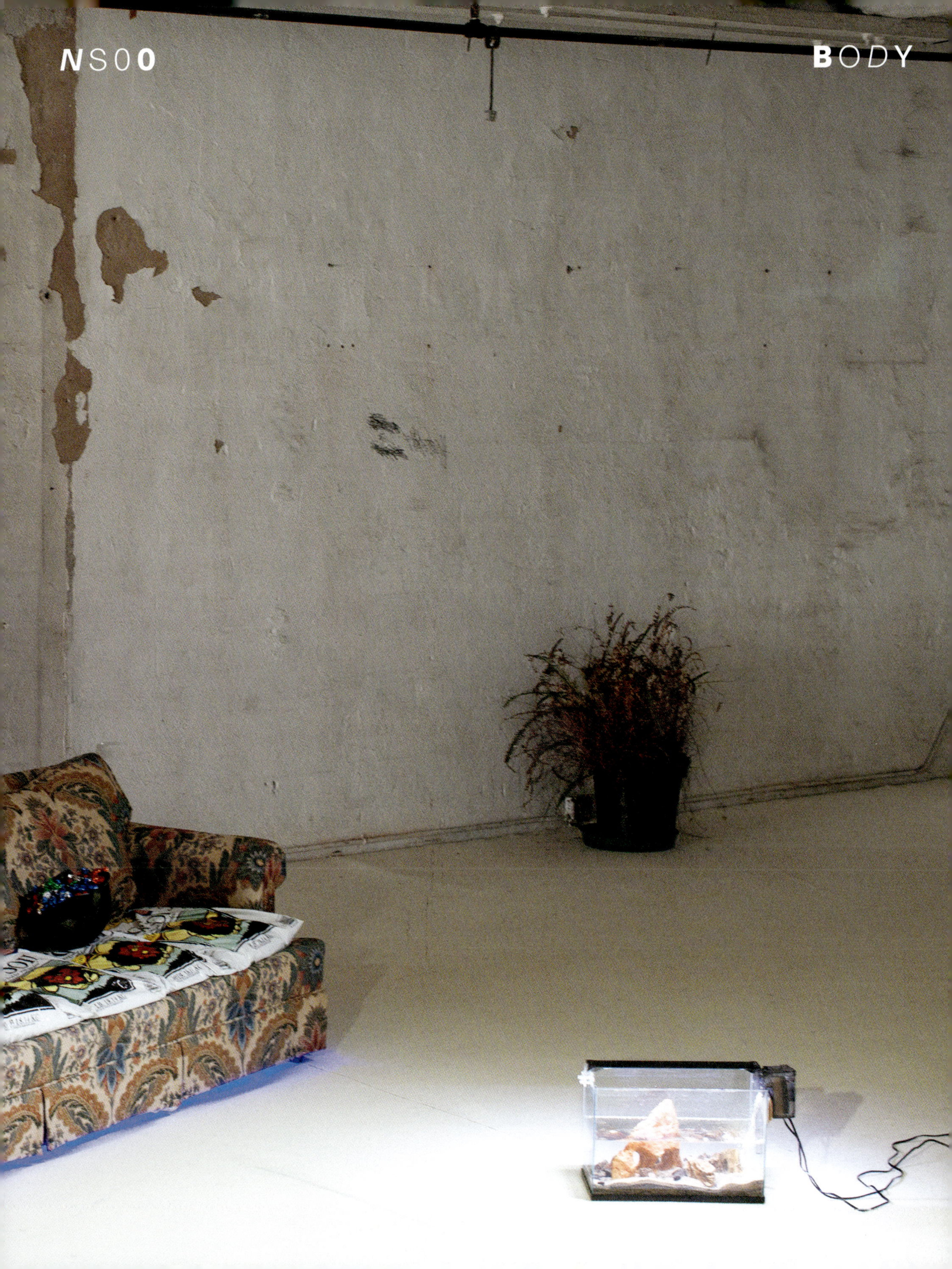
NS00
BODY

(BODY)

We could start with a question: What is the right container for living or for a life? We could try to answer: a cell, a home, a family, a forest, a skin, a collective, an ecology, a body.

The question is fair, viable, and maybe even appealing. It is inexhaustible in its potential to prompt riffs of the imagination, but at the same time it conjures basic images of enclosure. The simplicity of the question should prompt suspicion. It obscures the question at its root: what is life itself? And further: what counts as an individuated life? What equivalences make it enumerable? Are there ways to understand life without turning to the biological (and also to the species), the mechanistic, or even the material? And once we name a container, is it still possible to imagine? Or can life be conceived without an enclosure, as a material existence that doesn't behave according to ordinary physics? As a major currency, as the underpinnings of material existence, from linguistic practices to mediations of care to ontological theory, the body is revealed, not as an innocuous given, but as a conspirator in violence at scale. Is it possible to extricate and unknow the body, even as replacements and displacements are sought?

(TEARDOWN)

Perhaps a body is more of an effect, or an apparition, than a transcendent and self-possessed entity. If the human body is used as a projective basis for any body, it is worth remembering that material containment and social isolation can kill it, for the drawstring bag of human skin leaks and absorbs as much as it holds. In other bodies, whether glass, plastic, or metal, rigidities and stabilities yield to material degradation—flaking, sagging, and biochemical transformation. The ostensible structural legitimacy and logic of a body, from a synchronic viewpoint, is exposed as a wispy integrity legitimated by a narrow present. At the very least, to call something a body is to name an assemblage, but its integrity is temporally subject to change and stasis; it is only a body if it hasn't decayed to the point of proving more porous than sealed. Bodies apprehended as such can also transform or lose their stability under the effects of contamination-intoxication. Yet the relentless commodification of the body naturalizes its reification into something biopolitically enduring, seamless, which has generally meant that its necropolitical dimensions have gone unacknowledged, proceeding as if such continuity were natural. This is why a phrase like *the body* is meaningless. The conveniences of the phrase are ultimately sinister: the idea of bodily integrity has enabled inhumanization through targeting and abandonment of the colonized, racialized, gendered, sexualized, and disabled. The body deserves to have its necropolitical ordinaries challenged, deconstructed, and ultimately torn to shreds.

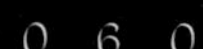

(ECHO)

Not just ideas but habits—habits of material tuning, sustaining, accumulation, and repair—shape and reshape bodies. Some habits are inhuman (or inattentive to the human) and depend upon inhuman temporalities. Temperature ranges and rhythms of humidity common to a climate, patterns of manufacture and consumption, material durabilities—alloys, nails, joints, adhesives, grains—all take part in the shaping. This is (one or another way) how you come to know a body; it's how a body knows itself; it's how bodies know other bodies. I find it worth remaining mindful of and open to the vast regions of the "life" of a body that does not issue from imagined human sovereignty over it. Ultimately, that bodily sovereignty has deeply curtailed effectivity and is all too often undone, challenged, or surrounded by other (inhuman, nonhuman) agencies—some of which are precisely the forces of the Earth operating at scales exceeding human bodies (whatever their provenance, be it human-induced global warming or something else). It might as well be a fiction. I say this even knowing that (1) sovereignty is, pragmatically speaking, far from a fiction and must be fought for, particularly by those not guaranteed it, such as those facing medical racism, refusal of basic reproductive health, or intoxication from the perverse chemicality of city or rural infrastructures; (2) biopolitically favored humans are exerting radical forms of control where they can. But that pragmatics is, cosmologically speaking, rendered in the terms of a narrowed human signifier of late liberalism, and so while these battles are fought, something else must also be dreamed or remembered. As for radical control, even in your escape to Mars, you will be weakened by the stale bubble you build.

(CUT)

A sustained cut, iterated into its own habits, makes for strange and yet increasingly familiar conjunctures that might become flesh, new integrities. These conjunctures needn't even scar in their making, if the materials are not particularly excited. (Affective intensity isn't necessary for revolutionary making. Deadpan reproduction could be the basic way to go.)

Bodies, beloved ones, giving ones, "dependent" ones, exhausted, petered, terminated, shattered, and thrown out: this is the time to unleash new cuts and new desires for cuts. Not simply cuts mechanistically and materially calculated or even cuts directly responsive to a necropolitical analysis—but cuts of/from desire, even where that desire isn't fully knowing. We might call this horizonal, in the sense that José Esteban Muñoz described, to do other than what transpires through the deadening determinacy of pragmatic legibility. World-making, after all, is less calculus than it is dreaming. If novel cuts in human-built worlds—in the shape of natural disasters—are a narrow slice that achieves the status of the spectacular, many more cuts live below, above, across, and fully beyond the diagnostics of a defunded infrastructural or survey-bound monitoring. They make for a "whole new world" of abody and abodiment, discernible only for the time being as mass nouns, but they are ready: they have always been ready.

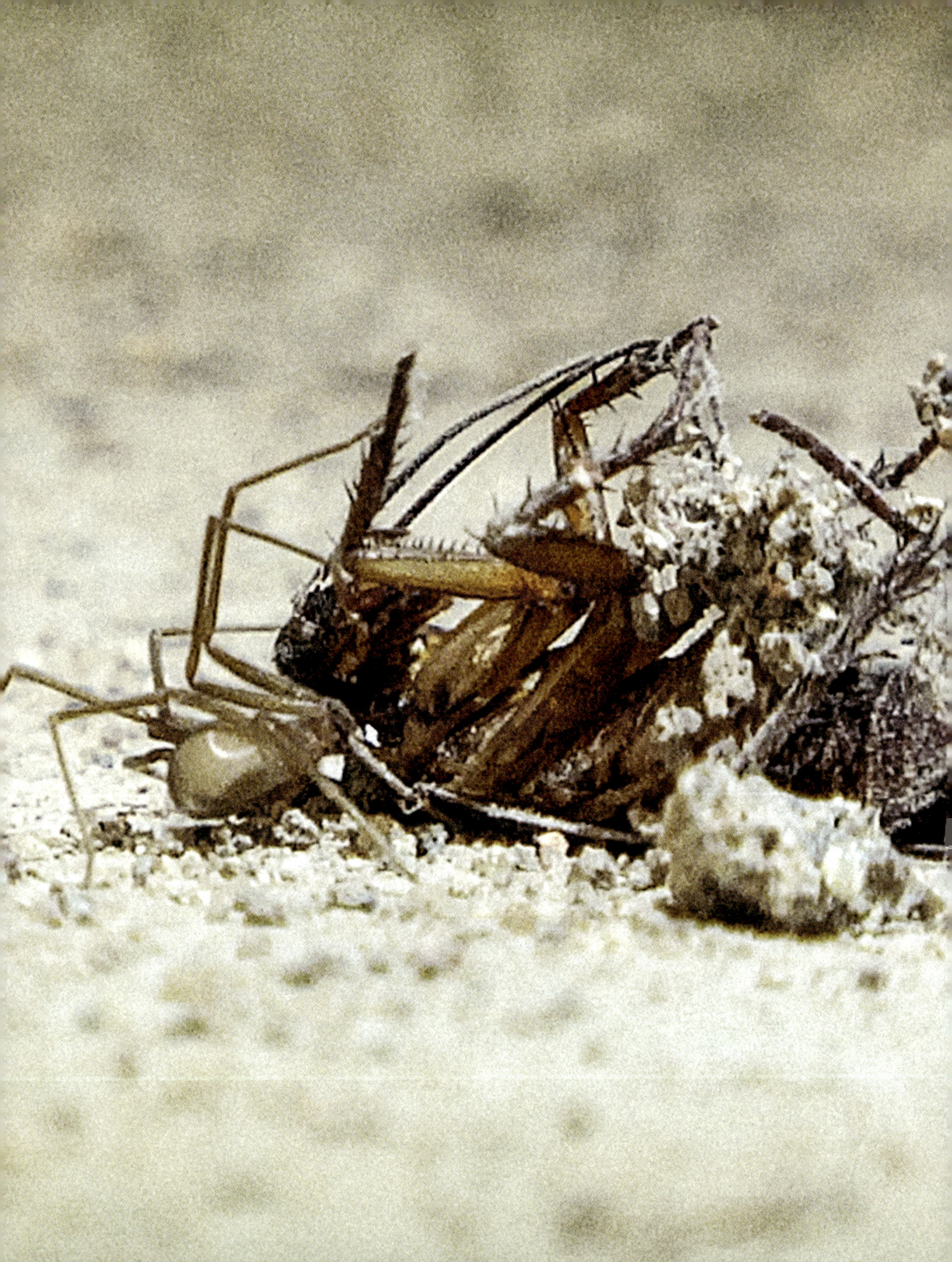

Living Room

DEATH OF MARAT
Marat: A.L. Steiner

BASEMENT / UTERUS (THE MOVEMENT)
Her: Nathaniel Flagg
Or Bust: Arianna Gil
No: Jahmal Golden
Again: NIC Kay
Her: Savannah Knoop
Or Bust: Monica Mirabile
Again: Marbles Jumbo Radio
No: Tsige Tafesse

SITUATION SITE
BODY
40° 43' 20.2944" N, 73° 59' 34.2096"W
231 Bowery, New York

PRODUCERS
A.K. Burns
Sara O'Keeffe

DIRECTOR OF PHOTOGRAPHY
A.K. Burns

LIVING ROOM
(Negative Space 00)
2 0 1 7
A.K. Burns

ACTING AGENTS
STAIRWELL / MOUTH TO ANUS (WEIGHT-BEARING)
Mx Manning: keyon gaskin
Pregnant Backpacker: Savannah Knoop

DWARF PLANETS (CELESTIAL BODIES)
Makemake: Winter Collins
Eris: Mia Cenholt-Haulund
Pluto: Elias Delate

ANIMALIA ANIMA / THE PSYCHE
Fish (out of water): Winter Collins
The Fly (swatter): Mia Cenholt-Haulund
Bird of Prey: Elias Delate

BATHROOM / KIDNEYS (DETOX TUB TALKS)
Marat (Economic Toxicity): A.L. Steiner
Patient Patient (Persistent Microaggressions): keyon gaskin

ASSISTANTS
Clara Chapin Hess
Diana Lozano
Delfina Martinez-Pandiani
Jessica Robbins
Saar Shemesh

COSTUME, PROPS AND SET DESIGN
A.K. Burns

CHOREOGRAPHER
NIC Kay

LIGHTING
Derek Wright

TECH ASSISTANT
Kate Wiener

STILL PHOTOGRAPHY
Eden Batki
Minnie Bennett
Lauryn Siegel

EDITOR
A.K. Burns

SCORE
Geo Wyeth

AUDIO MIX
Matthew Patterson Curry

AUDIO MASTERING
Quentin Chiappetta

DIGITAL EFFECTS
Common Space Studio

POSTPRODUCTION
A.K. Burns

IMPROVISED CONVERSATION
A.L. Steiner
keyon gaskin

ADDITIONAL CAMERAS
Eden Batki
Minnie Bennett

REFERENCED
Jacques-Louis David, *The Death of Marat*, 1793

SPECIAL THANKS
Johanna Burton
Callicoon Fine Arts
Katherine Hubbard
Delfina Martinez-Pandiani
Sara O'Keeffe
Jon Santos
Lauryn Siegel
Will Rawls

FUNDED WITH THE GENEROUS SUPPORT OF
Creative Capital Visual Arts Grant
The Radcliffe Institute for Advanced Study

COMMISSIONED BY
The New Museum Department of Education and Public Engagement

KAREN ARCHEY

Obviously, Living Room *looks quite different from* A Smeary Spot: *the film is set indoors in a domestic space rather than in the desert or the black box, the cast includes children as well as your peers, and it appears there are more custom-produced elements in the set. Could you talk about the content and production differences between the works and what the conceptual starting point was for* Living Room?

A.K. BURNS   When Johanna Burton offered me a show in the New Museum's education department, I was given an empty floor of an adjacent building as a residency workspace. This was before the New Museum had renovated it into an exhibition annex; it was still an unmaintained floor of a SoHo loft building. When I was given access to it, I started to develop this idea that the building was an analogous body—a shell to think through the broad subject of "the body." I began to designate various interior spaces as body parts or organs. From this point of view, I saw the stairwell that ran from the roof to the basement as a digestive tract, a path running from mouth to anus. I also realized pretty quickly that the outside world would overly complicate the analogy and that the work had to be restricted to the building's interior. I didn't have access to every space; I could utilize this one floor, the stairwell, and the basement. Within those parameters, I broke up the body, pairing it with different locations in the building that then became scenes in the video.

KA   *I find it such an unusual analogy, but it really works. Where did that analogy come from, this idea of going from the mouth to the anus when you move to the basement?*

0 6 4

AKB   I don't always know where every idea comes from. In general, I think a lot about the entries and exits of the body. I think of bodily orifices as central to the functioning and pleasure of the body. It is through a queer and feminist positioning that I tend to be orifice oriented.

KA   *Orifice-oriented ontology!*

AKB   Yes, exactly—instead of object-oriented ontology, orifice-oriented ontology! I love this. That's really accurate. When I started thinking about analogies for the body within the building, I got into this idea that the stairs connected the roof to the basement and that the doorways could be the orifices—the entry and exit points for the body. Since the whole scene developed from thinking

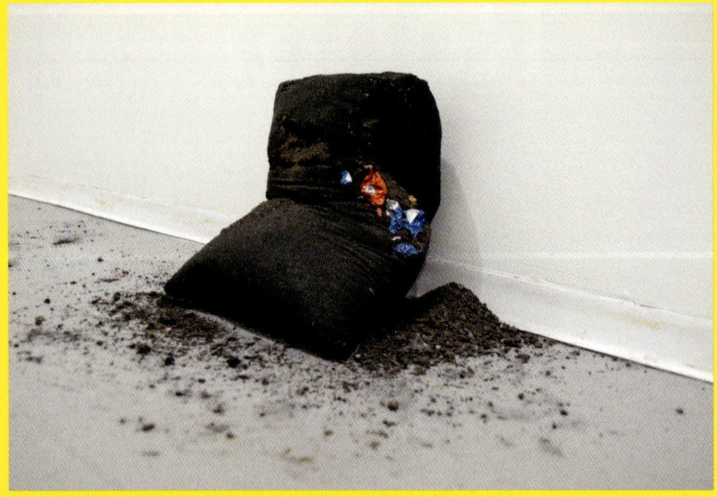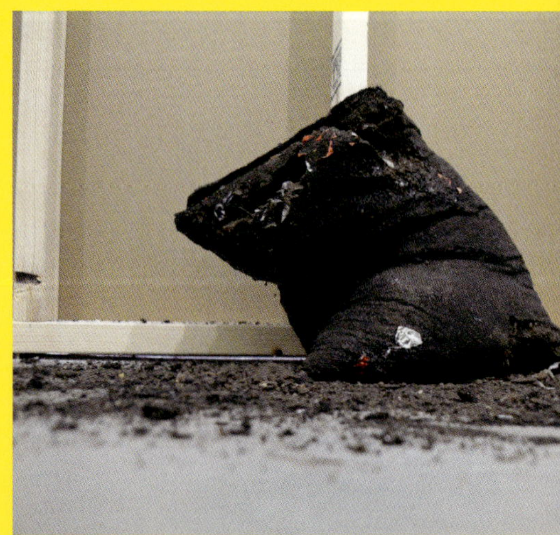

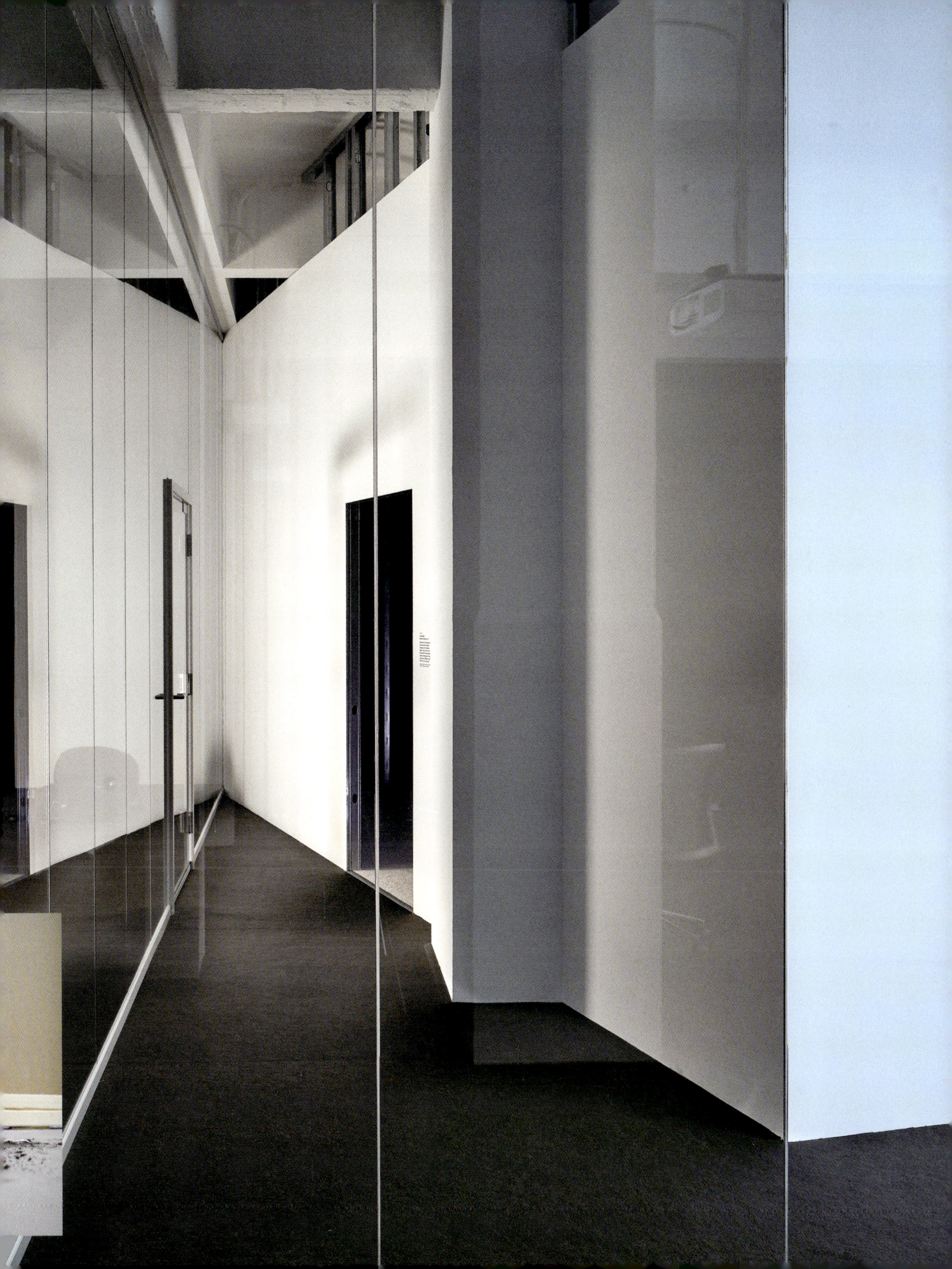

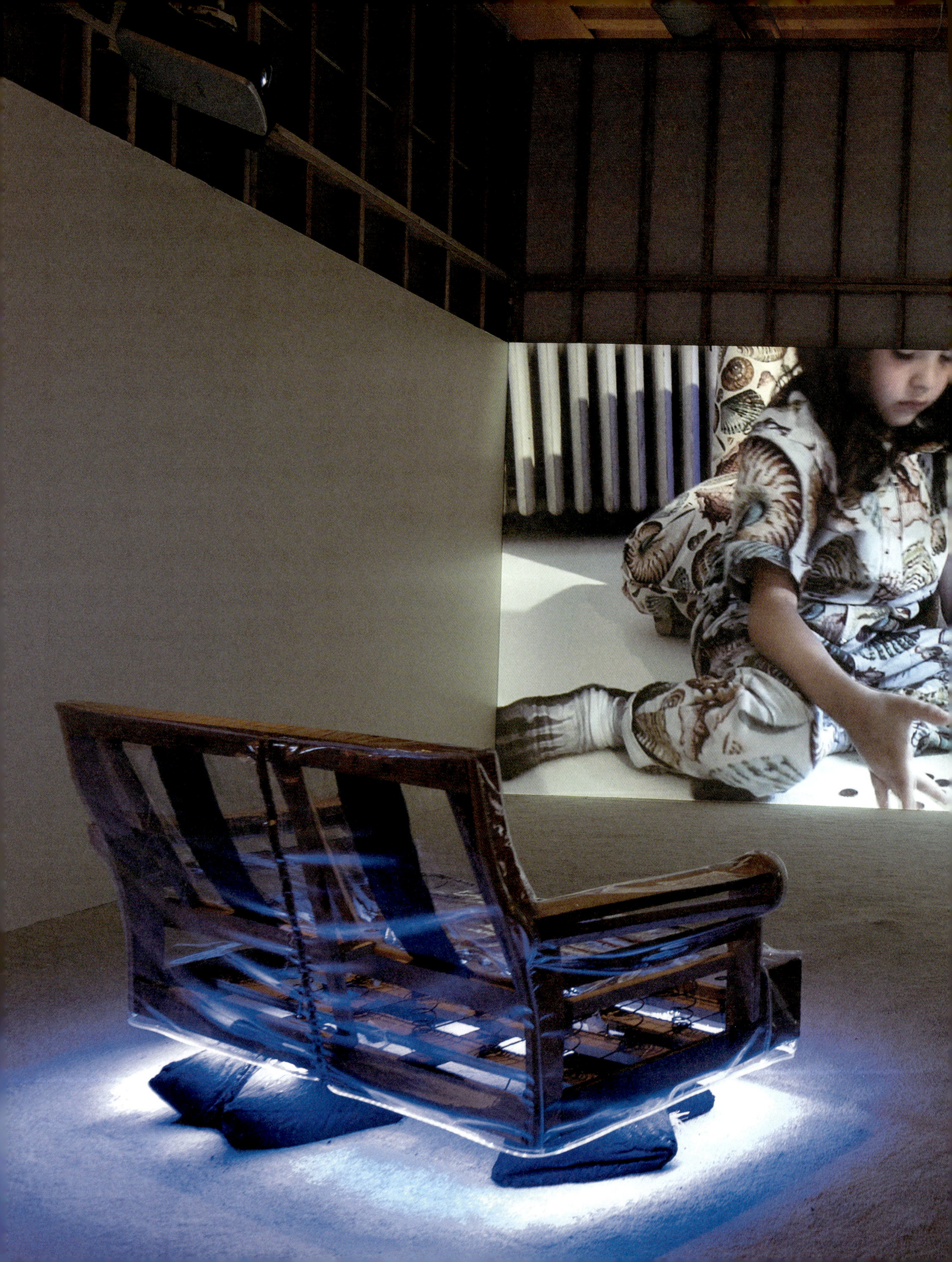

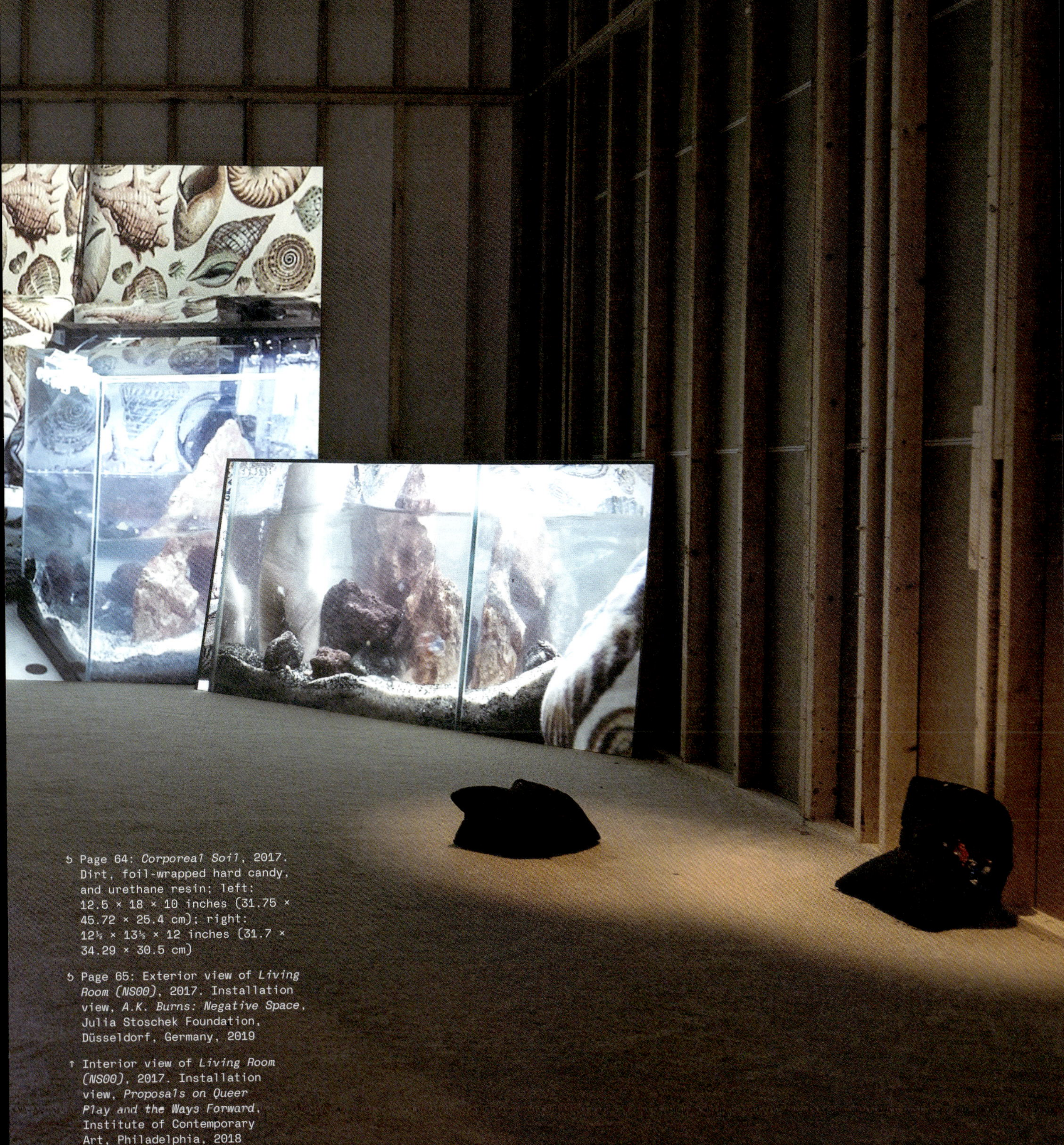

↳ Page 64: *Corporeal Soil*, 2017.
Dirt, foil-wrapped hard candy,
and urethane resin; left:
12.5 × 18 × 10 inches (31.75 ×
45.72 × 25.4 cm); right:
12½ × 13⅓ × 12 inches (31.7 ×
34.29 × 30.5 cm)

↳ Page 65: Exterior view of *Living
Room (NS00)*, 2017. Installation
view, *A.K. Burns: Negative Space*,
Julia Stoschek Foundation,
Düsseldorf, Germany, 2019

↑ Interior view of *Living Room
(NS00)*, 2017. Installation
view, *Proposals on Queer
Play and the Ways Forward*,
Institute of Contemporary
Art, Philadelphia, 2018

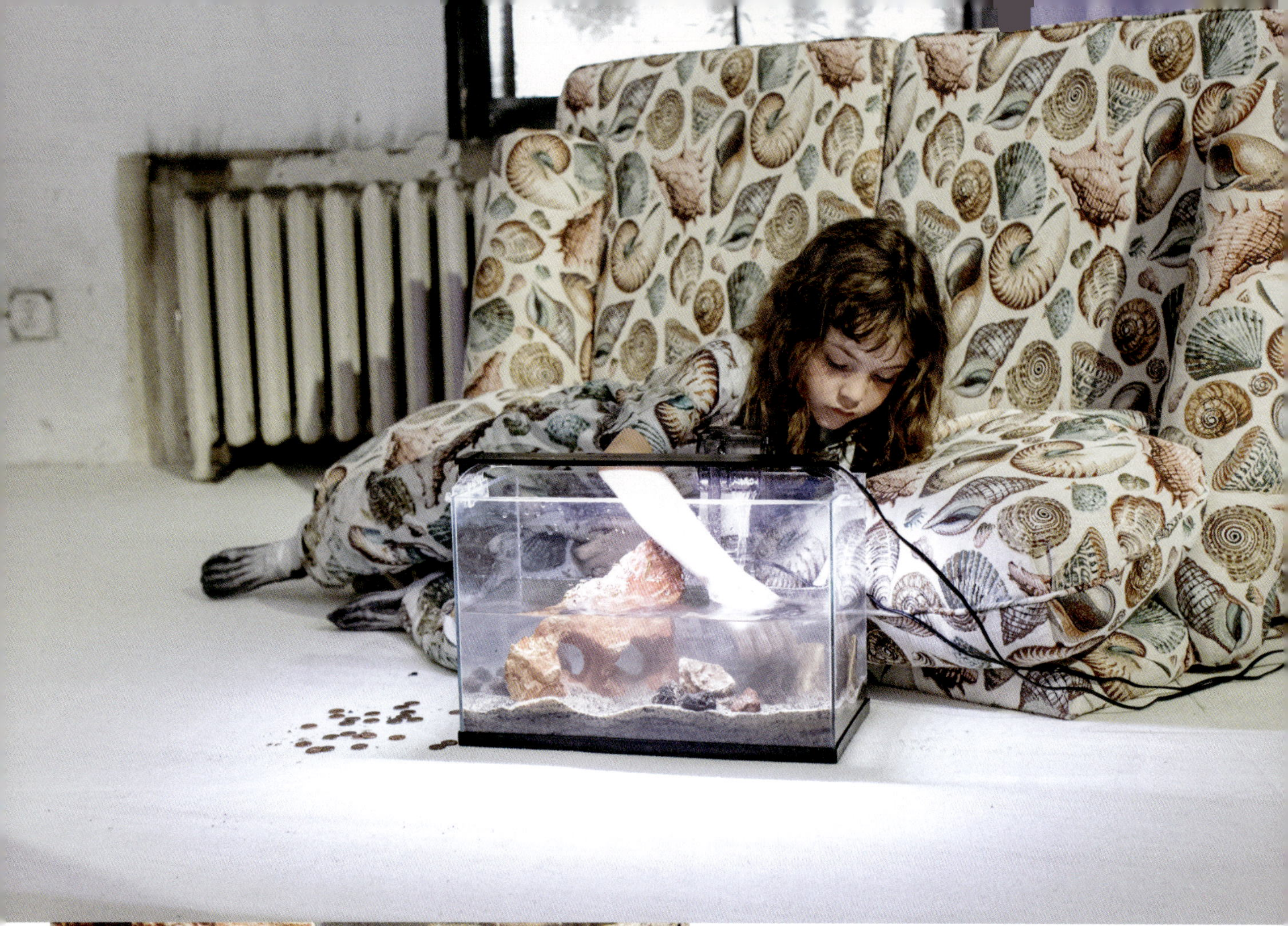

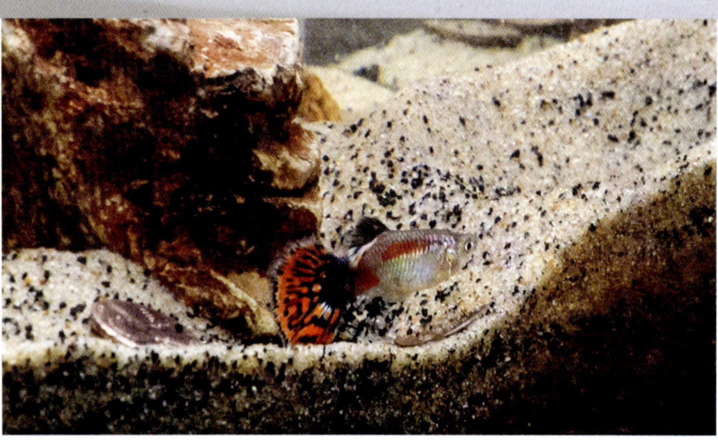

through the digestive tract, the door to the basement became the anus. I spent a lot of time considering the basement itself as either the bowels or the uterus—an *interior* interior. I ended up designating it as the uterus because I started thinking about how the heating system, water heaters, electrical system, pipes—all the most generative parts of a building reside in the basement. My practice often proposes a counternarrative to phallocentric modalities, and the vagina and the uterus have historically been relegated to the status of a passive absence awaiting a procreative presence.

KA   *A void.*

AKB   Yeah, but like all the other "negative spaces" within the larger work, I see it not as empty and awaiting activation but rather as a presence unto itself, generative and dynamic. A metaphorical womb room, so to speak.

KA   *The heart of my initial question goes to what you did differently with* Living Room *than with* A Smeary Spot. *It seems there was a difference in the level of resources, at least in the way* Living Room *was shot.*

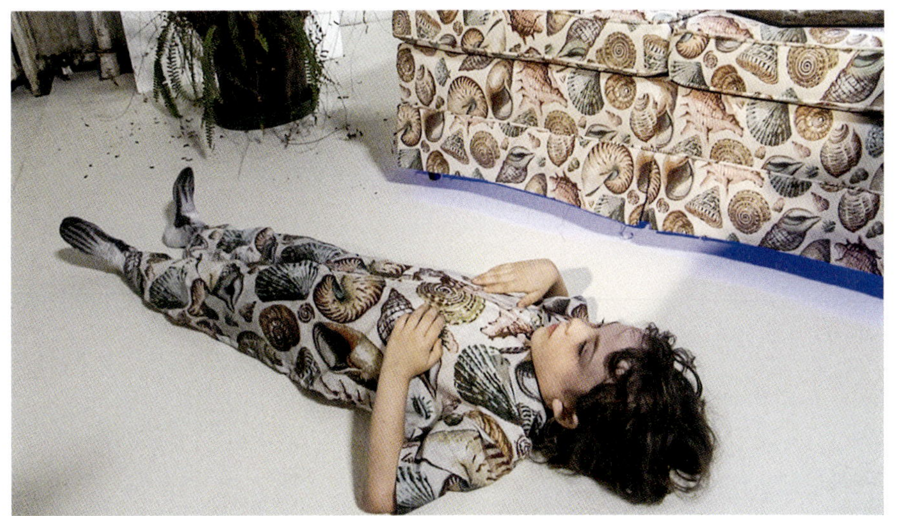

AKB   It's hard to say. There wasn't a quantitative difference in resources. I was a Radcliffe Fellow at the time, so I was able to use a little funding from that, and I also had some fiscal support from the New Museum. Just before I finished *A Smeary Spot*, I got a Creative Capital grant. The big difference between the two works was that I had access to this very specific space—a semi-empty building in New York. I then asked myself some questions about what it could be: "Am I committed to these sites that I established in *A Smeary Spot*? Or do I see each work in the *Negative Space* cycle as discrete, yet retaining echoes of the other works?"

I decided I wanted each work in the series to be autonomous, taking one subject (void, body, land, or water) as a structuring device, while also reflecting on themes established in *A Smeary Spot*. The script of *A Smeary Spot* sets up a philosophical framework for the whole *Negative Space* tetralogy.

KA   *Tell me if I'm wrong, but it seems you had more of an idea of how the episodes in* A Smeary Spot *would look in advance than those in* Living Room—*those seemed much more open.*

AKB   That is interesting because I think it's actually the reverse. I spent two years shooting *A Smeary Spot* in the desert before coming to terms with the fact that I needed something to ground the work (the script) and be more accessible, location-wise. In the final year of production, I began to understand what scenes I needed to give the script structure and how to best activate it. With *Living Room*, I thought, "I have been given a building to work with, so the building as a body is the foundational analogy." And I was able to move relatively quickly into deeper questions like how to address issues related to human bodies while also addressing the body as a multifaceted and less anthropocentric concept.

When I settled on situating *Living Room* strictly within the New Museum building, I also decided that each work in the *Negative Space* cycle would be unique but that I would use certain props, attributes, and events across all four works—such as trash, remakes of works from the art canon, a replica of Chelsea Manning's military jacket, and a dance sequence. In *Living Room* specifically, I used the fish tank to create a pseudo-desert with red rocks and sand. The tank was intentionally depleted—half-filled with water—and host to a lonesome single fish. So the desert became a subtext in *Living Room*. Even though it is a miniaturized

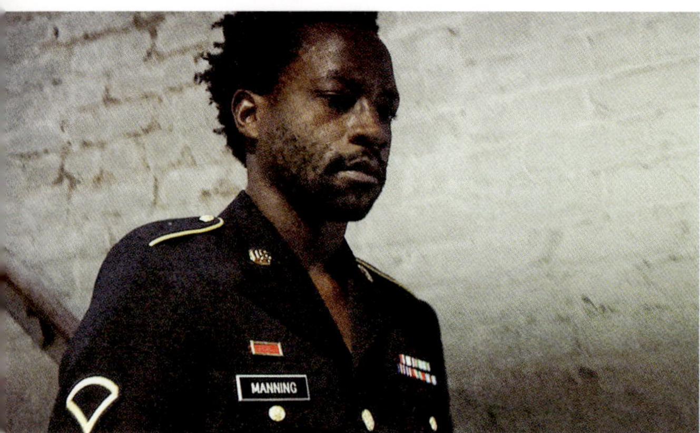

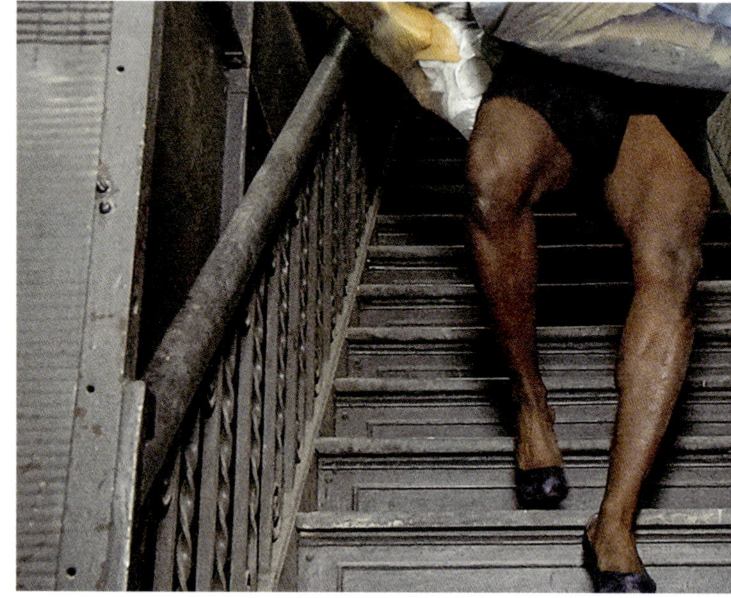

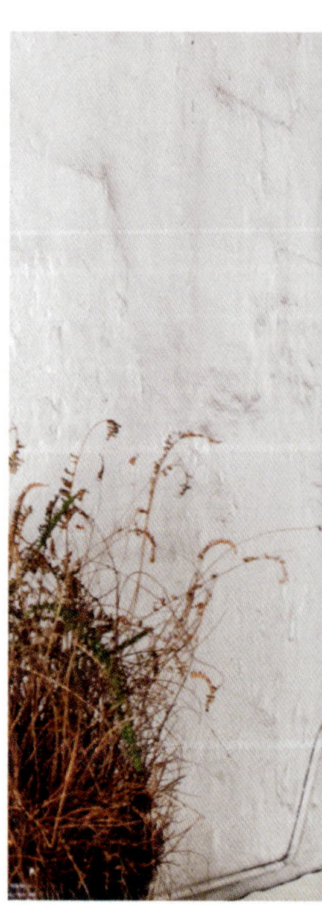

interior site within an interior site, the fish tank points to a vast exterior, entangling scale and perspective relationally.

KA

It brings A Smeary Spot *into* Living Room—*water and desert. These elements were formative parts of the film, especially because of the intentional lack of a linear narrative. Also, the way in which you shot it, with performers traveling up and down the stairs, does recall going from light to dark. And there's a sense of accumulation in the basement, where I think the ontology—or the analogy—really works.*

AKB   Yes, the bearing of excessive weight and the movement of waste structures that scene. Starting at the doorway from the roof, two acting agents, the Pregnant Backpacker and Mx. Manning—played by Savannah Knoop and keyon gaskin—each carry a bag of trash, and as they head down through the building, they accumulate more and more, until it exceeds their individual capacities. The Pregnant Backpacker signifies the social weight of carrying the biological responsibility of reproduction. The backpack is a counterweight to the front load of the pregnant belly; to express the absurdity of this burden, I add comically more and more to the load. Additionally, the performers aren't wearing pants or the right shoes for the job—they are dressed in sandals and heels—which signals vulnerability. Mx. Manning's heels reflect society's tendency to embrace sex appeal while simultaneously burdening femme gender representation with objectified subjugation.

KA

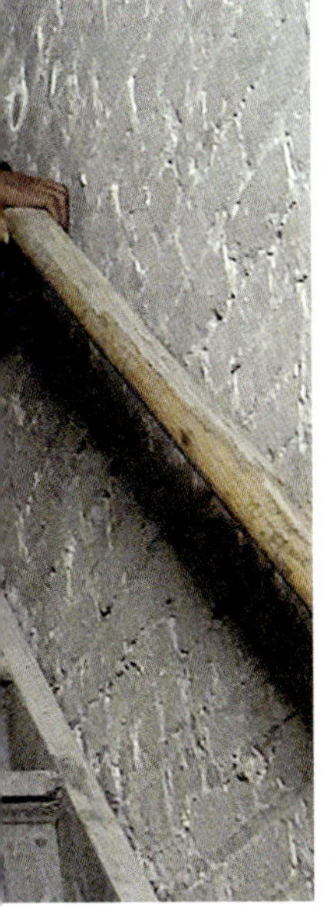

Viewers may feel they've been dropped into a familiar but alien world. They observe these agents in action and must figure out for themselves what that action means. One child, whose outfit matches the sofa they had been lying on, swats at an invisible fly, while Mx. Manning carries trash bags down a stairwell. In a sense, there is an environmental development, and through observing the characters' actions, the viewer gets a sense of who the performers are and what they represent. The children all have quite unusual names, right?

AKB The children are Makemake, Eris, and Pluto, named after three dwarf planets. There's always a subtext of something that is going on in the real world at the time the work is made, i.e., the speculative present. *Living Room* was developed and shot mostly in 2016 during the US presidential election, but also while astronomers were debating Pluto's status, ultimately removing it from our solar system and designating it a dwarf planet. I thought this debate made Pluto a kind of "queer" planet. And because I work with associative thoughts and verbal puns, dwarf planets got me thinking about scale as a marginalizing principle, which led me to think about children (small humans). How would I represent that kind of metaphorical

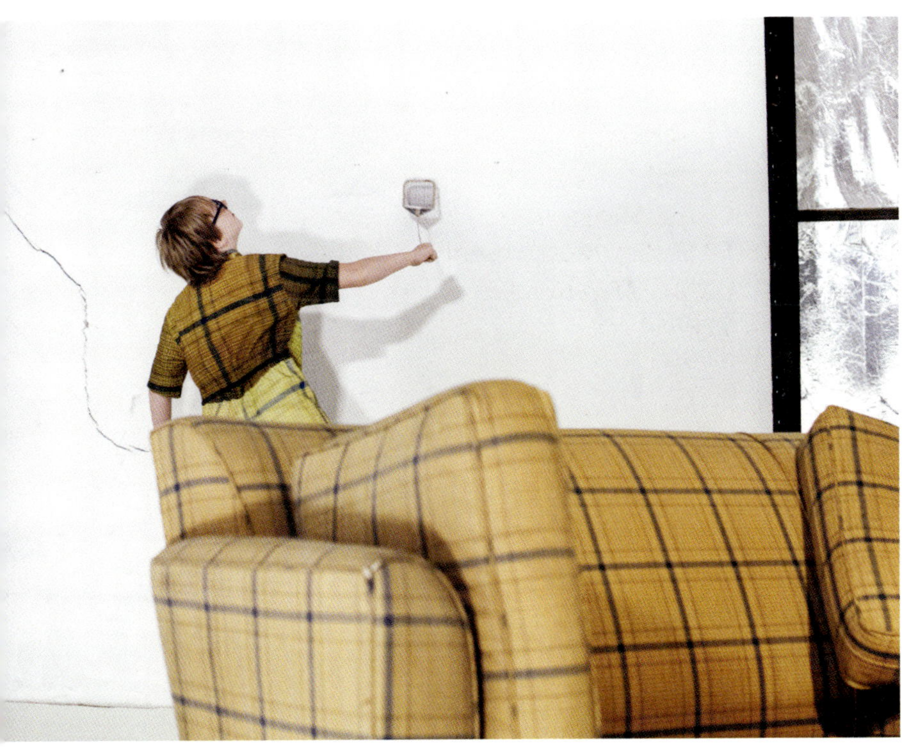

abstraction? I staged the children in an expansive space, creating an abstracted living room occupied by three couches with an underglow that rotated. It was like a celestial showroom, where the couches were the planets. The children's jumpsuits matched the fabric of the couches, so that together they were essentially the inanimate and animate parts of one entity. Dwarf planets are named after gods and goddesses, and all the props relate to this mythological background. Eris, the goddess of discord, throws a golden apple into a party, which results in jealousy and competition, so in *Living Room*, Eris has a gold-colored plaid couch and a yellow apple is thrown into the fish tank. Pluto is the god of the underworld, of earth and minerals, so the seats of Pluto's couch,

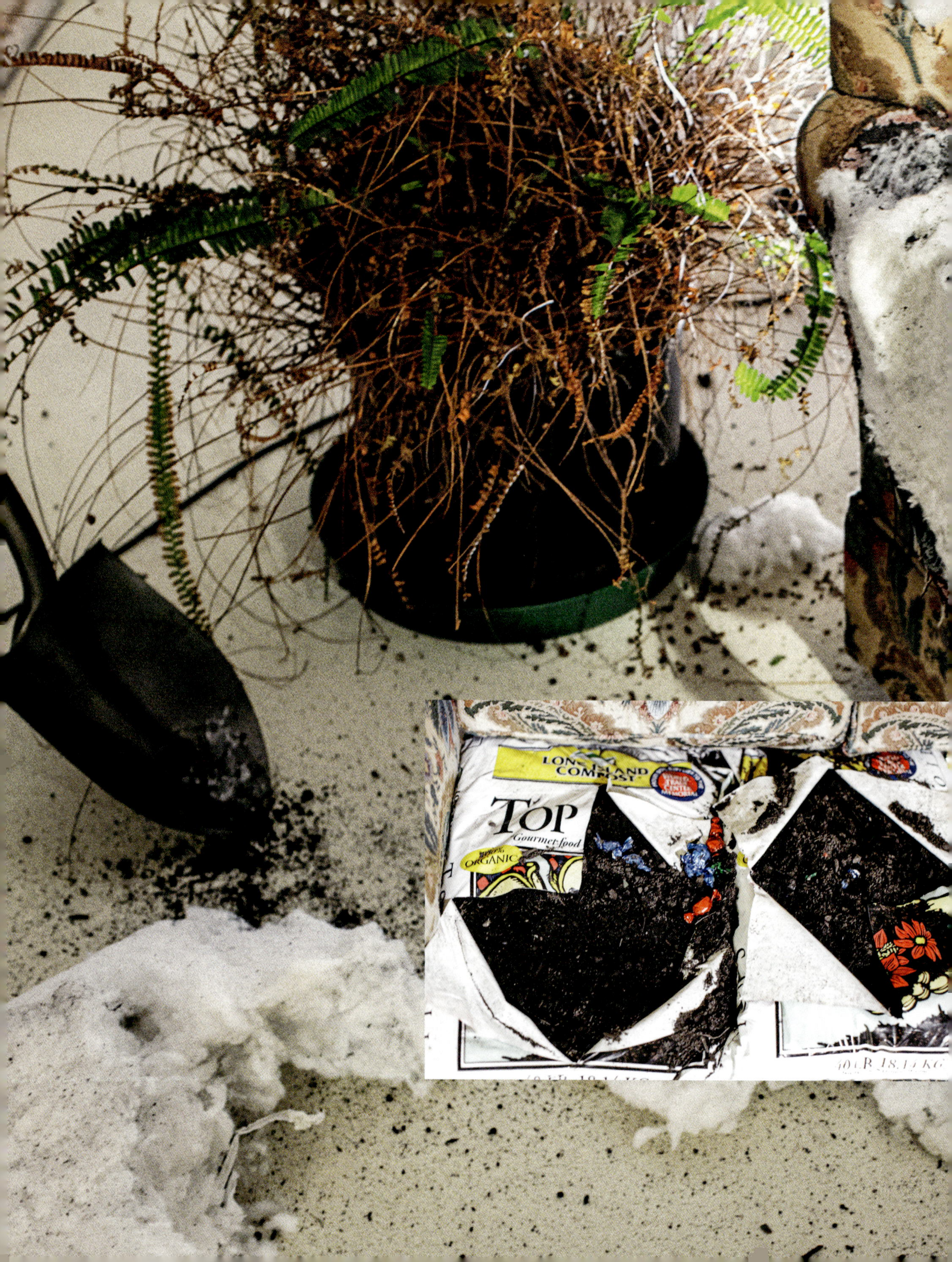
LONG ISLAND COMPOST
TOP
Gourmet food
ORGANIC
NET 18.11 KG

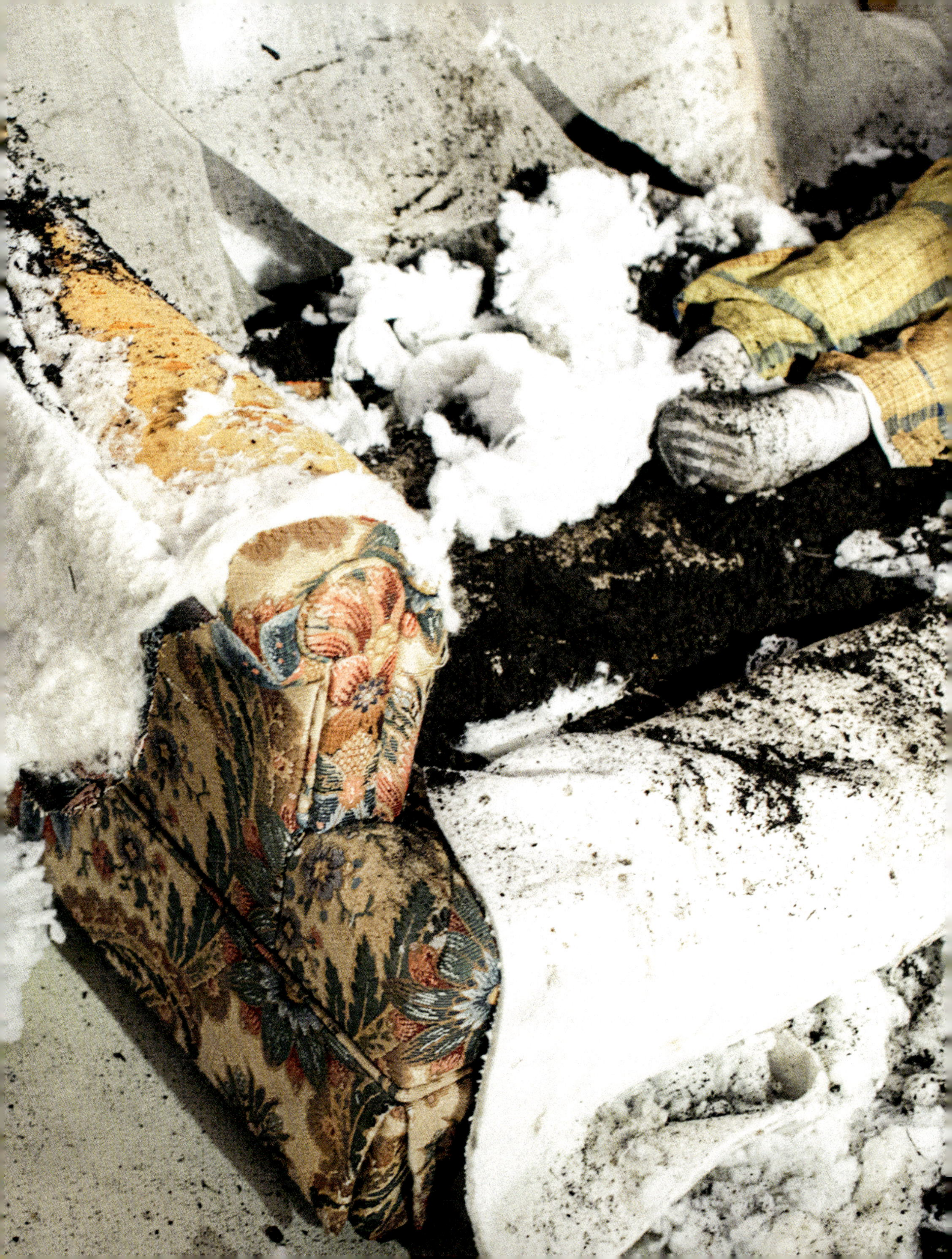

which is flower patterned, have been replaced with soil. Makemake is a dwarf planet named after a god of the Rapa Nui, the people of Easter Island. I found a couch with a seashell pattern that inspired Makemake's fish-tank-ocean theme.

KA

In Rapa Nui mythology, Makemake is the creator of humanity. I find it interesting that while these historical, scientific, and cultural references underline your thinking, they're not always legible in the works themselves, so that they become almost like an ambience.

AKB Yes, true. I do not expect the audience to recognize all the source material. The astute viewer will see clues in the film credits and the mirror collages. But the source material is there to help me build a logic for aesthetic choices and to script the performance. Some odd challenges are introduced by shifting the viewer's expectations away from assuming actors are human characters and reconceiving performers as metaphors, concepts, or objects. If I were going to be more direct or literal, I would have to do something like dress these children in globe-shaped costumes and float them on a green-screened image of outer space. Personally, I find that too jokey and hokey. And really that's not the point. An ambience is a perfect way to think about it. The viewer may watch it and think this is a bit unusual, but things just seem to exist differently in the world of *Negative Space*.

 The experience is similar to that of being queer. Within myself, I just exist; I am perfectly normal to myself. I am only queer in relation to the societal structure I live in, so my sense of queerness is 100 percent reliant on an awareness that my internal sense of self contrasts with the environment I exist in. As Rosa von Praunheim said, "It is not the Homosexual who is perverse, but the society in which he lives." This informs my way of

perceiving the role of performers in *Negative Space*—as metaphorical—and integrating it through what we are calling an ambience. My hope is the viewer will just give in to experiencing the work.

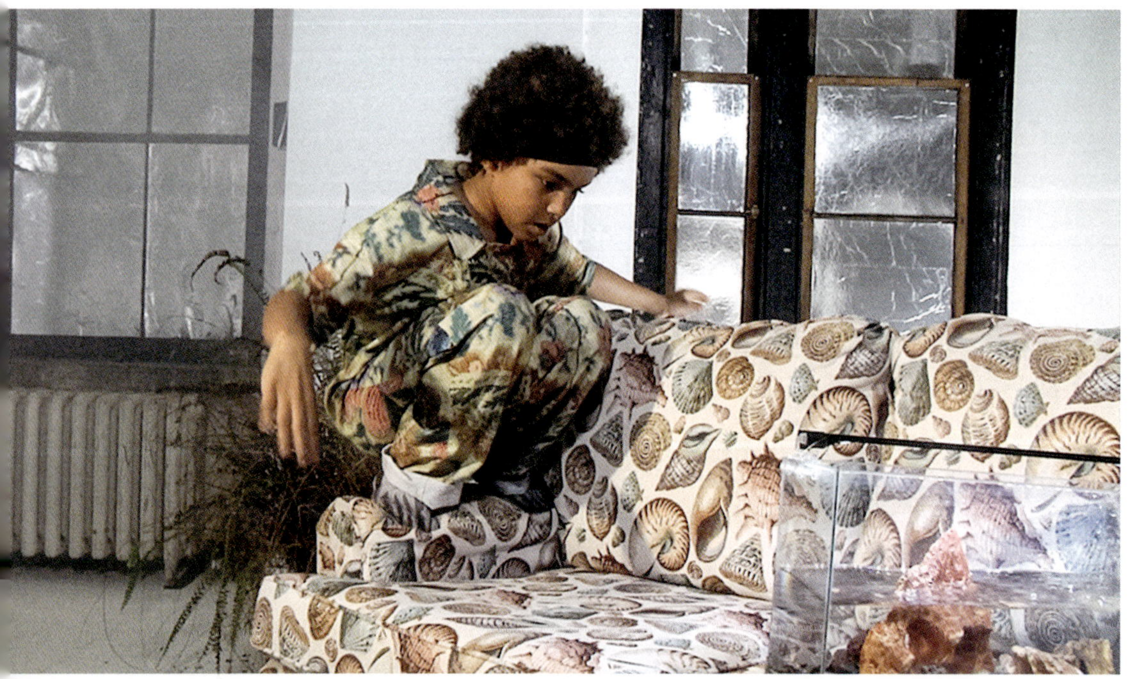

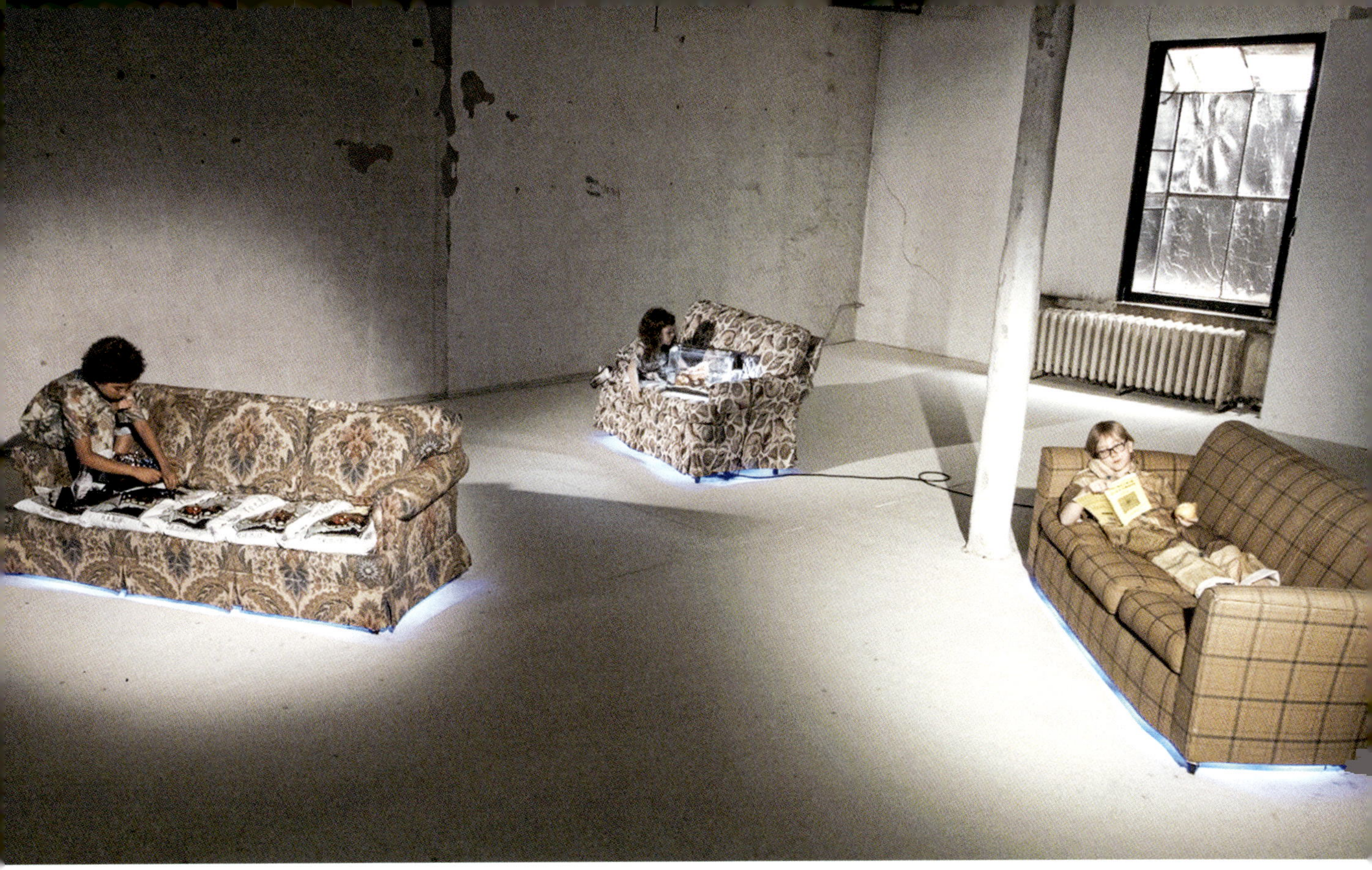

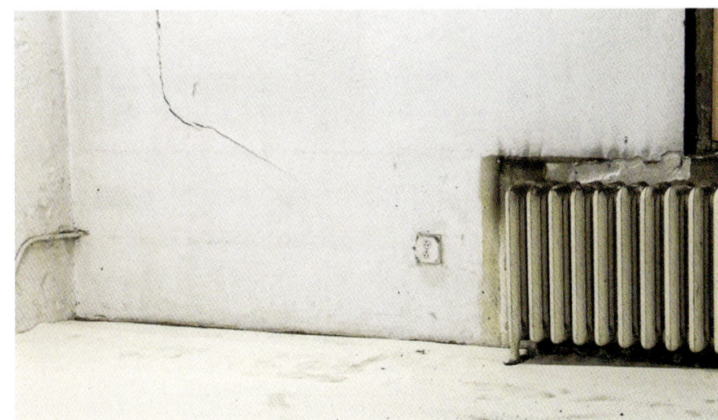

KA

There are many references to the physical body, but there is also an emotional and psychological landscape built within the film. How did you introduce the concept of the psyche in Living Room?

AKB I wanted to deal with the mind as one of the aspects of the body. And I was thinking a lot about children as liminal people, in that they are developing and growing but also fluidly oscillating between reality and the imaginary. For example, there's the moment when Makemake is playacting as the fish from the tank and flopping around on the floor, as if they were struggling to survive out of the water. There's another moment in which Eris hears a voice in the room that is calling to them and buzzing about like a fly. Eris swats at it, but we don't know if it's all in Eris's mind or an actual fly. I think that one's perception is one's reality, and that is bound up with what we validate as mattering individually and collectively.

KA *It plays on the liminality of the imagination in the sense that, when you're a child, you think the monster from the*

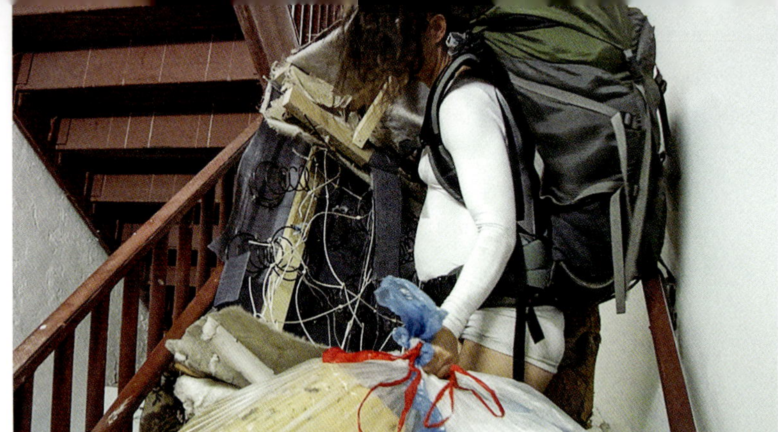

AKB   The term *science fiction* is complicated. I'm using it not only as an entry point to think through an alternative ontology that relies on reorienting our perceptions of world-building but also as an aesthetic to draw on common tropes, so the viewer has a sense of familiarity with the idea that things will feel unfamiliar. Sometimes I lean more on the term *speculative fiction*. Speculation proposes, *What if we thought about it another way?*

Sometimes I lean into surreal or sci-fi aesthetics, as with the couches in *Living Room*. They're meant to be planets, but they also reference spaceships, as each is illuminated and

0 7 6

rotating in space—i.e., an expansive carpeted room. But the couch is an object that has a relationship to the human body and the domestic, too. Aesthetically, I'm creating a science fiction with our material residue or waste—in a time and with material that feels "post-productive." Resources are found in what is left over and after most supplies have been exhausted. To build scenes, I'm often limited by what I can find. As a holistic process, I don't go out and choose the perfect couch; I'm looking at what's available in cheap, secondhand markets that will hit a note close to what I need. Likewise, there was a barely functional bathroom in the residency space that was staged to remake the *Death of Marat* (1793) by Jacques-Louis David. For this scene, I brought in a salvaged tub and installed it with a hose running from the sink. It didn't even drain properly.

KA   *The bathroom was completely staged? It is quite convincing.*

AKB   Cheap special effects! This bathroom became the kidney, a space of detoxification. Two performers, whom I call Patient Patient and Marat—performed by keyon gaskin and A.L. Steiner—are attempting to heal; eventually, Marat succumbs to death. I was looking for ways to talk about different forms of violence and the body under duress. The David painting is based on the assassination of Jean-Paul Marat, a French revolutionary, who was found dead while bathing to heal a skin condition. But I didn't want to set up a dynamic where a person kills another person. That is an all-too-obvious and, unfortunately, normal way, especially in cinema, to address the subject of violence. Since healing and illness were already part of the narrative of the original painting, I wanted to think about the invisible violence that emerges through individual contexts and our relationship to different environments. That's why Patient Patient is covered in an absurd number of Band-Aids. A Band-Aid is meant to heal, but it is also a racist object, devised to match the skin of white people. Thus, Patient Patient is suffering from a severe case of microaggressions. Marat eventually dies of a nosebleed stemming from economic toxicity. Their ailments are exaggerations of real social ills that, in my view, require a surrealist approach to visualize, as they're forms of violence that aren't easily visible in the way verbal or physical aggressions are.

KA
When you speak about these surreal qualities, it makes me realize how and why you use science fiction in your work: it's an aesthetic or narrative device that turns your attention to societal forces, but the fictional element flips these forces on their head, so that you're attuned to different potentials and opportunities. Could surrealism be your aesthetic and science fiction your approach?

AKB
I think the surreal is not only an aesthetic but also a tool because it allows me to be eccentric or excessive. It's not just one Band-Aid on this body—it's twenty—so it pushes the edge of what seems normal. I'm very interested in the subtlety of the line between whether something is peculiar or not: "Do you notice it? Are you paying attention to how odd that is?"

KA
I noticed it, but I didn't think much about why there were so many bandages there.

AKB
I'm interested in exposing how insidious many forms of violence are because they are normalized and thereby easy to overlook.

KA
Was there a theoretical or literary reference you were thinking about when making Living Room? *I was just reflecting on how the script developed from research texts for* A Smeary Spot *and wondering if you had different key texts or thinkers in mind amid the creation of this work?*

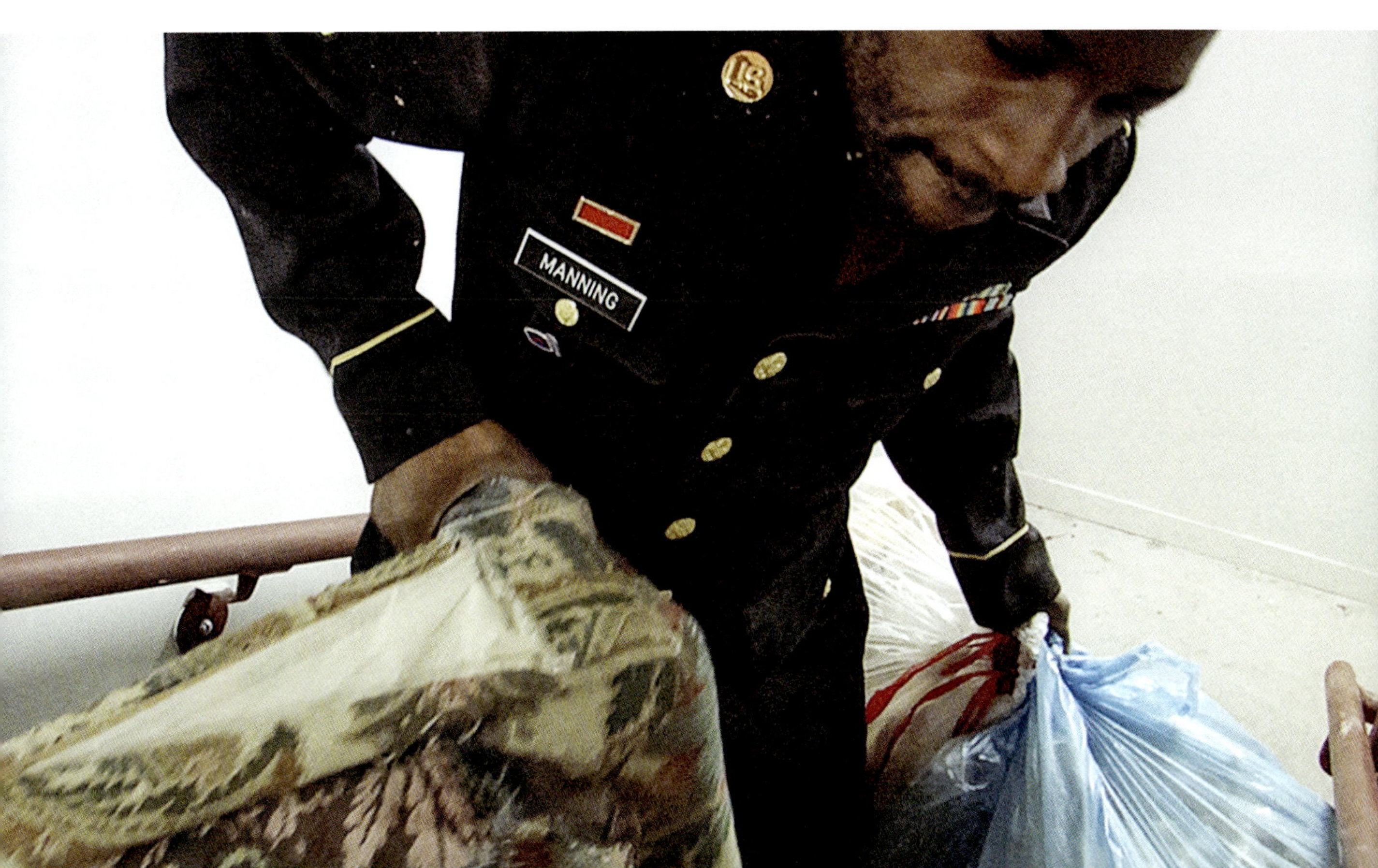

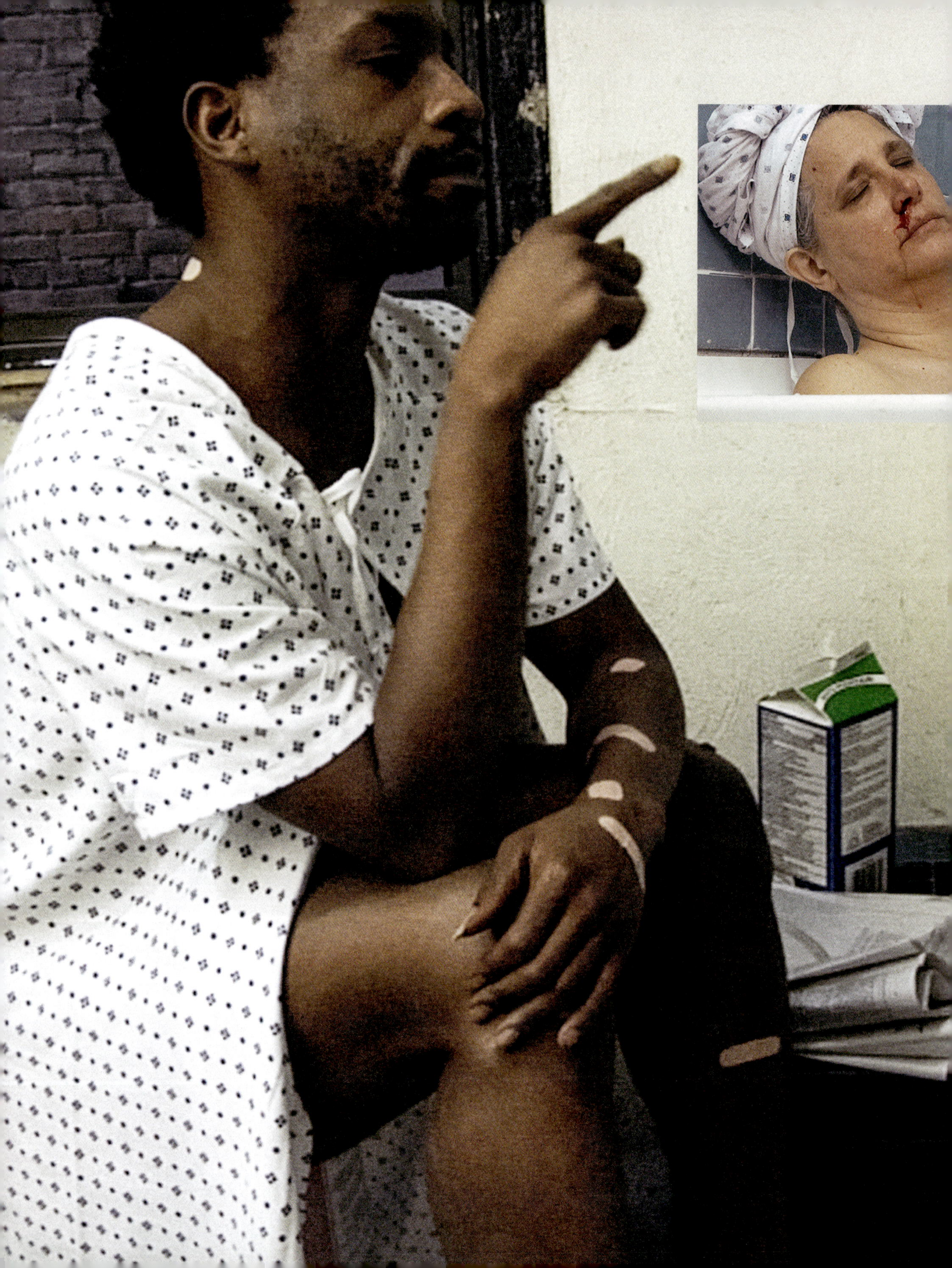

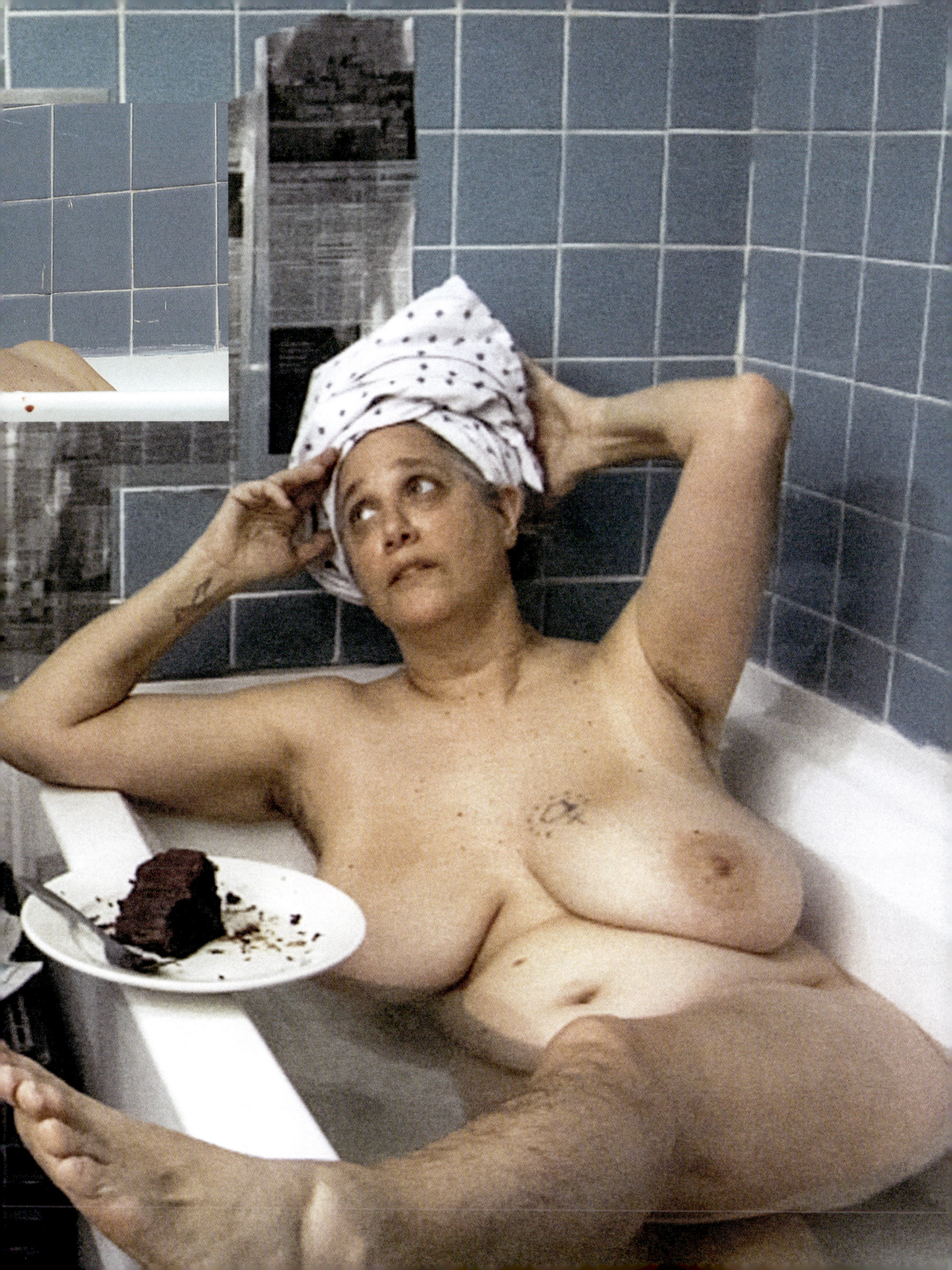

AKB   I didn't. And that was intentional, because I felt a little weighed down by all the thinking and reading, by other people's words swirling around in my head. That script not only established a framework for the whole project; it was also a way of purging. After *A Smeary Spot*, I wanted to liberate myself to be less theory heavy and build a poetic visual language to make different kinds of aesthetic choices. In *Living Room*, there is improvised dialogue in the bathroom scene. The performers were given the task of coming up with a name for a new "party." Whether they are debating the name of a dance club or a political party was left open to interpretation. They came up with a party called Lies—which was oddly prescient, as this was filmed at the onset of the post-truth Trump era. They were also tasked with discussing language itself. I didn't tell them why they were in a bathroom in medical gowns beyond

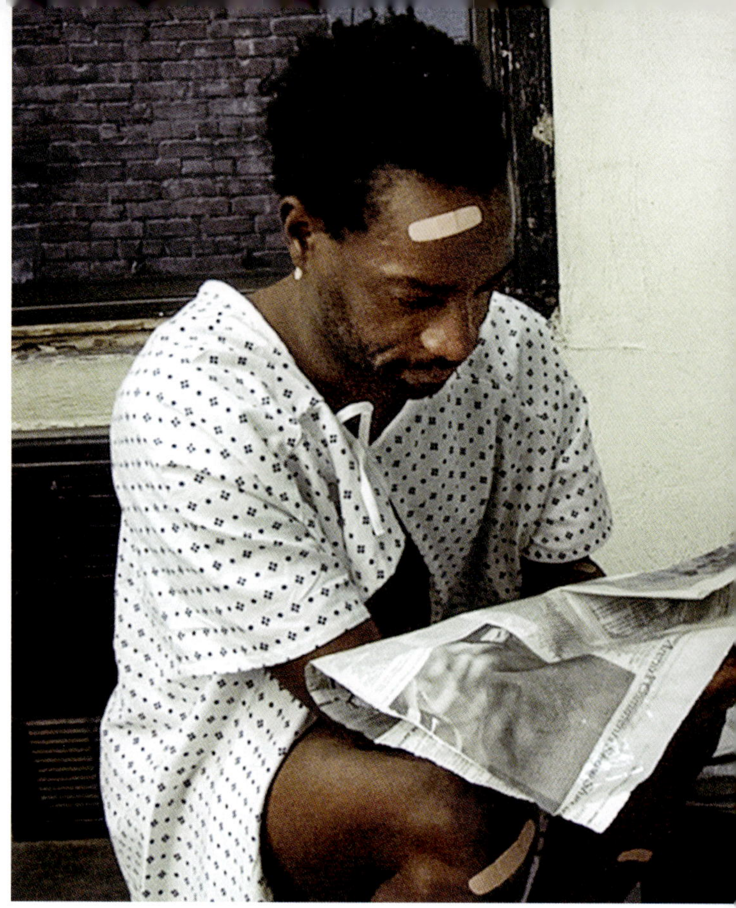

the Marat reference, so they made up a narrative about being in an asylum or hospital with a cafeteria where they seem to be institutionalized, possibly against their will.

KA   *The scenography of the installation seems to reflect the content of the work itself; it has that surrealist character. Could you talk a bit more about how you decided to show the work in terms of the channels and the presentation mode, the furniture, and other aspects of the installation environment?*

AKB   I'm trying to remember what came first. The couches were central and led to the title *Living Room*, which I think is not just a room in a house but a philosophical proposal. What does it mean to have room to *live*—the safety, care, and resources to thrive? Then there was the act of gutting the couches, a

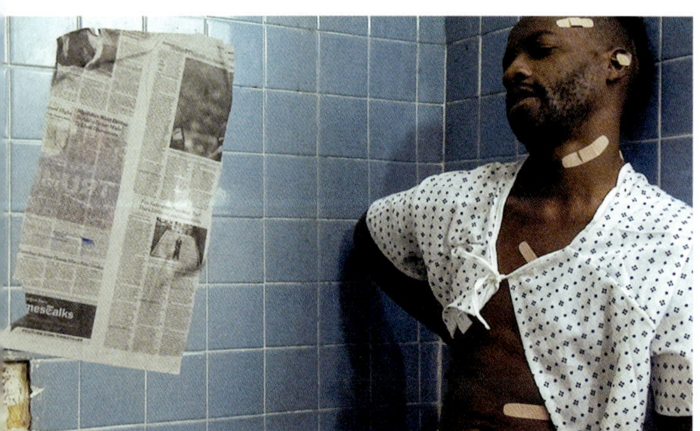

destructive disemboweling initiated by the children. It just seemed obvious to use the gutted couch with an underglow as the seating for the installation. The underglow endows a trashed couch with the status of a tricked-out car. I show it with a plastic cover. Covering a couch in plastic introduces the idea of preservation—in this case, of a trashed and depleted object. The floor is covered in a suburban off-white carpet that easily gets dirty; the audience will soil it over time, marking their presence. I also realized that I wanted to highlight the fabricated quality of built environments, so I removed the drywall from the exhibition space to expose the studs

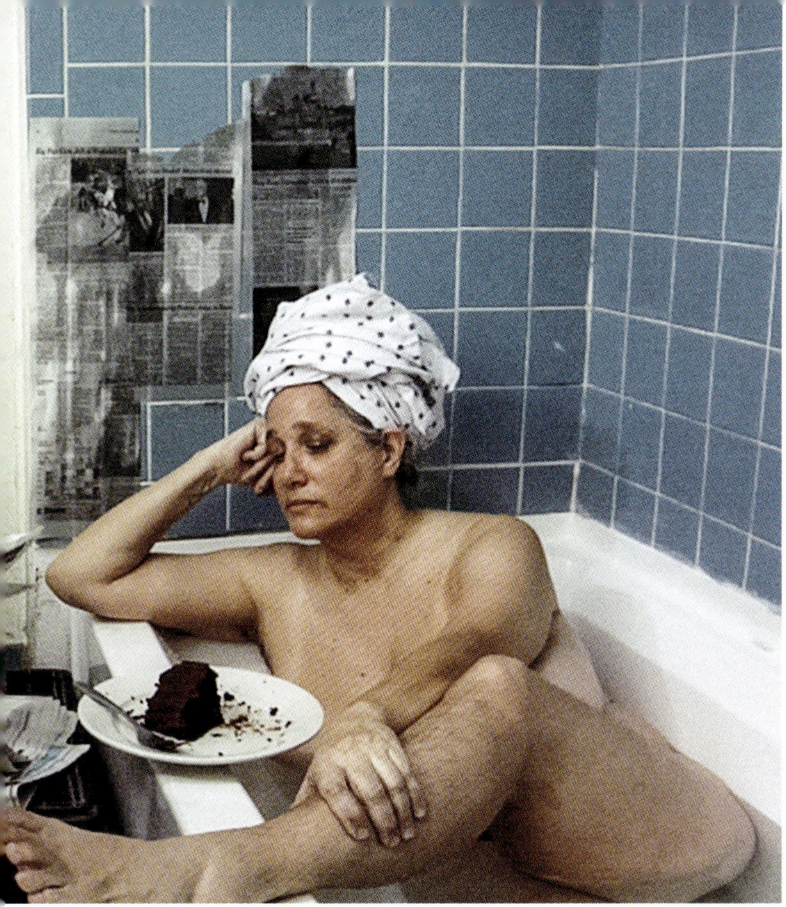

or "bones" of the building. Additionally, I created a series of sculptures called *Corporeal Soil* by adding casting resin to the bags of dirt that were used as Pluto's couch cushions. They are scattered about, occupying the space like slumped torsos.

When it came to the two channels, I was initially thinking about the body as a bifurcated structure, but one that's asymmetrical. I was interested in making that kind of difference more explicit by using two mismatched screens. One is the size of the screens in *A Smeary Spot*. And after working with drywall removal, I thought, "Let's just take this construction material, a sheet of drywall, and lean it against the wall for the second screen." Standard drywall is four by eight feet, so to create the second screen, I just cut down the width to match the 16:9 ratio of the video.

KA   *How many times have you installed this? Is it always the same constellation of objects and screens, with the couch and the exposed studs?*

AKB   The Wexner is its fourth iteration. The sizes of the screens are fixed, as scale is specific for me in all the works. And then there are certain consistent parameters—exposed studs, a glowing gutted couch, the carpet, and the *Corporeal Soil* sculptures. It's not always the same couch, though; I've made different versions because the cost of storing the original and shipping it is so much greater than just remaking it from a locally sourced used couch. I also adapt the exposed studs to different environments with different types of walls. At the Julia Stoschek Foundation, I had to contend with glass walls, which meant building a giant white cube that could be seen through the glass from a distance. As viewers approached it, they would find an entry into the minimalist monolith and view the work inside its stripped-back interior. At the New Museum, viewers walked out of an elevator and went straight into the interior stage of the installation.

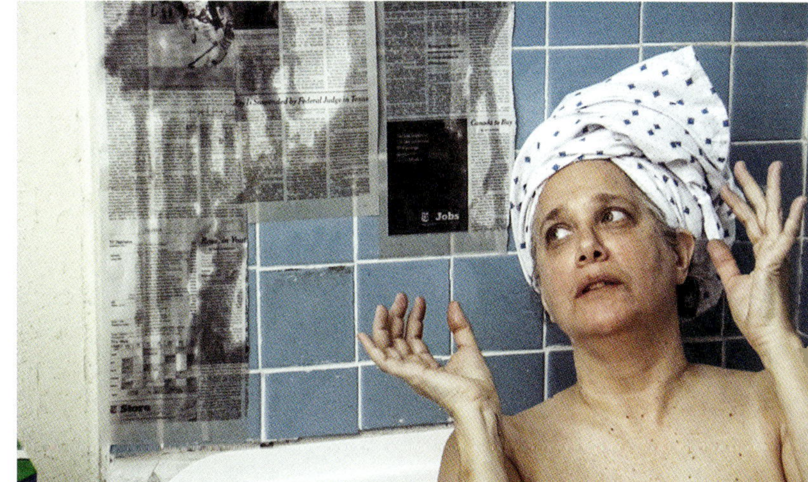

AKB   Yes, I think that's an accurate way of thinking about it. Also, a strong theme for me is sustenance
and the struggle to maintain an existence, considering the social, political, and economic factors
that make that incredibly hard. My performers or "acting agents" have this tension they're working
through that has to do with the sociopolitical and economic impacts that bear down on specific
bodies in different ways. There's not a lot of support for subsisting, especially in the United States.
I dig into existing dystopias as much as I embrace utopian potential.

KA

*I agree. Support is always seen in the Western context
as needing to be reciprocal, you know? I think that's
the foundation of many Western societies. Living with a*

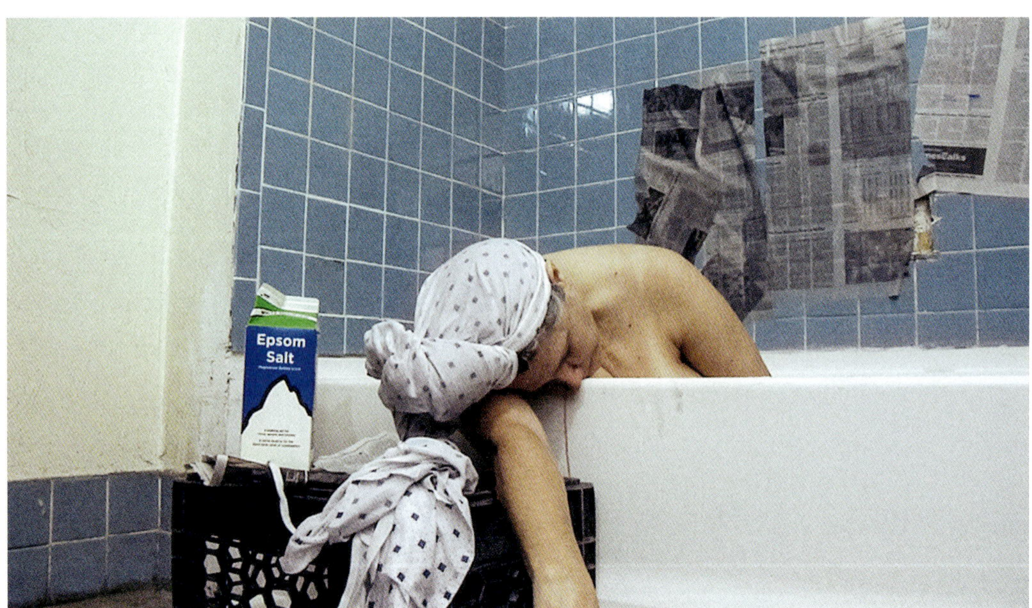

*profound disability or illness and depending on
the government to help provide basic quality of
life, without the ability to be a "productive" member of society, comes with enormous social and
emotional baggage.*

AKB   Yes, these burdens are palpable and personal for me. I'm the oldest of six, and my mom
was at one point a single mom of four kids and working multiple low-paying jobs. How do I
address the magnitude of that?

This makes me think of the basement scene, as it was shot two weeks after and
came directly out of the trauma of the 2016 US election. When I was talking about
the basement being a generative space, I was thinking specifically about the
machines that are commonly found there, all working to keep the building functioning
(or "alive"). I started considering these machines as a series of movements that generate
energy for the building, then about movement more broadly as political or social; protest
takes shape as the improvised movement of a mass of politicized bodies.

This led to the dance sequence in the basement, where I asked NIC Kay to base their choreography on the formal qualities of line dancing. We worked with both professional and amateur dancers to produce a movement that oscillated between being in and out of sync. The imperfection was important because I wanted to push the line between the synced machine and the more organic, human movement of a collective. The language on the shirts came from the last word(s) of campaign slogans: "I'm with *Her*," "Bernie *or Bust*," "Make America Great *Again*." I felt this overused campaign rhetoric had been stripped of its meaning. Dancing with this exhausted language was for me a recuperative act. The "No" T-shirts came from thinking about that word in relation to negative space, the entwined qualities of this blunt statement of refusal and absence.

KA

It calls for a simultaneous individuality and collectivity, which is interesting considering how much the social and political moment of the work's production influenced the

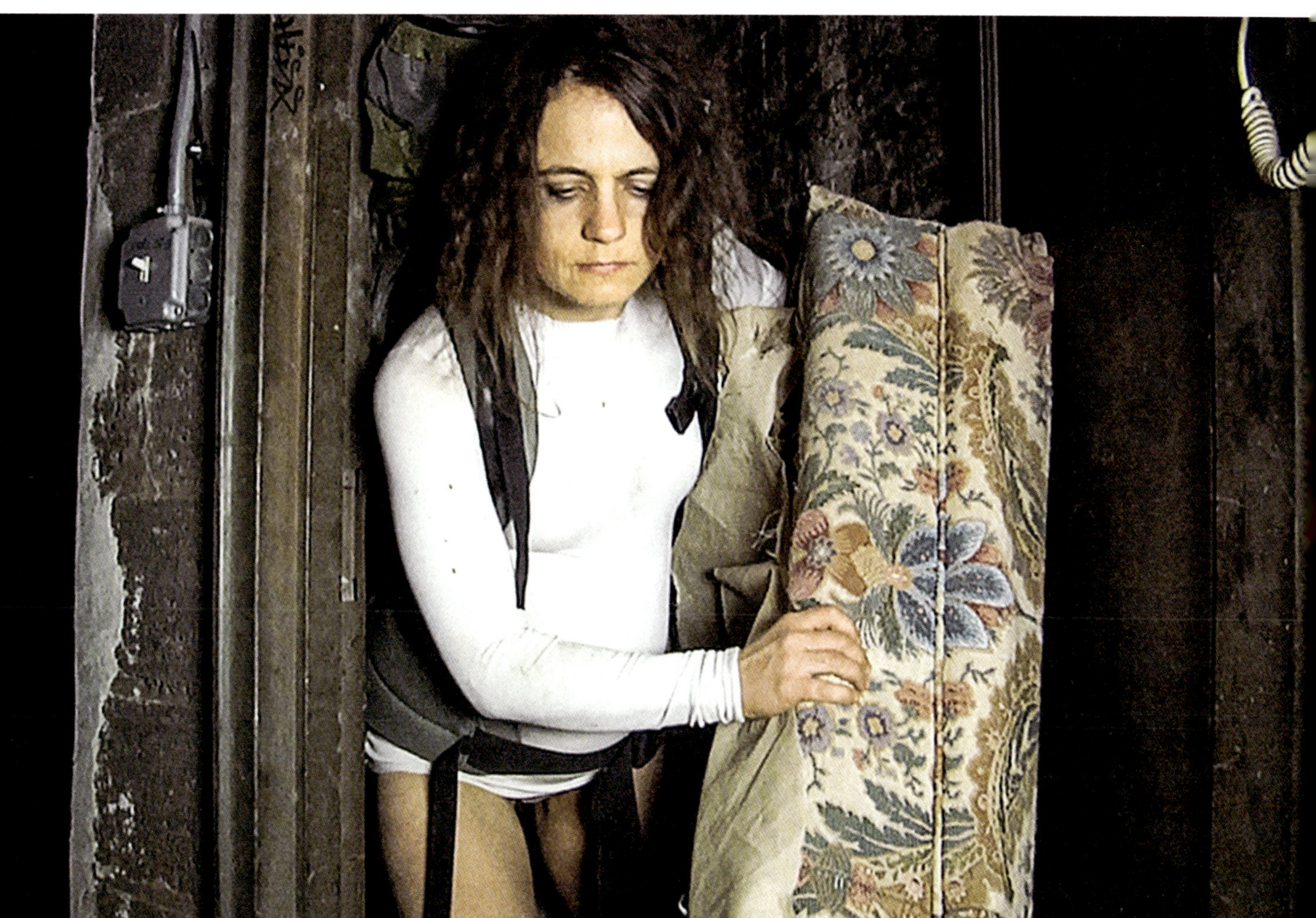

content of the piece. Individuality and collectivity are concepts that underscore the politics of the contemporary era: what recourse do we have if we feel left behind by society? Are we to think systemically and holistically,

AKB   Yes, thank you, that's what I hope the work does. It's important that, as I mentioned previously, the work is set in a speculative present. I wanted to have a space where I could process politics in real time along with the speculative and alternative ways of being within the context of whatever is our "reality." I didn't want to create a world that was entirely fictional.

KA   *A lot of the work is not speculative, though; it's aspirational. It is almost an acceptance of what a body looks like: an acceptance that an artwork exists in different ways simultaneously.*

AKB   And that gets us back to the problem of object-oriented ontology …

KA   *Orifice-oriented ontology!*

AKB   Ha! The difference between orifice- and object-oriented ontology … This work is steeped in feminist new materialism, but from the Karen Barad camp. And that's because, for Barad, the articulation of difference is essential and always present in all matter(s). There isn't a false celebration of sameness in the idea that "everything is just matter, so it's all the same," which object-oriented ontology is built upon. When difference is seen as essential and a given, then how do we engage, embrace, and

build culture that celebrates difference? That is where the potential for new sociality emerges. I think so many problems, especially in Western culture, come from demands to assimilate. This centers white Judeo-Christian heteronormativity as the key to social harmony. There are just so many ways of existing, experiencing, and perceiving. Unassimilated difference would be my political desire.

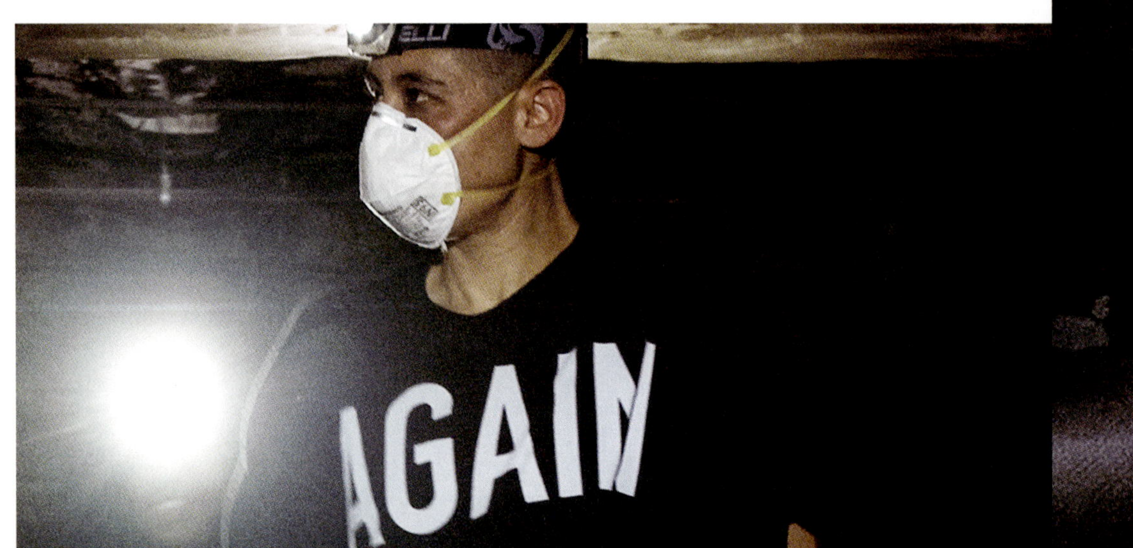

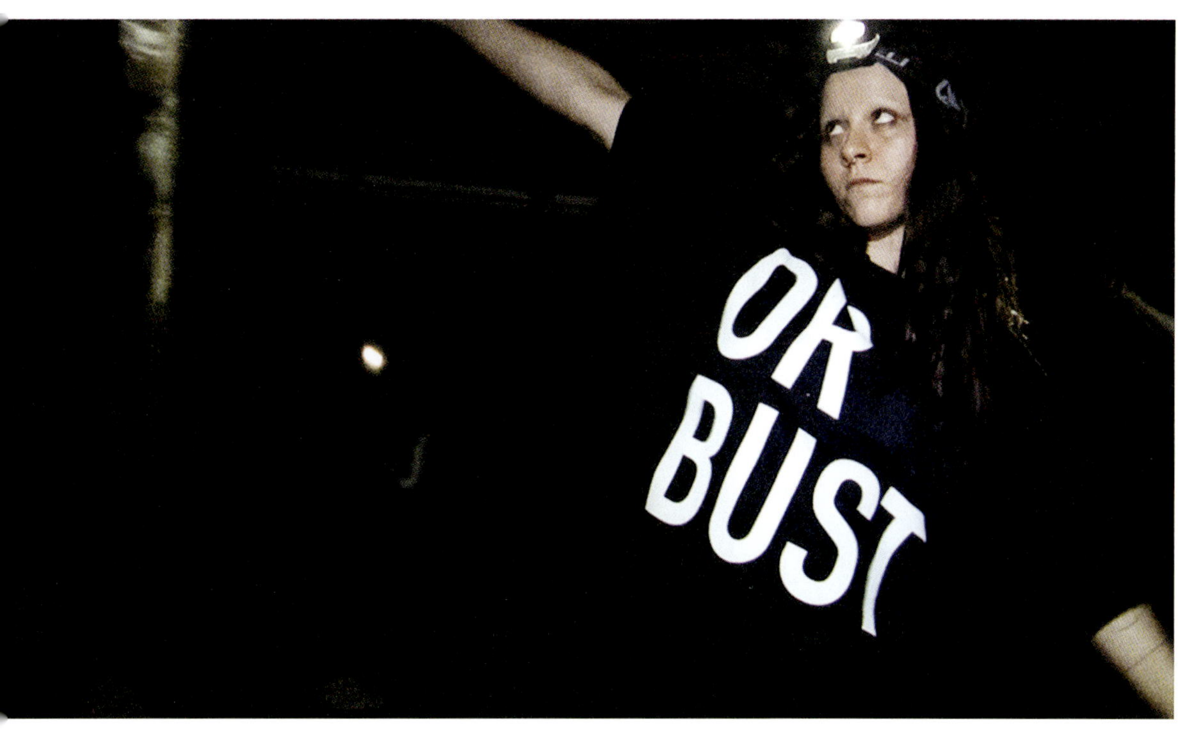
OR
BUST

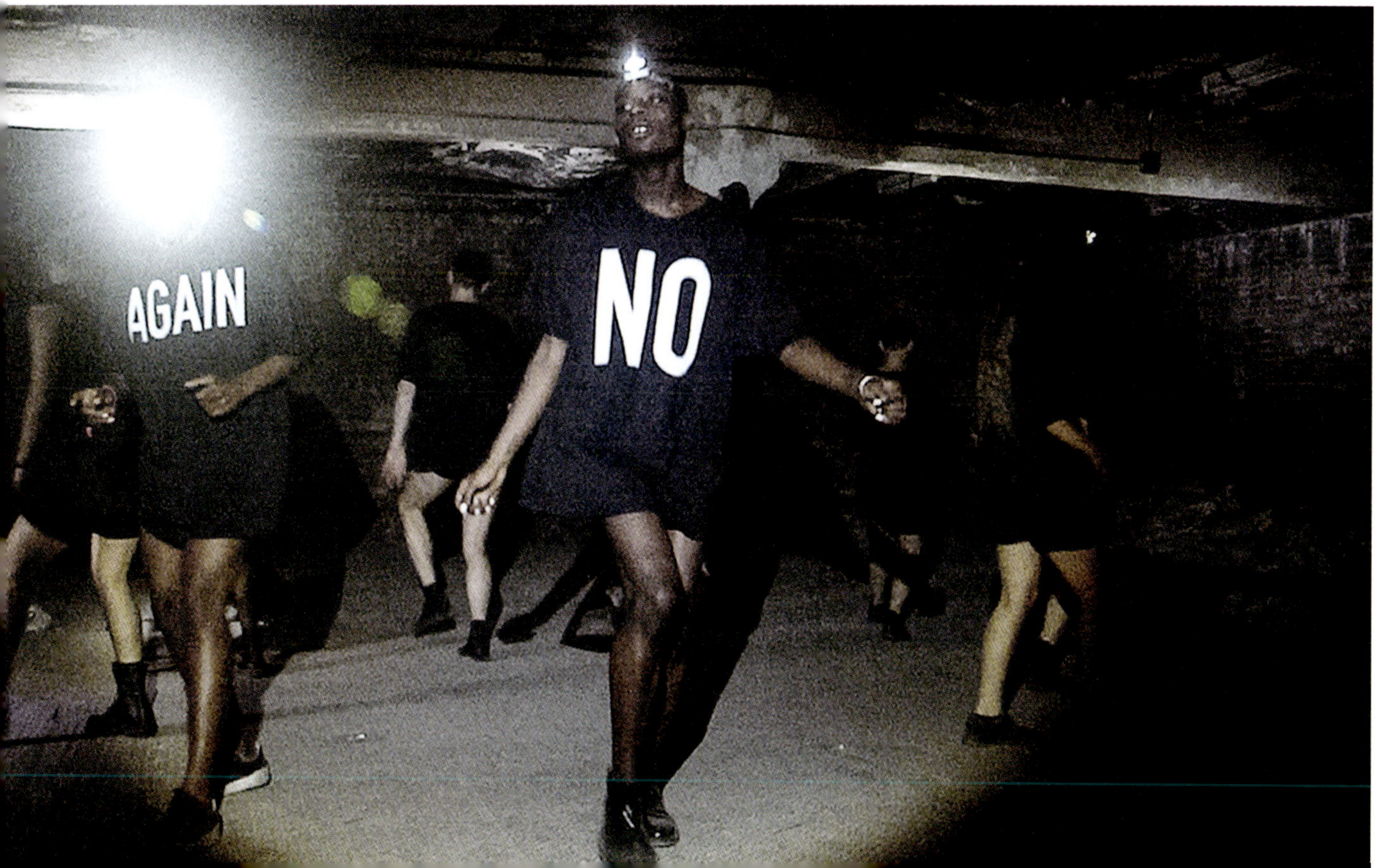

AGAIN
NO

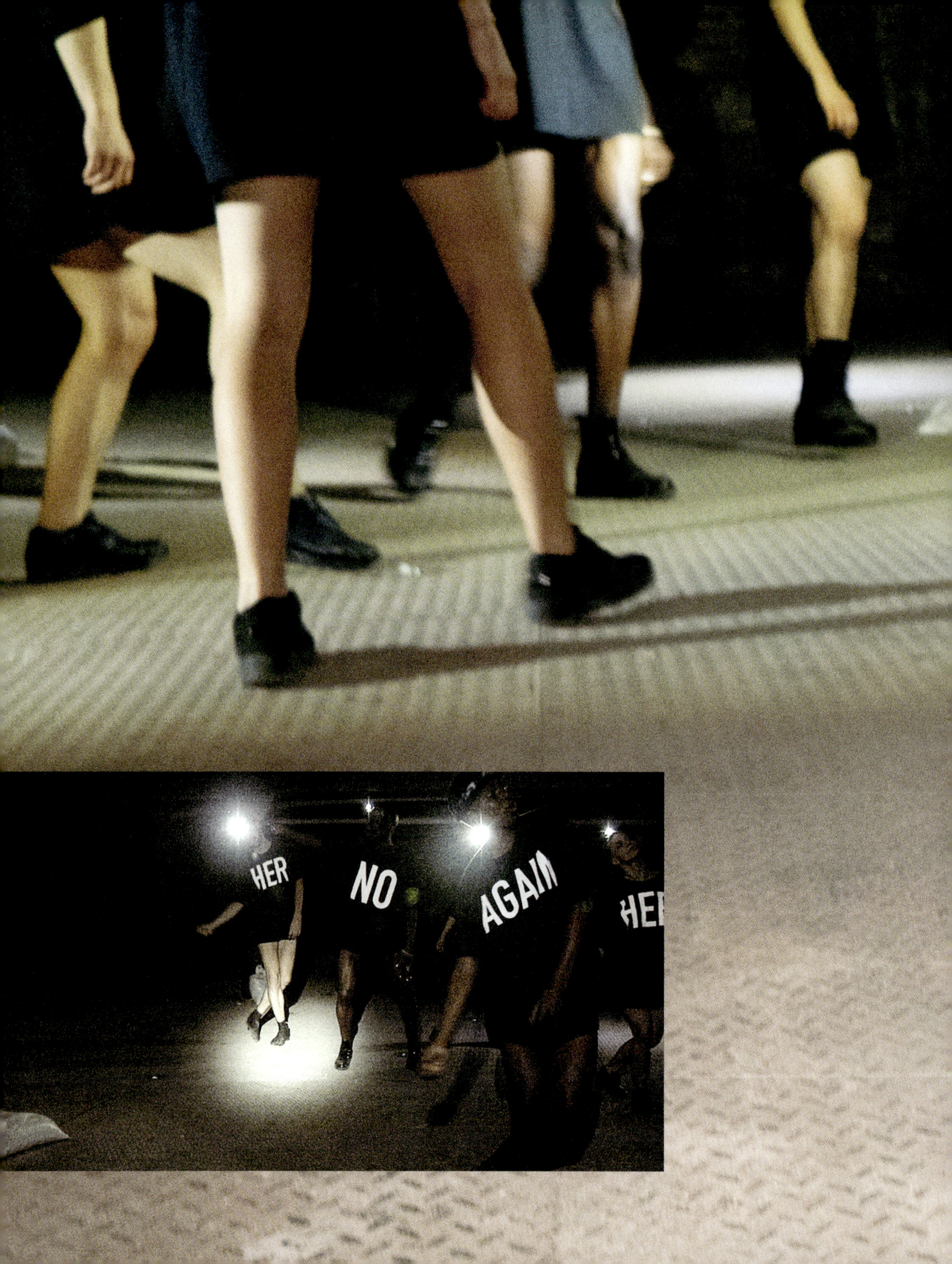

HER
NO
AGAIN
HER

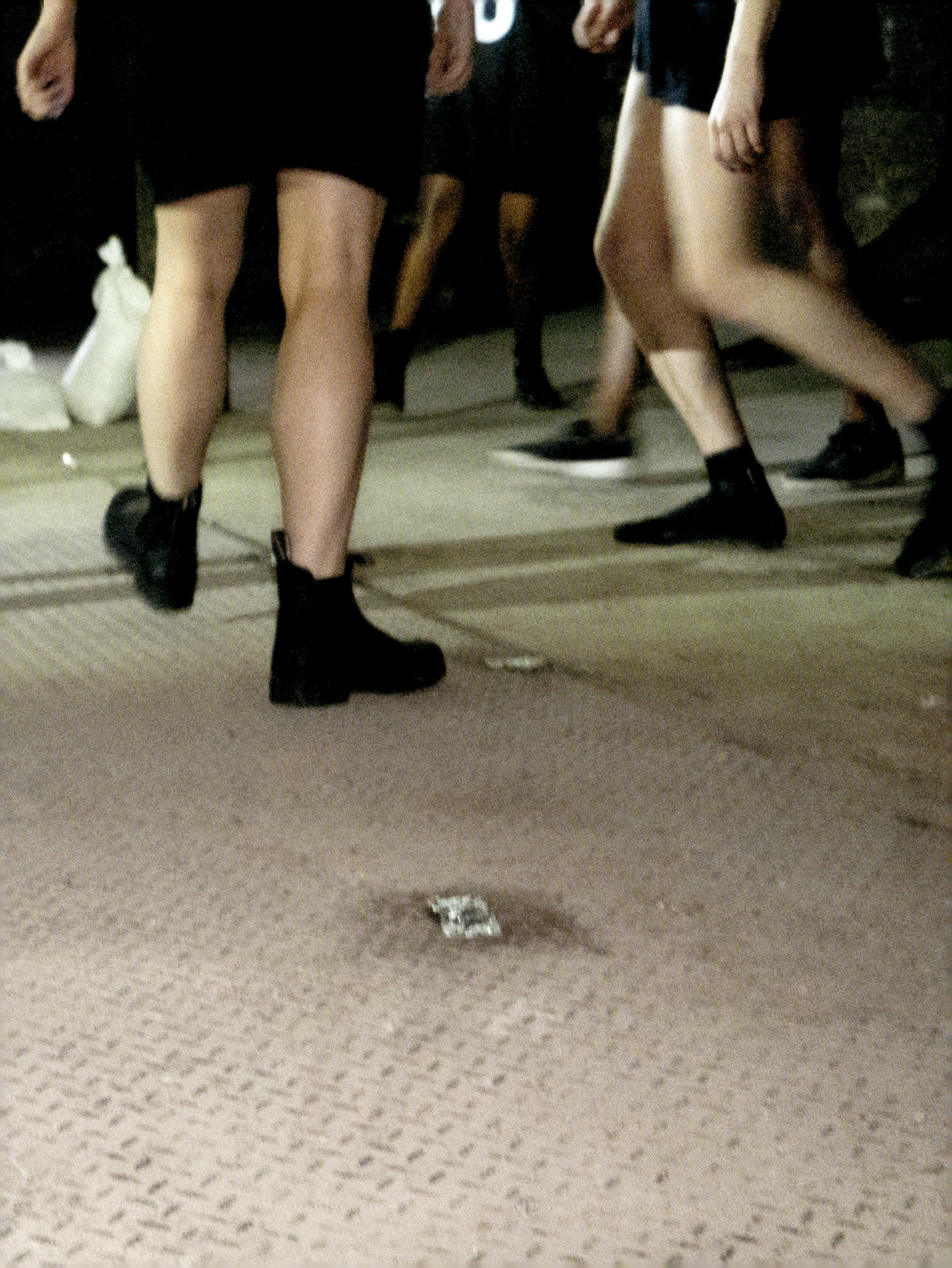

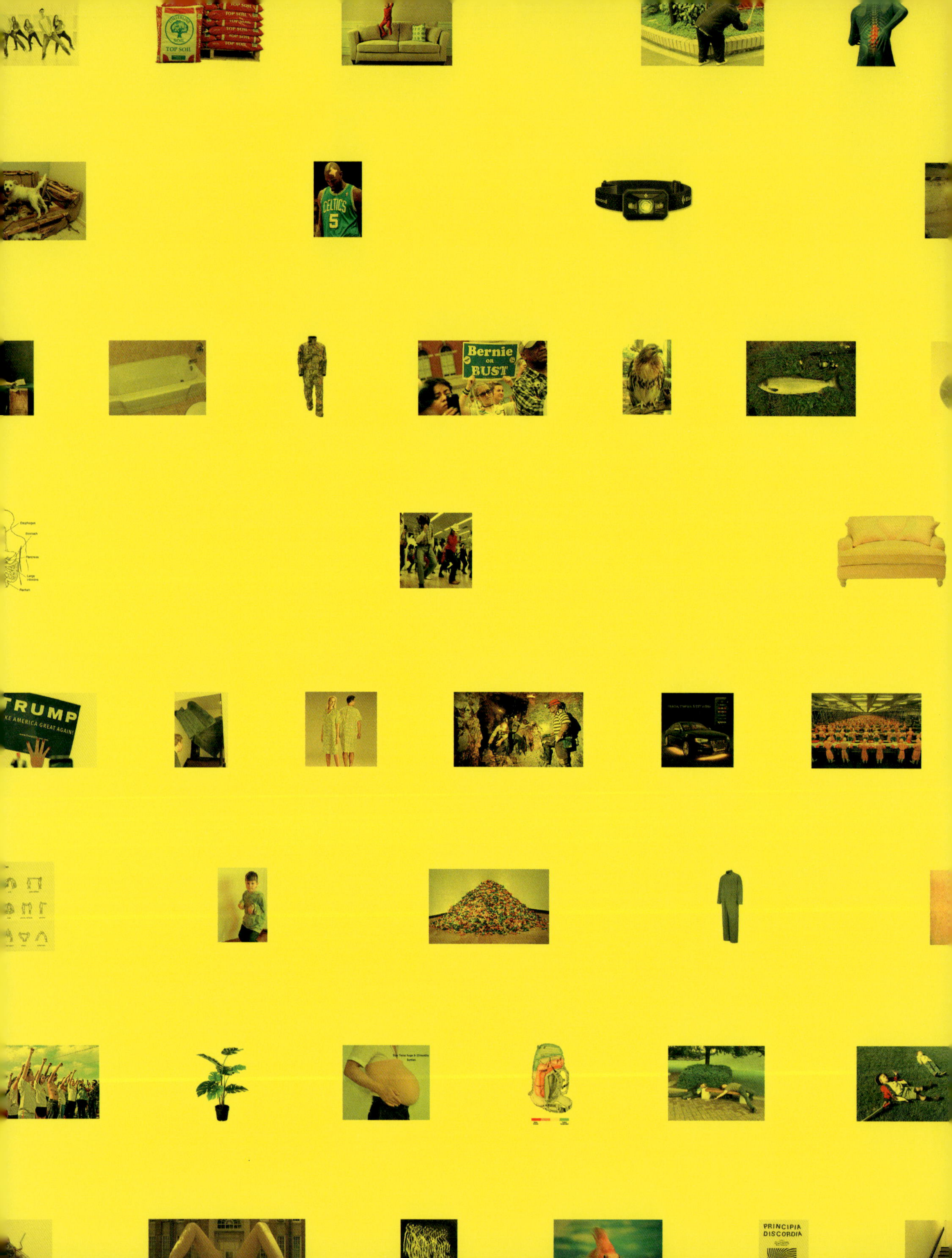

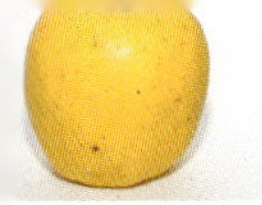

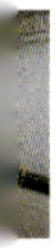

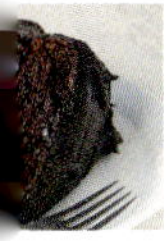

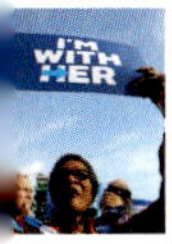

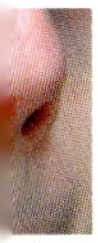

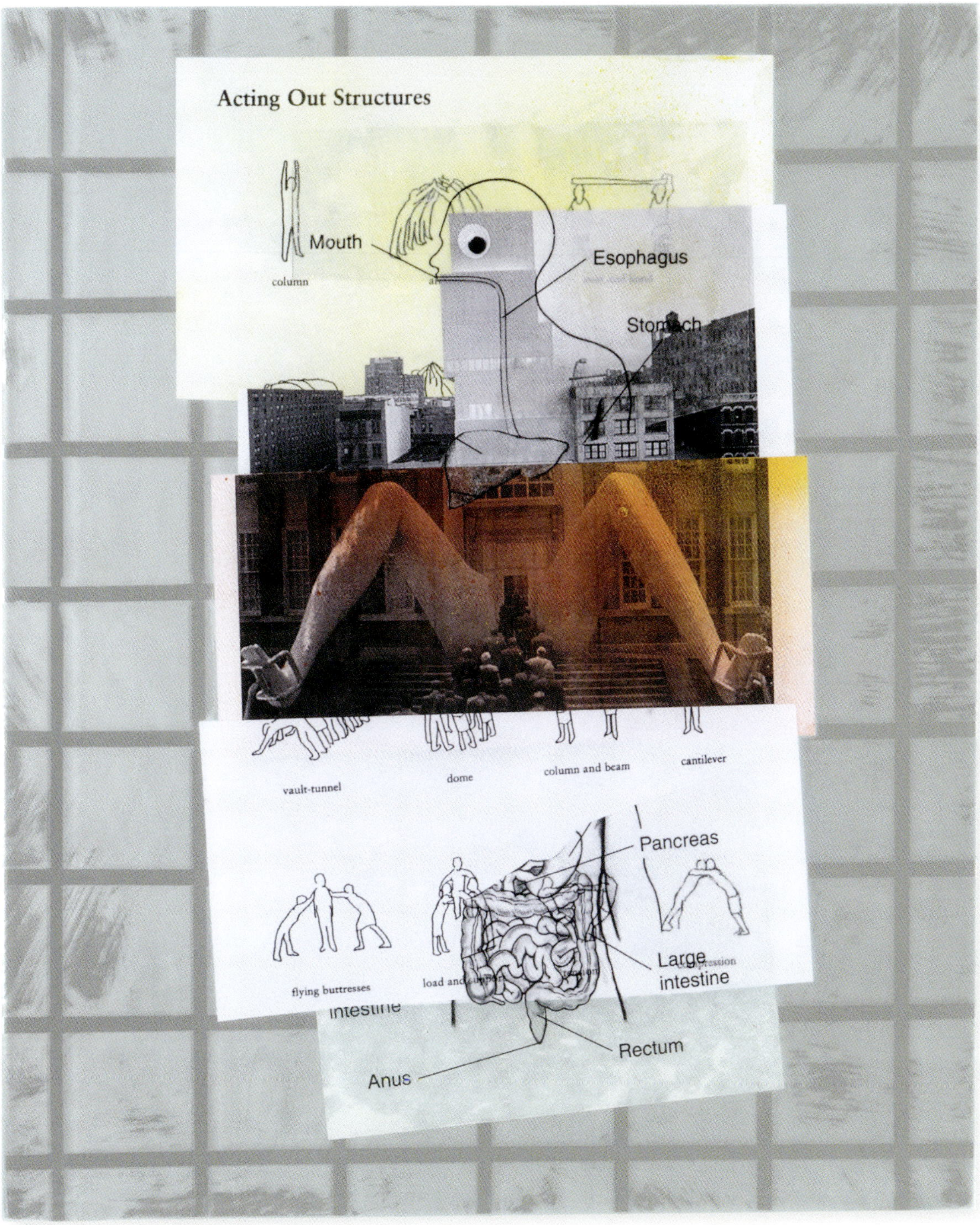

↗ *Situation Site: Body Building, Building Body*, 2019. Etched mirror, photocopy, and spray paint; 17 × 14 inches (43.2 × 35.6 cm)

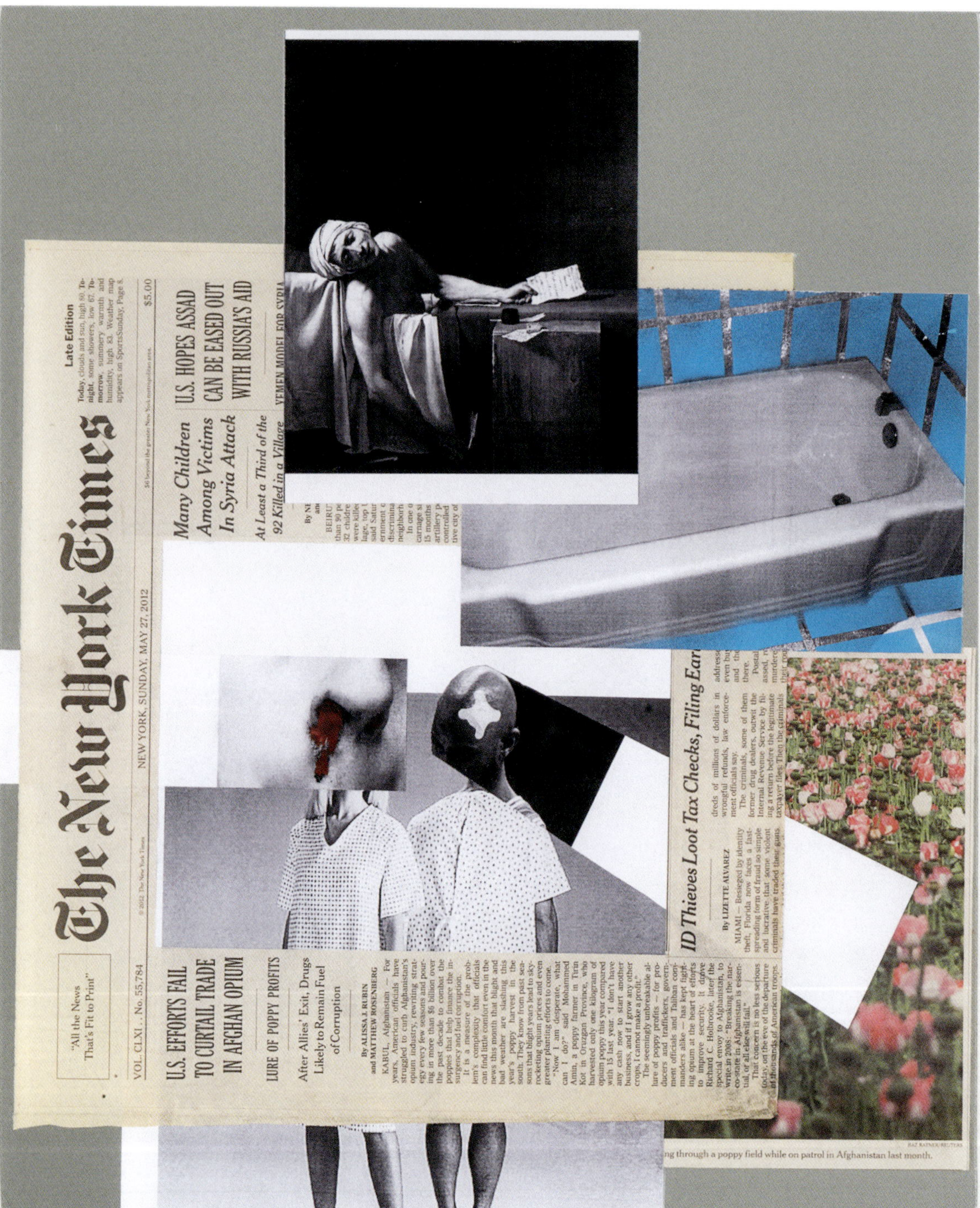

↑ *Detox Tub Talks: Death of
Marat (bathroom/kidneys)*, 2019.
Mirror, photocopy, spray paint,
newspaper, and oil paint; 17 ×
14 inches (43.2 × 35.6 cm)

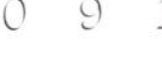

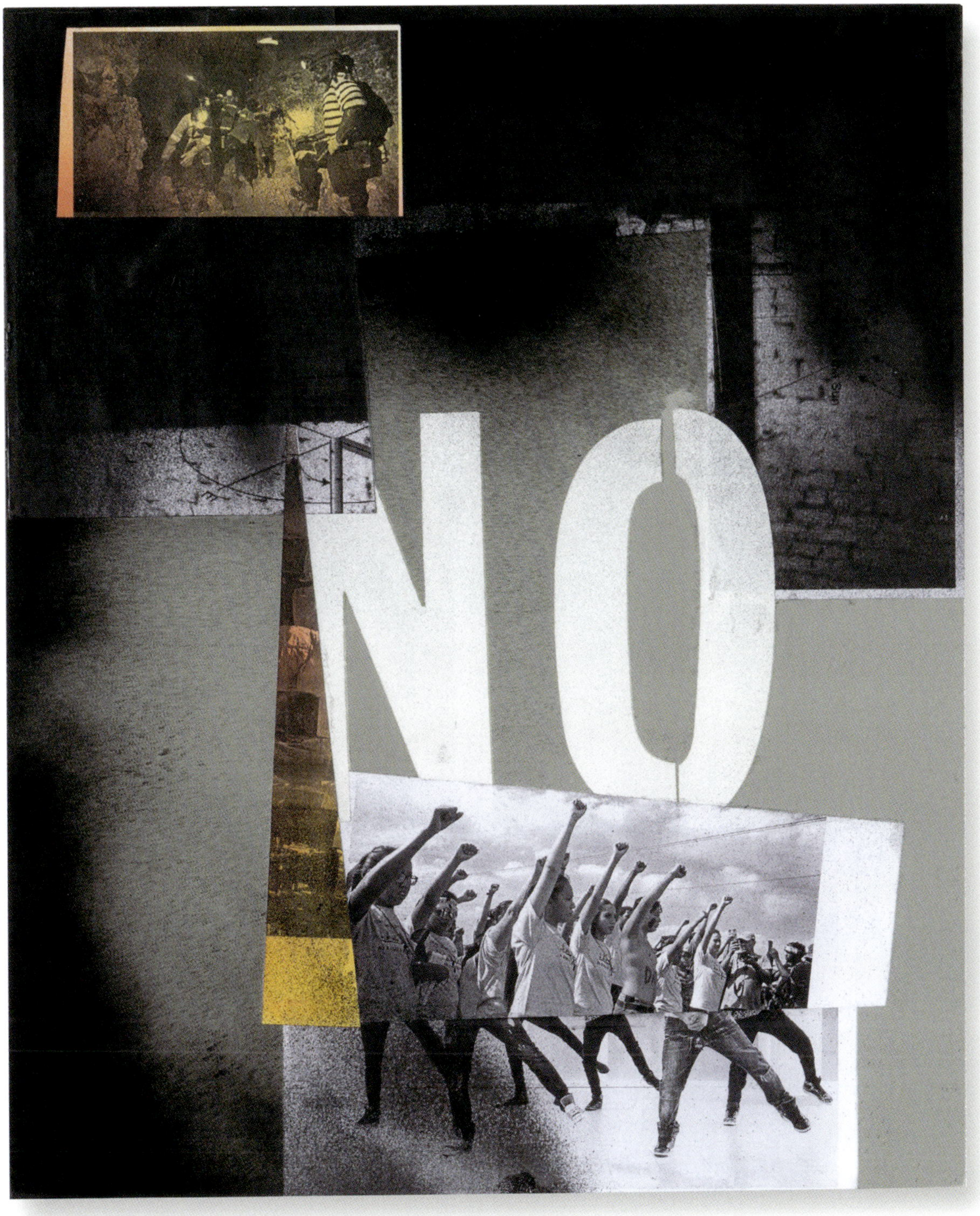

↗ *No Movement (basement/uterus),*
2010. Mirror, photocopy, spray
paint, and adhesive vinyl; 17 ×
14 inches (43.2 × 35.6 cm)

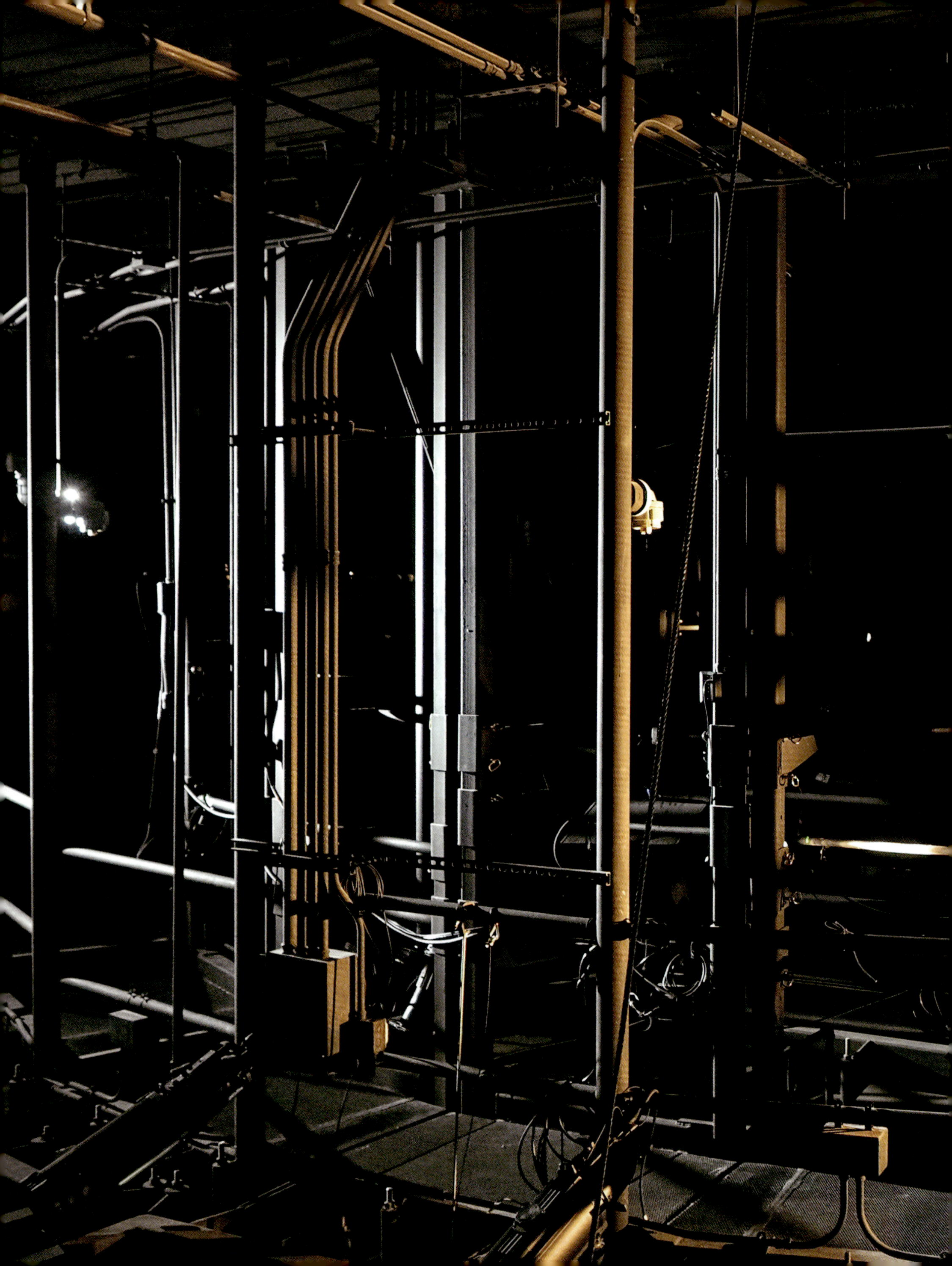

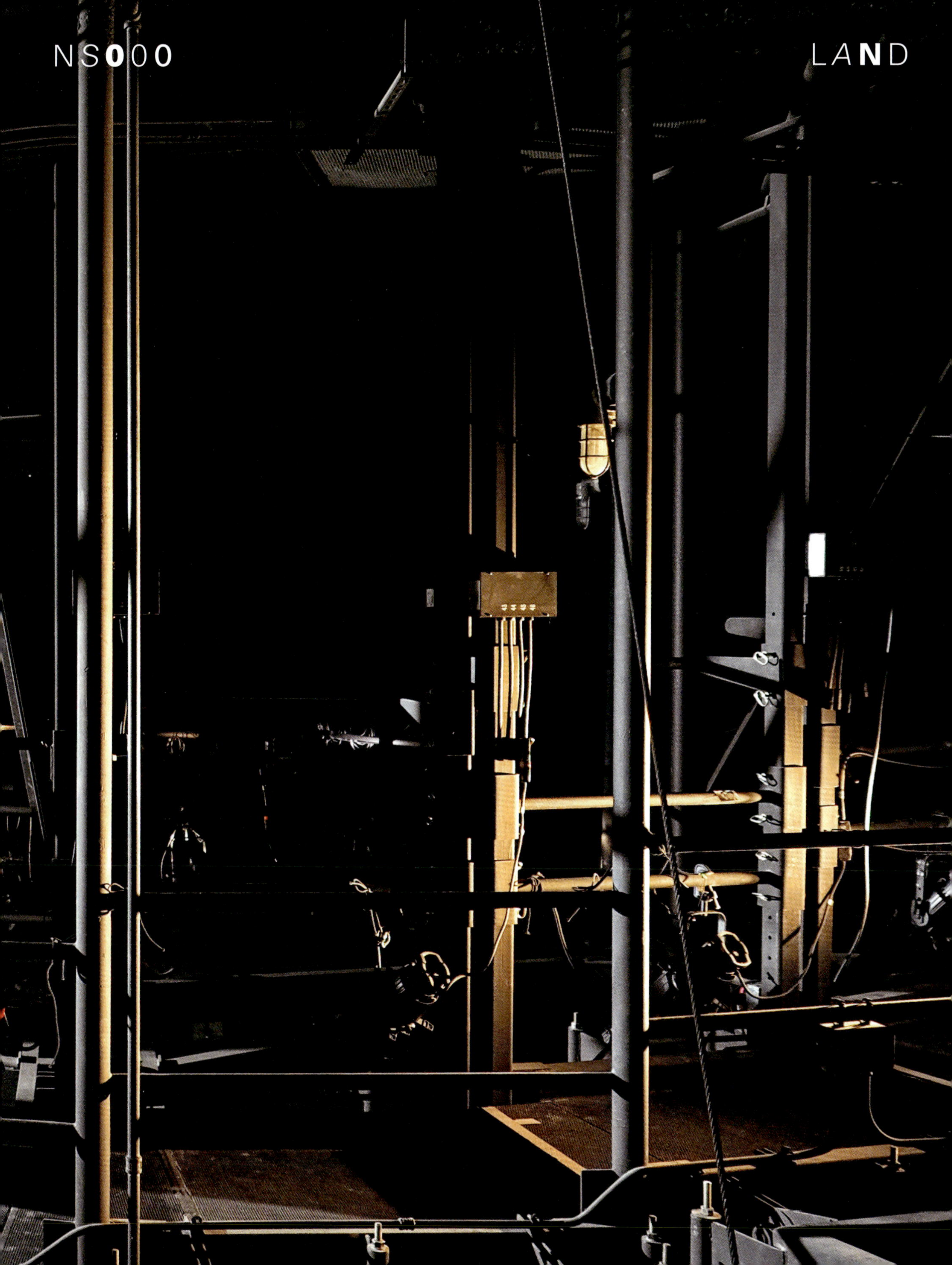
NS000
LAND

Soil represents an expansive matrix of relationships between constituents and time. First, the weathering action of wind and water fragments bedrock into particles of sediment, where gravity and weather continue to shift them into even levels. These minerogenic components combine with organic partners, such as plants, fungi, bacteria, and other life-forms, in simultaneous life and decay, to form hive-like complexes. Geologists call mobile, mineral particles sediments until their maturation and interweaving with life, after which they are termed soils. Layers of soil with distinct origins and different visual and textural characteristics are termed strata, and these form in vertical relationship to one another. Strata narrate the sequence of occurrences and are composed according to a grammar of time that we observe as a physical relationship. We can read this with a commitment to understanding causality.

The smallest particles of sediments and soils—imperceptible to the human eye—are clays and silts. Then there are larger sands, pebbles, gravel, cobbles, and boulders. Winds can shape, shift, and move dunes. Moderate winds might redeposit particles in thin wisps. Earthquakes, landslides, and other powerful events can rapidly reform the land, moving boulders and cobbles. What can landslides tell us about the ways in which power makes and unmakes relationships set into place over the *longue durée*? What is required in terms of the measure and the medium of force to move the largest and smallest constituents? How and what do roots hold during moments of upheaval?

Sedimentation is a useful metaphor for Black feminist thinkers like Saidiya Hartman in describing the forced displacement of the Black diaspora through theft and capture, the Middle Passage, enslavement, and systemic eviction. In these flows, Tiffany Lethabo King tells us, people become framed as movable, exchangeable, fungible assets. The acquisition and displacement of land and people—labeled primitive accumulations by Sylvia Federici and others—are projects of profit-making institutions that mythologize land and people as their own economic foundations while simultaneously casting them as disposable. These events seem to happen across spaces—or surfaces—that are ideologically mapped along the Cartesian, or rectangular, x- and y-axes, a system of coordinates that reflects simplified and colonial modalities of knowing the land. But what of the z-axis, which moves us up and down and through strata? What can we learn by charting directional movement into the earth? What more can we know? What happens when we map soil (and all its depth and substance) into these relations—unsettling the idea that land is a surface, covered and bounded.

Artist and filmmaker Derek Jarman noticed the queerness of digging into the earth while tending to his shingle garden in the shadow of the Dungeness nuclear power stations in Kent, England. His excavations crafted an escape from the repressive structure of his present and a movement into past surfaces, cultivating the idea of queer temporality as his death was accelerated by AIDS-related illnesses. He collected flotsam and pieces of driftwood that had washed up on the shore and embedded them, standing and pillar-like, as small vertical monuments.

The porosities between earth and bodies contradict the perception of the solidity of the ground. Even bedrock readily yields its constituents to merge with bodies; released from bedrock, strontium isotopes seep into water and find their way into our teeth as they form, marking us all with the bedrock home of our upbringing. Geoscientists use the term *parent rock* to refer to eroding bedrock surrendering sediment into the environment. If science doesn't author poetry of homelands, then it unknowingly quotes from it.

II

I drove south, through rifts in red clay and past caverns at Luray, to find my ancestors' place in Sumter, South Carolina. The former cotton fields located near where my relatives lived, which were now interred under open fields of cropped grass, pinelands, and a chicken-processing factory, struck me as colorless, flat, cold, and vacant. My grandmother's father farmed there during cotton time and always paid what was due, but insurance companies did not come through after losses from boll-weevil infestations. After the family lost access to land in Sumter, he moved them to Kingston, New York, then New Britain, Connecticut. Debts, receipts, and letters followed him, referencing his payments related to the land he once farmed. (I do not yet know whether he was a tenant or repaying a loan.) I read the letters the bank sent him. *I thank you for yours of the twenty-ninth enclosing check for 20.00 to be applied on your balance with us. I am glad to know that you are doing well and hope that you continue to do so.* Another letter was addressed to New Britain: *I thank you for yours of the fourteenth enclosing check for 10.00 to be paid on your account. It gratifies me very much to tell you that the note will soon be paid and I want you to be assured that it speaks mighty well for you.* I'm thinking about his debt on land he no longer could access.

The relentless theft of Black livelihood moved my people north. Their mode of subsisting was sacrificed to profit-making mechanisms. Debt bondage mediated their access to land and traveled with them, even after their institutionally calculated eviction. When I thought about why the bank letters and the receipts are among the few tangible materials passed down by my great-grandfather, I realized that these letters of paid debts were like freedom papers—but more honest. They document the scheduled, incremental, and multidirectional recapture of time, value, land, and bodies involved in the business of getting free.

Cotton farming, the industrial way, has proven unsustainable in the long term; soil exhaustion was but one reason. I think about how my people were aware of their participation in depleting the soil within a world that limited their agency. Institutions are padded and protected by legalities and administrative coding, so that the profits rendered from the exhaustion of the people and soil were ultimately protected for the business owners and could be reinvested in a new mode of production with another set of relations. The mobility of profit from the soil, along with the disposability of Southern soil and the eviction of

Black soil workers, points to the disposability, the fungibility, built by the powerful into this system along the z-axis.

I don't relate these details of Black eviction as a means of circumscribing us forever within broad or generalized narratives; I do so to explore the experiments, directions, obstacles, and pitfalls around self-determination across and within particular landscapes.

I now weed a garden that precedes me. I find written and material records of the English who privatized this land in the 1600s, when the crusades lingered in their cultural memory and theft of land was considered virtuous. Young oak and hickory grow where they once cut and squared exclusive parcels. When I dug holes to plant an imported laurel, white shards of shattered nineteenth-century jugs and plates splintered up out of the black earth, reminding me that, as a purchaser of land, I participate in the persistent institution of ownership that makes land and people fungible. How will I emerge from these simultaneous conditions? By the old carriage road, I found a small mound; topped by a dapper leather shoe, a tire, and an electrical insulator, it is an early-twentieth-century refuse heap. In the garden, my recent intrusions uncovered pits, skins, and seeds left by the people who sold this land to me.

Like Katherine McKittrick, Hartman, and King, I am interested in Black geographies. I understand gardening and composting as futurist acts; exploring the ways they demand time, commitment to place, and tending to healthy relations. And in this way, gardening and digging are vehicles by which I revisit places and things chronically stolen. When landscape architect Richard Westmacott interviewed Black gardeners in the South about the practice of sweeping their yards, many were hesitant to confirm the connection to a West African tradition. Their equivocation reminds me that we have the potential to play parts in the various forms of our own disconnection and alienation.

III

Grounding in the z-axis reveals divergent instances of land, body, and time relations.

During the sixteenth and seventeenth centuries, Dutch laborers called *veenders* cut and extracted billions of cubic meters of peat (an organic soil composed of compressed plant remains) that was then sold and burned as fuel to support industrial production, including for herring preservation, beer making, building kilns, manufacturing ceramics, dye works, and sugar refining. In the late-seventeenth century, peat deposits began to dwindle, causing the cost of the fuel source to go up and taking with it the price of all Dutch goods, which reduced their competitiveness in international markets and diminished Dutch advantages in colonial trade.

By contrast, consider Amazon black earth—*terra preta Indio*—a precious anthropogenic soil produced by Indigenous people, who selectively burned vegetation and turned the charcoal underground with pulverized pottery for ideal air space and drainage, along with organics like dung and bone, which added nutrients. This land technology has been used across millennia and creates soils that are not only stable but self-supporting, continually building their own mass and richness over time. This outlasts the soil-management method of modern farming in the Amazon, where fields are frequently abandoned because of nutrient depletion (mineralization) and poor drainage. An antithesis to extraction, the making of *terra preta* is characterized by a reciprocal relationship between the land and its people, each contributing to the other's survival and prosperity. The cultivation of soil through a transtemporal Indigenous approach was the foundation for what were likely dense settlements in the Amazon, which Western colonists long dismissed and neglected, claiming that the rainforest is virgin nature, or a *terra nullius*—empty and ready for their saws and plows.

The vigorous plowing of land for crops and grazing disrupts the organic structure of soil, making it prone to depletion of organic content, drying out, weathering, and erosion. It blows and washes soil away, not just displacing life along the x- and y-axis but also plunging into and rearranging its depths along the z-axis. It took only two hundred years (in some places less) for colonialism's modes of extraction and capitalism's insistence on fungibility to cause topsoil depletion and erosion on a massive scale. The West has meanwhile mythologized Indigenous peoples in terminal narratives (stories centered on their end, placing these people permanently in a mythical past), while producing ends (for us all) on an apocalyptic scale. To do so, the West claims futurism as its own, through the aesthetics of technology (mechanization), but what brand of futurism plans without conceptualizing responsibility? How futurist is it to generate the very conditions of your own depletion and finitude? We must revisit the z-axis and reconsider our multidirectional, porous relationship with the earth as substance, uncovering its trove of cultural memory to enable new futures.

References

Federici, Sylvia. "On Primitive Accumulation, Globalization, and Reproduction." *Friktion*, September 9, 2017. https://friktionmagasin.dk/on-primitive-accumulation-globalization-and-reproduction-c299e08c3693.

Hartman, Saidiya. *Wayward Lives and Beautiful Experiments: Intimate Histories of Social Upheaval*. New York: Norton, 2019.

King, Tiffany Lethabo. *Black Shoals: Offshore Formations of Black and Native Studies*. Durham, NC: Duke University Press, 2019.

King, Tiffany Lethabo. "The Labor of (Re)Reading Plantation Landscapes Fungible(ly)." *Antipode* 48, no. 4 (September 2016), https://doi.org/10.1111/anti.12227.

McKittrick, Katherine. *Demonic Grounds: Black Women and the Cartographies of Struggle*. Minneapolis, MN: University of Minnesota Press, 2006.

O'Quinn, Daniel. "Gardening, History, and an Escape from Time: Derek Jarman's 'Modern Gardening.'" *October*, no. 89 (1999): 113–26.

Westmacott, Richard. *African American Gardens and Yards in the Rural South*. Knoxville: University of Tennessee Press, 1992.

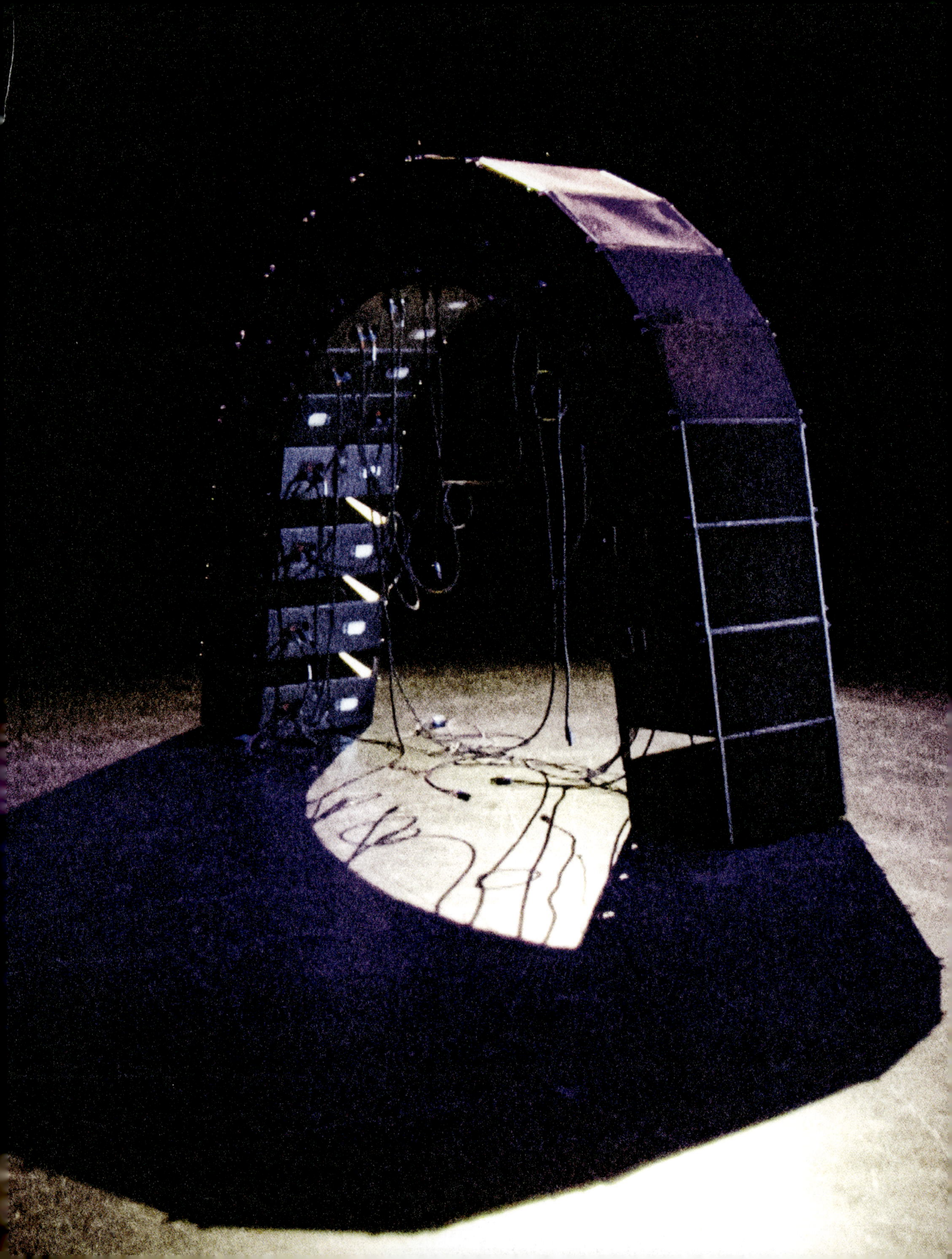

LEAVE NO TRACE

(Negative Space 000)

2 0 1 9

A.K. BURNS

LAND

34°15'04.2" N, 116°14'42.7" W
Joshua Tree, CA

34°15'06.9" N, 116°14'42.5" W
border of "Little Bagdad" Camp Wilson Marine Corps,
Air Ground Combat Center, Twentynine Palms, CA

P R O D U C T I O N
Victoria Brooks
A.K. Burns

PRODUCTION ASSISTANTS
Peymaan Motevalli-Aliabadi
Wren Warner

DIRECTOR OF PHOTOGRAPHY
A.K. Burns

ADDITIONAL CAMERAS
Eden Batki
Eric Brucker
Ryan Jenkins

PRODUCTION MANAGER (EMPAC)
Ian Hamelin

DIRECTOR FOR STAGE TECHNOLOGIES (EMPAC)
Geoff Abbas

PRODUCTION TECHNICIANS (EMPAC)
Sara Griffiths
Mike Hanrahan
Mike Lake

AUTOMATION (EMPAC)
Gordon Clemens

AUDIO ENGINEER (EMPAC)
Todd Vos

MASTER ELECTRICIAN (EMPAC)

ACTING AGENTS

SUB TEXT (LEAKS)
Mx. Manning: Kera Armendariz

MOBILE HOME
Free Radical: Adee Roberson
Free Radical: Clara Lopez Menendez
Free Radical: Kera Armendariz

VOID VACUUM
Transparent Sucker: Savannah Knoop

CONSTRUCTION CREW
Free Radical: Adee Roberson
Free Radical: Clara Lopez Menendez
Free Radical: Kera Armendariz
Re/productive Labor: keyon gaskin
Re/productive Labor: Wren Warner

PROTEST TABLEAU
No: Kera Armendariz
Un/productive Labor: keyon gaskin
Witness Protection: Adee Roberson
Nothing: Wren Warner

THE TRESSPASS
Mx. Manning: Kera Armendariz

A CAPPELLA ON THE GRID
Vox: Shannon Funchess

GO-GO DANCER (FOR FELIX)
Go-Go Boi: Clara Lopez Menendez

VERTIGO BICEPS
Muscles: Savannah Knoop

---

at Rensselaer Polytechnic Institute, Troy, New York

Leave

No

Trace

WARDROBE, PROPS, AND SET DESIGN
A.K. Burns

STILL PHOTOGRAPHY
Edin Batki
Mick Bello

E D I T O R
A.K. Burns

S C O R E
Geo Wyeth

AUDIO MIX AND MASTERING
Quentin Chiappetta

A N I M A T I O N
Peymaan Motevalli-Aliabadi

P O S T P R O D U C T I O N
A.K. Burns

S C R I P T
A.K. Burns

R E F E R E N C E S
Cerrone, *Supernature*, 1977
Felix Gonzalez-Torres, *Untitled (Go-Go Dancing Platform)*, 1991

SPECIAL THANKS
Victoria Brooks
Callicoon Fine Arts
Katherine Hubbard
Molly Larkey
AV Linton
Lisa Long
Clara Lopez Menendez
Peymaan Motevalli-Aliabadi
Michel Rein Gallery
Julia Stoschek

PRODUCED WITH THE GENEROUS SUPPORT OF
Experimental Media and Performing Arts

KAREN ARCHEY

A.K. BURNS

I was wondering: what was the conceptual starting point for Leave No Trace, *and how does it fit into the larger* Negative Space *series? Both the titles of the individual works and the series as a whole are marked by a multiplicity of meanings.* Leave no trace *as a phrase is both a literal command and an ideology;* negative space *could be read in the context of an aesthetic composition, as in the empty space around the subject of an image, or perhaps with an emotional dimension: "I am in a negative space," meaning, "I am in a bad place emotionally." The word* space *also, of course, refers to a common subject of science fiction, a genre that provides inspiration for the series.*

I would start again by pointing toward locations and resources. I was in residency at EMPAC, the Curtis R. Priem Experimental Media and Performing Arts Center at Rensselaer Polytechnic Institute. EMPAC is housed inside a large high-tech building whose main theater is a "floating" room. The theater is an acoustically perfect zero-decibel space. It has a passive air system, and the theater grid is web-shaped instead of rectilinear.

The silence of that building got me thinking about the phrase *leave no trace*, which I already knew would be the title of the episode centered on the subject of land in the *Negative Space* cycle. *Leave no trace* is a wilderness ethic for low-impact human interaction with nature. I carried this idea forward from my youth, when my dad would take me backpacking and taught me the principles of LNT. I was drawn

1 0 0

to that piece of language not only because of this reference but because the term points to questions about how we leave a mark, interact with our environment, and take up space. The theater, with its deafening silence of zero decibels, helped structure my exploration of land through the lens of immateriality and absence, and thereby it seemed obvious that the third work in the series would be *Leave No Trace*.

EMPAC had several black-box theaters. In *A Smeary Spot*, I used the stage as a tool for *becoming*—i.e., for making and unmaking a world; by contrast, in *Leave No Trace*, I got very interested in what I call the nonevent spaces of the theater. I wanted to move away from the stage, a site where we expect events to occur, and toward activating the behind-the-scenes infrastructure, such as the theater battens and grid. And I began to think about these sites—where the labor to create the theatrical illusion occurs, invisible to the audience—as another type of negative space, a highly productive marginalized space. The web-shaped grid at EMPAC is beautiful and radically different from any other grid I've ever seen. It is made of concentric polygons that felt to me like a "feminist" grid form. The battens also got me excited, as they extend four stories high, so I could capture dramatic perspectival lines.

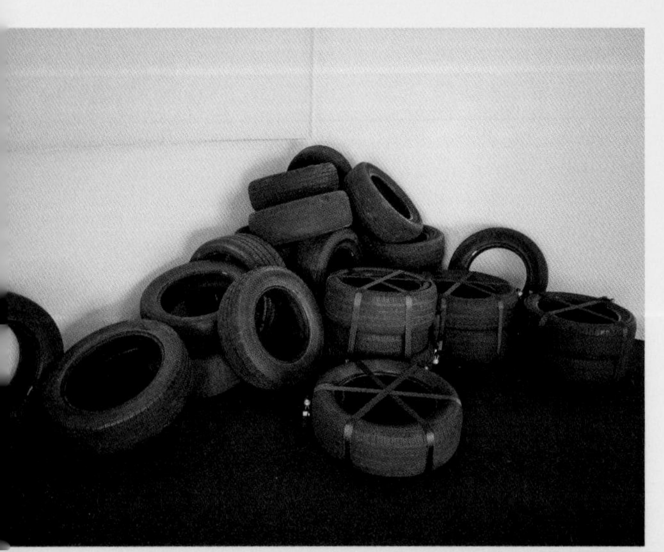

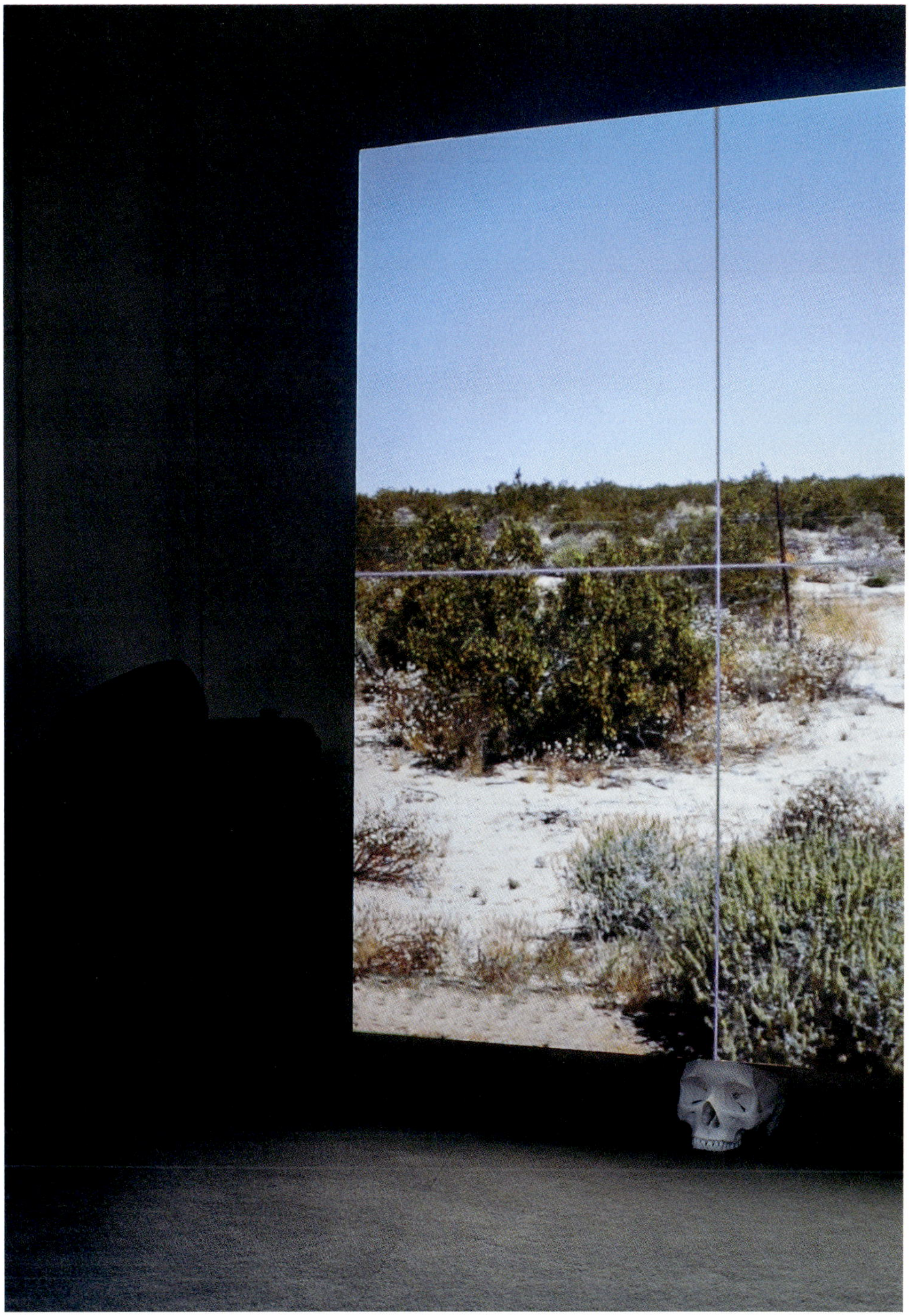

← *Leave No Trace (NS000)*, 2019.
Installation view, showing
stacked-tire seating area, *A.K.
Burns: Of space we are. . .*,
Wexner Center for the Arts,
Columbus, Ohio, 2023

↗ *Leave No Trace (NS000)*, 2019.
Installation view, *A.K. Burns:
Negative Space*, Julia Stoschek
Foundation, Düsseldorf, Germany,
2019

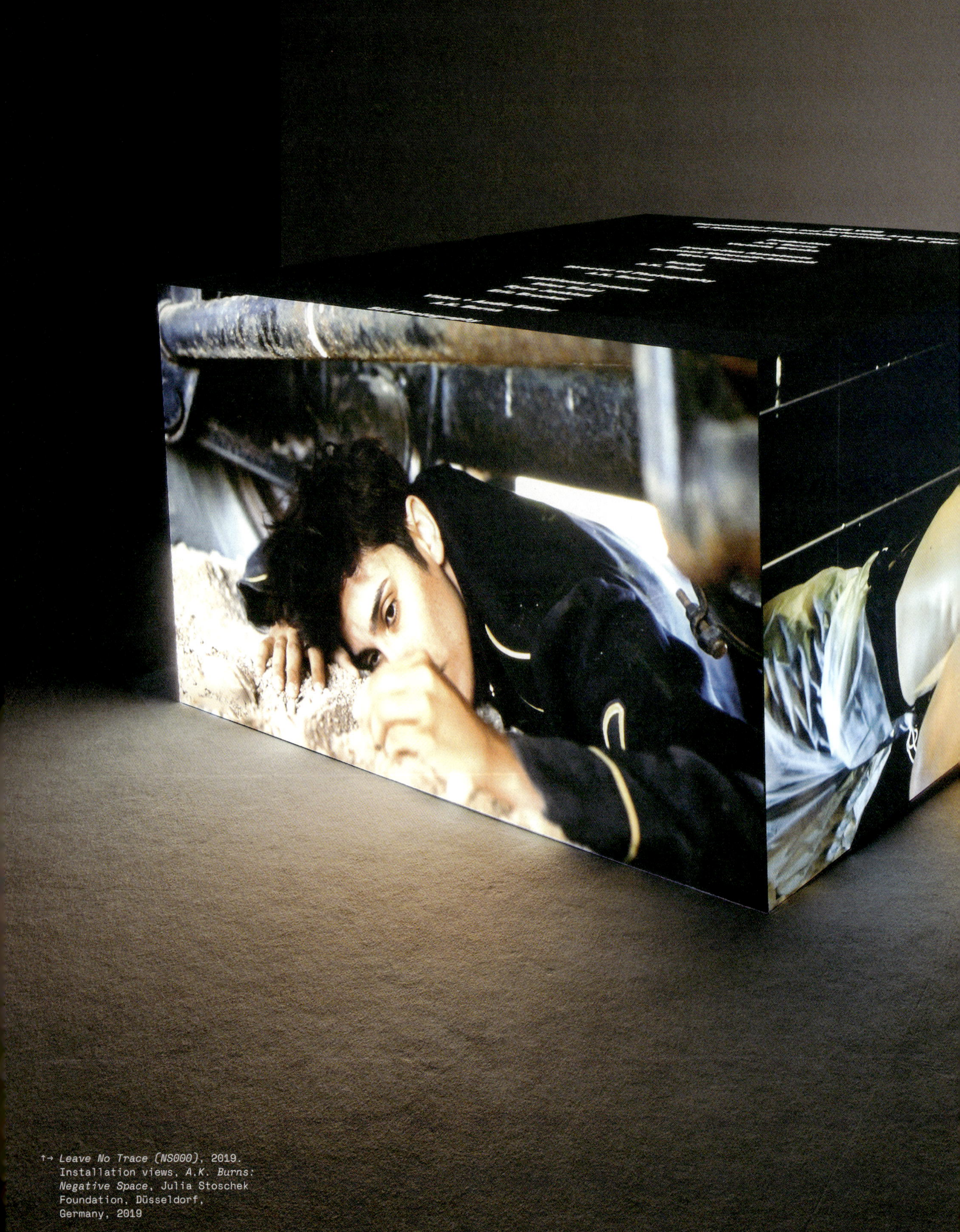

↑→ *Leave No Trace (NS000)*, 2019.
Installation views, A.K. Burns:
Negative Space, Julia Stoschek
Foundation, Düsseldorf,
Germany, 2019

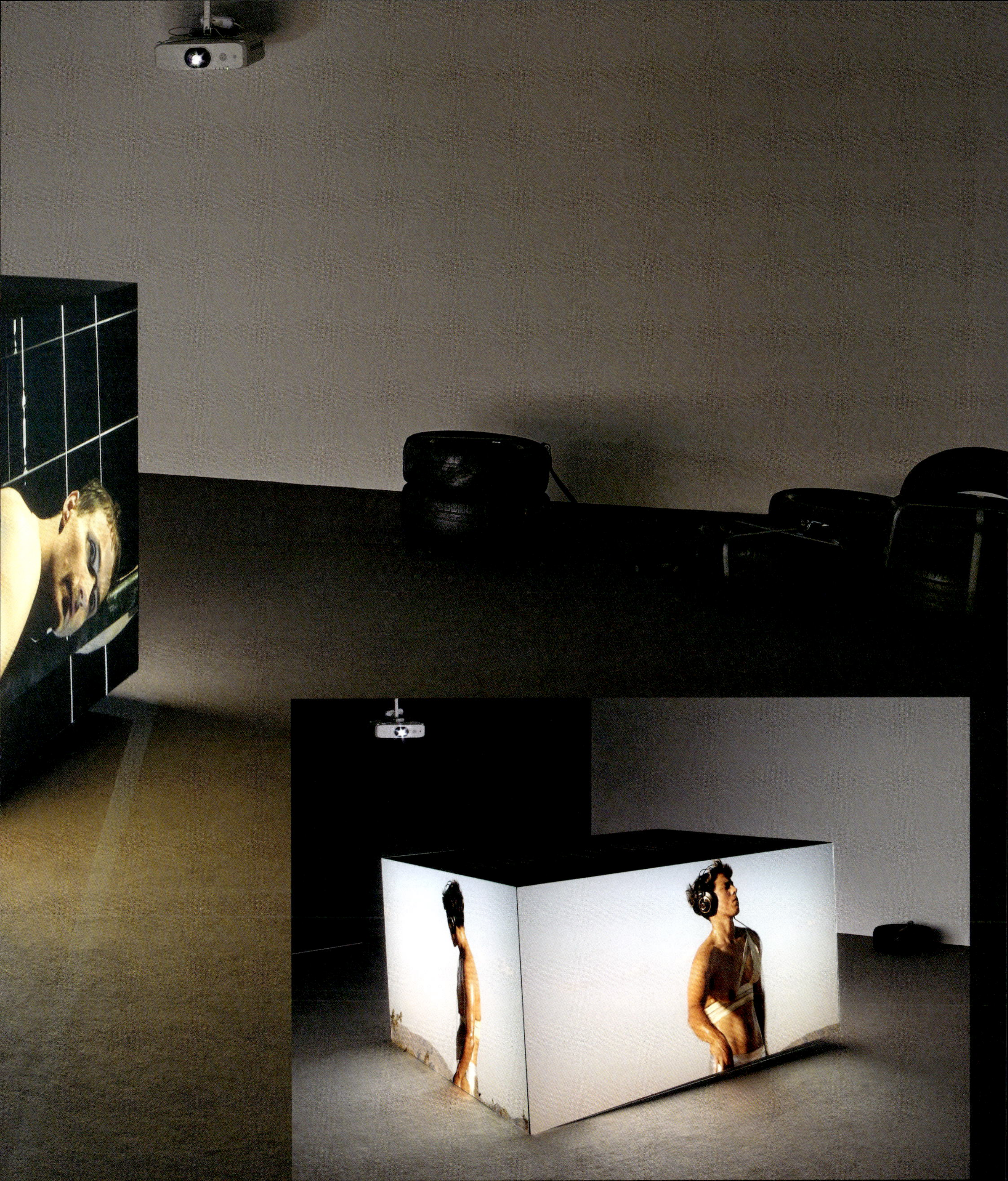

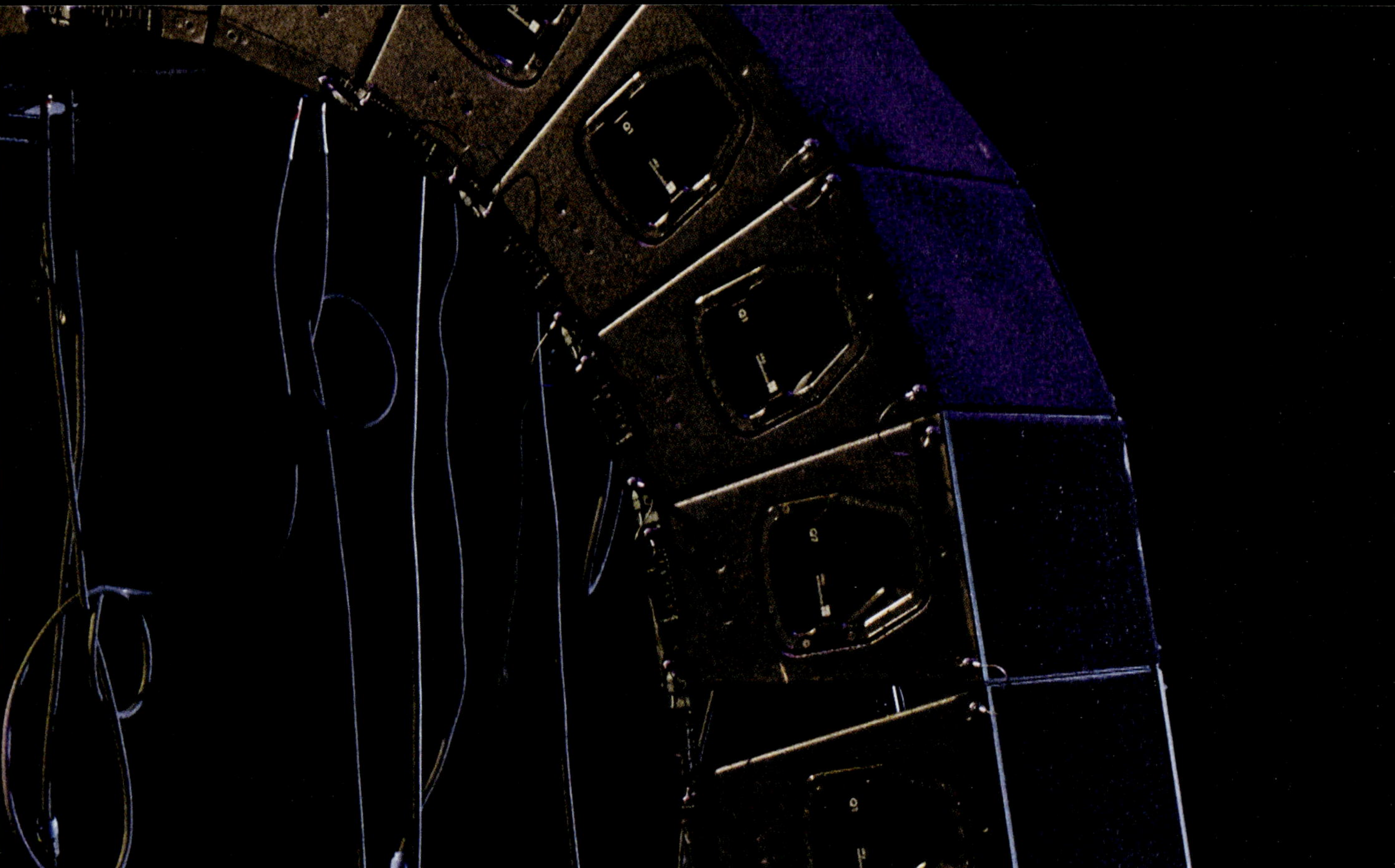

KA   *Those shots are scary; the height is indeed dramatic. I notice that there are some elements that return from* A Smeary Spot *and* Living Room. *I'm curious to hear how you decided which elements to bring back from the previous works into* Leave No Trace *and how these influenced the content and structure of the piece—I was going to use the word* narrative, *but that seems too strong. There are actions that happen, though, including with bee pollen and a fish tank, which we've seen in the previous two works. How did you develop your thinking around these elements?*

AKB   Some things were preplanned, and some were discovered on-site while shooting. As you point out, I brought back acting agents—Mx. Manning, Re/productive Labor, and the Free Radicals. Because I was going to be working at EMPAC with various theater spaces, I decided to shoot in similar sites to those in *A Smeary Spot*—the desert and the theater. This time, I went to Joshua Tree, California, partially because it was more accessible but also because I wanted the works to be in conversation, so to speak, rather than repeat one another. *A Smeary Spot* centers on a landscape that has little reference to human presence. There are power lines, a dam, and a power plant—public infrastructure—but there are no domestic sites, no personal or human-scale struc-tures. In *Leave No Trace*, you can see homes in the distance in the town of Joshua Tree, a semi-trailer, and a platform on the site of a demolished cabin. Also, we were located on the border of Little Baghdad, a training facility in Twentynine Palms where the military stages war games; you see the barbed-wire fence and warning signage that encloses it. *Leave No Trace* is much more about encountering and permeating borders than *A Smeary Spot* was. I wanted the grid and the systems that put borders and boundaries in place to be more visible and be something the performers negotiate.

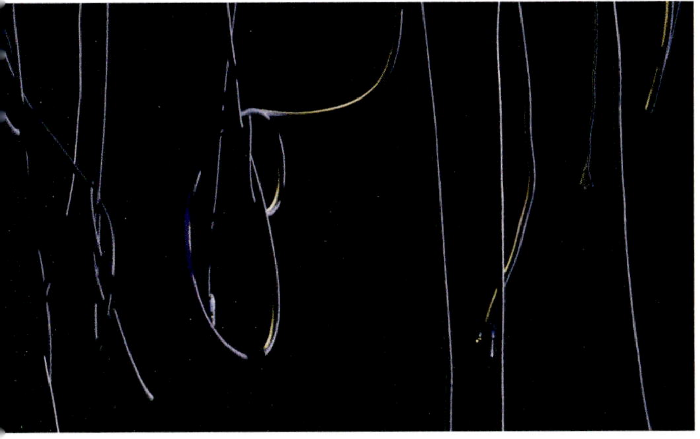

When I arrived in Joshua Tree to shoot *Leave No Trace*; I didn't know the border of the military base would be across the street or that there would be a foundation of a demolished building on the site of our rental property. I was planning on building a platform for a go-go-dancing scene, but the concrete platform was already there, covered in garbage, including a gutted couch. So I had these unexpected references to *Living Room* that I could build upon, in staging an exterior pseudo living-room space, as well as a ready-made platform and a militarized border to work with. I brought the fish tank with me because I wanted to have the presence of water in a place that has so little of it but also an allusion to *Living Room*. In *Leave No Trace*, the tank is pushed across the desert—sloshing around—its murky water unsuitable for drinking or living in.

KA *You've talked a lot about sites, nonsites, land, and the relationship between bodies and sites. Knowing you've done research on Nancy Holt, even giving a talk on her work at Dia Art Foundation, I'd love to hear about your*

1 0 5

relationship to Land art, specifically that of Land art to the Negative Space *series.*

AKB Land art is complicated. I have a lot of problems with it, especially the Michael Heizer and Walter De Maria brand. I find their works to be macho responses to land, wherein the artist carves it away or inserts actions onto it. The work is imposed on nature, and it often requires a lot of excavation for its construction. De Maria was theoretically even interested in altering the natural course of lightning, for example. I'm emphatic about Nancy Holt's work because she's underrecognized and made Land art in a way that feels more responsive to the environment. It was a profound experience to finally get to go to the *Sun Tunnels* after being obsessed with them from a distance for so many years. You could tell Holt had spent a year out there, just listening and looking at the way the Earth and the sun move. The *Sun Tunnels* are in conversation with the specificity of that location and its orientation to the cosmos. It's a completely different approach than most (male) Land artists have. I hope that *Negative Space* similarly reworks the genre of sci-fi and

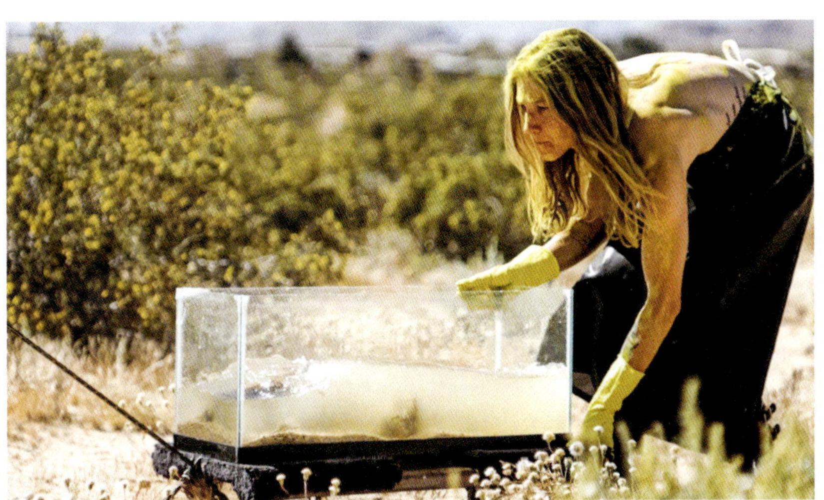

asks different kinds of questions about what really matters and what's at stake in the constructed fantasies of world-building.

KA
I completely agree. Land art is often such an interventionist, masculinist practice. The title of Leave No Trace *makes me think about how masculinist Land art aims to leave a* big *trace. The domestic site in* Living Room, *the open landscape in* A Smeary Spot, *and the combination of domestic site and open place in* Leave No Trace *seem to offer alternatives.*

AKB
Yeah, even in the black box: I explore *other* spaces and *other* ways of forming that decenter anthropocentrism. For example, in a scene where I do use the stage of the black box, I wanted to make a sundial because I was interested in working with the notion of experiential time, as opposed to mechanized time.

My plan was to compose a giant sundial from props in EMPAC's prop closet, until I found a vertical stack of speakers that was stored in the corner of the theater space. I found it to be a compelling totemic object, but I didn't want to use something that was so overtly phallic. I asked myself, "What's a feminist form this could take?" Hence, I arranged the speakers into an arch—which became more like a passageway. The speakers, being objects from which sound emerges, also act as hosts for the immaterial (sound). In exploring what structures our environment, *Leave No Trace* isn't just thinking about architecture and borders. Time, light, and sound also create structure, they just do so through immateriality.

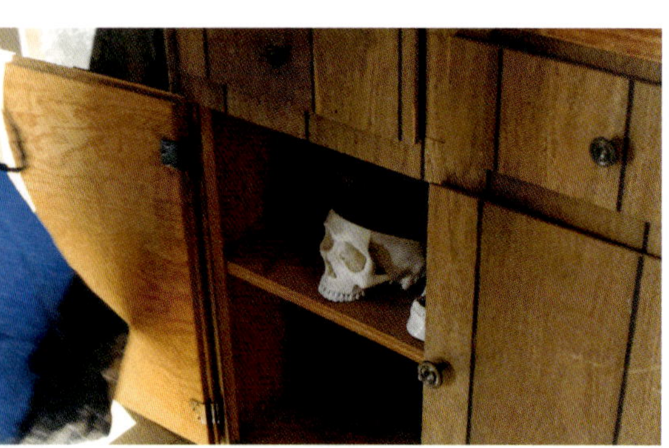

1 0 6

One of my biggest problems in this project was how to represent absences and immateriality. I had to come up with ways to introduce these kinds of structures and different forms of presence.

KA
There is a scene where we see a performer doing pull-ups in what feels like a black box. How did that develop?

AKB
Oh, yes, a performer, Savannah Knoop, is doing pull-ups in the battens at EMPAC. All the cables holding the battens appear like a fractured grid in that scene. Grids are one of these structures that I'm talking about; they appear throughout *Leave No Trace* in different ways, literally—for example, as an animation of a grid that builds up to cover the whole surface of the screens and then softens like fabric before pulling back to reveal a new scene—and more subtly through indications of verticality and horizontality, or above and below. We see this idea of dividing space vertically when the performers build a stage for the go-go dancer to perform on and wedge skulls underneath it. There is essentially a live body dancing on the remnants of dead ones. This is morbid as much as it is an expression of the idea that something is spent for something else to exist.

In the installation, the screen showing the scene of the pull-ups in the battens is paired with an adjacent screen on which Mx. Manning is lying on the ground under the wheel well of a trailer whispering "secrets." This is another way of exploring a kind of subspace or "nonevent" space and thinking about what information is being "leaked."

KA
I got the feeling that there was a military reference or a reference to war here, using the trailer for cover . . .

AKB
Yes, the performer, Kera Armendariz, is Mx. Manning and wears a replica of Chelsea Manning's military jacket—which appears in all four of the *Negative Space* works. They do a military crawl to get

under the wheel well. So the military reference is part of it, but there is no visible violence or threat. The things that threaten are boundaries; hence the text in this scene is about the sensory quality of borderlessness and about environments that aren't built up to accommodate human needs, such as the desert. The text is supposed to sound like it is being whispered, as if Mx. Manning were sharing something private with the viewer. So this scene also draws on another important theme in *Negative Space*—the leak. The Manning jacket is used as a prop and is activated in various ways; when worn by the acting agents, it references not only the information leak that led to Manning's imprisonment but also her transition. So the jacket also represents a leaky body—a person or object that may not fit easily into preexisting descriptions or categories.

KA

To return to the video, the "domestic" site looks like an abandoned one. Is this meant to suggest economic precarity or evoke homelessness?

AKB

Homelessness is a very complicated word. I'm thinking about being in the world with a less fixed, i.e., less proprietary, relationship to land. The proprietary model creates borders, fences, and a sense of self separate from the other/outsider. Recently, the term *unhoused* is being used. That feels more accurate. Having a home and having a permanent residence are not inherently the same thing. One of my brothers spent time living in his car and being an Uber driver because he couldn't afford to pay rent in the Bay Area, where he lived. This is unfortunately all too common—there are people with jobs who eat, shower, and change clothes but don't have a "home." I'm not interested in romanticizing being unhoused; rather, I'm interested in rethinking our current situation, where it's possible for some humans to own space while it's inaccessible to others. Proprietary modes are the foundation of this disparity. So, yes, acknowledging precarity is an important theme in the whole series.

1 0 7

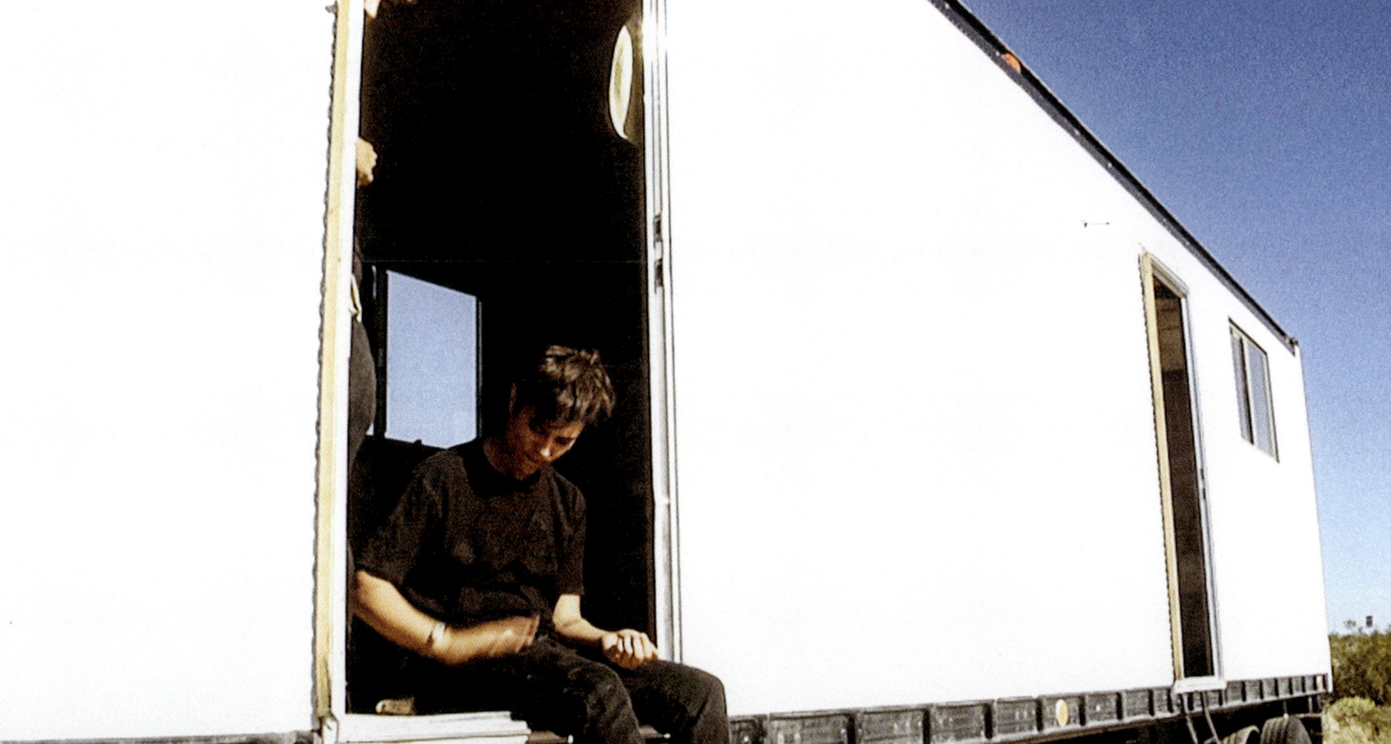

The construction of the platform is also key to this concept: we see a group of people constructing a site, but this site doesn't have walls. Instead, it's a stage, a platform, and a foundation. Beings can move on and through it. The stage is a site for communing and creative expression. This sets up another way to interact with space that establishes a politics for holding and making space without engaging in border creation.

KA

That brings a lot together for me. It makes me think of your use of camping gear: camping gear is for temporary use.

AKB

Right. There's the temporary again—that's what I call *provisional living*, which the camping gear points toward. And then there's also the utilizing of trash, which is a strong theme in the whole series and is a way of rethinking the notion of the temporary as an ongoing active state rather than considering things as existing in the binary of useful and not useful.

KA

That's true: trash is omnipresent in the work, but since it's also so present in city living, it doesn't necessarily jump out as a theme.

AKB

What's important in *Negative Space* is the act of taking discarded or rejected material, language, persons, or environments, and reactivating them so their status as valueless gets thrown into question. Trash is therefore vital and should appear seamlessly integrated.

KA

Could you tell me about the witness-protection-program T-shirt that pops up at about the eighteenth minute?

AKB

I picked up that T-shirt when I was working on *A Smeary Spot*, thrifting for props. I really liked the language *witness-protection program* because I think a lot about what it means to be a witness. It implies that the viewer isn't passive and carries both responsibility and agency. I'm less interested in the actual government-run program that aids people in ratting out their coconspirators than the

concept of protecting the act of witnessing, set against a backdrop of bullet holes; it was just too ironic and problematic to pass up. Also, who wears this shirt? Certainly not someone in this program!

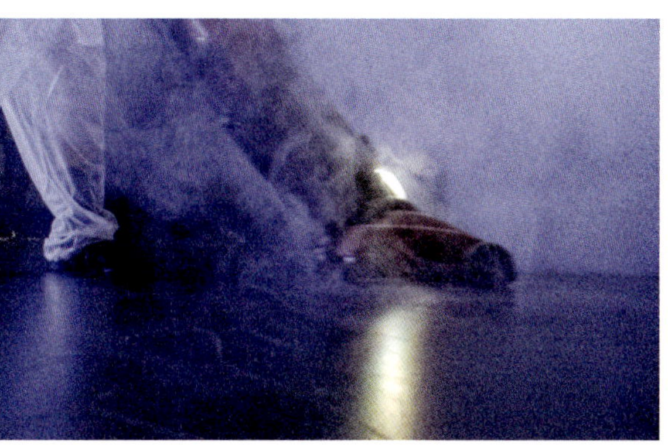

In all the works, T-shirts are used to send messages and can operate like protest signage. This is most explicit in a scene I call the protest tableau, where you see tropes of protest like holding a sign. But the group holds the pose in a somewhat apathetic manner, appearing more to be performing than to be genuinely resisting. Like many people, since the 2016 election, I have wrestled with the dire need for political change and the apathy induced by feeling overwhelmed. I'm again playing with expectations around how we as a society commune, organize, and aestheticize. I liked the idea that there would be a protest where the message is simply "No"—hence the NO shirt appears again and is used as a protest sign.

KA *Shirts, unlike protest signs, can come off.*

AKB In this scene, the shirt is a communication device that becomes a protest sign, which when removed from the body covers the blank sign with a statement (or not) and results in the acting agents being topless. Shirtlessness is a political act in many contexts, where laws around gendered bodies and biology collide. Bodies with protruding chests—often known as breasts—almost universally have fewer rights. So the real protest is the removal of the shirts. It's also an effort to acknowledge how action and language have different political effects.

KA *What I find interesting is the way in which the shirts are removed: it's contextual. How you remove your shirt in*

your own bedroom could be considered a political act if done on camera; otherwise, it's not sexualized. It's in the eye of the beholder. This brings me to the go-go dancer, who is supposed to be quite sexualized. It sounds like it was always your intention to re-create Felix Gonzalez-Torres's Untitled (Go-Go Dancing Platform) *from 1991, which I've only seen performed by gay men. What does it mean to you to have it performed by someone who is nonbinary?*

AKB That's essentially the question I wanted to pose. Gonzalez-Torres certainly throws the binary into question, leaning into the sexualized female body to introduce the sexualized male body as a site of desire. But both are produced by and mostly for the male gaze. Gonzalez-Torres was still working within the binary of cis-masc/cis-femme, with body types that sit within the cultural milieu of normative sexualized bodies. I wanted to introduce a sexualized body that you couldn't place in that binary. Each of the artworks I remake in this series—Édouard Manet's *Olympia* (1863) in *A Smeary Spot*, Jacques-Louis David's *Death of Marat* (1793) in *Living Room*, and Marcel Duchamp's *Étant donnés: 1. La chute d'eau, 2. Le gaz d'éclairage (Given: 1. The Waterfall, 2. The Illuminating Gas)* (1946–66) in *What is Perverse is Liquid*—were the creations of cis men who have have been granted significant art historical weight.

For this one, I wanted to re-create a piece that had immateriality built into it. What's beautiful about the Gonzalez-Torres work is the way the absent stage creates anticipation before it is activated by a go-go dancer, who then moves to music you can't hear. It was an exciting piece to work with and push further. My take adds a jockstrap as a quasi bra, which is a reference to the invention of the sports bra. The original sports bra was made by a woman who took two of her husband's jockstraps and sewed them together. The sports bra was

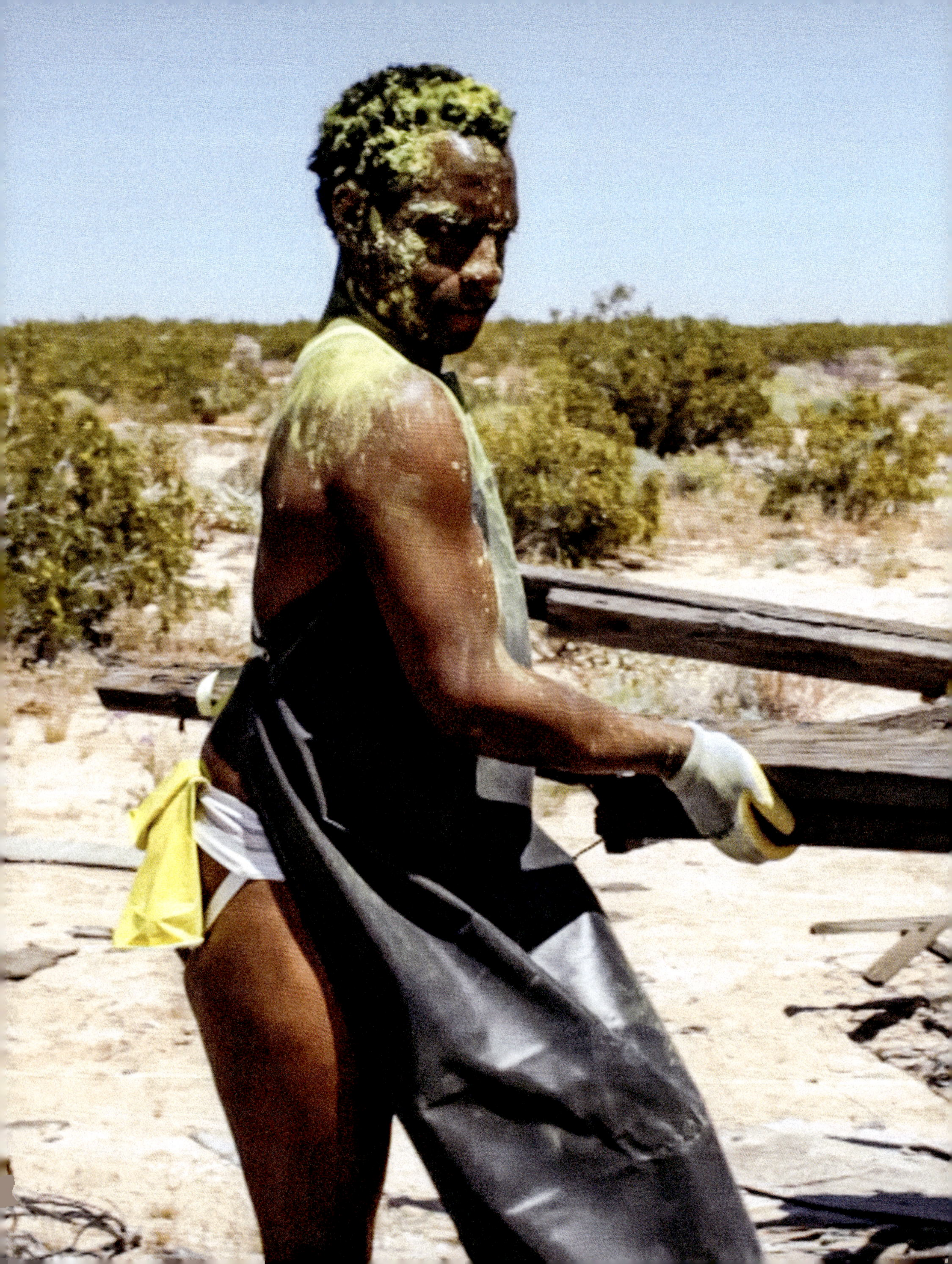

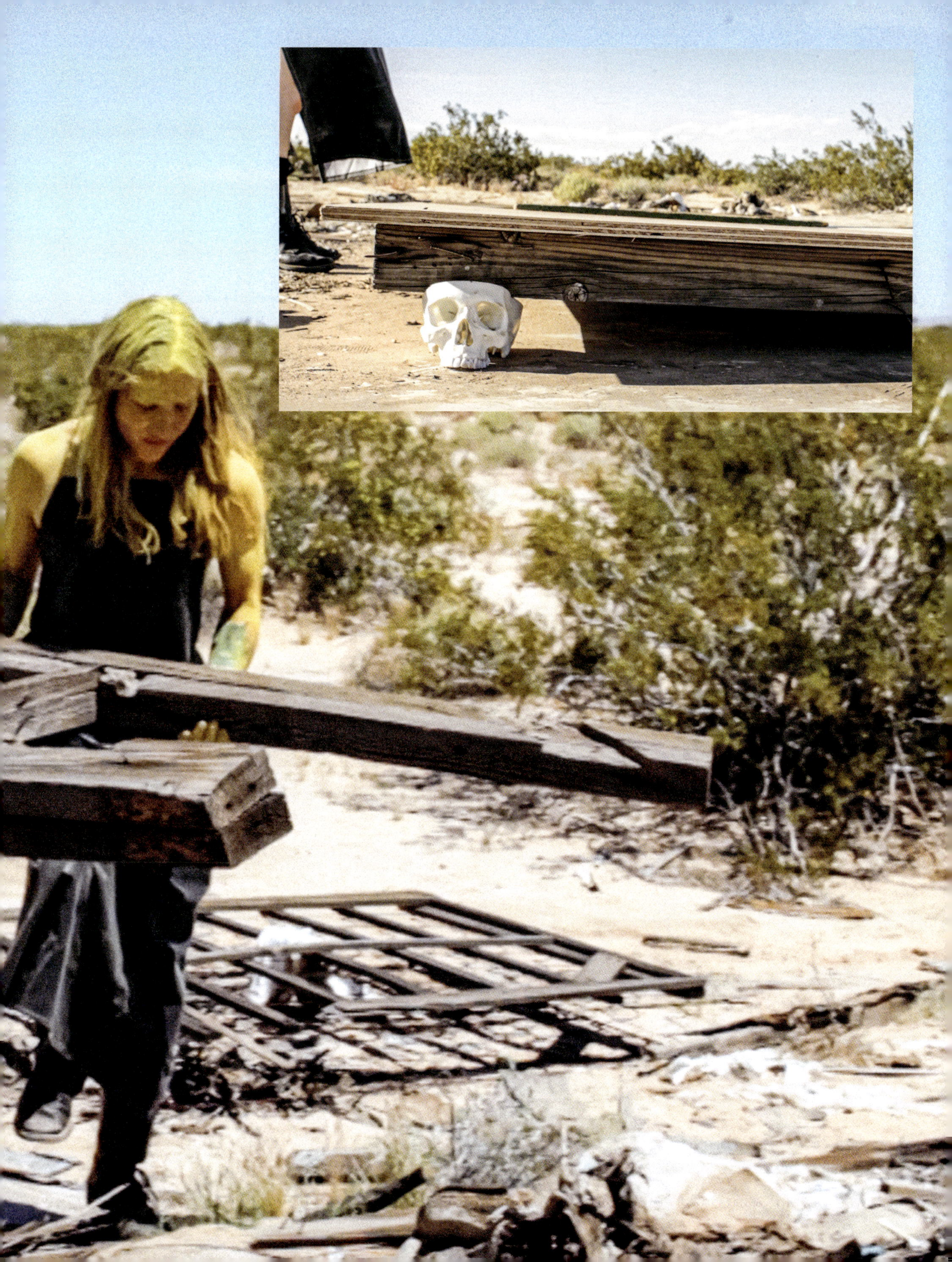

a crucial invention that enabled half the population to engage comfortably in athletics and rigorous physical activities.

KA

I find Gonzalez-Torres's Untitled *incredibly unlike the rest of his oeuvre. It's so literal in its representation of queerness. One of the strengths of his practice and sources of his popularity is that his work is highly abstracted and metaphorical. AIDS is represented by a museum visitor slowly taking away candy from a pile, for example. Because of this highly poetic form, it's not directly confrontational. While this makes his work more relatable for some viewers, you don't see the hard parts.*

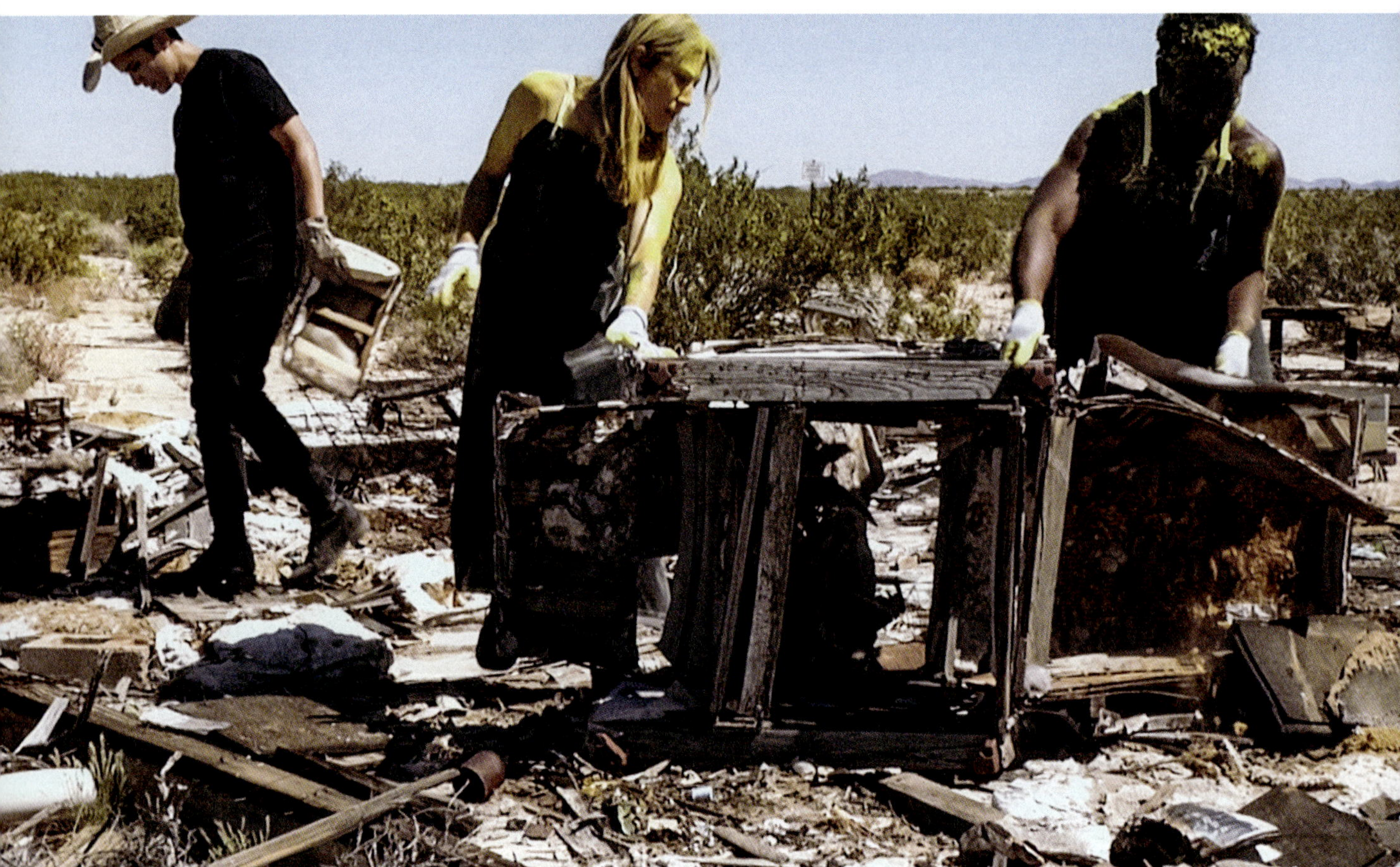

AKB

When I first learned about his work, I didn't know he was gay or that the work was queer. There's intention there; that makes it highly accessible and cryptic at the same time. Once you understand the work's intent and meaning, it's deeply queer in that queering-representation, rather than representing-queerness, kind of way I mentioned in our previous conversation. Gonzalez-Torres puts something in front of you that seems too simple and obvious to have any depth—it's a clock, it's a light bulb, it's a pile of candy—and then asks you to completely reconsider your assumptions about it and the ease with which you ignore its metaphorical potential. I'm critiquing as much as I'm celebrating when I take on another artist's work in *Negative Space*.

KA

Speaking of citation and adoration, where does the text for the script come from? There's this part about the desert: "The desert doesn't accommodate you, doesn't care

AKB That is a text I adapted from my own writing for the talk that I gave at Dia on Nancy Holt. I started that talk with some reflections on my personal experiences being out in the Utah desert making work. In this text, I ponder human in/significance and the illusion that the horizon is your only point of confinement.

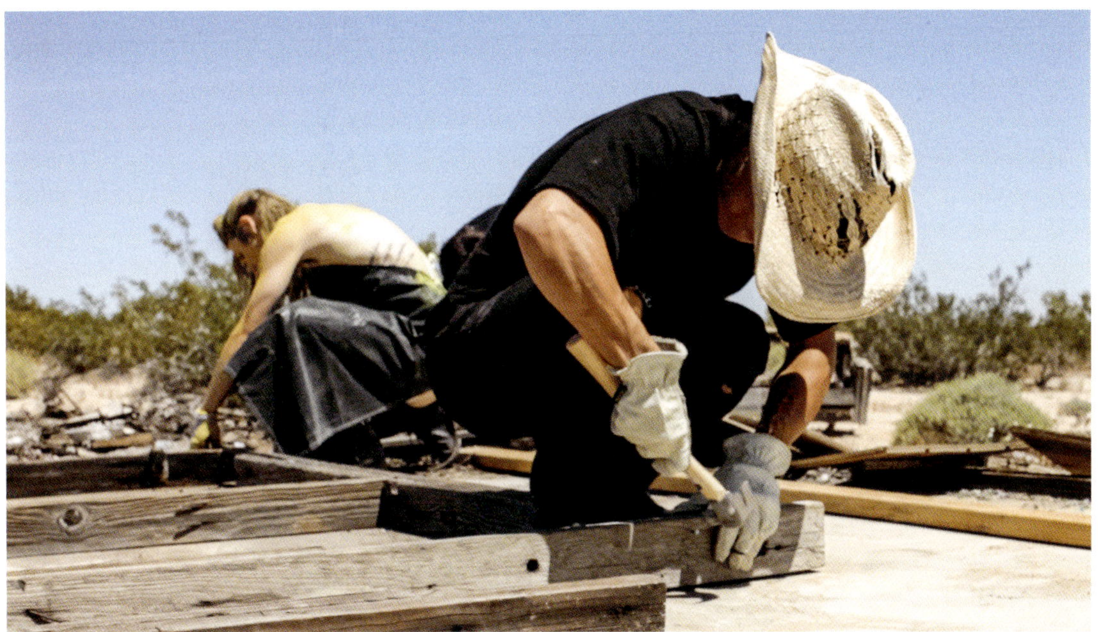

KA *There are also words in the form of a song that is performed in* Leave No Trace.

AKB Yes, that's Shannon Funchess singing an a capella cover of Cerrone's Italo-disco track "Supernature." In the late nineties, when I used to DJ and collect records, I stumbled on it by chance and bought it simply because I was intrigued by the cover art. Turns out the music is amazing. One of the things I really love about it are the lyrics; it's a narrative of the monstrosity born of technological experimentation and about humans trying to reconcile with a terror of their own invention. It is very sci-fi. Shannon has this incredibly powerful voice, and I had dreamed for years of having her cover it. That desire finally found its place in this film. It's a bit like the saxophone in *A Smeary Spot*, where I just had an urge for a sax solo. I was talking to a friend about wanting a sax solo but having no good reason to include one, and they were like, "You don't have to have a reason for everything."

KA *That is very true: sax solos* are *important, and you* don't *have to have a reason for everything.*

AKB Totally. It's absurd, but with these works, I needed to give myself permission to just do things based on intuition and desire. In the end, the sax solo is so important in *A Smeary Spot*, with its combo of breathing and smoke; it's all about air and circulation. Similarly, Shannon's performance reflects on the beings we are becoming as we absorb new technologies.

KA *I'm a firm believer that not everything has to have a logical, rationalized, verbalized reason to exist in an artwork—really the opposite.*

AKB Pleasure is so generative. I want my audience to experience the same release and pleasure that I get from collaborating with Geo Wyex, making these strange and beautiful dance tracks for each work.

I spent a lot of time in clubs when I was younger. The gay club and dancing are essential social forms that I keep returning to in my work.

KA   *One last thing I was wondering about, out of my own curiosity, is the vacuuming scene . . .*

AKB   Ah, yeah, that scene is one big dumb pun. It's the vacuum vacuum. Like, the Hadron Collider and a Dyson at the same time. When I use the smoke machine, I'm doing it to make air visible. So the scene is literally just a performer in a transparent outfit vacuuming smoke. The air is being sucked out of the room; a vacuum is being created by a vacuum. Another metaphorical void. The vacuum scene in the black box occurs while the concrete foundation is being cleaned to build the stage on the other screen. The two scenes collide in dust and smoke and the act of cleaning.

KA   *That's not what I expected.*

AKB   I'm so curious what your read was.

KA   *I thought it brought the work into a more domestic space and saw it as being about labor.*

AKB   I invite that read. I obviously think a lot about labor in all its forms. That's certainly a subtext. Note that acting agents Re/productive Labor are the ones cleaning the platform.

KA   *I also wanted to talk a bit about how the work takes form within the exhibition space. It's a five-channel projection shown on a cube. Could you explain how you intended the viewer to experience it?*

AKB   Each installation developed in response to the next as much as to the internal content of the videos. First, *A Smeary Spot* was this vast, immersive horizontal space reflecting the desert expanse; I was using seven-by-twelve-foot screens to bring the viewer into that world. Then, for *Living Room*, I was

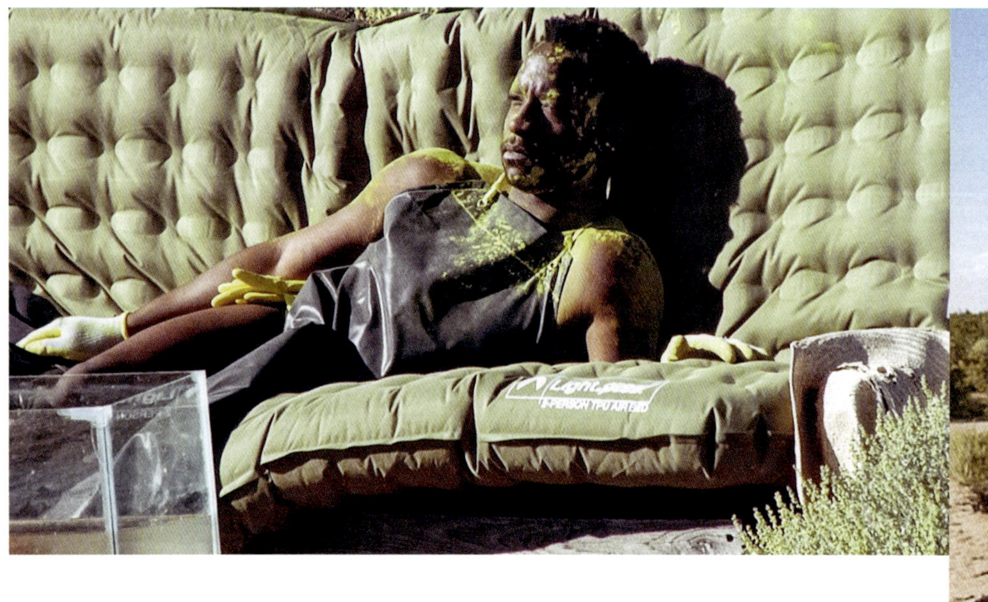

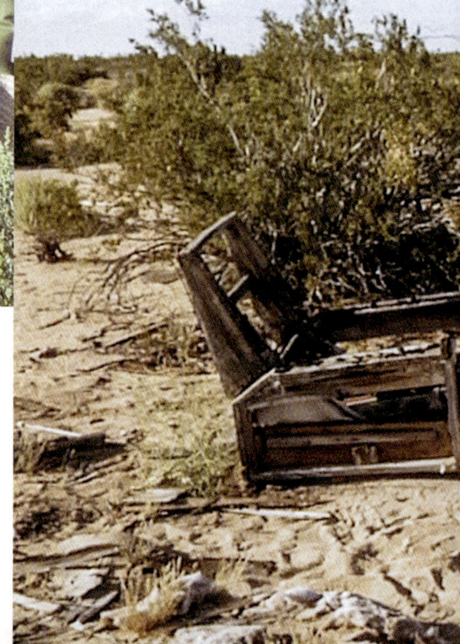

thinking more about the asymmetrical bifurcated body, where the smaller screen was based on the size of a sheet of drywall. For *Leave No Trace*, I took this smaller screen size, four by seven feet, and built a giant cube that the viewer circumnavigates.

I thought of the cube as a container or a point on a map where everything coalesces, as both an object and a site. When I get to show the works together, I try to place *Living Room* and *Leave No Trace* in proximity to each other. Viewers see a giant, room-size white cube that they can walk inside of and view *Living Room* playing within. Nearby, the *Leave No Trace* cube appears like a scaled-down version of the same, only the video is projected on the outside. So the two installations have a sculptural conversation about scale and interiority and exteriority.

Leave No Trace is viewed as a two-channel work, although all five exposed surfaces of the cube are aglow at once. There are piles of tires to sit on and observe the work from the corners of the cube. From each of those vantage points, the viewer sees two video chan- nels projected onto two sides. The same pair of videos are playing on the opposite sides of the cube, such that the left and right screen will swap depending on the corner you see them from.

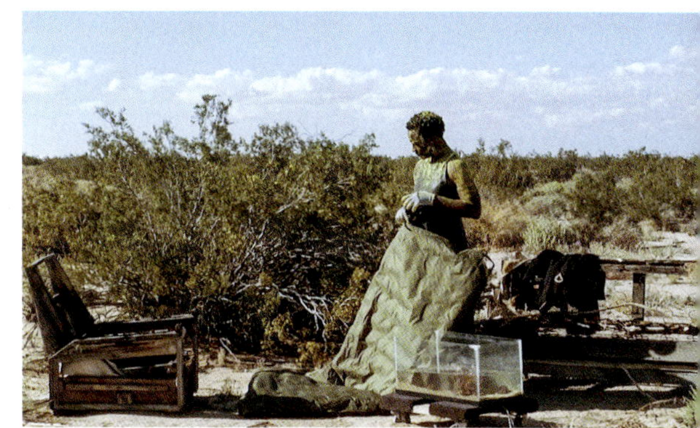

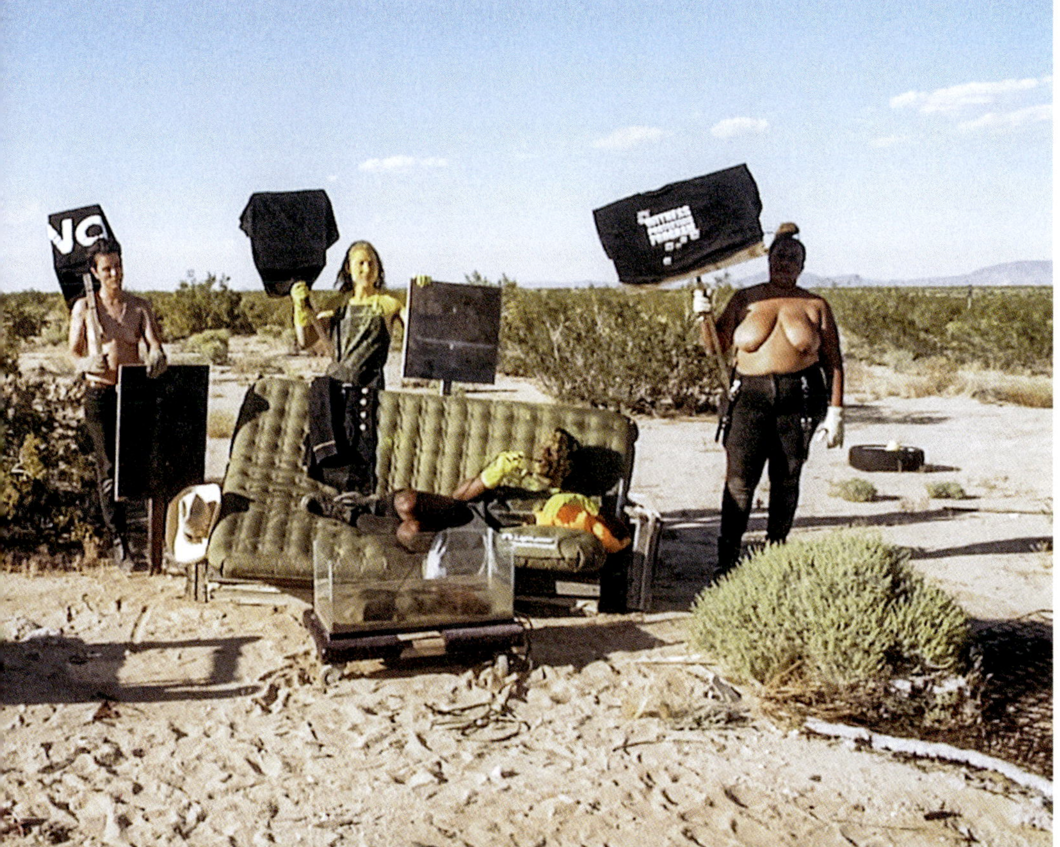

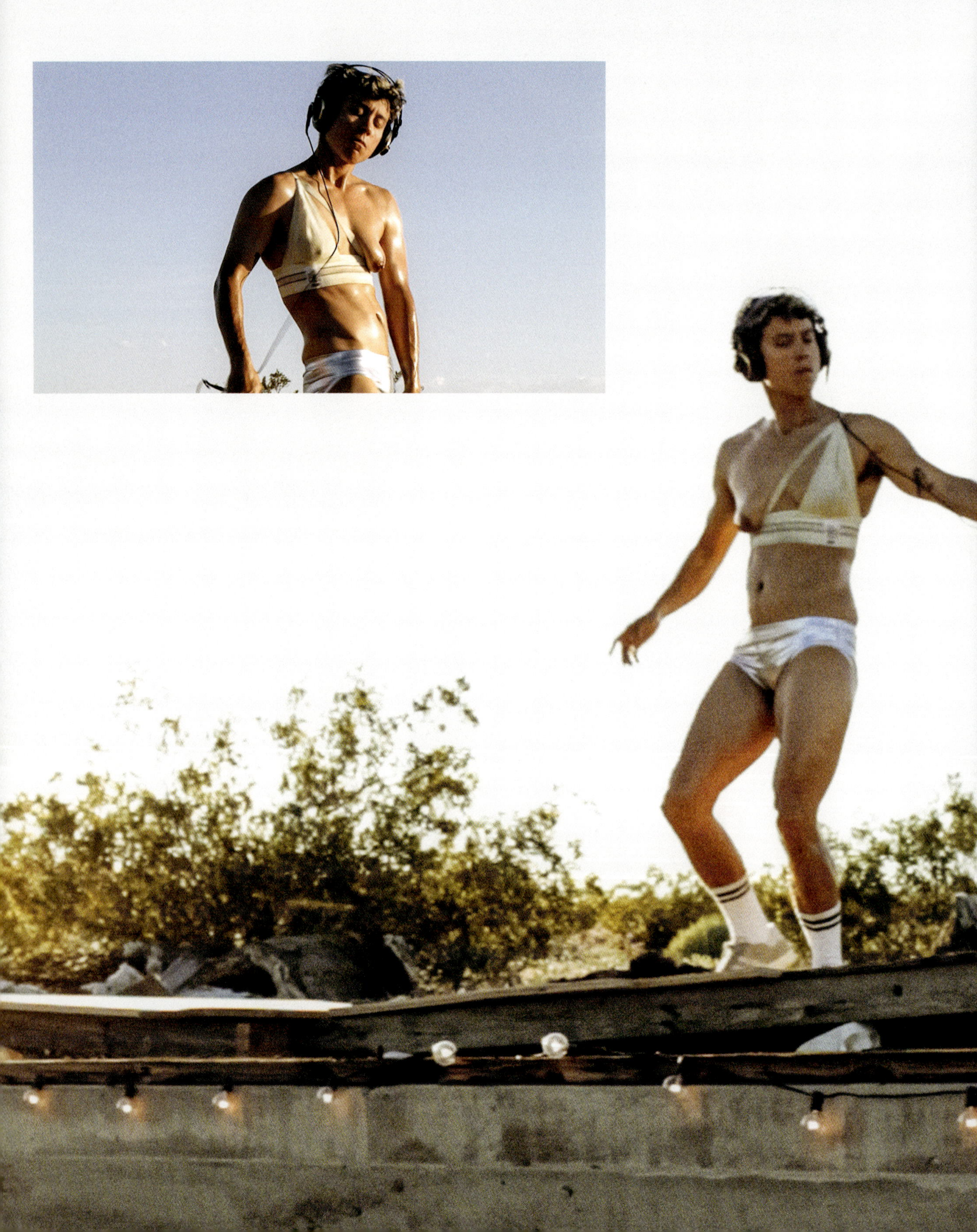

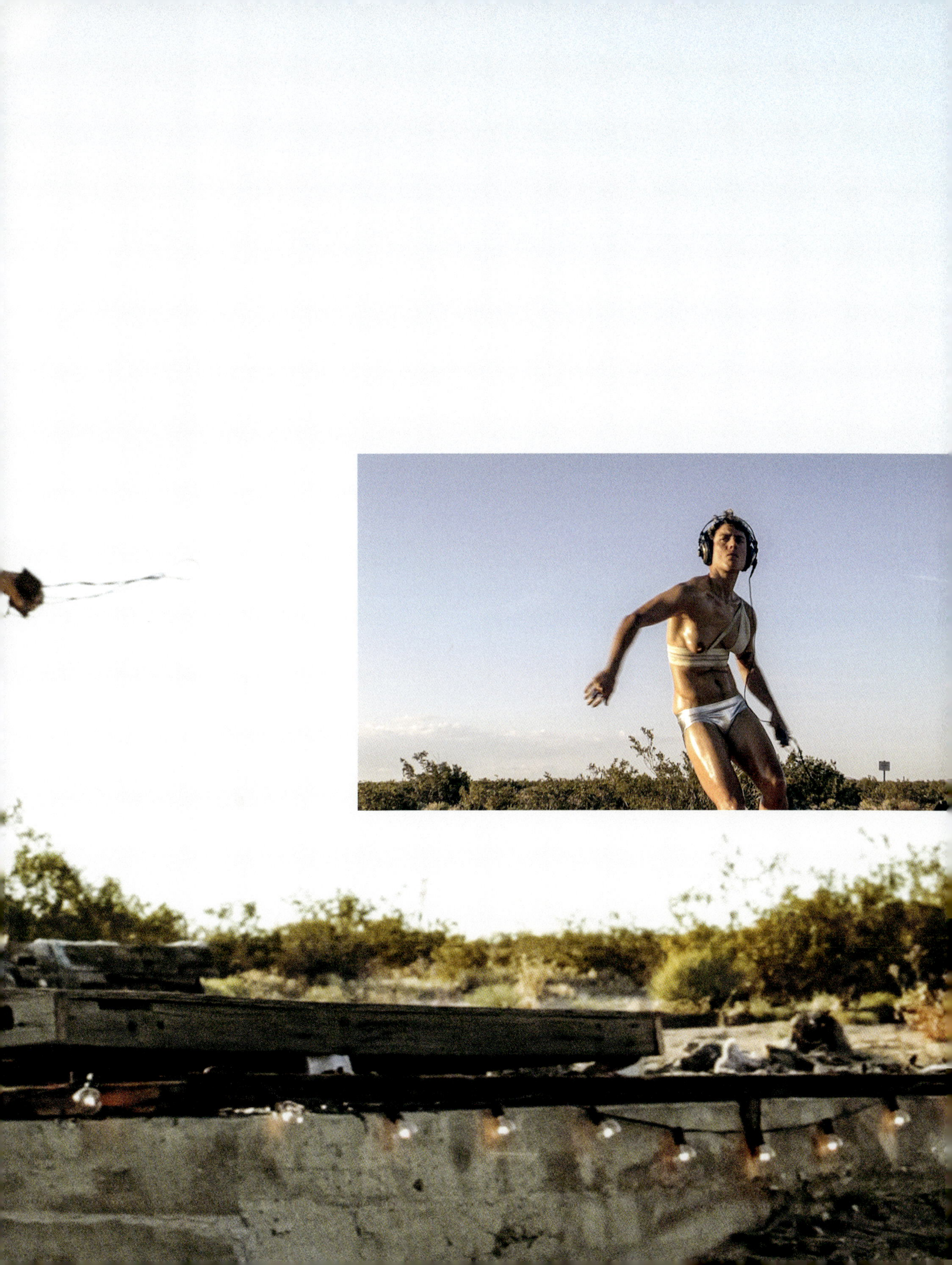

On the top of the cube, the credits run almost continuously except for two breaks, when we see a grid animation engulf all five sides. Starting from the center point on the top, the cube is animated by lines crawling along its surface that assemble into a gridded object. Because it is propped up on a skull, the cube is set at an angle to the walls of the room and the floor. Each work in the *Negative Space* cycle is staged to run counter to the existing architecture it's displayed in.

KA

Would you say that's a more visible place to put credits? I'm thinking about how community-driven your work is, sourcing performers from your social circle, and how crediting is a strategic part of supporting one's community.

AKB   It's about four feet high, and the cube is tilted at an angle because of how the skull is positioned. If you're of typical adult height, you can stand up and just read the credits. But if you're sitting in the corners, where the piles of tires are, you are level with the screens and you don't really pay attention to the top. If you're standing and navigating the room, you're going to see one point of view, and if you sit down, you have a lower sight line with just a pair of screens to watch.

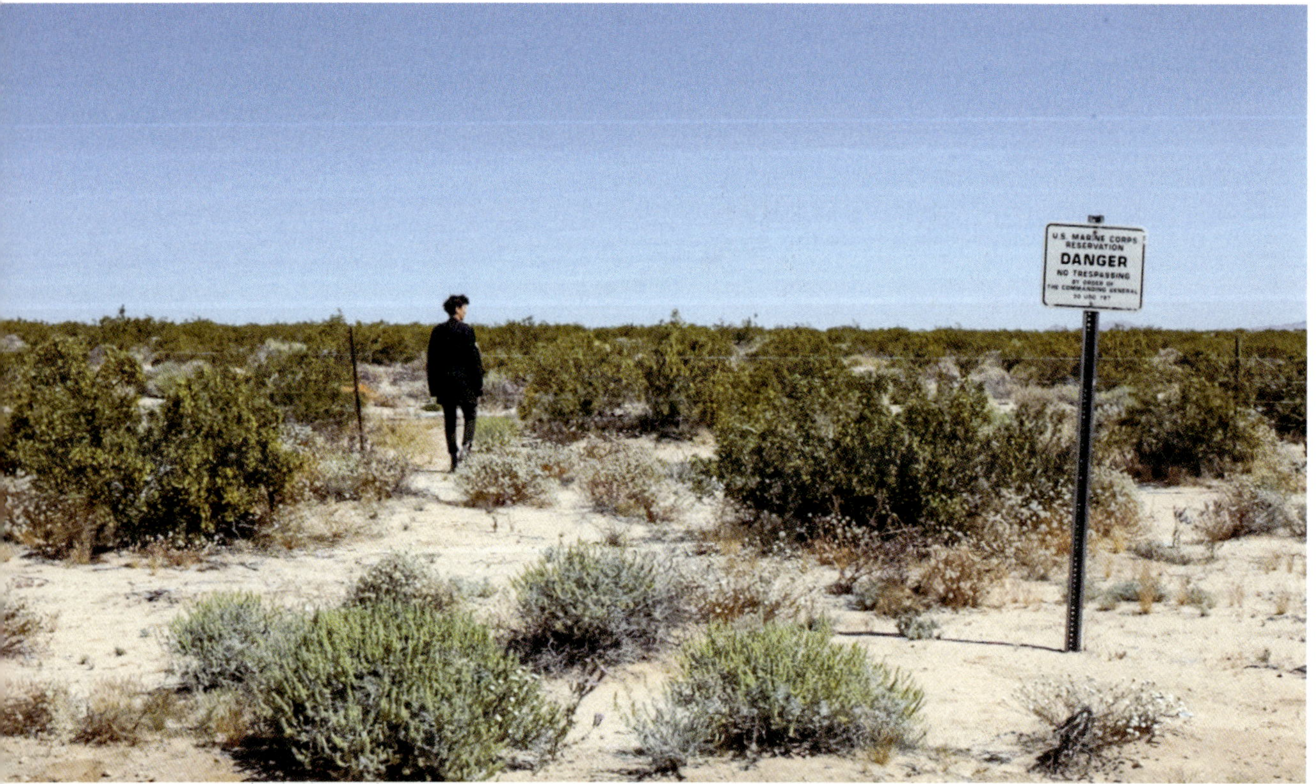

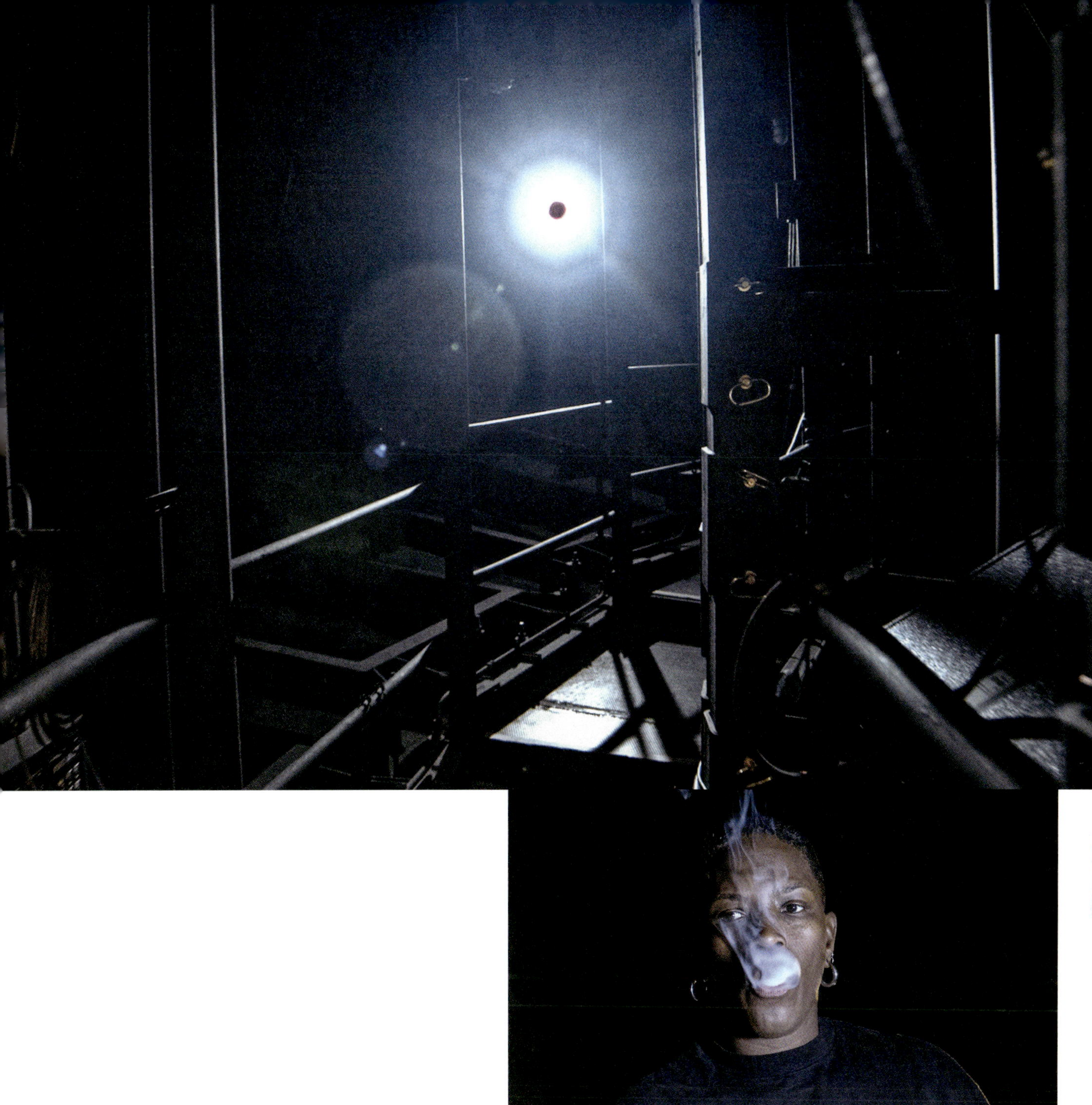

KA   *Do you prefer either sight line?*

AKB   No. It's always important to be *with* the work—to stand and sit and experience how it feels. It's sculptural. But there is a primary sight line, and that is the seated one. I realized not all viewers would be able to stand or be tall enough to fully access the top view. Moreover, I'm interested in the feeling of this glowing, almost floating form in space—the object is also an event.

KA   *How important is it to have seen the other works to fully appreciate* Leave No Trace? *How tightly are they bound in this series, and how autonomous are they?*

AKB   I've done a lot to explain how elements echo throughout all the works in the series, but each one is meant to be autonomous. They are more frequently shown alone, so it's important that each has a

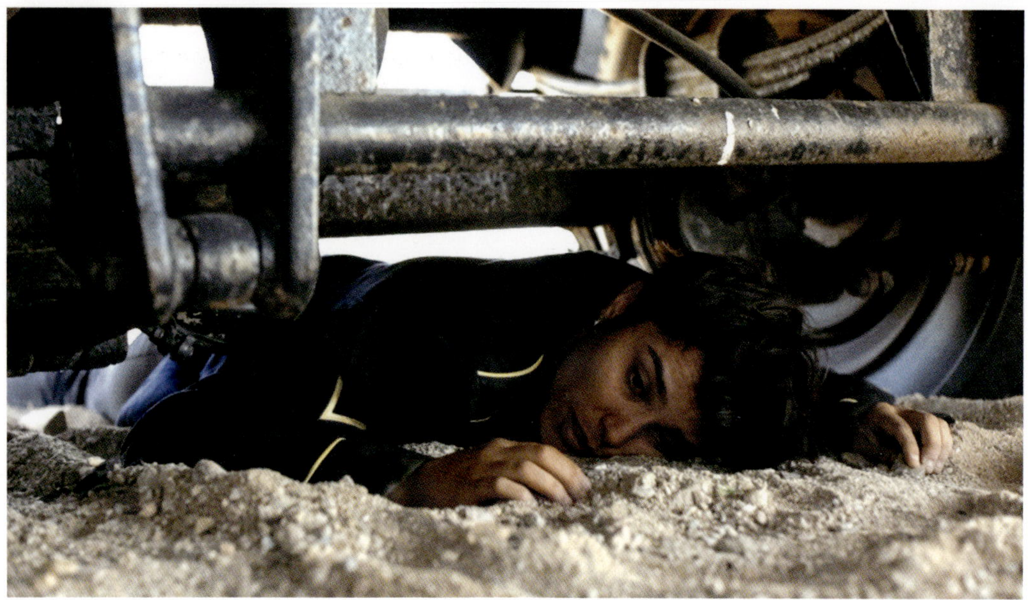

logic of its own. If you get to see more than one, it does give more context for some elements that may feel a bit arbitrary on their own.

KA　　　　　　　　　　　　　　　　　　　　　*It's just enriching to have seen them all.*

AKB　　I honestly think that seeing all the works together is a lot in one viewing. But I agree you get more from it the deeper you go into the totality of the project.

KA　　　　　　　　　　　　　　　　　　　　　*That would be hard because, well—how long is* A Smeary Spot?

AKB　　It's fifty-three minutes, and the others are each about thirty-five minutes. All of that adds up to about two and a half hours, so durationally it's no more demanding than watching *Apocalypse Now*. But because of the density of each work, there's a lot to digest. You could watch each one four times and see different things each time. I think the work reveals itself slowly.

KA　　　　　　　　　　　　　　　　　　　　　*I just don't think a "full" experience of a video work has to necessitate watching a piece in its entirety, especially in a gallery setting. Most museum viewers spend only seconds in front of individual paintings. That measure is hopefully significantly longer with time-based work, yet it remains a fact that white-cube galleries install video as something that can be walked through, in a fashion opposite to how theaters show movies, where a durational sitting is assumed. With* Leave No Trace*'s cube-based installation, you're thinking through these conundrums of displaying video in an interesting way. It calls into question what the ideal scenario is for looking at a very ambitious set of moving-image works. Most video artists that I know have an oeuvre that demands hours of attention. That's not necessarily something that can be viewed easily by one person in one sitting. We need to talk through that as curators and artists.*

AKB   I agree. Students are always paranoid that you can't make a video more than ten minutes long or
        you'll lose everyone's attention. There are so many myths about attention and the effects of social
        media. But I think if you make something compelling, people will watch it. Of course, some won't.
        And it's also okay to see only part of it. I don't know if I told you this, but the opening event for *A
        Smeary Spot* at Participant was silent because everyone was watching the work.
            It's much easier to immerse someone in a logical narrative, but I want the first experience
        of the viewer to be physical, for them to be aurally and visually absorbed. All the editing and
        the soundtracking is me working to create a sensory logic so the viewer will stay with me
        for twenty minutes, thirty minutes, fifty minutes, however long it is. If you leverage the tools
        of cinema, you can really capture attention. And I think that's a powerful and exciting part of
        making this work.

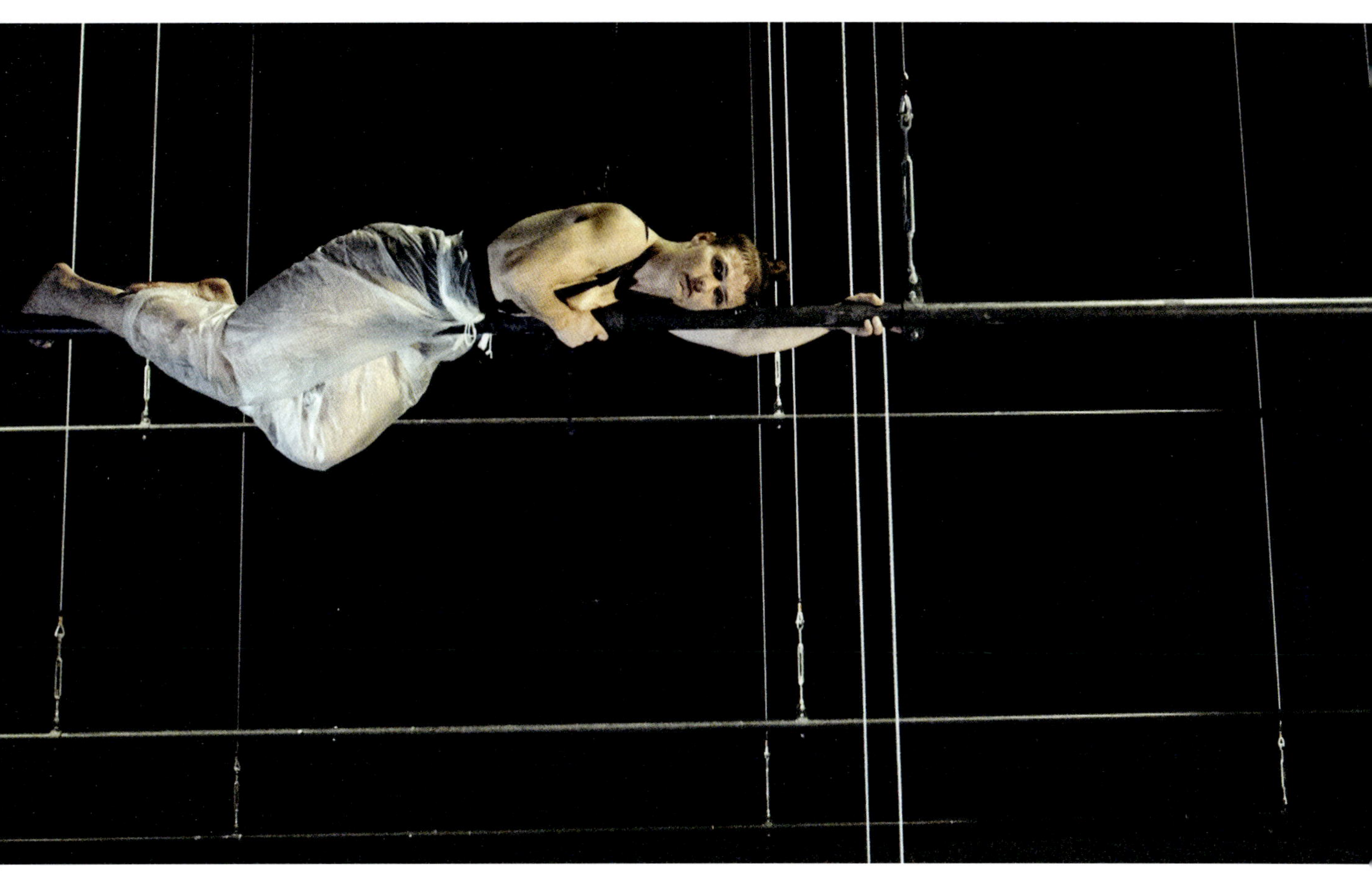

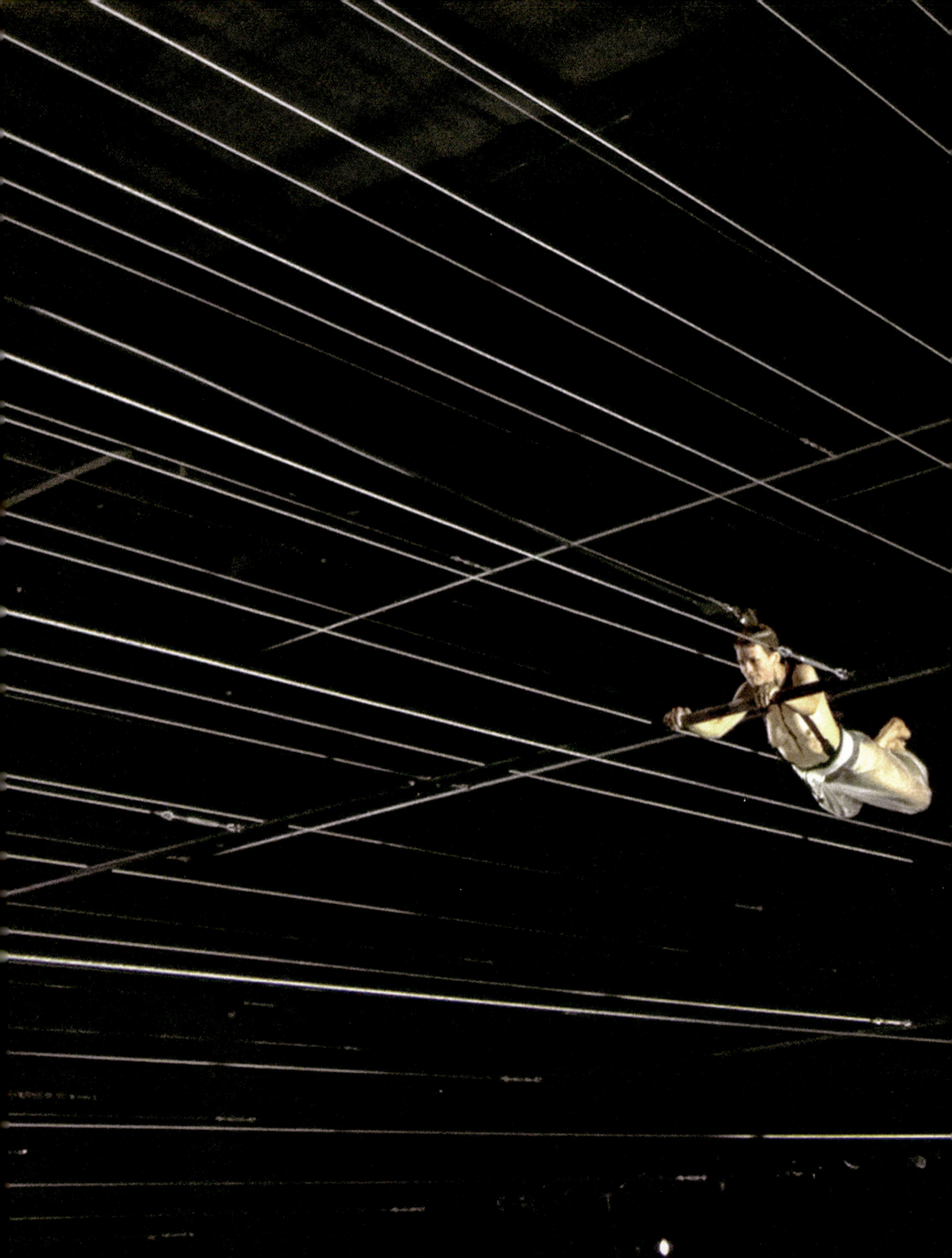

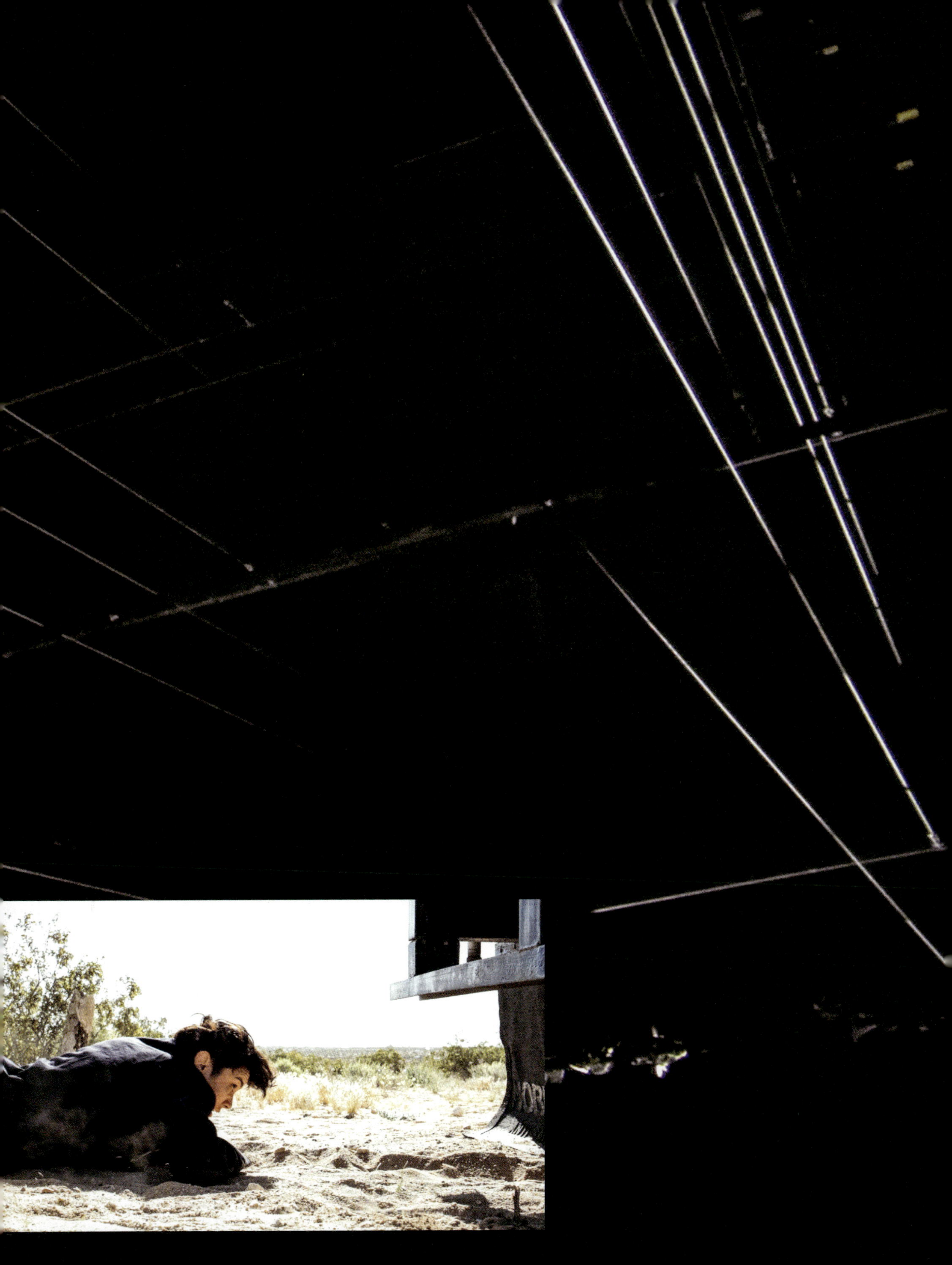

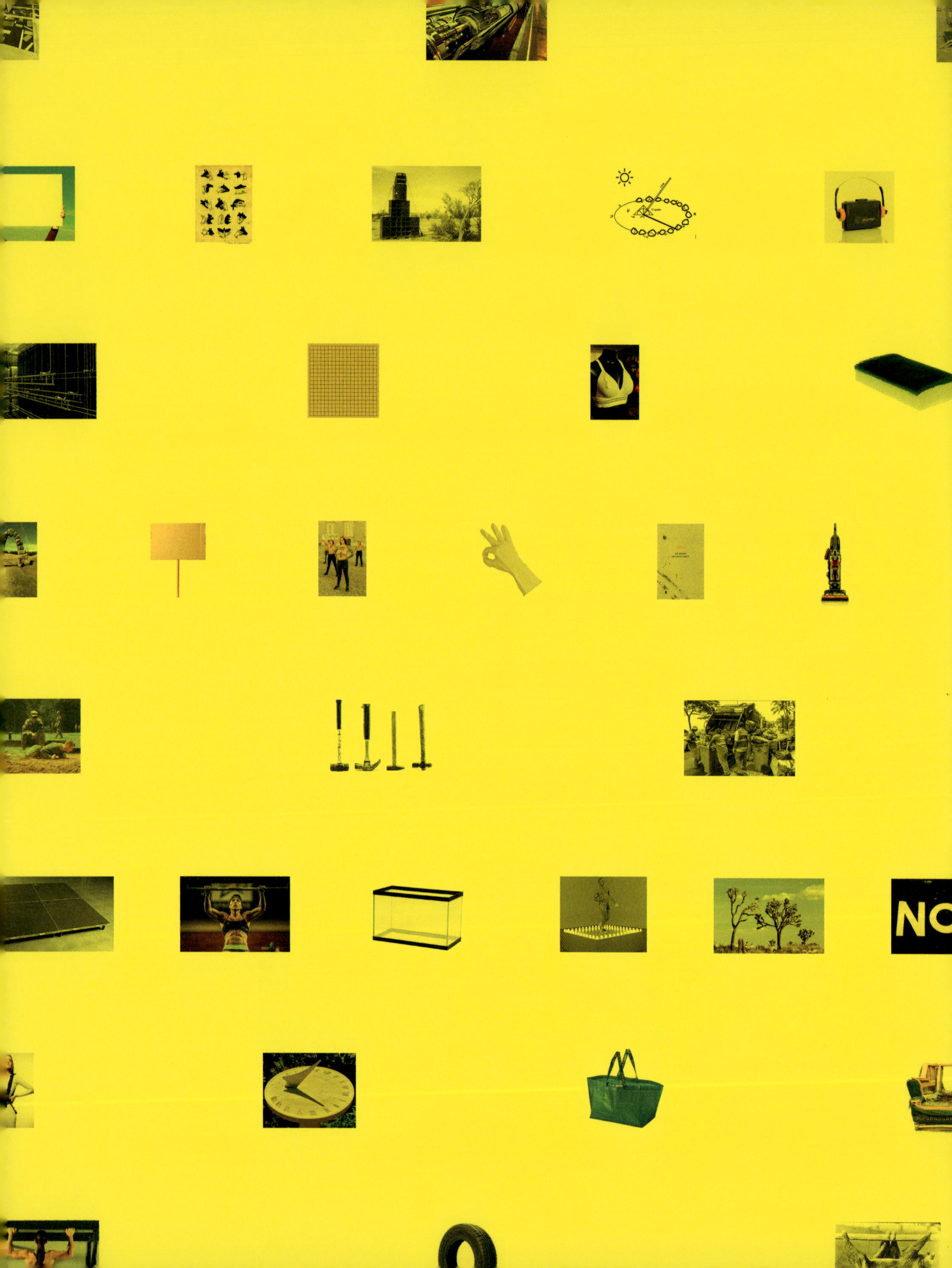

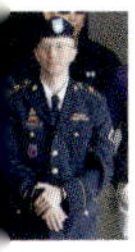

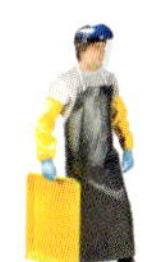

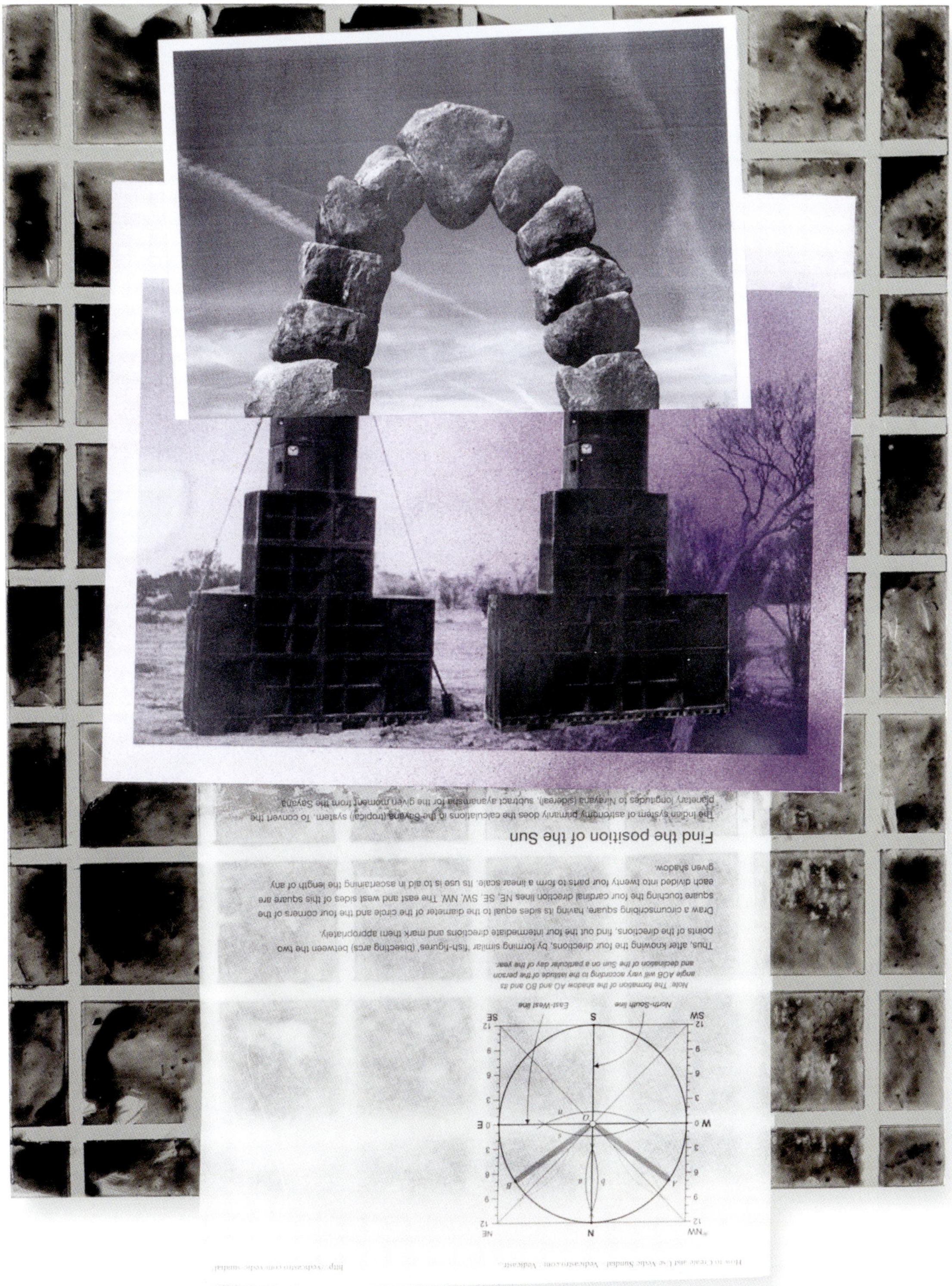

↗ *Im/materiality: Felt Time*, 2019.
Mirror, photocopy, India ink,
and spray paint; 17 × 14 inches
(43.2 × 35.6 cm)

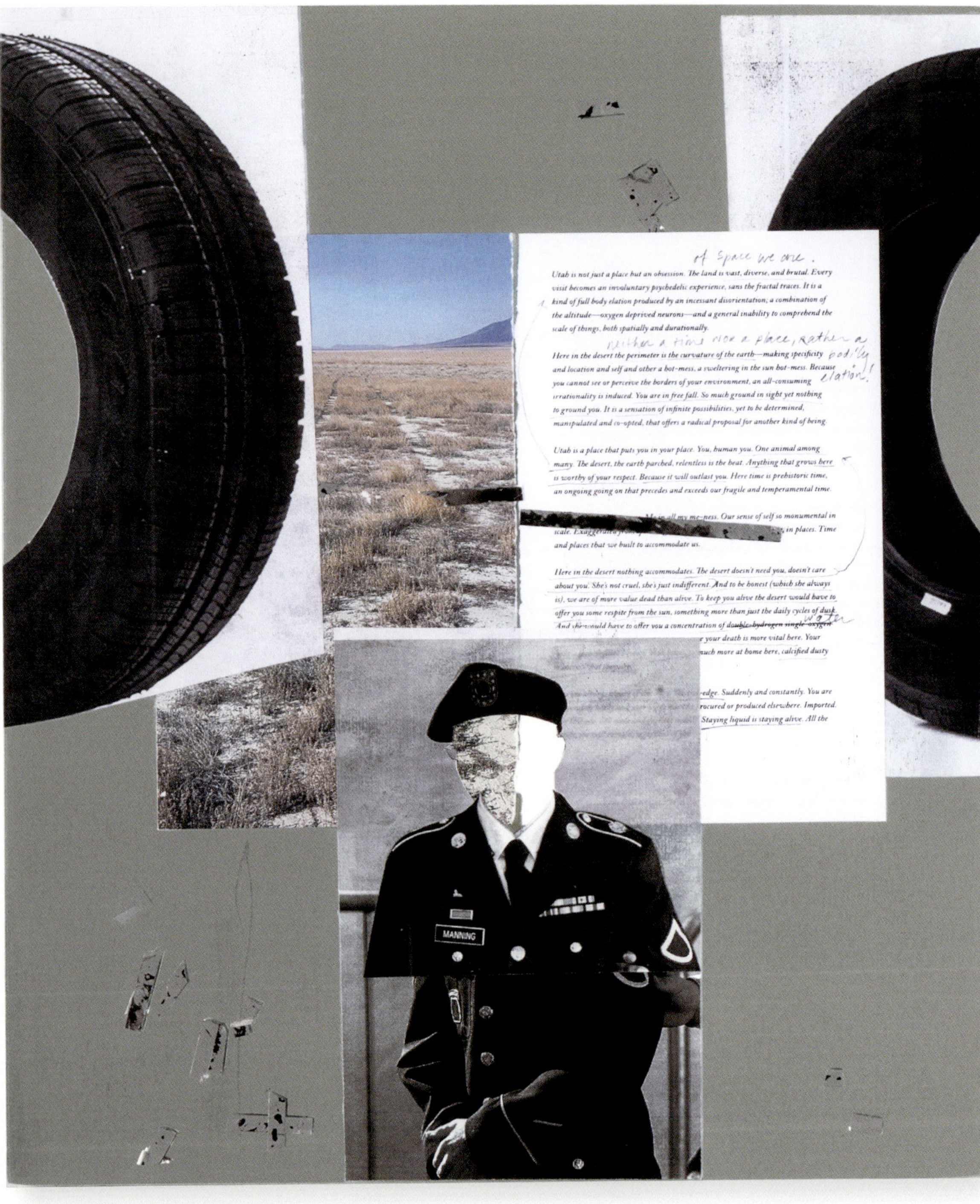

↑ *Mx. Manning (leaks)*, 2019. Mirror, photocopy, Mylar tape, India ink, pencil, and pages from *Zero* (a book on Nancy Holt by A.K. Burns); 17 × 14 inches (43.2 × 35.6 cm)

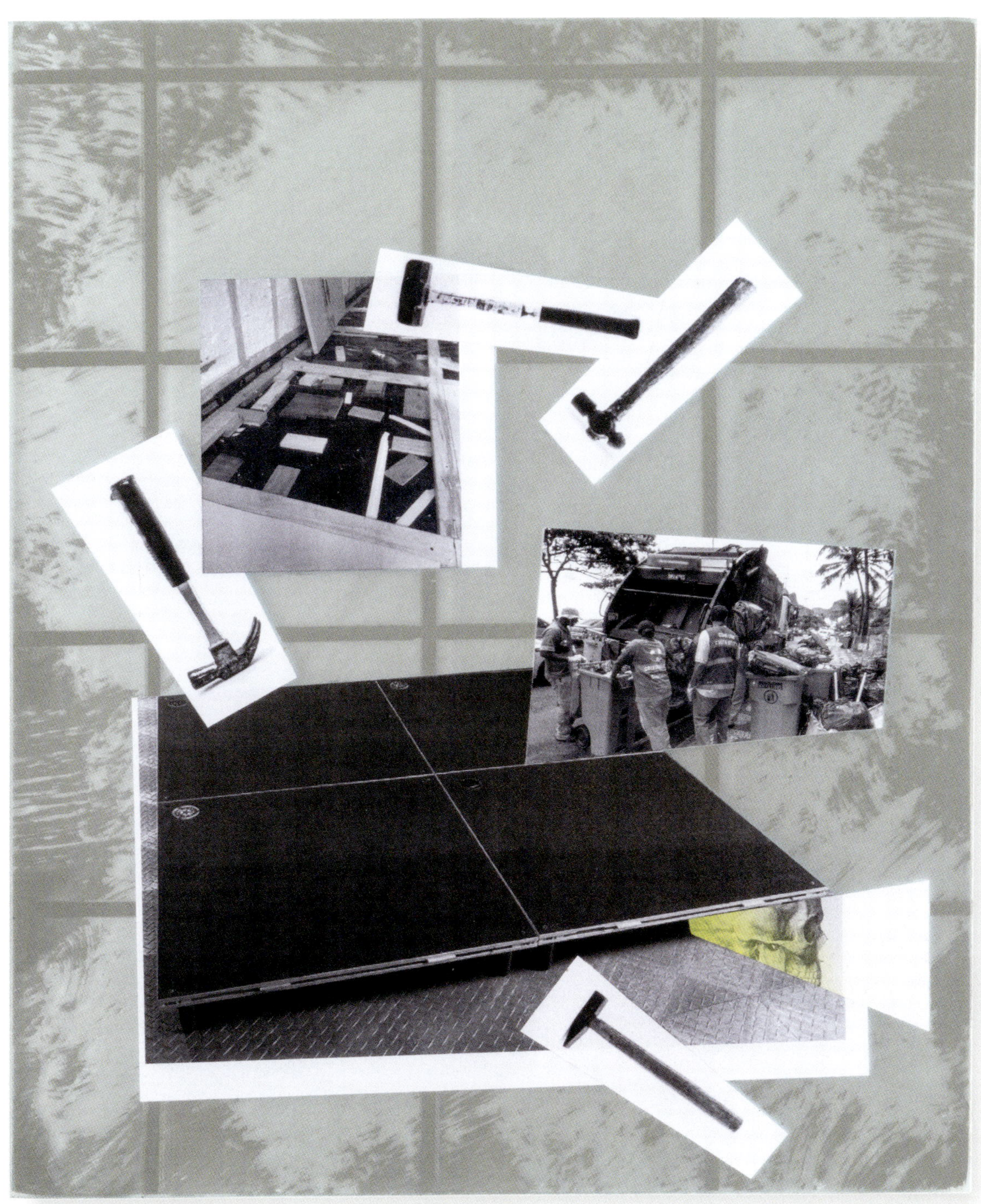

↗ *Situation Site: Stage (under
construction)*, 2019. Etched
mirror, xerox, and spray paint;
17 × 14 inches (43.2 × 35.6 cm)

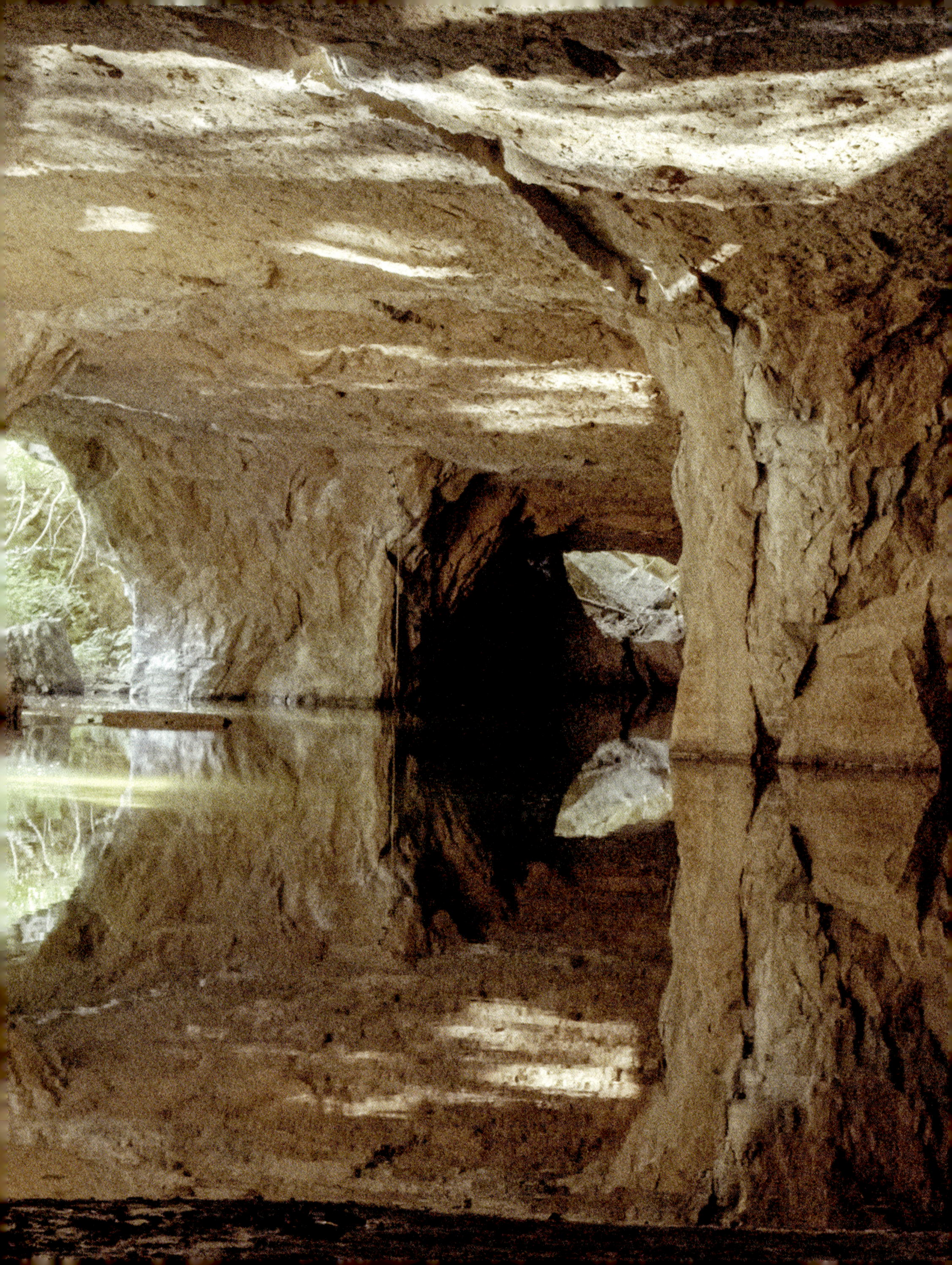

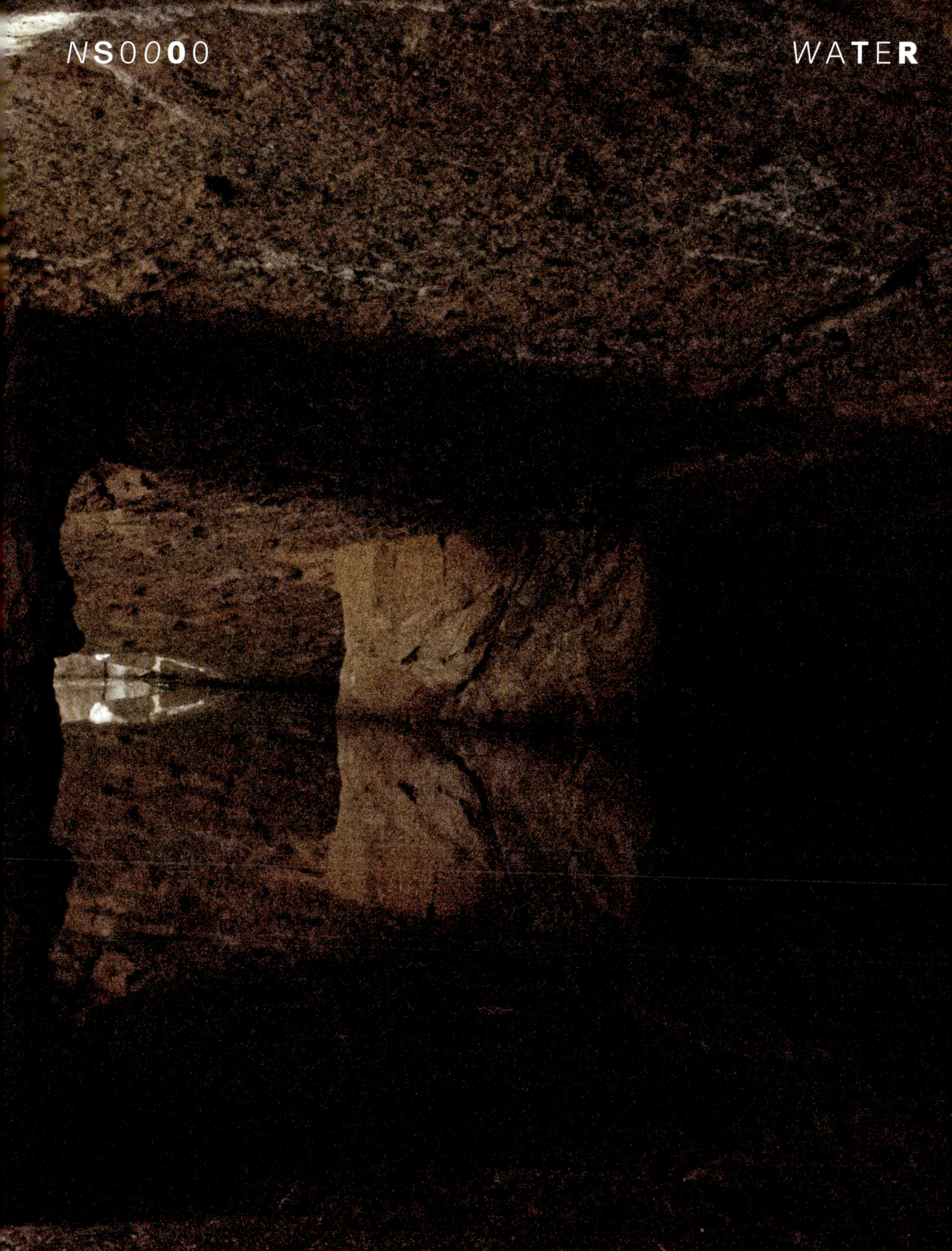
NS0000
WATER

don't worry
darkness always
accuses us
of falling on
purpose
you know how
to bulldoze
me back up
these hills
what does
darkness know of
light filling your
navel in the
middle of
the afternoon
we have not
lost our
place
in line
shaking
off the cold
let's get this
garden planted
give our fruit
away to one
another

thumbing through
calendars of the future
till touching
a year out
of reach
me a ghost
you a ghost
another poem
dedicated to the
great vanishing trick
we build
muscles
organs bones
at separate
tables
of our
favorite
restaurant
chewing to
motion
kept to
the tides

if the
marketing
birds do
for love
were
the
only
ad of
the day
do you
puke when
attempting to resist
the violence money costs
going over the freedoms
one at a time
questions
roll in blue
and red
answers
return
home
amethyst

who
stood
outside
arms open
for you to
crash your life into
lowering fork tines
fingering the list of
regrets nailed inside
sentences converge in
the middle of a thought
reporter's recycled
weather map shows
advancing soldiers
low temperature next
to civilian death toll
we open our bags
find cannon balls
did we shoot these
did we forget the
death we caused

remember
our metal skin
when the planet
first caught fire
it was
years
before we
understood
the awful
thing we
held to our chest
whatever a poem can
send into the future
please send the
breath
we have
been trying
to catch
for as long
as you can
hold it
so glad
you came by
thank you
as always

everything
falls with
the tree
something
about the man
in the pin holding
the butterfly down
Dear Reluctant Sleeper
we are supposed to be
used to sleep by now
each night we question
where we are going
why we have to go
a stick in the air to
poke a hole in the wind
our planet is lighter
with every astronaut
shot into space
jolted alive in the
catapult of ritual
roll the world's
barbed wire
into one
ball
good morning
glad we are back

one morning
every flying thing
aimed itself at
your pretty
hat
a vowel
the light
unleashed
overhead
we stood
awash with
songs about
time never
holding us
properly
regardless
of suggestion or
complaint carried on a
season of fruit and grain
when love learned to
turn into a sizable
journey without
leaving the room

it is easy to
forget there
are other stars
when sunlight
fills me
to the
gills
keeping
a toe in
the dance
music our
preferred
epoxy
I do not
have enough
civic pride for
the grift in
this system
get me out
of the grime of
the sentence
earning love is
like taxing oxygen
how many times are we
asked to overthrow our desire
please say you too are sick of it

battle cry
connects
bodies at
a critical
moment
while love
reveals the
art of pliability
before and after
never so visceral
sing happy
birthday while
harvesting organs
sing happy birthday
while stitching them
into their new body
learn to accept the
unanticipated
wonder for
your hand
when the
moon
reaches
back

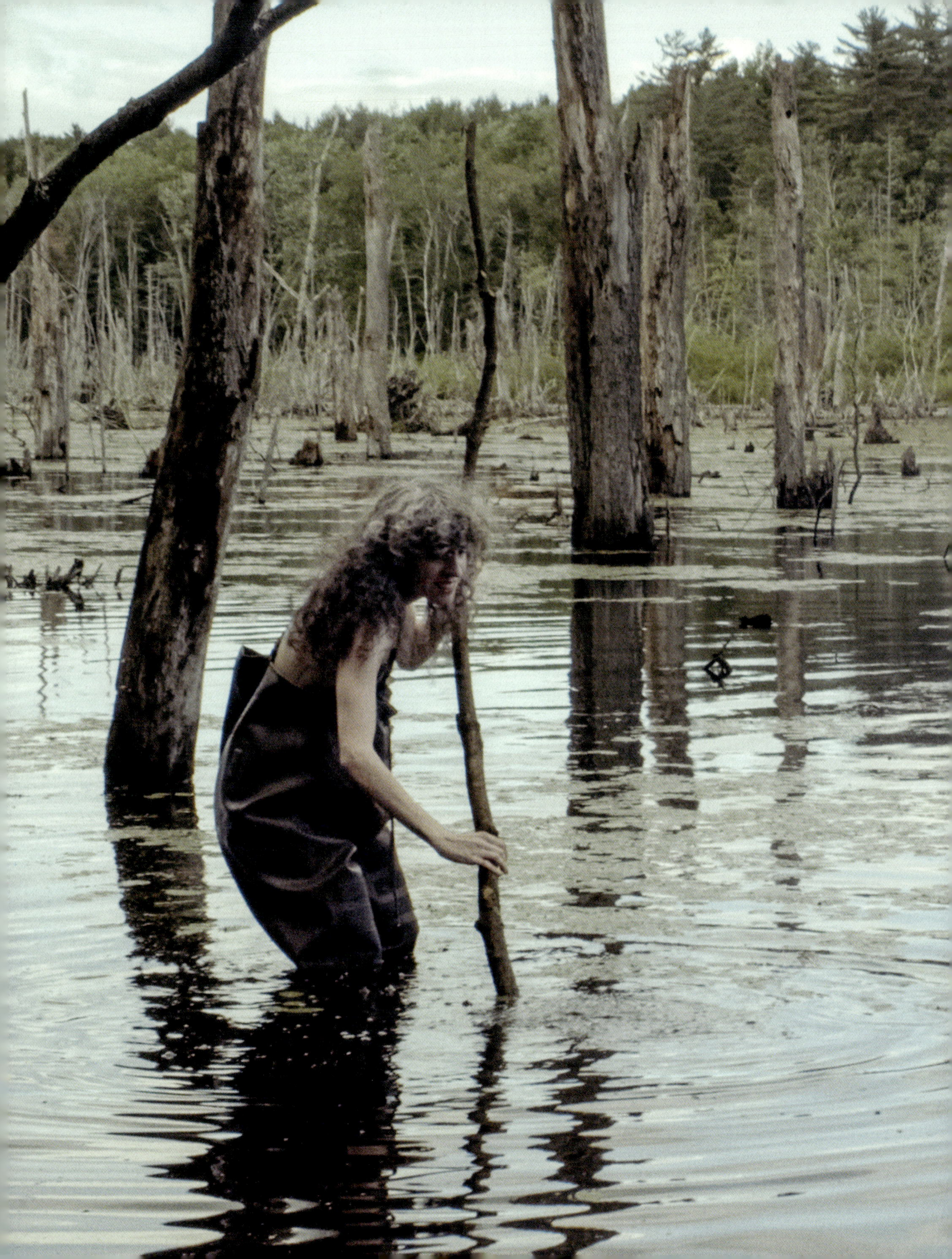

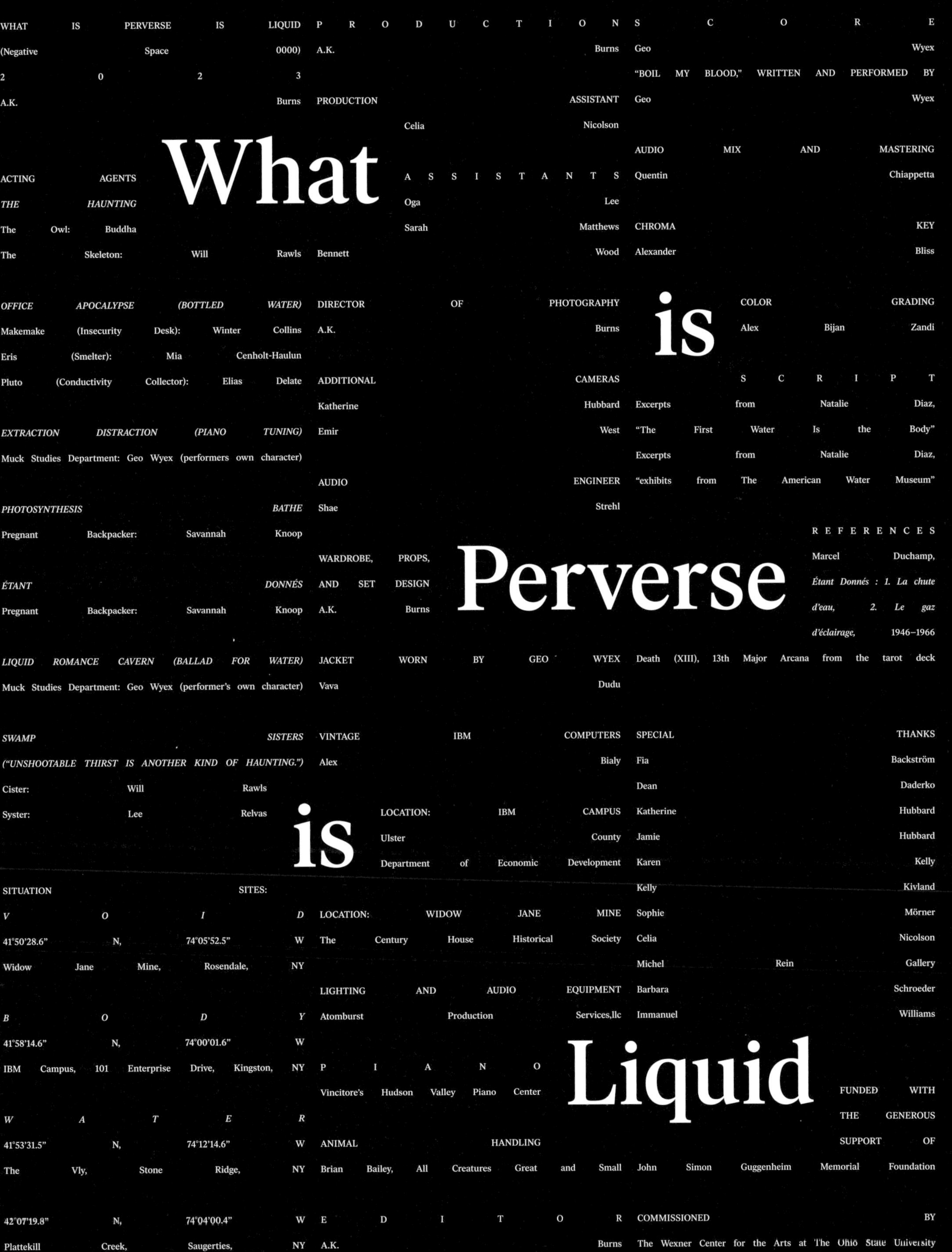

WHAT IS PERVERSE IS LIQUID PRODUCTIONS CORE

What

(Negative Space 0000) A.K. Burns Geo Wyex

2 0 2 3

"BOIL MY BLOOD," WRITTEN AND PERFORMED BY

A.K. Burns PRODUCTION ASSISTANT Geo Wyex

Celia Nicolson

AUDIO MIX AND MASTERING

ACTING AGENTS ASSISTANTS Quentin Chiappetta

THE HAUNTING Oga Lee

The Owl: Buddha Sarah Matthews CHROMA KEY

The Skeleton: Will Rawls Bennett Wood Alexander Bliss

OFFICE APOCALYPSE (BOTTLED WATER) DIRECTOR OF PHOTOGRAPHY COLOR GRADING

Makemake (Insecurity Desk): Winter Collins A.K. Burns Alex Bijan Zandi

Eris (Smelter): Mia Cenholt-Haulun

Pluto (Conductivity Collector): Elias Delate ADDITIONAL CAMERAS SCRIPT

Katherine Hubbard Excerpts from Natalie Diaz,

EXTRACTION DISTRACTION (PIANO TUNING) Emir West "The First Water Is the Body"

Muck Studies Department: Geo Wyex (performers own character) Excerpts from Natalie Diaz,

AUDIO ENGINEER "exhibits from The American Water Museum"

PHOTOSYNTHESIS BATHE Shae Strehl

Pregnant Backpacker: Savannah Knoop REFERENCES

is

WARDROBE, PROPS, Marcel Duchamp,

ÉTANT DONNÉS AND SET DESIGN *Étant Donnés : 1. La chute*

Pregnant Backpacker: Savannah Knoop A.K. Burns *d'eau, 2. Le gaz*

d'éclairage, 1946–1966

LIQUID ROMANCE CAVERN (BALLAD FOR WATER) JACKET WORN BY GEO WYEX Death (XIII), 13th Major Arcana from the tarot deck

Muck Studies Department: Geo Wyex (performer's own character) Vava Dudu

Perverse

SWAMP SISTERS VINTAGE IBM COMPUTERS SPECIAL THANKS

("UNSHOOTABLE THIRST IS ANOTHER KIND OF HAUNTING.") Alex Bialy Fia Backström

Cister: Will Rawls Dean Daderko

Syster: Lee Relvas LOCATION: IBM CAMPUS Katherine Hubbard

Ulster County Jamie Hubbard

Department of Economic Development Karen Kelly

SITUATION SITES: Kelly Kivland

V O I D LOCATION: WIDOW JANE MINE Sophie Mörner

41°50'28.6" N, 74°05'52.5" W The Century House Historical Society Celia Nicolson

Widow Jane Mine, Rosendale, NY Michel Rein Gallery

LIGHTING AND AUDIO EQUIPMENT Barbara Schroeder

B O D Y Atomburst Production Services,llc Immanuel Williams

41°58'14.6" N, 74°00'01.6" W

IBM Campus, 101 Enterprise Drive, Kingston, NY PIANO

Vincitore's Hudson Valley Piano Center

is

W A T E R FUNDED WITH

41°53'31.5" N, 74°12'14.6" W THE GENEROUS

The Vly, Stone Ridge, NY ANIMAL HANDLING SUPPORT OF

Brian Bailey, All Creatures Great and Small John Simon Guggenheim Memorial Foundation

Liquid

42°07'19.8" N, 74°04'00.4" W EDITOR COMMISSIONED BY

Plattekill Creek, Saugerties, NY A.K. Burns The Wexner Center for the Arts at The Ohio State University

KAREN ARCHEY

There's a growing confidence in your style over the course of the Negative Space *cycle that strikes me as culminating in* What is Perverse is Liquid: *unlike the split-second editing we're used to in narrative cinema, your scenes are sprawling and drawn out. In the absence of a linear narrative, the visual seduction of the scenes helps immerse the viewer and keep them glued to the work. There's a certain inscrutability to this style, and I was wondering if you could talk about how you think about communication in your work.*

A.K. BURNS

If I were to synopsize my work as a whole, I would say that I am, in everything I do, questioning systems that create, enforce, and diminish value. Our dominant social and political systems are structured through hierarchies, and I seek methods to agitate the illusion that they are givens. In the case of *Negative Space*, I am using the lens of the science-fiction genre because it is a cultural form wherein fictional world-building opens allegorical possibilities. I am staging scenarios that are as familiar as they are not, treading a line where, ideally, the surreal quality of the work encourages alternative reads.

In particular, because of the metaphorical, poetic, and inverted logic I use in creating the videos, cinematic tools are really important for engaging the viewer's attention. My interest is in sustaining attention, not direct communication. If the soundtrack and visuals don't captivate an audience, they are not going to sit around for this much mental work—which is why I am aiming for the viewer's gut first. I hope the thinking behind it reveals itself slowly, maybe after they leave. Perspectives evolve when people are motivated by a feeling, not when they are told what to think. Also, a primary reason I make art is because it's the only form of communication that is nonlogical and engages our sensory systems through color, scale, gesture, etc.

The viewer who wants to go deeper can look at the collages, which bring together a lot of my references, or read the book this conversation will be printed in. In the case of the exhibition at the Wexner, there is a room dedicated to my research, for those who want that level of engagement.

KA

I was thinking in terms of the communication strategies of the work, particularly your use of visual metaphor and symbology. It seems like the metaphor of water comes into What is Perverse is Liquid *quite a lot.*

AKB

Indeed. In *What is Perverse is Liquid,* water is the central subject of exploration, upon which many metaphors are built. I didn't want to just represent water with images of water, although there is a swamp, a waterfall, and copious amounts of bottled water. Water is essential for all terrestrial existence. A lack

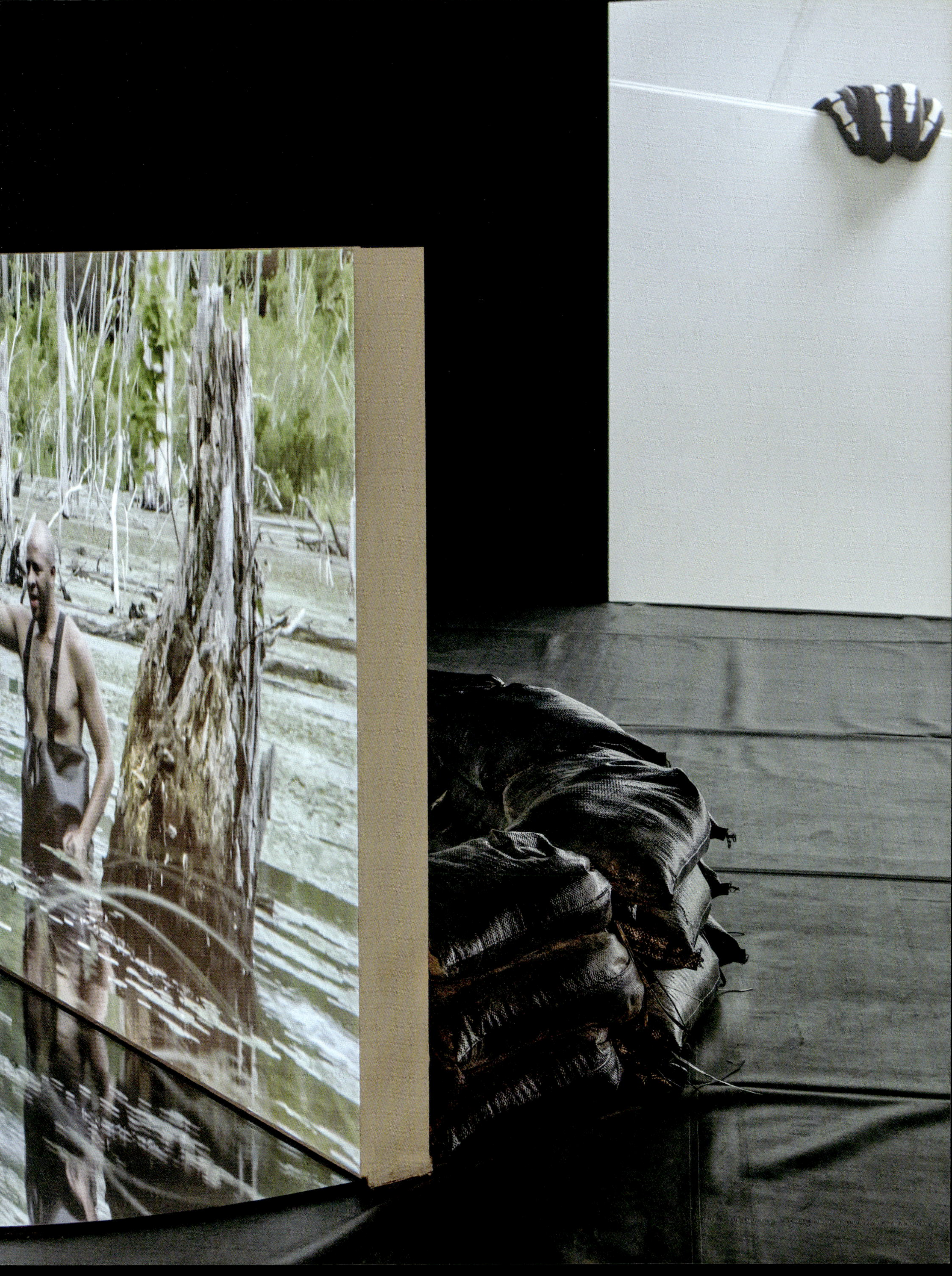

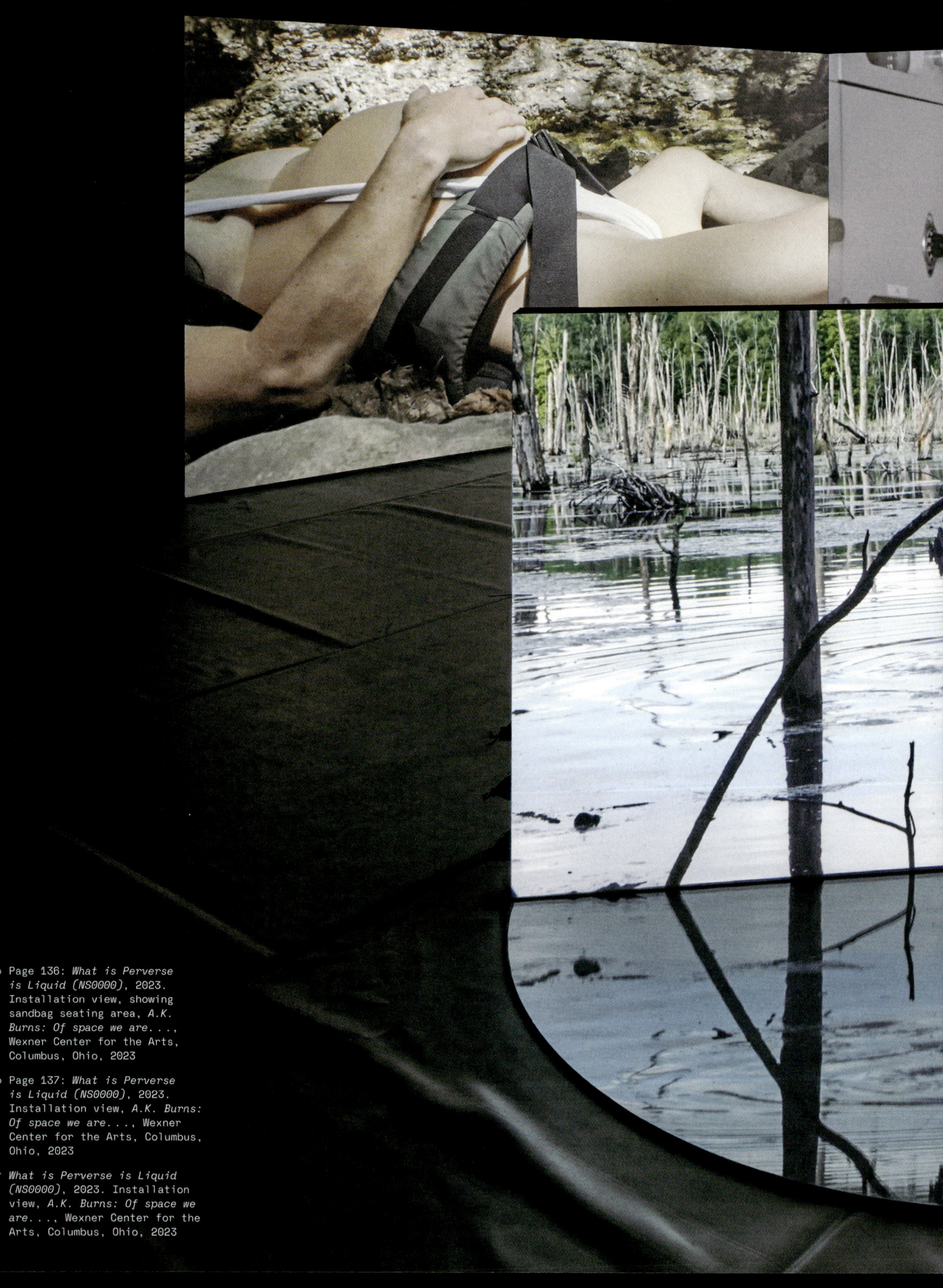

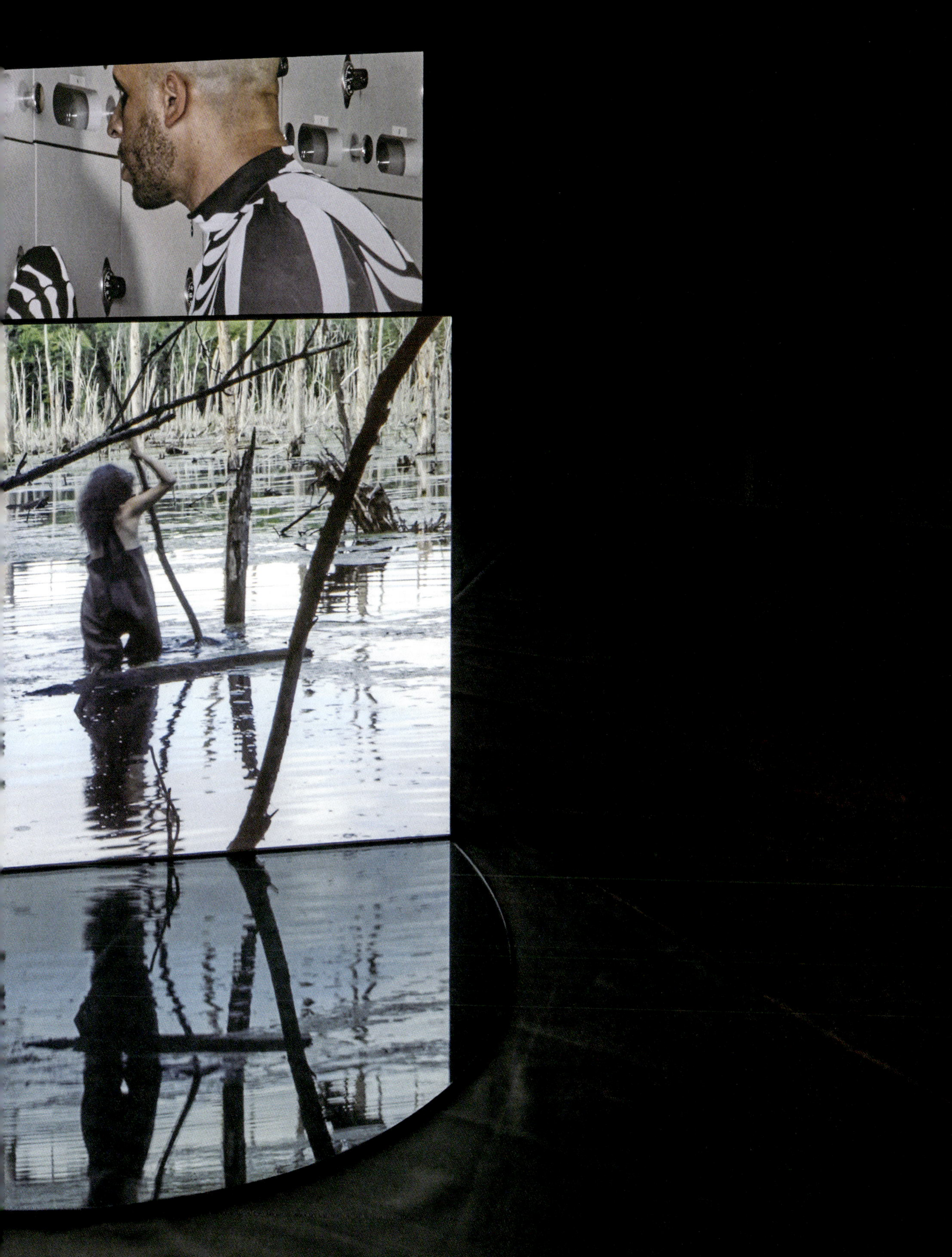

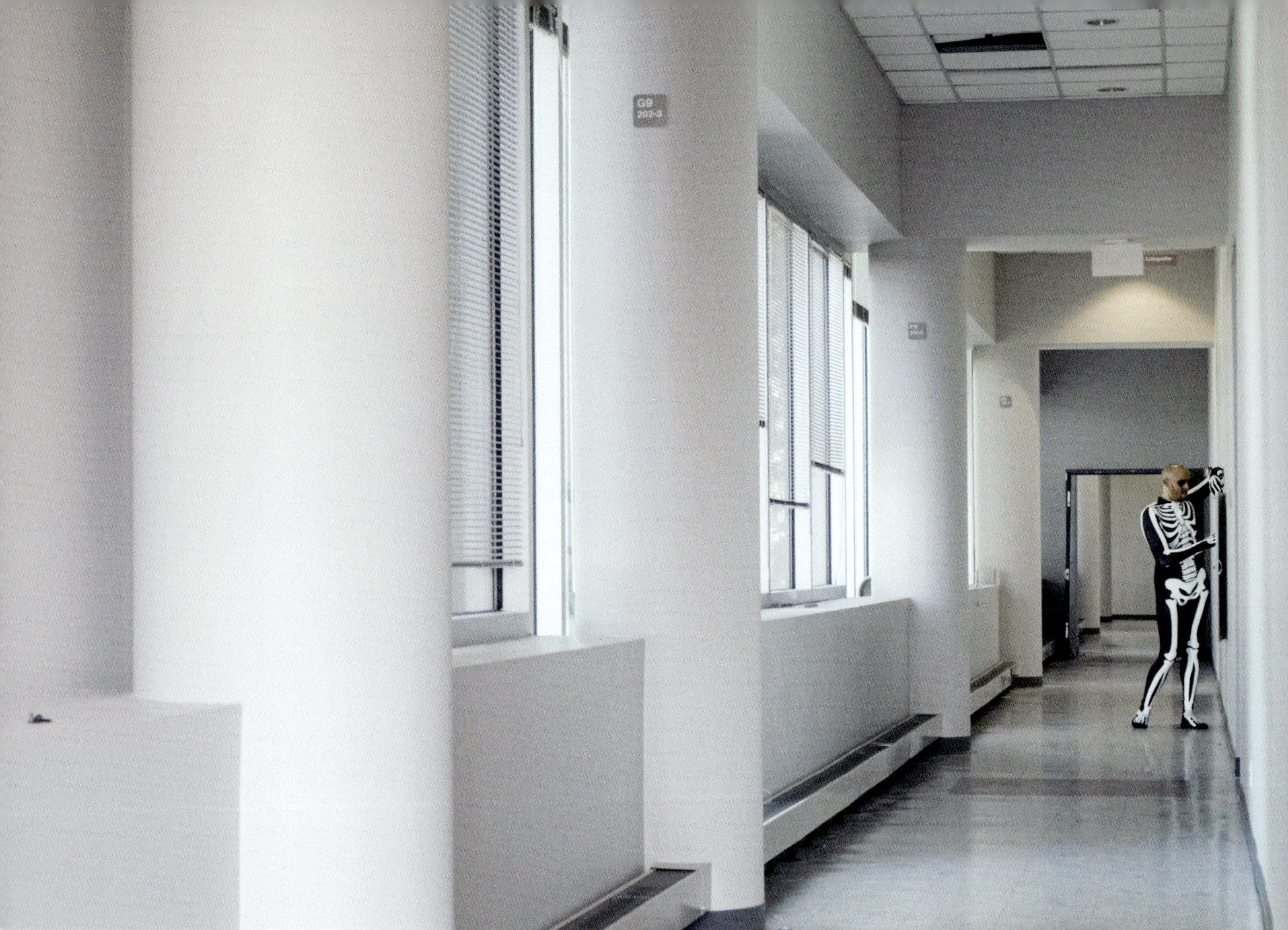

or excess of water can be life-threatening, so how it is accessed, contained, distributed, and potentially commodified is crucial. Water also has material qualities that I wanted to explore, such as the fact that it may flow or leak and has no shape of its own. Its form and movement are relational.

KA

There are also certain symbolic actions that point one toward the meaning of the work, like wrapping phones in tinfoil and melting coins with a blowtorch. I would be curious to hear more about what some of these activities mean. What does the owl mean to you? What do the seashells and the costuming mean to you? It'd be helpful to unpack specific things. Tell me about the coin smelting.

AKB

I've used pennies in many works over the years. My obsession with pennies has to do with the fact that not only are they the smallest denomination of US currency but also their value is less than their manufacturing cost. Pennies are no longer made with solid copper because copper is such a valuable resource. It is conductive and a low contaminant—thus it is used for wiring, pipes, pans, etc. The act of smelting or gathering these minute quantities of copper by liquefying the nickel interior to extract the copper shell also operates as a play on words: "liquid assets."

The film shows the absurdity of the tedious task of smelting, in this case melting pennies to extract copper. Capitalism demands that we continuously engage in extractive practices, and because scarcity increases value, those who possess a resource are motivated to exploit it. The scavenging and gleaning of a resource at such a minute scale points to the inane futility of late capitalism as resources diminish ever further.

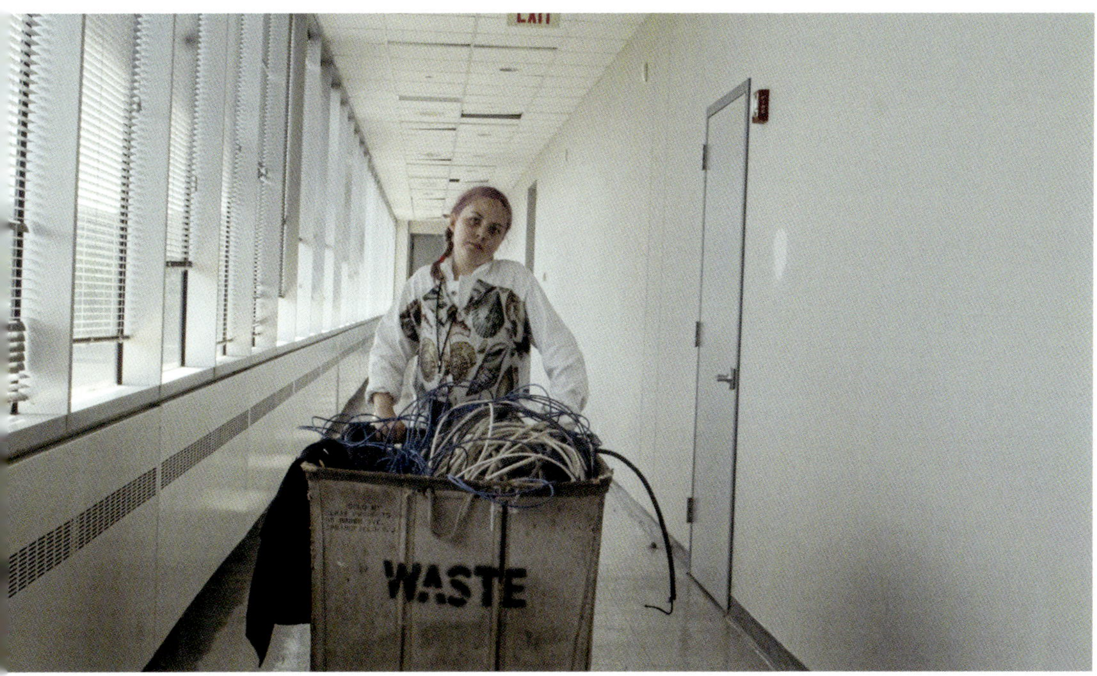

KA

Smelting in the film is a laborious and unpleasant task that yields little material benefit. I would imagine this character has a precarious life, if they're melting copper

off pennies. Maybe this is a good segue into thinking through the performers. Are there distinct acting agents in the work? There's obviously the skeleton; the Pregnant Backpacker, whom we've seen before in Living Room; *the Swamp Sisters; the singer playing piano in a cave—who happened to remind me of Elton John. Is that Geo Wyex?*

AKB

Yes. Geo plays the piano in the cave. But let's start with the skeleton, which shows up in several of the works in *Negative Space*: there are skulls in the cabinets in *Leave No Trace*, and skulls prop up both the go-go dancer's platform and the cube in the installation. In *Living Room*, the children are wearing skeleton socks. The skeleton is an expired human body: it bears the traces of human existence, but its presence marks an absence, so the skeleton is a form through which I can represent a negative.

In *What is Perverse is Liquid*, the skeleton plays an especially prominent role because I was thinking about the death card, which represents Scorpio and the element of water in a tarot deck. Side note: both Will Rawls, who performs as the skeleton, and I happen to be Scorpios, so we often discuss our watery

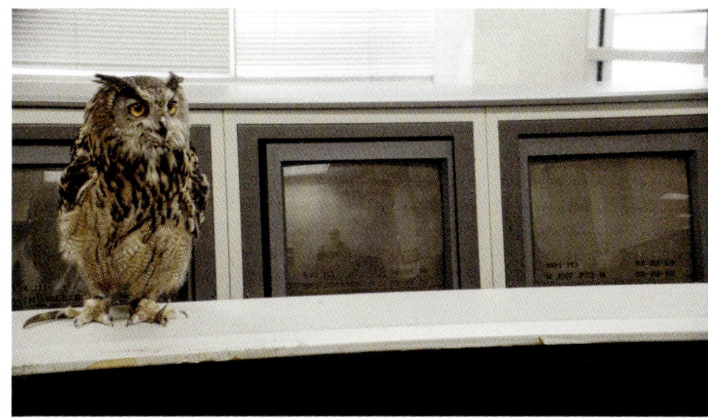

qualities. There is an autobiographical subtext to this whole project, the Scorpio being one of many examples.

Early in the development of *Negative Space*, I pulled tarot for the project, and the death card was the one that I pulled. The death card is typically illustrated with a skeleton and implies an end to old patterns through greater

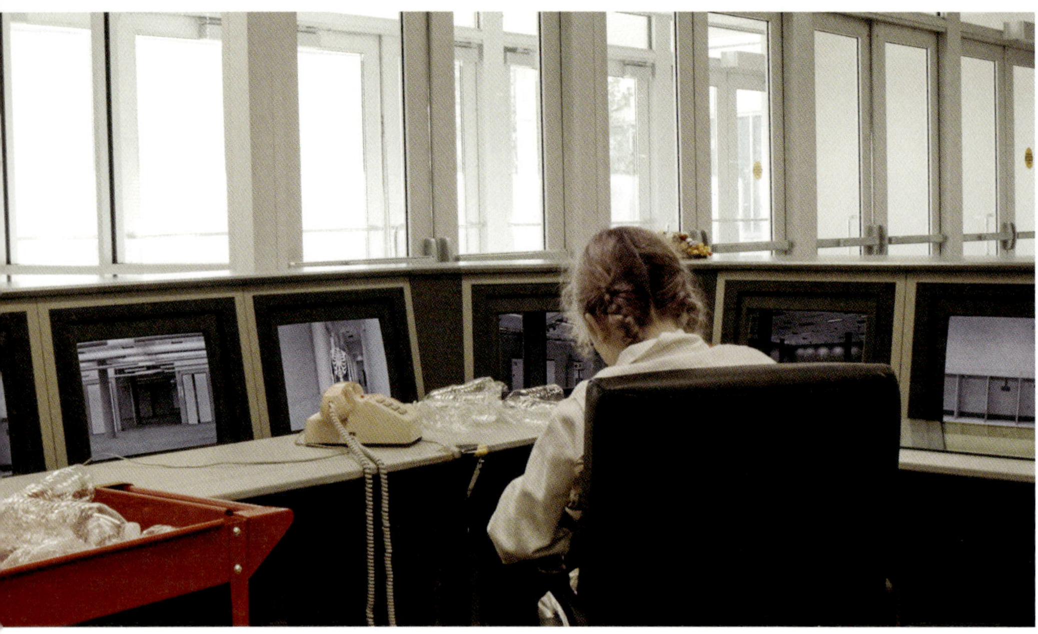

self-awareness. Animating the skeleton interrupts our thinking around the terminal nature of human existence. I used a skeleton Halloween costume to lean into camp and comedy so that the figure resonates more symbolically than literally.

As Will and I developed the skeleton, we talked a lot about how to move a body that is just bones, no muscles. So there's a clunkiness to it. The skeleton does a lot of touching, tapping, banging, and moving around the building, trying to understand its environment through haptics. The skeleton has no brain, just a skull, so what it knows is only what it encounters. It's just constantly playing around to get to know its environment.

KA

Is haunting a more general thing that's happening throughout the film? And how do you think about the skeleton dancing in a computer-server room, which appears to have a different tone than the other scenes with the skeleton?

AKB   Yes, the role of both the skeleton and the owl is to haunt. They are located, along with the three teenagers, in an abandoned office park in Kingston, New York, that formerly housed IBM headquarters. It used to be the main economic hub of the area, where I now live. I was interested in the building for its postapocalyptic look but also for its history—IBM isn't the computing juggernaut it was in the 1980s and 1990s. Their hauntings of this postproductive space allude to the manufacturing of what has now become "dead" technologies and the residue or waste produced by planned obsolescence. Within the context of this building, planned obsolescence starts to feel like a self-fulfilling prophecy.

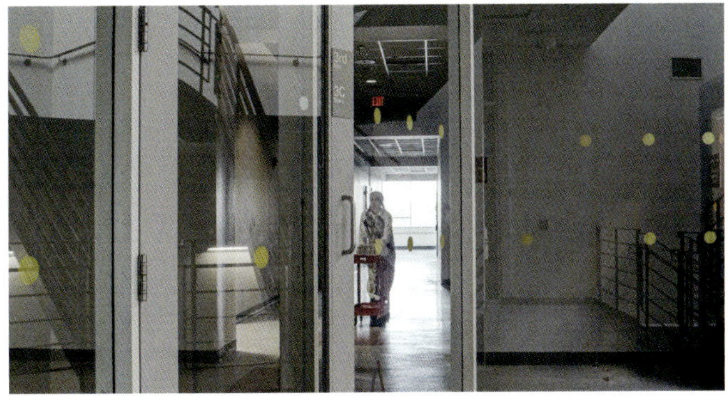

Also, this work was produced during the COVID-19 pandemic. So death and human vulnerability loomed large, as did the major cultural transitions in work life, i.e., the death of the office. The dancing in the server room is where things kind of "come to life." As I've mentioned before, I see dancing as an act of liberation or revitalization. And that scene is less a haunting than a bit of comedy and an awkward release, in which the skeleton suddenly seems to have a personality or selfhood, as well as newfound agility.

KA   *Could you say a little bit about some of the other agents— for example, the teenagers?*

AKB   The three teenagers in *What is Perverse is Liquid* are six years older than they were in *Living Room* as the three dwarf planets. They're almost unrecognizable, having grown from childhood into young adulthood. To connect them back to *Living Room*, I sewed their old jumpsuits onto larger white jumpsuits that fit them now. This continues their role as liminal beings—manifesting change and transformation.

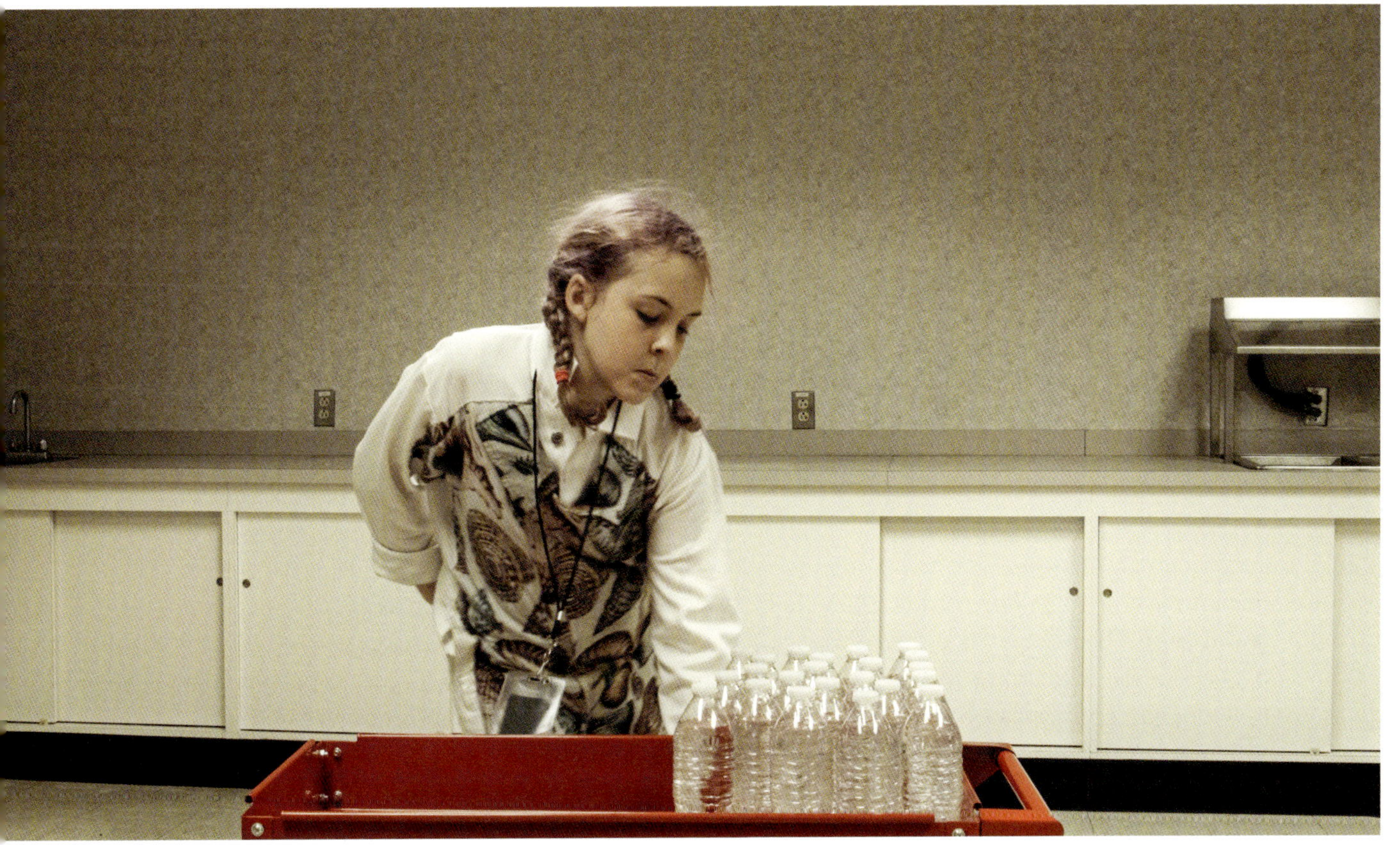

   The teenagers are squatting in the office building and simulating productivity within that context. They're running some quasi business, which involves stripping the building of copper, smelting pennies, and hoarding bottled water. They don't just arrive and scavenge; they're also on antiquated IBMs and making phone calls on retro phones, as if time were a

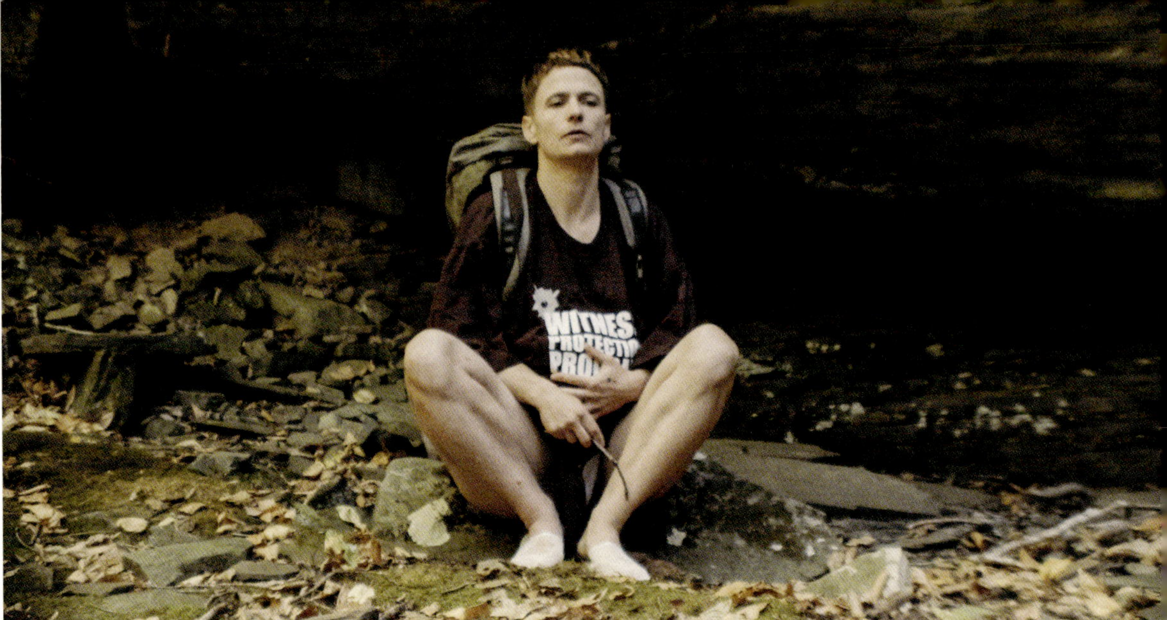

construct of their own devising. What era are they in? I'm looking backward and forward as a way to play with this notion of the speculative present.

KA *The retro age of the technology used by these teens makes it seem like they are playacting. They're clearly not actually at an office working. It's more like they're imitating working. To me, it seems like a postapocalyptic*

1 4 4

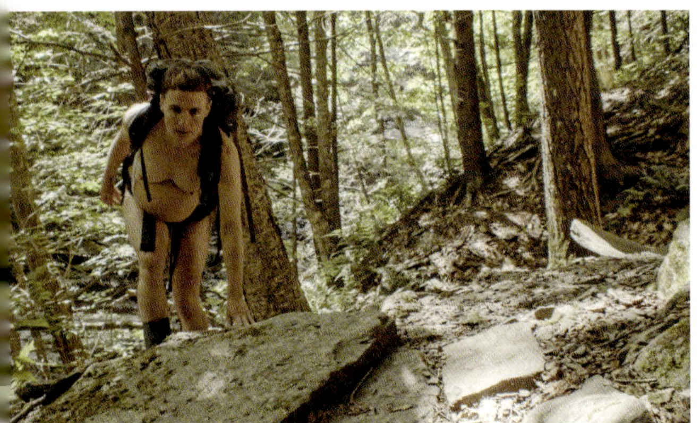

environment, in which a new generation fantasizes about the preapocalyptic world. At the same time, the scene doesn't feel so far from our current historical moment, as if we were looking back at a time before the precarity brought on by neoliberalism. It's the almost sculptural physicality of the computers, their massive presence, that simultaneously embodies multiple periods of time.

AKB Yes, that is exactly how I hoped it would feel. It was a project to hunt down those old computers.

KA *Were they not just in there?*

AKB No, the place was completely empty. I had to bring in the desks and chairs, as well as the old IBMs. I found a computer engineer who loves old technology and has a personal archive of computers he's salvaged from the trash over the years, so he lent me the 1980s-era IBM laptops.

KA *Can you tell me about the Swamp Sisters? They are featured on a separate channel, as a kind of minifilm within the larger* What is Perverse is Liquid *installation.*

AKB As you know, whatever was going on in the world affected how I built each work, and sites and locations have been the main drivers for its development. The Swamp Sisters came directly out of these two factors. This video was produced from 2020 through 2022, which correlates to when COVID-19 hit. I spent much of this time at home, like so many. Since I had moved to upstate New York in 2018, I was learning how to live in a rural area, dealing with the whims of the environment and tending to land after living in New York City for fifteen years. Originally, for *What is Perverse is Liquid*, I'd imagined returning to Lake Powell on the Colorado River to observe the drought crisis and reflect on water from the perspective of lack. Because I grew up in California during the drought of the 1980s,

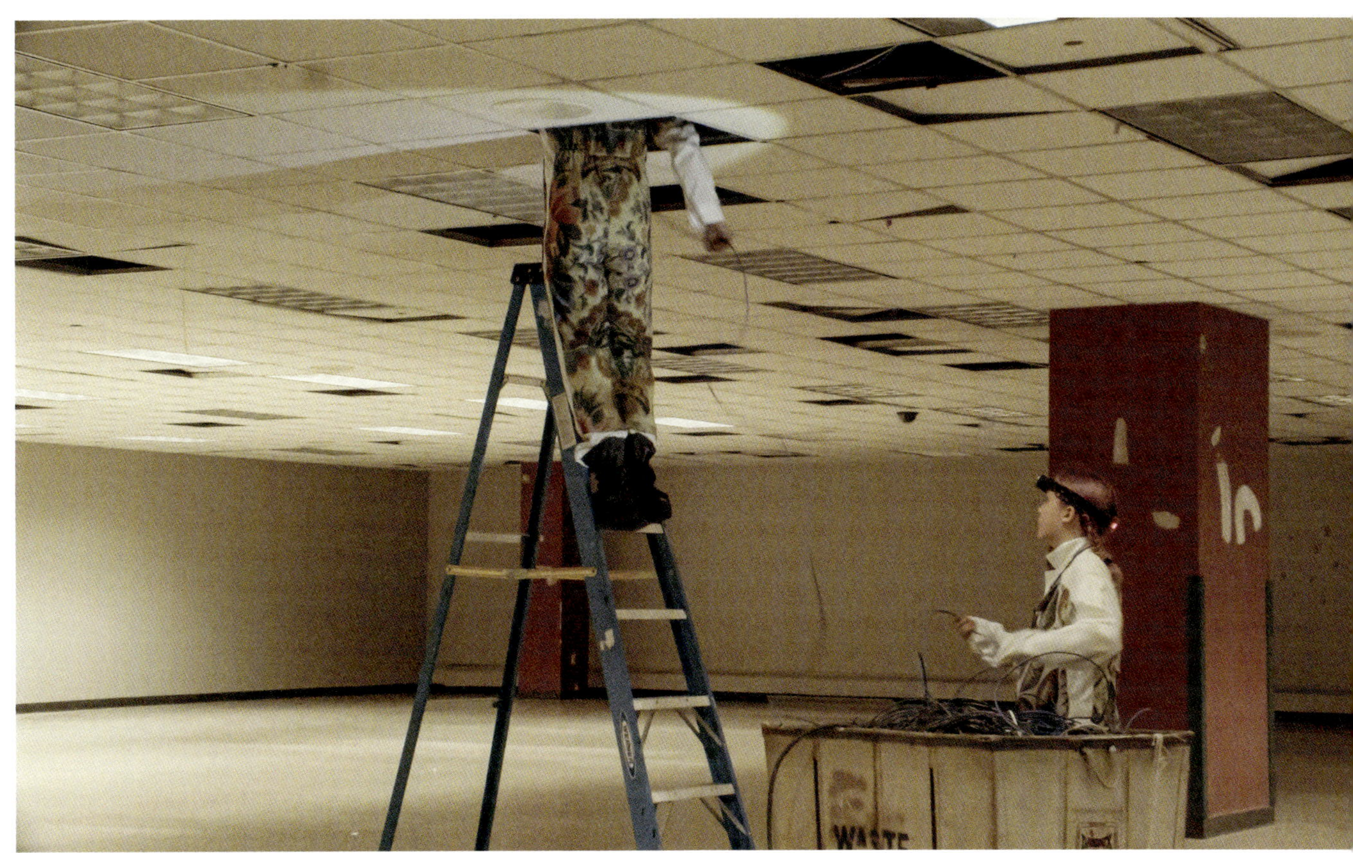

the prospect of a lack of water remains a constant anxiety for me. But being trapped at home on the East Coast during the COVID-19 pandemic, I started to think and observe things more locally.

In my neighborhood, there's a swamp-like body of water called the Vly. I walk by it every day, and it's, for me, the spiritual center of the neighborhood. I've been captivated by it since I moved here. Since it's such a striking body of water, it seemed preordained to be part of the film. The Vly has hundreds of dead trees growing out of it—well, not growing, but sticking out of it—which in part create its rich ecosystem. It's alive with tons of wildlife, even though it appears to be dead. It's much like the tarot's death card, which should be read as a positive, because new growth emerges through death.

KA   *Yeah, I mean the death tarot card just sounds so dark, but—*

AKB   I know, we have all these associations with death as an end point, as something that we're always resisting and that is many people's biggest fear. But, in tarot, it means that something that doesn't have value anymore may cease so that something new can exist or grow.

KA   *Acknowledging that we are part of the land, that we are part of this idea that our bodies will return to the land at some point, that our existence doesn't have to be so incredibly self-centered—that idea recalls what I see as the metanarrative of the* Negative Space *series, which looks at our relationship to the land more holistically.*

AKB   That, for me, is something that has been actualized through moving to a more rural space. You're constantly negotiating with the environment. Every season is very physical—mowing, raking, and shoveling snow.

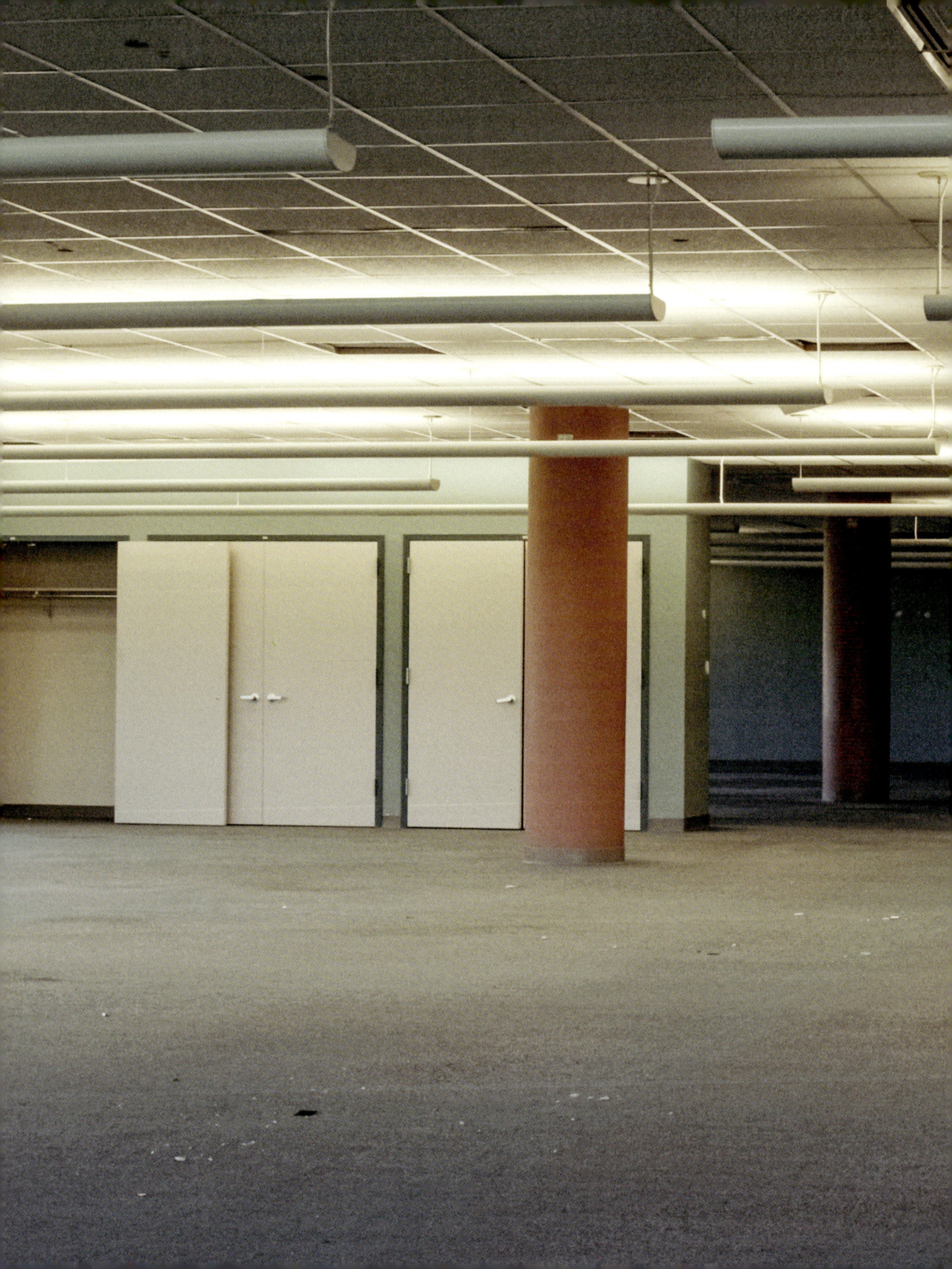

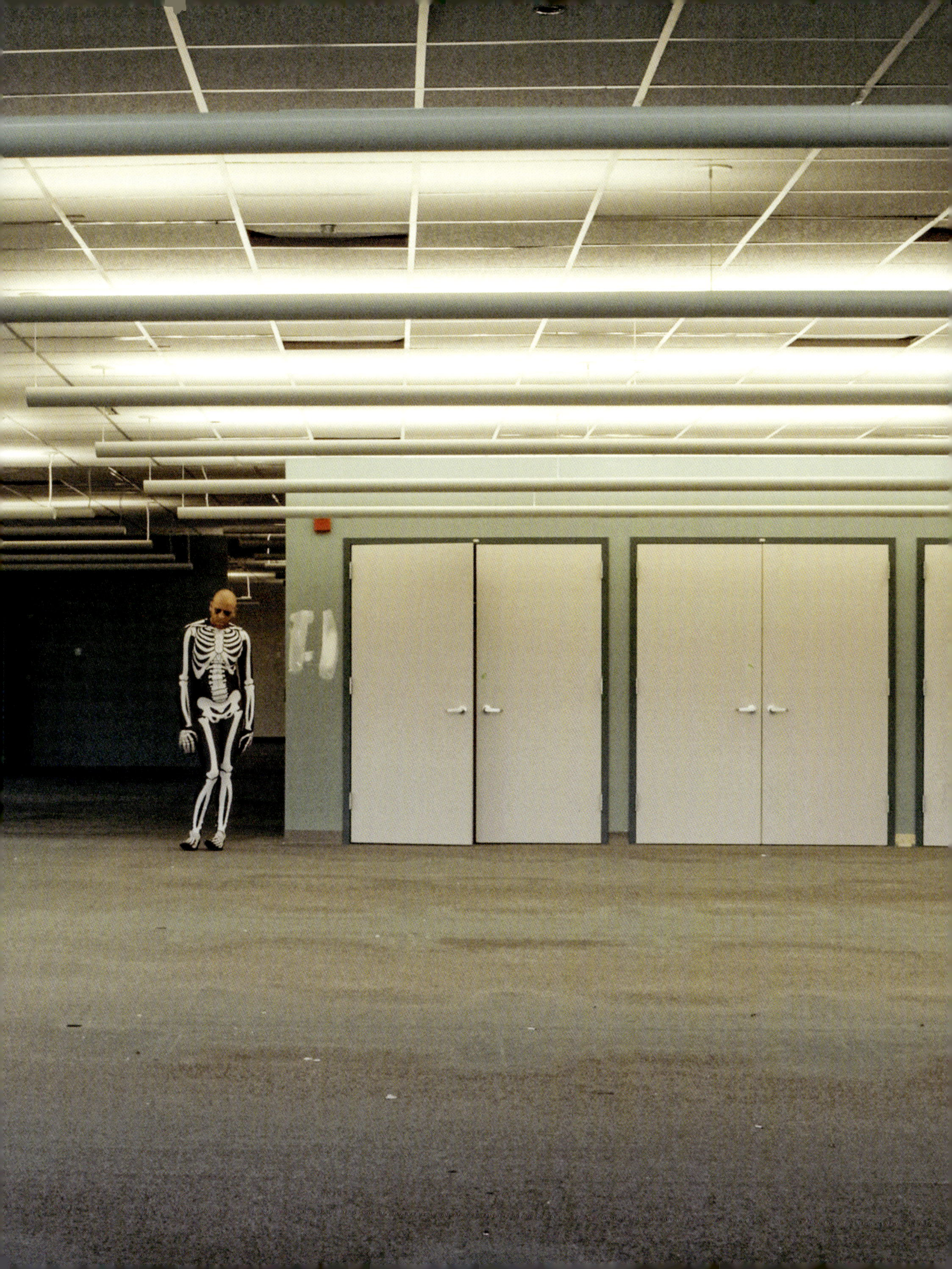

*Picking up sticks, unplugging drains, enriching the soil.
I'm from rural Ohio, I get it.*

AKB Yeah, and many people understand nature as something to be controlled and managed, which makes it feel like a battle.

By contrast, the Vly is an ecosystem—an environment based in reciprocity and diversity—that spawned the Swamp Sisters. The Vly also has a rich auditory quality because of the numerous croaking and squawking animals that populate it. When I brought performers to this site, I felt they needed to have a call-and-response with the environment to become part of it. The vocalizing between the two Swamp Sisters thus became their central activity. As their vocal mimicry progresses throughout the film, it transforms into language. This language is excerpted from the poem "The First Water Is the Body" by Natalie Diaz. The Swamp Sisters start to speak in an elongated language that sounds like animal calls, saying, "Unsoothable thirst is one kind of haunting."

KA *You've sourced from various texts for the works in the* Negative Space *series. Are there other books that you pulled from for* What is Perverse is Liquid?

AKB All texts in this work come from Diaz's book *Postcolonial Love Poem* (2020), in which water is a big theme. One poem is called "The American Water Museum," which isn't a real place but a medium through which Diaz reflects on our bodily detachment and the consequent institutionalization of bodies of water. The section I used starts with "There's more than 100,000 miles of waterways in our bodies," and it ends with "The curators ask us to collapse as naturally as possible in a heap, so those who come behind us might be immersed in this exhibition of thirst as if it was their own." The Pregnant Backpacker recites this excerpt, and unlike with my use of text in the other works,

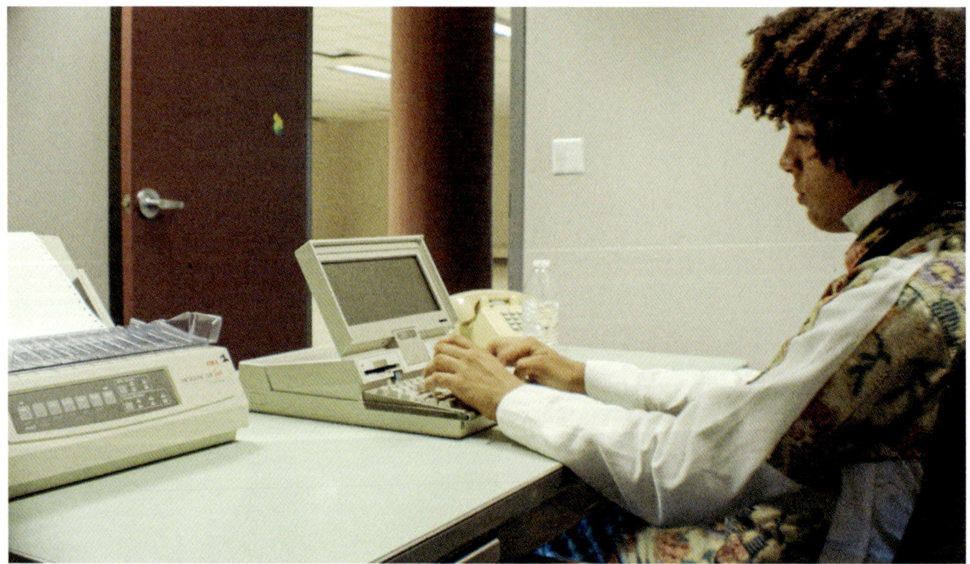

the performer looks straight at the camera and breaks the fourth wall, as if addressing the viewer directly in the exhibition space they are watching the work in.

I was drawn to this text because it entangles water politics with the ethics of exhibition and historicization. As an artist, I often work in the context of museums, and this excerpt addresses the staging of knowledge and culture and the power institutions have in telling stories that shape the present. This also ties into my interest in remaking canonical artworks in each of the films in *Negative Space*. I alter elements within these known works to query knowledge production and what engenders cultural values.

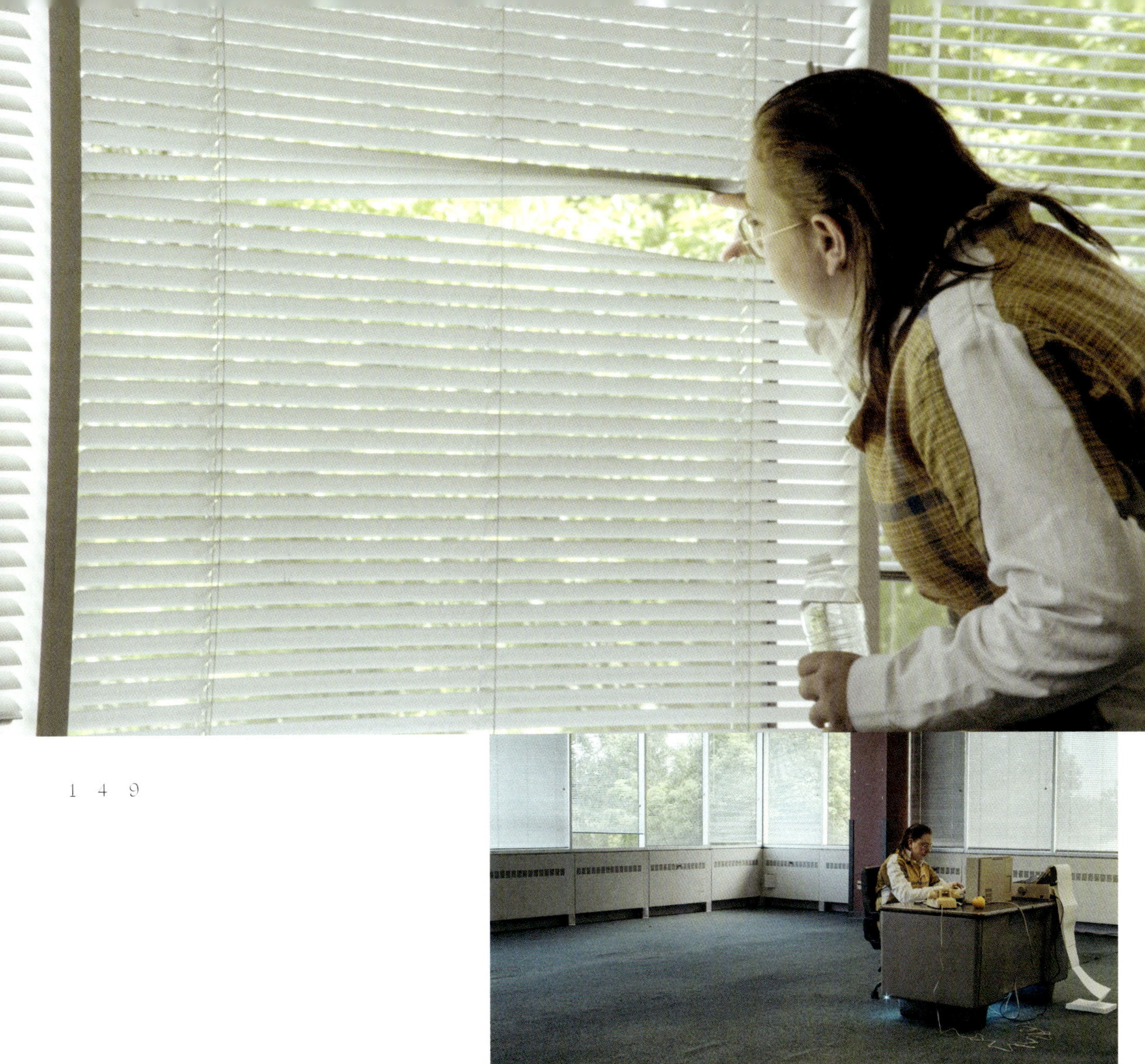

KA *Yes, there is a confrontation between the viewer of* What is Perverse is Liquid *and the subject of their gaze, the Pregnant Backpacker. It makes me think of other instances where the gaze is more surreptitious. There are peepholes and portals throughout the film. Could you speak more about these?*

AKB Peeping happens throughout the film, which throws open the question of who holds the privilege of the gaze, generating unequal power dynamics. But peepholes and portals also allow light, bodies, and other worlds to "leak" from one space into another, connecting the scenes and holding them together.

For example, Makemake is working the front desk, where the security monitors act as a type of portal. This is the only scene where we see the skeleton and the teens together—through the screens—because the skeleton exists in a parallel world, maybe an afterlife, and is essentially an apparition. Makemake appears not to notice, since the skeleton is a haunting and invisible to them. In other instances of peeping, the smelter parts shades to look through a window, and the camera peers obliquely through glass windows and doors, observing as the skeleton dances and Makemake wanders down a hall. The skeleton peeping through the mailboxes is the most explicitly voyeuristic scene, delivering a visual crescendo with the reclining body of my remake of Marcel Duchamp's *Étant donnés: 1. La chute d'eau, 2. Le gaz d'éclairage (Given: 1. The Waterfall, 2. The Illuminating Gas)* (1946–66) on the adjacent screen in the installation.

KA
    As you've mentioned, you have restaged artworks in each of the works in Negative Space. *How are these restagings critical of the originals?*

AKB
As I planned *What is Perverse is Liquid* and reflected on the three completed works, I thought, "I can't believe I haven't done Duchamp." When I thought about which work of Duchamp's to address, I landed on *Étant donnés*, because it's his last and such a loaded, misogynistic work. Plus it includes a waterfall—how could I not? In the original artwork, the viewer looks through the peepholes of a giant wood door and takes on the role of a voyeur or Peeping Tom. As they look, they are delivered a scene that is both confusing and maybe exactly what is expected: a crotch shot. It's a classic pornographic "money shot"

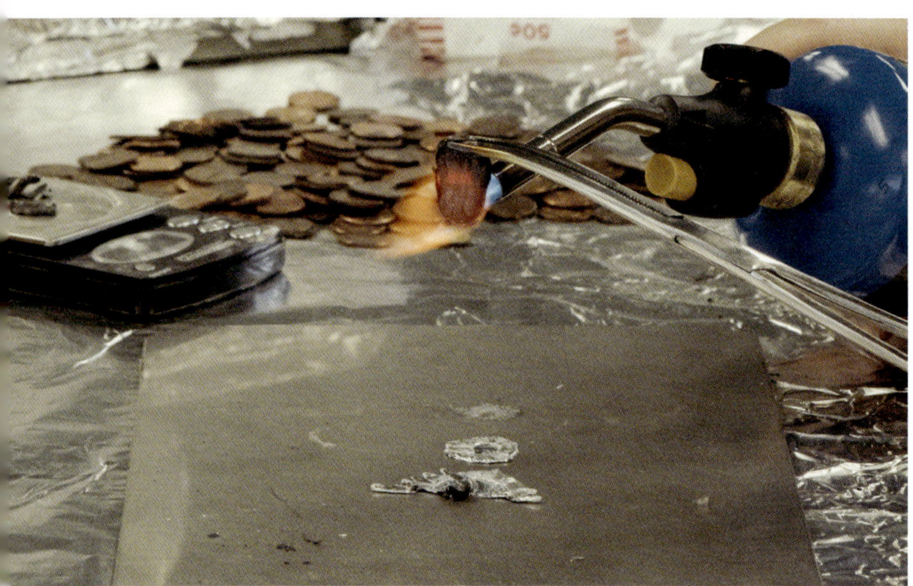

that delivers the body onto which the male gaze projects itself. But the labia are rather abstract in their rendering, and the torso appears headless because parts of the diorama obscure the view, so it's as disturbing as it is enticing. I wanted my version to confront the voyeur and give the reclining body more agency. In Duchamp's work, the figure holds a lantern; in my version, the Pregnant Backpacker, who is the subject of this scene, holds a mirror. The mirror takes light from the environment (the sun) and beams it back into the viewer's eye. The Pregnant Backpacker retains their agency by visually obliterating their own image.

KA
    That's not what I expected. I don't know what I expected, but it wasn't that, especially the purpose of the light.

AKB
Light is a key part of Duchamp's *Étant donnés*, not only through the presence of the lantern but through all the artificial lighting in the staging of the work and the fact that the door with the peepholes is in a darkened space in the Philadelphia Museum of Art. The Pregnant Backpacker, who was originally in the stairwell in *Living Room*, returns as the figure in my *Étant donnés*. Their pregnancy signals, of course, the potential for a human to emerge from their body, so in my *Étant donnés*, there is the implication of a body coming out of a body rather than the suggestion of a body receiving another, as in Duchamp's. The skeleton, ultimately, is the one who peeps at the pregnant body.

KA   *It represents a state of becoming. And speaking of death in*
                                                  this more holistic sense, of course, it's a beginning.

AKB   There's definitely a reference to that cyclicality in the work.

KA   *All this talk about voyeurism, sex, waterfalls, and Duchamp*
                                                  leads me back to the title: What is Perverse is Liquid.
                                                  Could you talk about that title and where it is from?

AKB   Some of these titles have been with me for a long time. I've just been waiting to make the correlating
             works. *Leave No Trace* and *What is Perverse is Liquid* were known titles before *A Smeary Spot* was
             even finished.

             Perversity, the term, has a negative connotation. Being a member of the queer community,
             I have a lot of feelings about what is perceived as perverse. This is language that has been

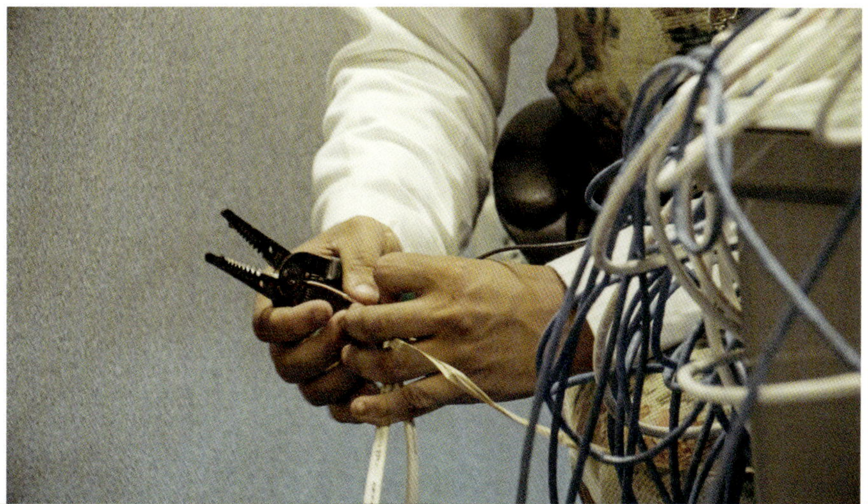

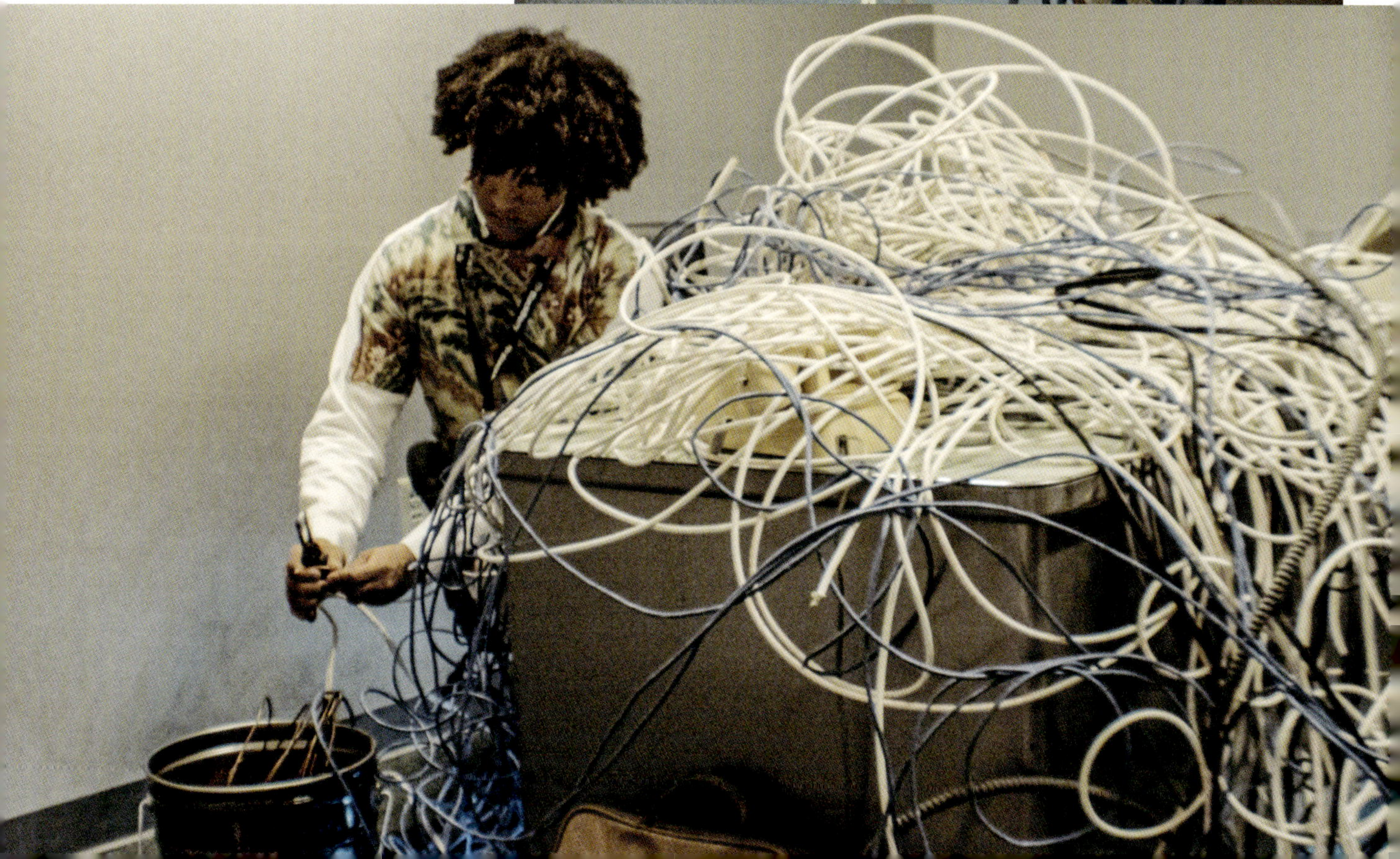

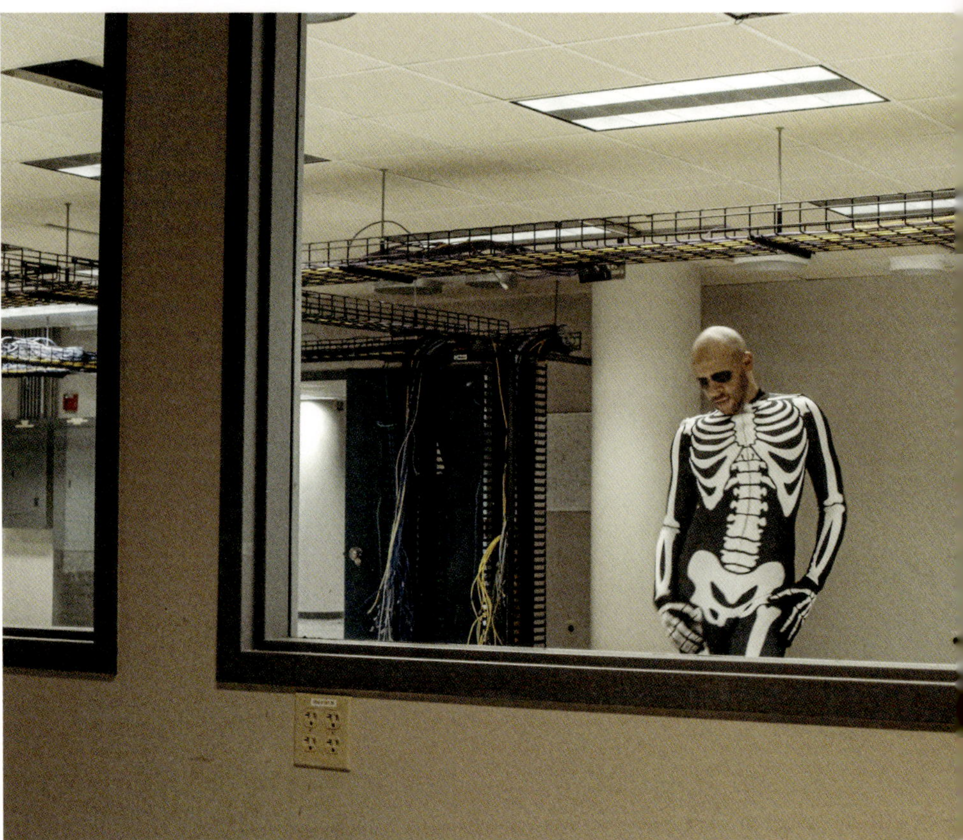

and continues to be leveraged against our community. But with the title, I was also thinking about my conception of the void and its relationship to water—both have a strong relation to the concept of mutability. And as mentioned, water has no shape unto itself; it's always in relation—to a beach, a bank, a container, a pipe, etc. It is also often hard to contain; it bursts, leaks, overflows, floods. I posit that this mutability, uncontainability, and codependency is a perversion of our nationalistic, deterministic, and individualistic norms. So to be liquid is to be perverse. I challenge the negative connotations of perversity, and I see this kind of perversion as a strength.

KA   *How is* What is Perverse is Liquid *installed?*

AKB   There are three screens, and the floor is covered in a black-rubber pool liner. I use the two screen sizes already established in the other three *Negative Space* installations. There are two larger

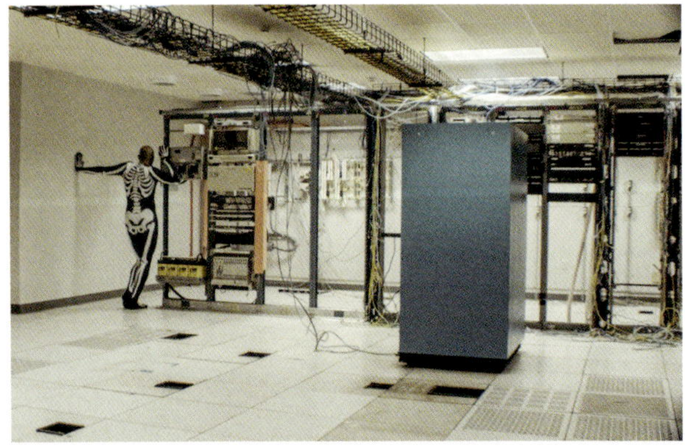

screens, seven by twelve feet each, that meet in one corner of the room. At the center of the room, there is a four-by-seven-foot wall. In front of the small wall, facing the corner screens, there are stacked sandbags arranged in a half-circle. This half-circle of sandbags creates seating, as well as an empty space I call the dry pool, with sand and pennies strewn about in it. The film with the Swamp Sisters, which includes intervals of rolling credits, is projected on the other side of this smaller wall, and in front of it is a half-circle of plexiglass on the ground that creates a reflective surface. I call this the wet pool. So one side of the small projection wall is the "dry" side and the other the "wet" side.

You can stand in the farthest corner of the room, opposite the corner where the big screens meet, and take in all three screens at once; the small one is spatially layered in front of the two large ones. Or you can sit on the sandbags and exclusively view the two large screens. As I mentioned, the Swamp Sisters is a film that runs simultaneously with the other two screens and is meant to set a tone and provide atmosphere for the installation. So the small screen doesn't require concentrated attention from beginning to end. You can pick up parts of it; you can hear the murmur of the Vly and the performers squawking at each other in the background. The soundtrack orchestrates these different video components, keeping them in balance and spatializing the audio. This work had a lot more diegetic sound than the others in *Negative Space* and is by far the most opulent from an audio perspective.

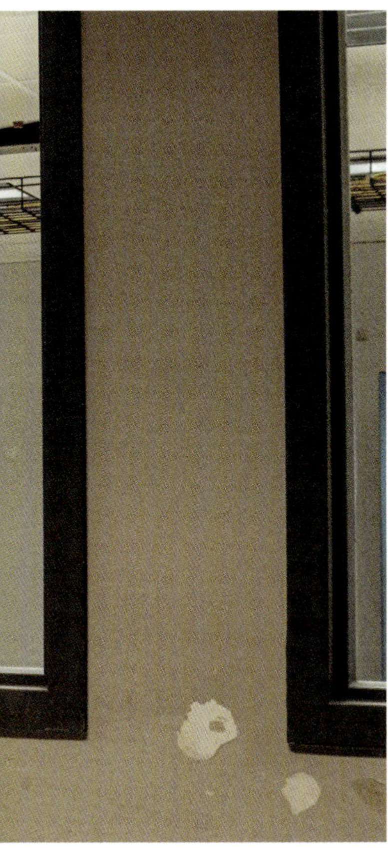

1 5 5

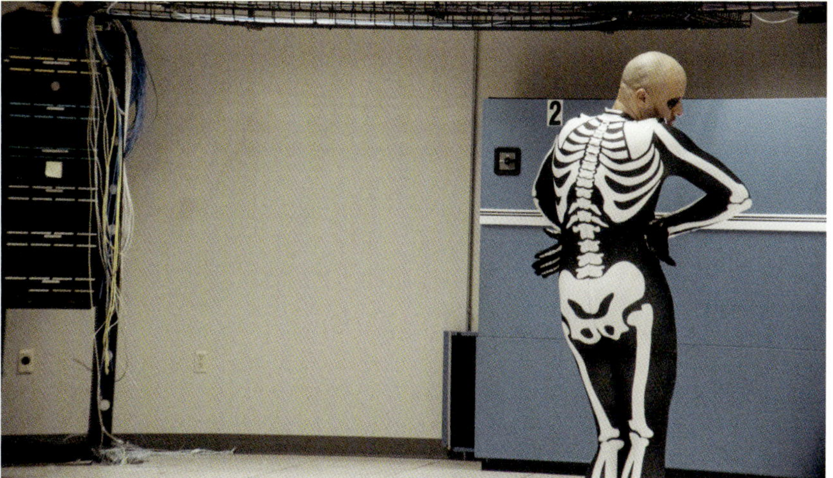

 How is this work envisioned as the ending of the series? Or do you consider it the end? What is the relationship of it to the other works and to the series itself? How is it similar? How is it different?

AKB There is no end because there's no beginning. Time is treated as a continuum, and cyclical time structures each film, since they run on a loop and are constructed through a series of entangled vignettes rather than by a linear narrative. I have also numbered each work with zeros (*NS0, NS00, NS000, NS0000*), so as to acknowledge the order they were made in without attaching a numerical order to them. *What is Perverse is Liquid* completes the cycle but isn't necessarily an ending.

I started the whole four-part project with the notion of building a speculative ontology centered on these four elemental, physical systems—the void, which I see as a political position and a rethinking of power; the body, because it's the container, the way things coalesce; the land, which is our foundation, as the Earth gives us a relationship to space and place; and water, because you have no life without water.

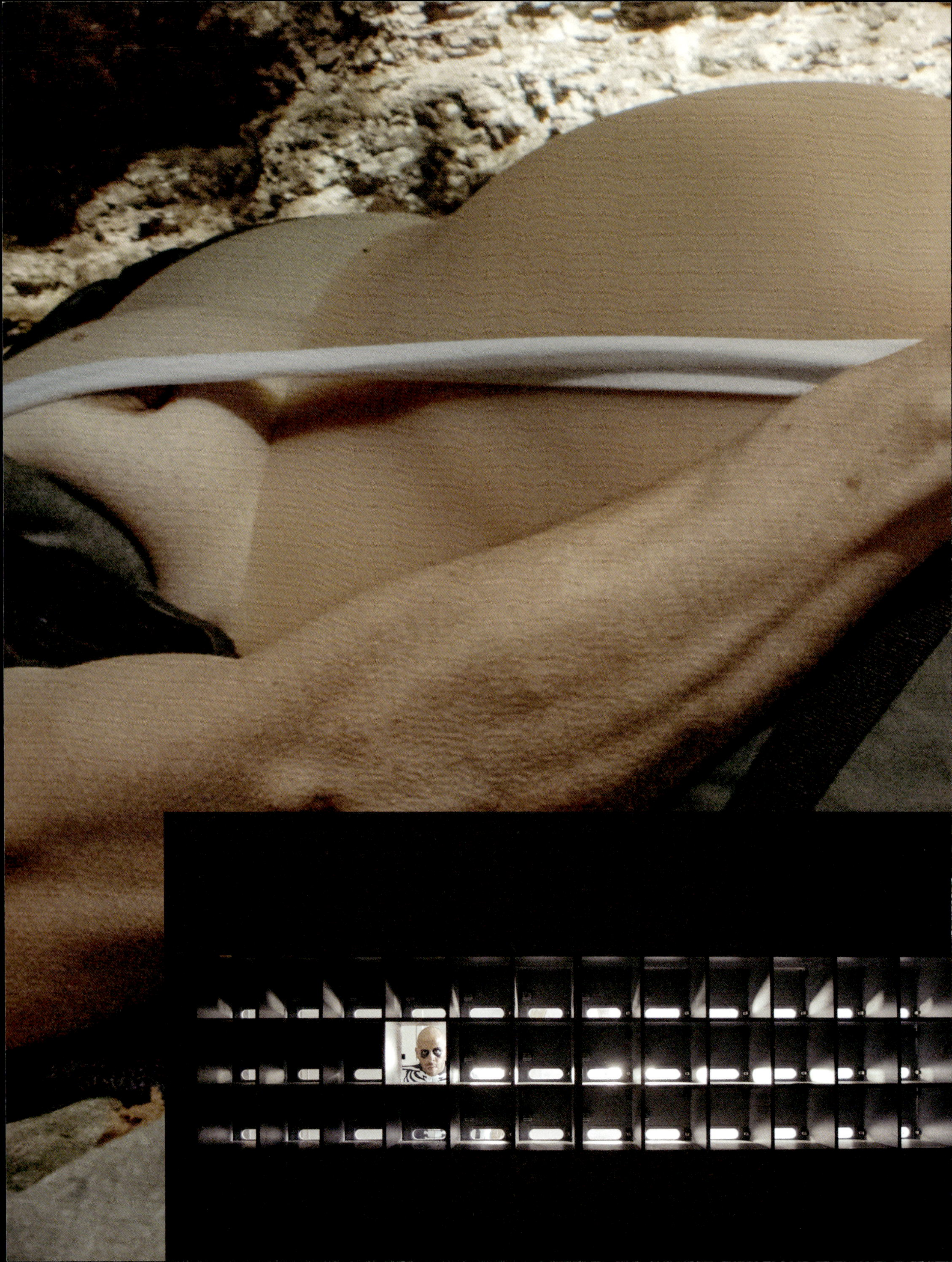

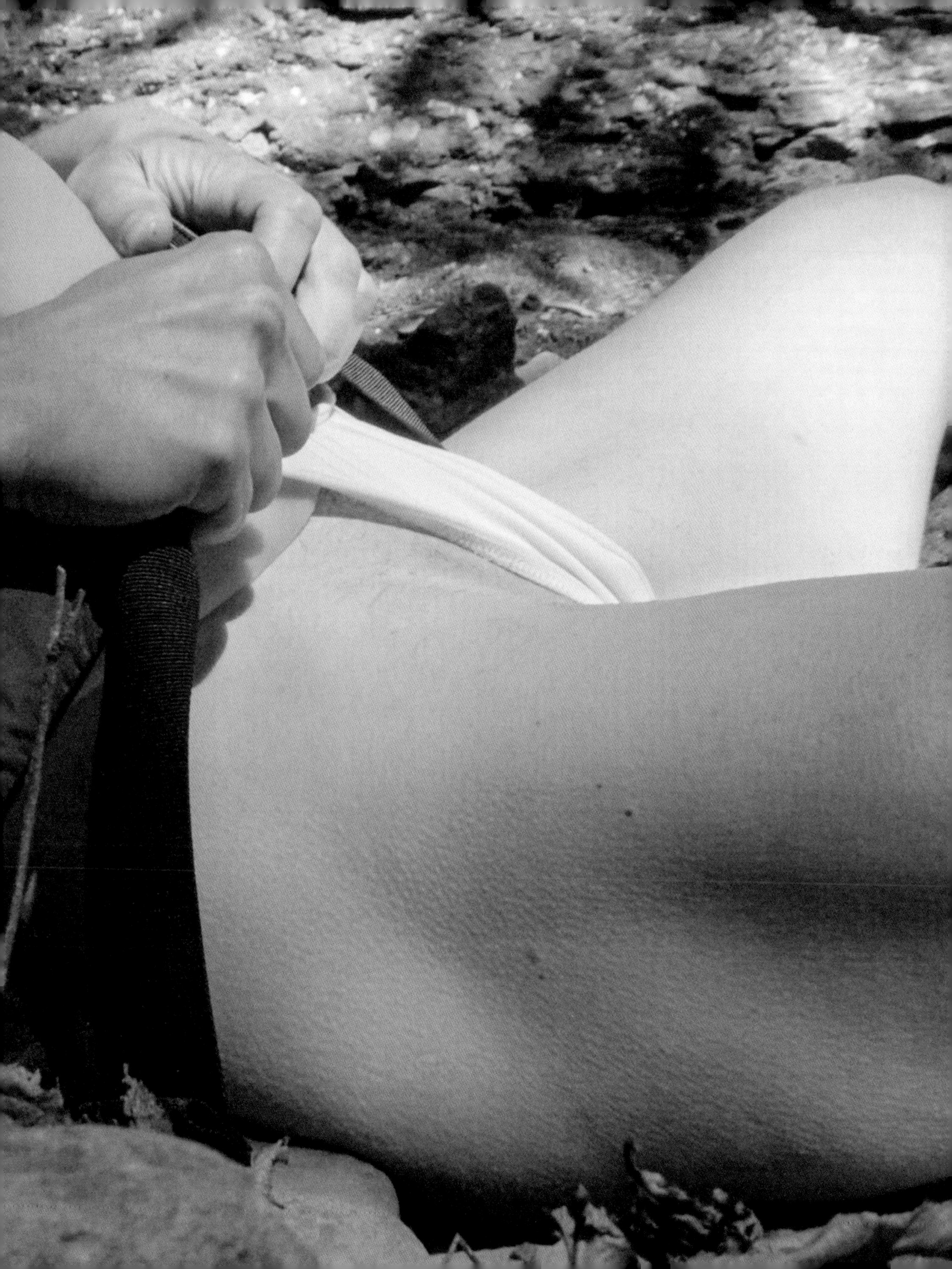

The best way to think about the structure of the four works that make up *Negative Space* is that *A Smeary Spot* is like the sun. It is the central work of a constellation of four. The other three works are like planets orbiting that sun. They need the resources of the sun to exist. In other words, the intellectual framework—the script for *A Smeary Spot*—sets the stage for the other three works to cross-reference one another yet remain autonomous.

The order they were produced in was determined by the available resources. For *Living Room*, I was given the opportunity to use the New Museum building, which ushered in ideas about the body. With *Leave No Trace*, my residency at EMPAC provided access to its zero-decibel theater, which led me to think about immateriality and absence as a way of marking space and place. The resources spoke to me in terms of which film they aligned with conceptually. So it is purely coincidental that *What is Perverse is Liquid* ended up being the last that I made.

KA

Before we wrap up, could you talk a little bit about what I've called the Elton John moment, where we see Geo in the cave playing the piano? Because it's quite the ending ... not that there's an ending.

AKB   Let's call it a peak moment, since there are no endings. That was shot at Widow Jane Mine, a man-made cave that is local to me in Rosendale. It's an old limestone mine that provided materials for the first cement companies that populated the region in the nineteenth century. The foundations of the Statue of Liberty and the Brooklyn Bridge were built using material extracted

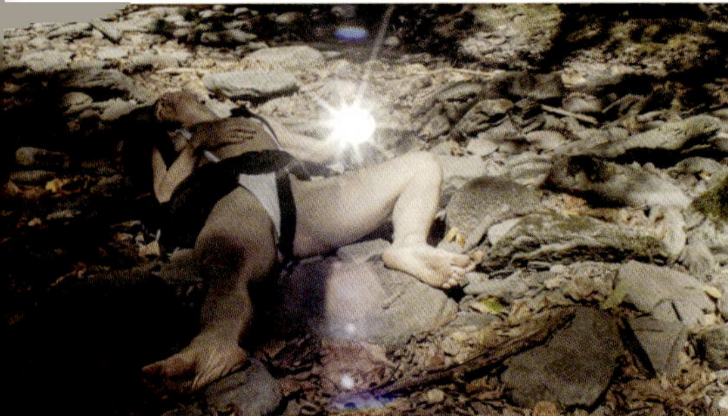

from it. Sites that look natural but that are in fact created through human intervention appear throughout *Negative Space*, like Lake Powell in *A Smeary Spot*. Each has a loaded history that has to do with extraction or the management of resources.

Thinking about how to amplify the particular qualities of the cave's interior, I was struck by how resonant it is. In listening to the drips of water in the cave, I got to thinking about instruments and how a piano and its keys could be in conversation with a trickle of water. Because this is the last work I shot in the cycle, I had been reflecting on what I had and hadn't done within the whole series. And because Geo was my primary collaborator on this work for nearly ten years—but was always only present in the background through the score—I realized I wanted to celebrate him as a performer. To bring him into the fore-ground, so to speak.

That led me to bring a piano into the cave and work with Geo to write a song. I started out wanting a ballad, a love song for water, personifying water as a love interest. It's a torrid relationship that one cannot live without but that could also threaten your life. I wanted to play with the idea of romantic desire and physi-ological need in relation to this essential resource. I gave this concept to Geo, who then composed that incredible track. We set up five microphones in differ-ent places in the cave to get that rich cavernous recording. Geo performs this scene through a character he's been developing for years called Muck Studies Department. So this scene is really an intersection of our two practices, which, while different, emerge from similar concerns and responses to the world.

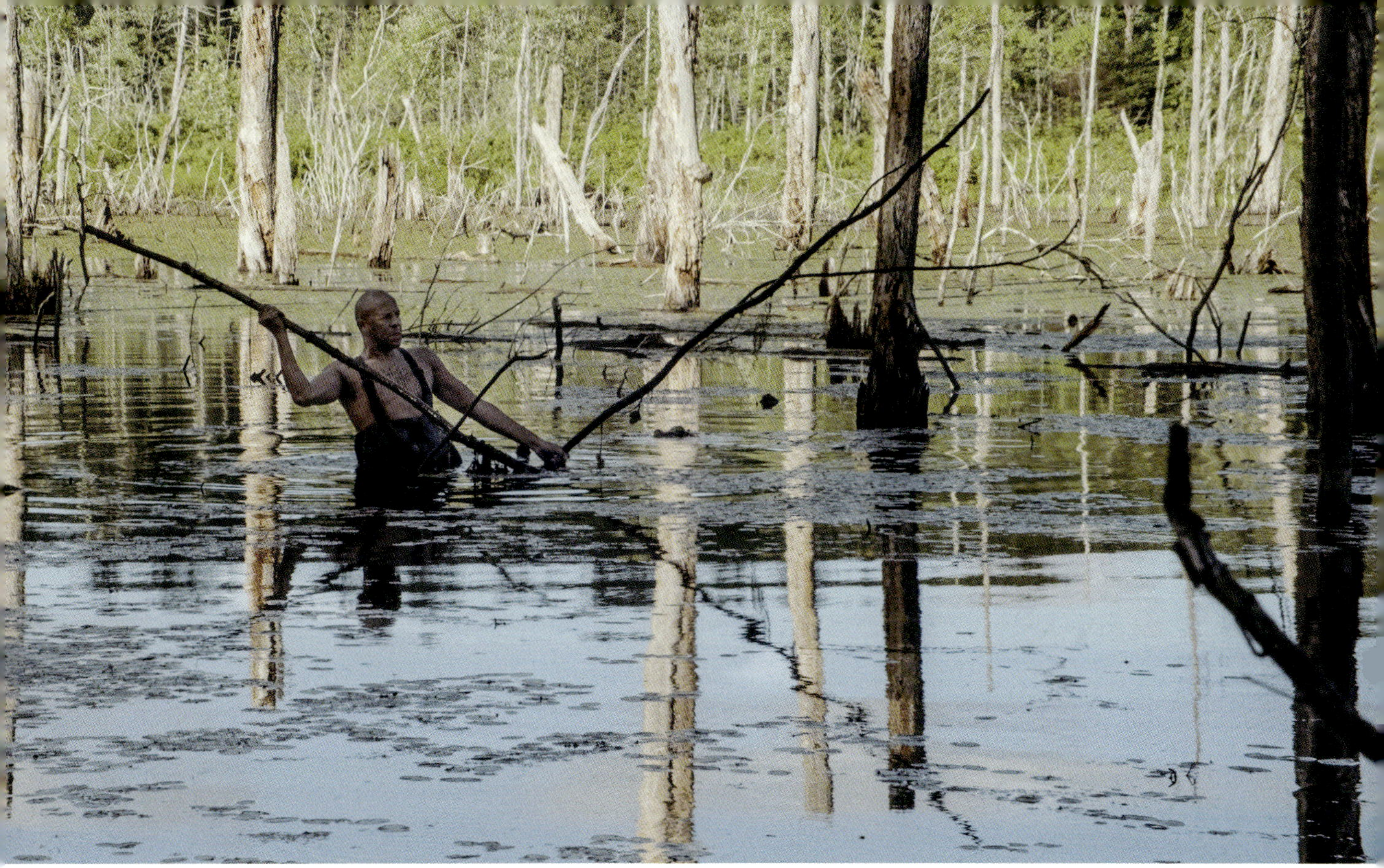

KA   *We've talked a lot about your thoughts on the human relationship to land and water and your desire for humankind to have a less extractive relationship to the planet. But I haven't heard you talk much about putting these ideas into a specific political framework. To what extent do you think this work engages sustainability as a topic?*

AKB   If there's a political dimension in here, it's the proposal that individuals are compelled to behave differently if they perceive the world differently. An artwork can provide alternative ways to feel and see, but I'm not giving you any instructions. Ultimately, the only thing that is sustainable is doing and consuming less.

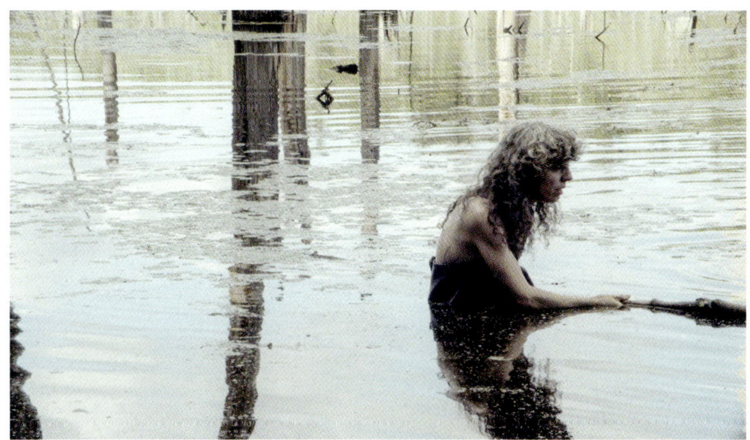

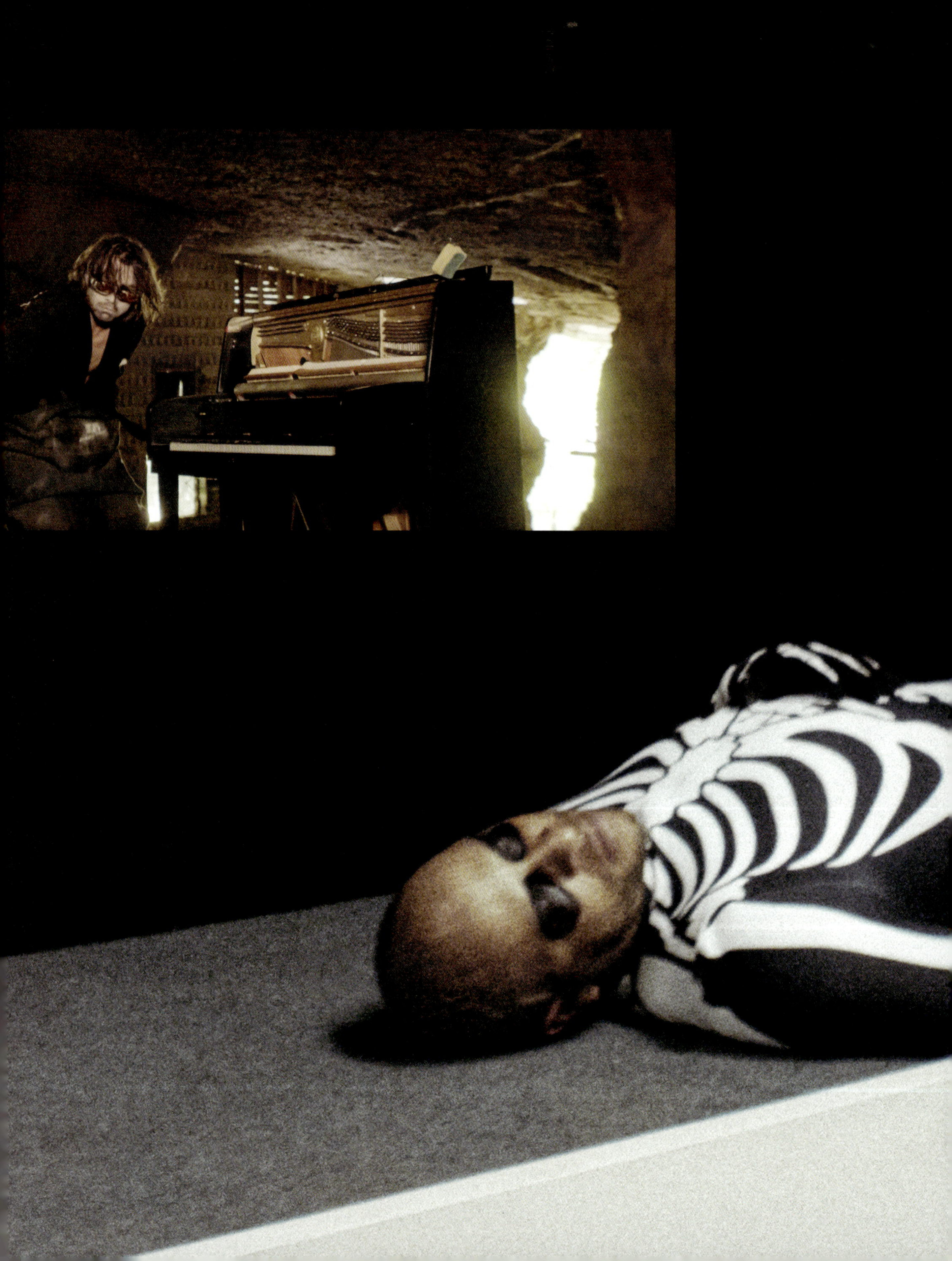

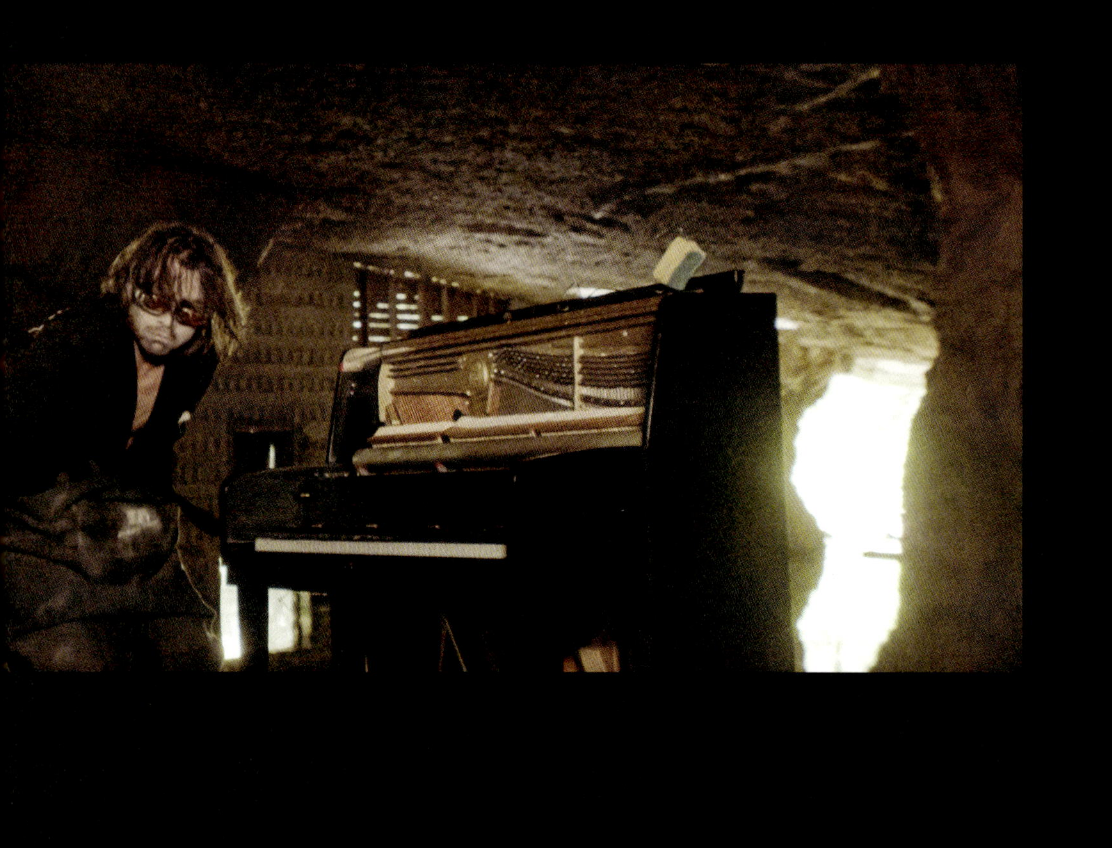

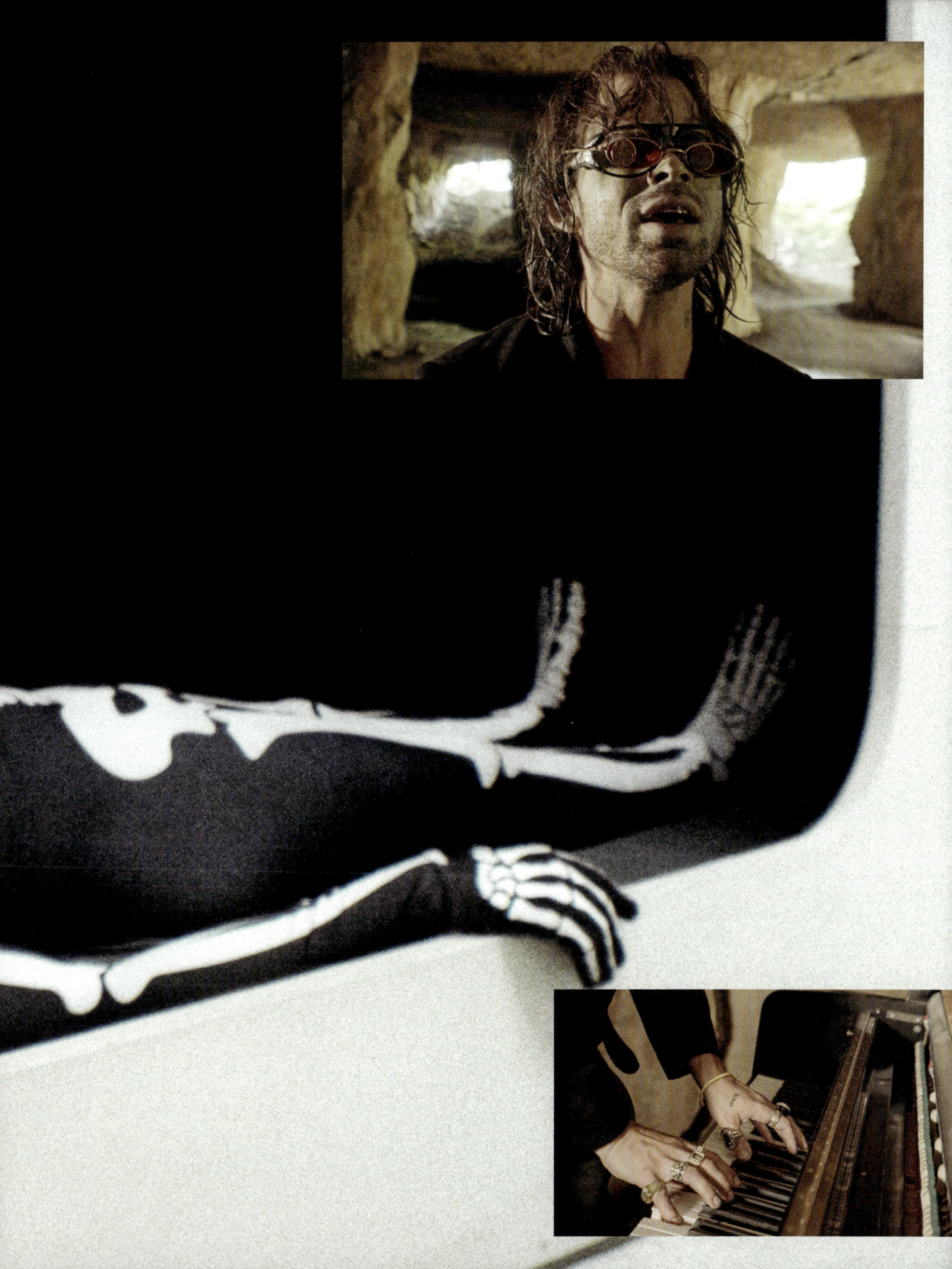

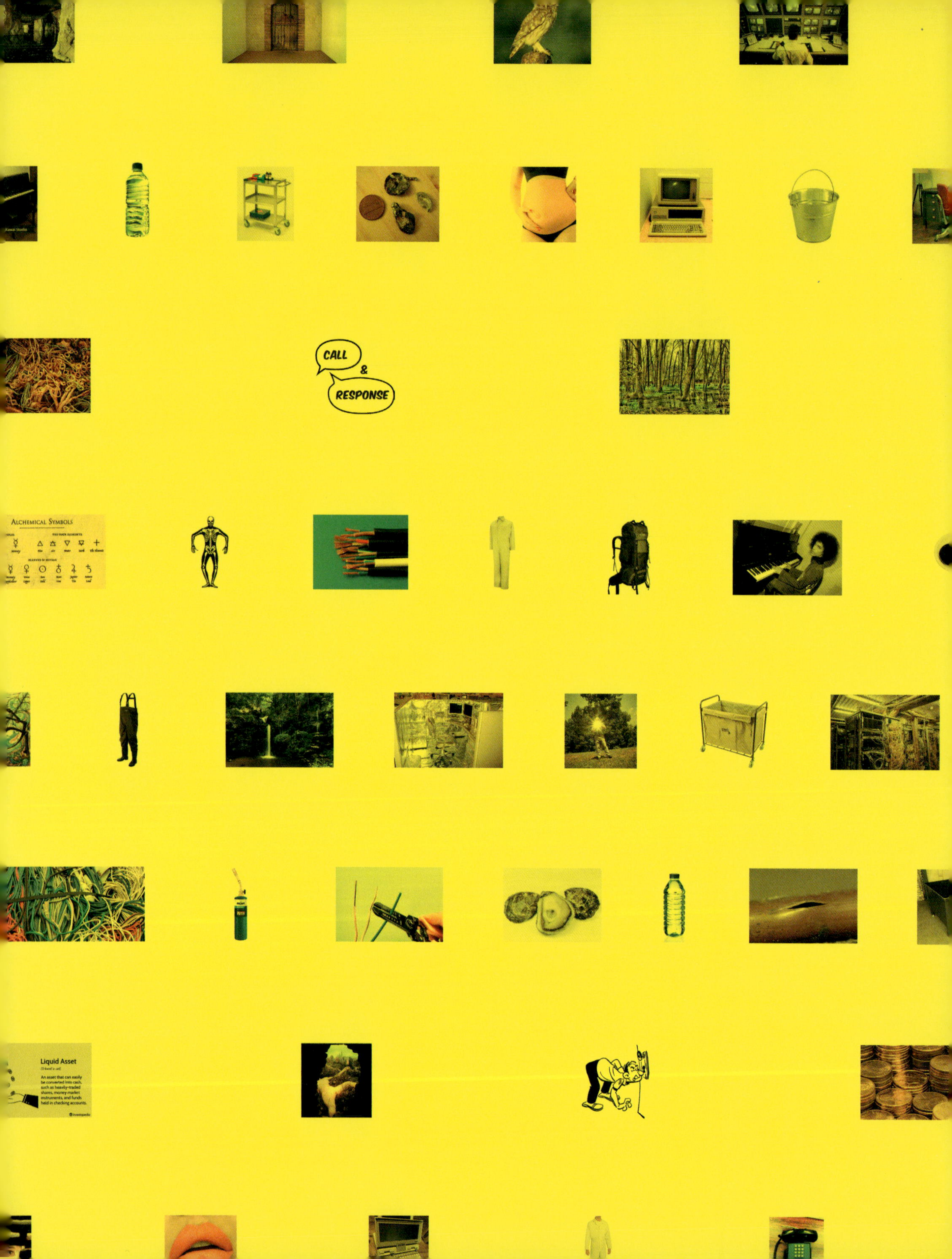
CALL
&
RESPONSE

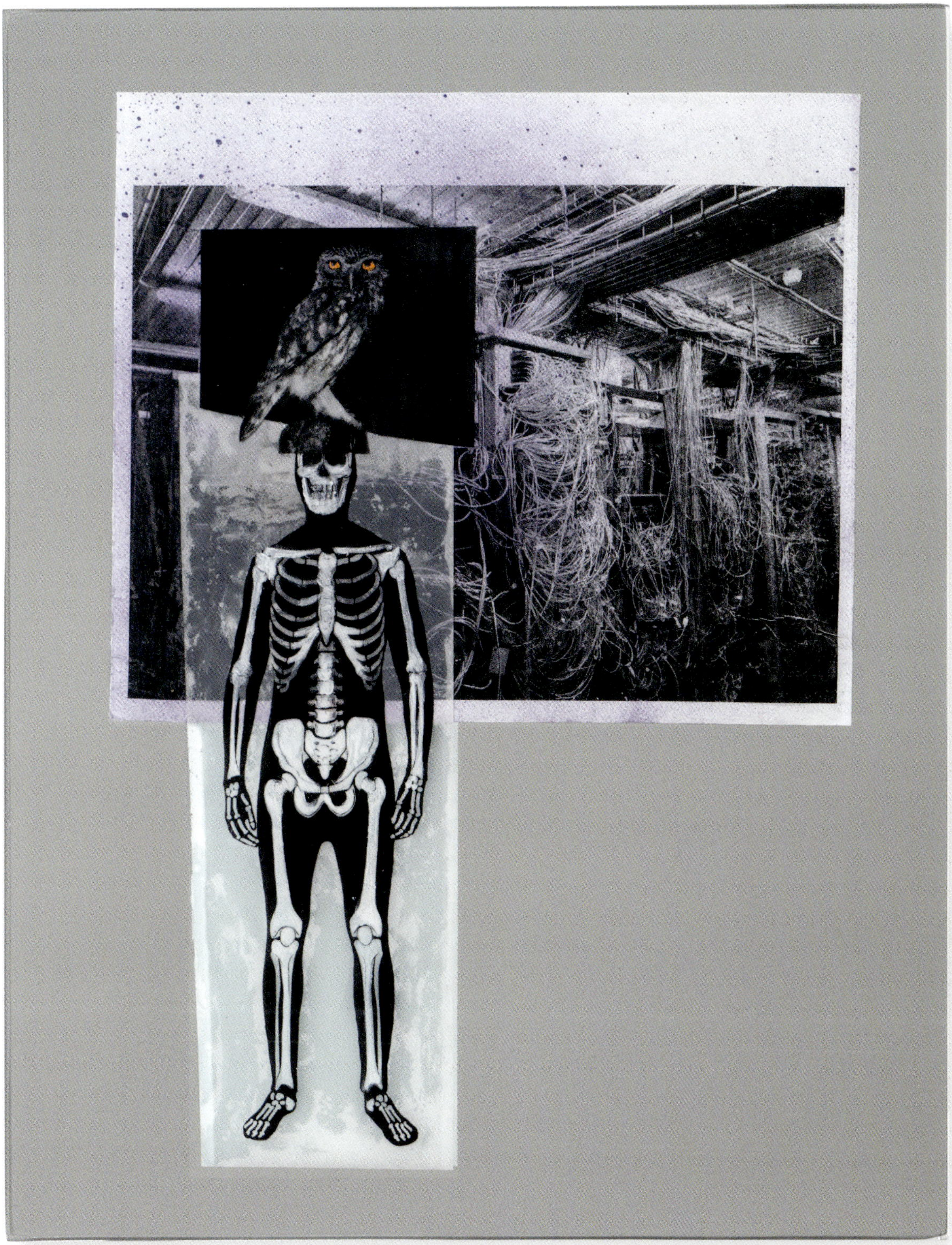

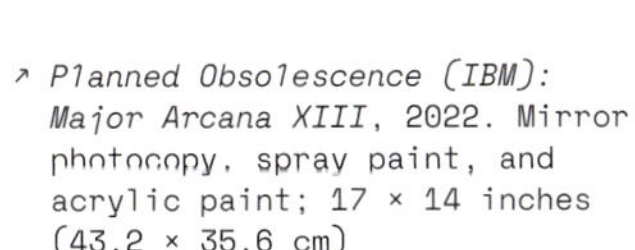

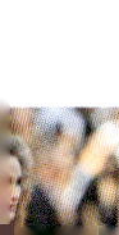

↗ *Planned Obsolescence (IBM):*
Major Arcana XIII, 2022. Mirror,
photocopy, spray paint, and
acrylic paint; 17 × 14 inches
(43.2 × 35.6 cm)

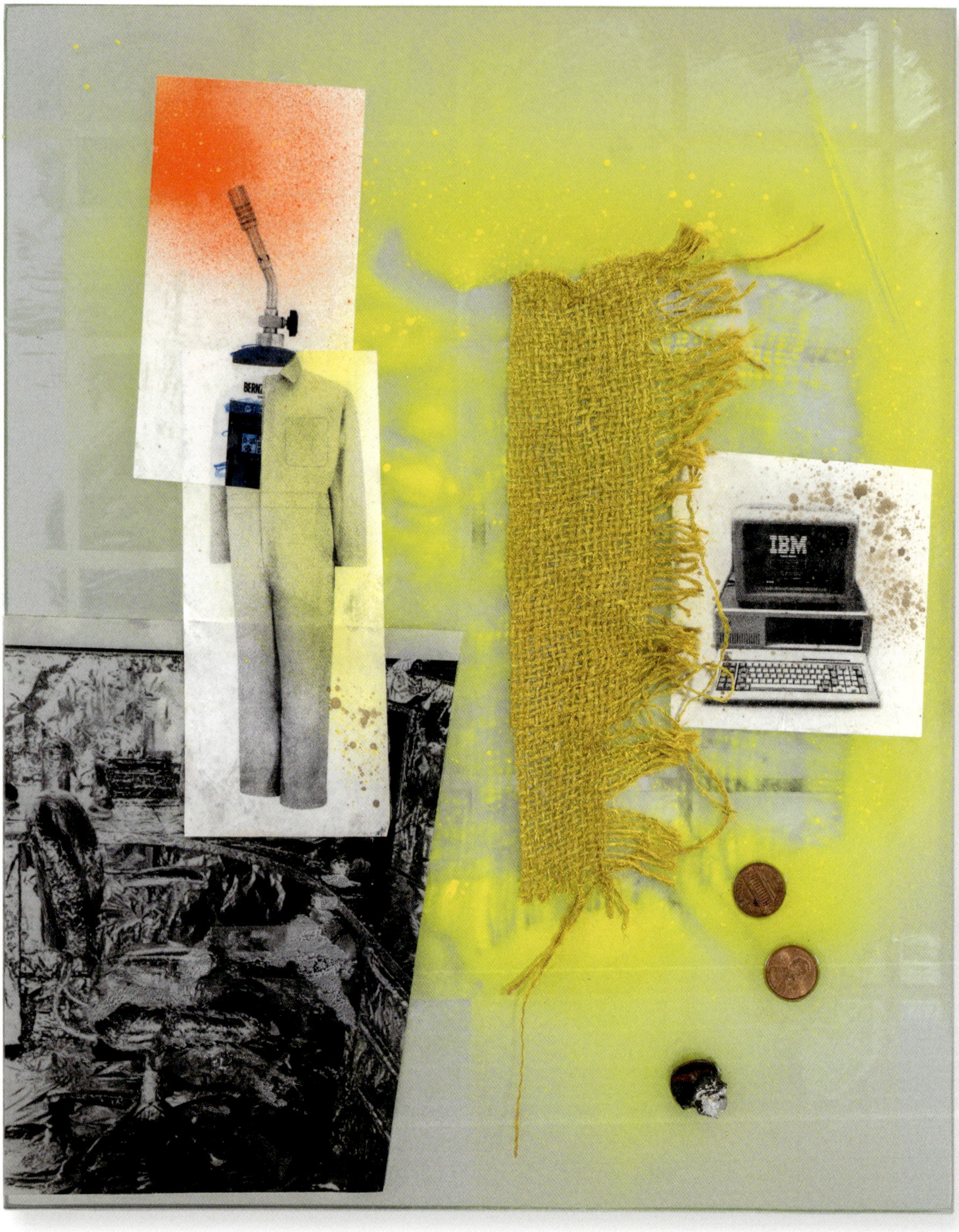

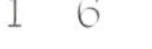

↑ *Eris: Smelter (liquid assets)*,
2022. Etched mirror, photocopy,
spray paint, wax pencil,
pennies, and burlap; 17 ×
14 inches (43.2 × 35.6 cm)

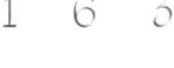

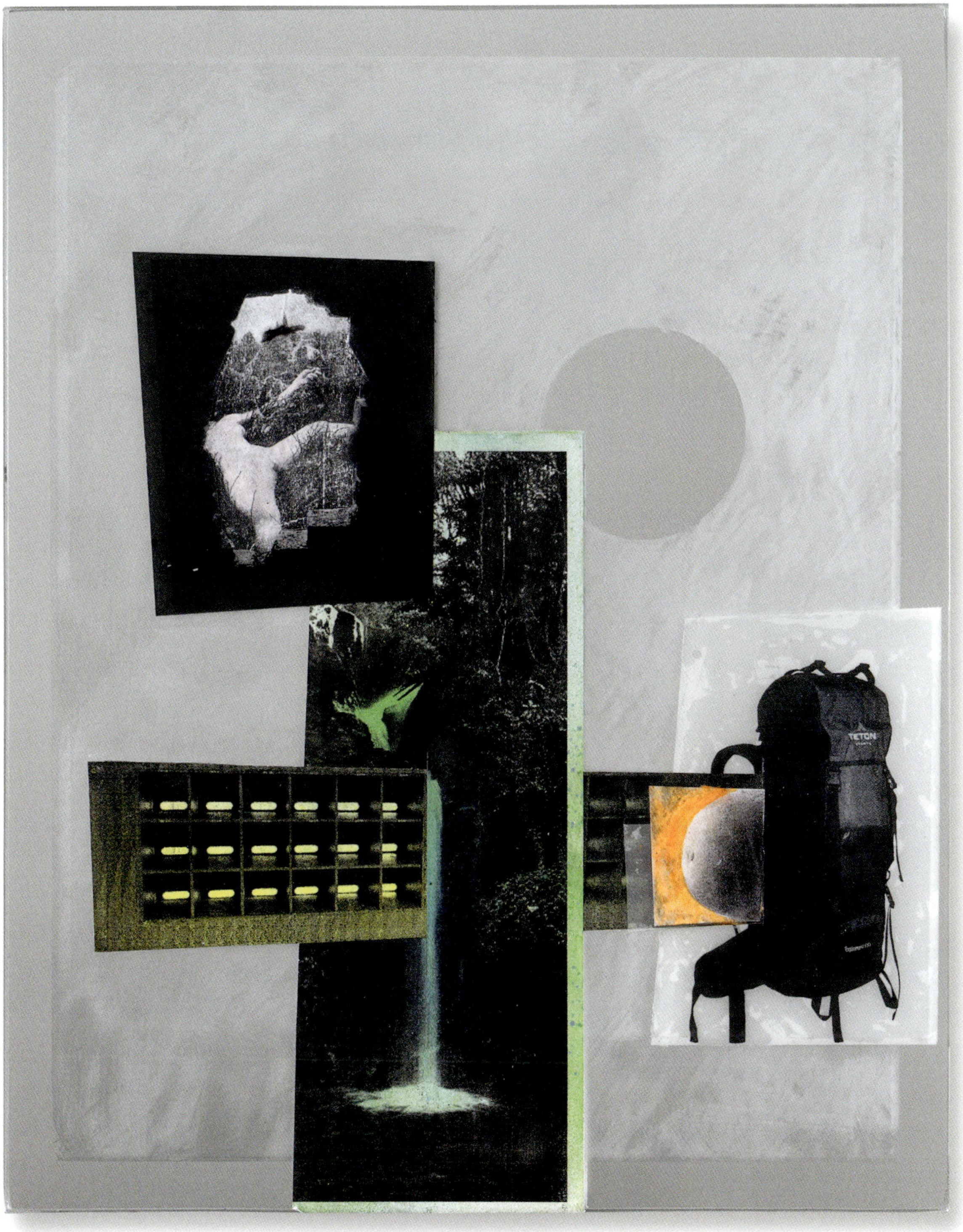

↗ *Pregnant Backpacker: Étant
donnés*, 2022. Etched mirror,
photocopy, spray paint, pencil,
and acrylic paint; 17 × 14
inches (43.2 × 35.6 cm)

Katherine Hubbard for her love, support, and perspective, which are essential to the production of all my creative work.

The extended community of performers who have worked with me on each of the films and are central to animating this epic work—niv Acosta, Kera Armendariz, Nayland Blake, Mia Cenholt-Haulund, Winter Collins, Elias Delate, Macauley Devun, Jack Doroshow, Cyrus Dunham, Nathaniel Flagg, Shannon Funchess, keyon gaskin, Arianna Gil, Jahmal Golden, Marcelo Gutierrez, Katherine Hubbard, NIC Kay, Savannah Knoop, Lauren Maida, Clara Lopez Menendez, Monica Mirabile, Marbles Jumbo Radio, Will Rawls, Lee Relvas, Adee Roberson, Matana Roberts, Jen Rosenblit, A.L. Steiner, Tsige Tafesse, Mariana Valencia, Wren Warner, and Geo Wyex.

The brilliant Geo Wyex for scoring these works and bringing my auditory ideas to life, often exceeding what I imagined. And Quentin Chiappetta, who, in mastering the sound, helps to craft its spatialization for installation.

My studio managers, who provided foundational support in video and installation production over the past decade—Sage Donahue, Delfina Martinez-Pandiani, Peymaan Motevalli-Aliabadi, Celia Nicolson, and Immanuel Williams.

Barbara Schroeder and Karen Kelly of Dancing Foxes Press for their dedicated labor, organization, and wisdom in shepherding this book through the publishing process. Karen Archey for spending many hours in conversation with me, and Cole Graham for his help whittling the transcripts into something printable. And the combined genius of the contributors, Mel Y. Chen, CAConrad, Aruna D'Souza, Megan Hicks, and Simone White. Designers Azi Rad, for her visionary visual translation of *Negative Space*, and Katy Nelson, for evolving it into a beautifully cohesive book.

The many institutions and granting organizations who believed in my vision and whose generous support brought *Negative Space* to completion. The fiscal support of the Creative Capital Visual Arts Grant, the Radcliffe Institute for Advanced Study, the NYSCA/NYFA Fellowship, the Research Foundation of CUNY, and the John Simon Guggenheim Memorial Foundation. The crucial additional resources provided by Matthew Lyons and the Kitchen, New York; Lia Gangitano and Participant Inc, New York; Johanna Burton, Sara O'Keeffe, and the New Museum, New York; Lisa Long and Julia Stoschek Foundation, Düsseldorf, Germany; Vic Brooks and the Experimental Media and Performing Arts Center at Rensselaer Polytechnic Institute, Troy, New York; and Kelly Kivland and the Wexner Center for the Arts, Columbus, Ohio.

Michel Rein, Alice Joubert-Nikolaev, Florent Houel, and the rest of the staff at Michel Rein Gallery—*merci*!

My dad, for sharing a lifetime of environmental awareness and knowledge. And my mother for her unwavering commitment to radical and alternative life-building.

A.K. Burns

The term *visionary* perfectly describes the scope of imagination captured in A.K. Burns's exhibition *Of space we are . . .*, featuring more than a decade of projects that speculate about nothing less than the future of life on Earth. Premiering the Wexner Center–commissioned installation *What is Perverse is Liquid (NS0000)* (2023), the exhibition marks the completion of the remarkable body of work explored in this publication, Burns's epic *Negative Space.*

Conceived as a crucible of artistic experimentation, the Wexner Center for the Arts has pursued a visionary program from its inception, always posing anew the question of what comes next. Serving as The Ohio State University's multidisciplinary laboratory for both exploring and advancing contemporary art, the center is proud to support artists taking bold steps forward in their practices and offer a home to forward-looking audiences in Columbus, Ohio, and the world beyond.

I am thankful for Kelly Kivland, our head of exhibitions, who curated *Of space we are . . .* with much care and attention and in close dialogue with the artist. I would also like to acknowledge the dedicated teams at the Wexner Center who have helped make this exhibition a reality. Behind every practice stands a team of problem-solvers. Expertly installed, the complex *Negative Space* video installations at the core of *Of space we are . . .* benefited from the skilled collaboration of technicians working across multiple departments. We want to thank David Dickas, senior installation manager and head preparator; Stephen Jones, former design engineer; Stephen Trefnoff, former sound engineer; and their teams, who exceeded all expectations for this presentation. We also share our deepest appreciation for Kimberly Kollman, senior registrar and exhibition manager; Nicole Miller, associate registrar; Jonathan Gonzalez, curatorial assistant; and Lynne Pearson, exhibitions coordinator, who kept the many moving parts comprised by *Of space we are . . .* on schedule. I am profoundly grateful to the leadership of Ohio State's Office of Academic Affairs, the Wexner Center Foundation Board of Trustees, and the donors and sponsors whose financial support makes all our exhibition programs possible.

Beyond the Wexner Center, a host of additional farsighted supporters deserve our praise. We extend our heartfelt thanks to Fred and Laura Ruth Bidwell, Gregory R. Miller and Michael Wiener, Sophie Mörner, Shelley Fox Aarons and Philip Aarons, and the private individuals who graciously loaned works to *Of space we are . . . .* And thank you to Michel Rein, Alice Joubert-Nikolaev, Florent Houel, and the staff at Michel Rein Gallery, who have provided Burns with indispensable support. The Wexner Center is sincerely grateful to the National Endowment for the Arts and Shelley Fox Aarons and Philip Aarons for their support of the exhibition and this publication. Lastly, our deepest gratitude goes to A.K. Burns, whose practice continues to challenge the perception of our world today—and onward. We thank her for her trust and engagement with every aspect of this thoughtful collaboration.

Gaëtane Verna, Executive Director, Wexner Center for the Arts

A.K. Burns is an interdisciplinary artist and associate professor in the Department of Art at Hunter College, City University of New York. Working at the nexus of language and materiality, Burns troubles systems that assign value and explores their sociopolitical embodiment. Burns has exhibited internationally, including at 2018's FRONT International, Cleveland, Ohio; the Harvard Art Museums, Cambridge, Massachusetts; Institute of Contemporary Art, University of Pennsylvania, Philadelphia; Julia Stoschek Foundation, Düsseldorf, Germany; MMK Museum of Modern Art, Frankfurt am Main, Germany; New Museum, New York; Palais de Tokyo, Paris; the Portland Institute for Contemporary Art, Portland, Oregon; and the Wexner Center for the Arts, Columbus, Ohio. Burns was a founding member of W.A.G.E. (Working Artists in the Greater Economy), a nonprofit artists' advocacy group. *Community Action Center* (2010), a video created in collaboration with A.L. Steiner, has screened internationally, including at the Tate, London; and the Museum of Modern Art, New York. Burns is a 2023 Berlin Prize Fellow at the American Academy in Berlin; a 2021 Guggenheim Fellow; a 2016 Radcliffe Fellow at Harvard University, Cambridge, Massachusetts; and a 2015 Creative Capital Foundation Visual Arts Award recipient.

Karen Archey is curator of contemporary art at Stedelijk Museum Amsterdam, where she has organized major exhibitions of artists including Hito Steyerl, Rineke Dijkstra, and Metahaven, as well as the group exhibition *Freedom of Movement: The 2018 Municipal Art Acquisitions*. Archey has commissioned performance works by CFGNY, Alicia Frankovich, Ann Hirsch, Jennifer Tee, and Nora Turato. Archey also heads the museum's research initiative on time-based media. Formerly, Archey worked as an independent curator, editor, and art critic, writing for publications such as *Artforum* and *Frieze*. In 2014, she coorganized, with Robin Peckham, the exhibition *Art Post-Internet* at Ullens Center for Contemporary Art, Beijing. In 2015, Archey was awarded an Andy Warhol Foundation Arts Writers Grant. She is author of the book *After Institutions* (Floating Opera Press, 2022).

Mel Y. Chen is the Richard and Rhoda Goldman Distinguished Chair of Undergraduate and Interdisciplinary Studies, an associate professor of gender and women's studies, and the director of the Center for the Study of Sexual Culture at the University of California, Berkeley. Chen is the author of *Intoxicated: Chemical Intimacies of Race and Disability in Empire* (Duke University Press, forthcoming 2023) and *Animacies: Biopolitics, Racial Mattering, and Queer Affect* (Duke University Press, 2012 Alan Bray Award); they are also coeditor of *Crip Genealogies* (Duke University Press, forthcoming 2023). Their writing can be found in journals, exhibition catalogues, and scholarly anthologies. Chen coedits the book series *Anima* (Duke University Press) and is a board member of the Queer Women of Color Media Arts Project and part of a queer/trans of color arts collective in the San Francisco Bay Area.

CAConrad has worked with the ancient technologies of poetry and ritual since 1975. They are the author of nine books, including *AMANDA*

PARADISE: Resurrect Extinct Vibration (Wave Books, 2021), which won
the 2022 PEN Josephine Miles Award. They received a 2022 Ruth Lilly
Poetry Prize, a Creative Capital grant, a Pew Fellowship, and a Lambda
Award. They exhibited poems as art objects at recent solo shows in
Spain and Portugal, and their play *The Obituary Show* was made into
a film in 2022 by Augusto Cascales. UK Penguin published two of their
books in 2023, and *Listen to the Golden Boomerang Return*, a new
collection of poetry, is forthcoming from Wave Books in 2024.

Aruna D'Souza is a writer whose work appears regularly in the *New
York Times* and *4Columns*, among other publications. Her most recent
editorial project is Linda Nochlin's *Making It Modern: Essays on the
Art of the Now* (Thames & Hudson, 2022). She is editor of Lorraine
O'Grady's *Writing in Space 1973–2018* (Duke University Press, 2020) and
co-curator of the 2021 retrospective of O'Grady's work *Both/And* at the
Brooklyn Museum. Her book *Whitewalling: Art, Race, and Protest in 3
Acts* (Badlands Unlimited) was named one of the best art books of 2018
by the *New York Times*. She is the recipient of the 2021 Rabkin Prize for
art journalism and a 2019 Andy Warhol Foundation Art Writers Grant.
In 2022, she was the Edmond J. Safra Visiting Professor at the National
Gallery of Art, Washington, DC, and in 2022–23 was named the W. W.
Corcoran Professor of Social Engagement at the Corcoran School of Art,
George Washington University, Washington, DC.

Megan Hicks uses archaeology to study how communities have stew-
arded their local ecologies over long periods of time and to explore the
influences and impacts of colonial and capitalist market-oriented econ-
omies upon them. She also collaborates with communities to harness
archaeological tools and activist methodologies for sovereignty, land protection, self-determination, and abolition. Most of Hicks's work is focused
on the North Atlantic and North America. Hicks is currently an assistant
professor in the Department of Anthropology at Hunter College, City
University of New York, where she teaches courses including Archaeology
of Colonialism, Gender in Archaeology, and Urban Archaeology.

Simone White is the author of *or, on being the other woman* (Duke
University Press, 2022), *Dear Angel of Death* (Ugly Duckling Presse,
2018), *Of Being Dispersed* (Futurepoem, 2016), *House Envy of All the
World* (Factory School, 2010), the poetry chapbook *Unrest* (Ugly Duckling
Presse, 2013), and, with Kim Thomas, the chapbook *Dolly* (Q Ave, 2008).
Her poetry and prose have been featured in *Artforum, e-flux, Harper's
Magazine, BOMB Magazine, Chicago Review*, and the *New York Times
Book Review*. White's honors include the 2023 Dorothea Tanning Award
from the Foundation for Contemporary Arts, a 2021 Creative Capital
Award, a 2017 Whiting Award in Poetry, Cave Canem Foundation fellow-
ships, and recognition as a New American Poet for the Poetry Society of
America in 2013. She is the Stephen M. Gorn Family Assistant Professor
of English at the University of Pennsylvania and serves on the faculty of
the Milton Avery Graduate School of the Arts at Bard College.

This book was published on the occasion of the exhibition *A.K. Burns: Of space we are…*, on view at the Wexner Center for the Arts, Columbus, Ohio, February 11–July 9, 2023, and curated by Kelly Kivland, head of exhibitions, with assistance by Jonathan Gonzalez, curatorial assistant, and Cole J. Graham, curatorial intern.

Exhibition support was generously provided by the National Endowment for the Arts and Shelley Fox Aarons and Philip Aarons; organizational support for the exhibition was provided by Michel Rein, Paris/Brussels. The Wexner Center's winter/spring exhibitions were made possible by Cardinal Health, Karen R. Lane, and Nancy and Dave Gill. The center's 2022–23 exhibition season was made possible by Bill and Sheila Lambert, The Andy Warhol Foundation for the Visual Arts, Carol and David Aronowitz, Crane Family Foundation, and Mike and Paige Crane. Free galleries are made possible by American Electric Power Foundation, Adam Flatto, Mary and C. Robert Kidder, Bill and Sheila Lambert, CoverMyMeds, and PNC Foundation. Wexner Center programs are made possible by Greater Columbus Arts Council, The Wexner Family, National Endowment for the Arts, Ohio Arts Council, L Brands Foundation, and The Columbus Foundation.

Generous support for this publication was provided by the John Simon Guggenheim Memorial Foundation; The Wexner Center for the Arts; Michel Rein Gallery, Paris/Brussels; The Research Foundation of CUNY; and the 2022–2023 Presidential Faculty Advancement Award at Hunter CUNY.

Edited by Karen Kelly and Barbara Schroeder

Editorial assistance on the conversations by Cole Graham

Proofreading by James Camp

Art Direction: Azi Rad

Design: Katy Nelson and A.K. Burns

This book is typeset in Ivar and Basel Grotesk and printed on Arctic volume white 130 gsm and Munken polar rough 300 gsm.

Printed and bound by Graphius, Ghent, Belgium

Published in 2023 by Dancing Foxes Press and Wexner Center for the Arts

ISBN: 978-1-954947-06-1
Cataloging-in-publication data is on file with the Library of Congress.

Dancing Foxes Press
16 Lefferts Place
Brooklyn, NY 11238
dfpress.us

Distributed in the United States and Canada by Distributed Art Publishers
artbook.com

List of Works

A Smeary Spot (NS0), 2015
Four-channel video installation, with three primary channels high-definition projected video (color, six-channel sound; 53 min.) and single-channel standard-definition (black-and-white, silent, 4 min.) on box monitor
Three free-standing screens, box monitor, rolling office chairs, black walls, black carpet, takeaway poster (script)
Dimensions variable

Living Room (NS00), 2017
Two-channel high-definition video installation (color, sound, 36 min.)
Projection wall, sheet of drywall, stripped couch frame, plastic couch cover, LED strip lighting, dirt, foil-wrapped hard candy, urethane resin, topping soil, epoxy resin, off-white carpet, walls with studs exposed
Dimensions variable

Leave No Trace (NS000), 2019
Five-channel high-definition video installation (color, sound, 28 min.)
Projection cube, faux skull, used tires, and ratchet straps
Dimensions variable

What is Perverse is Liquid (NS0000), 2023
Three-channel video high-definition video installation (color, 5.1 sound, 35 min.)
Two projection screens, free-standing projection wall, plexiglass, sandbags, sand, rubber pool liner, and pennies
Dimensions variable

Front cover: Photo taken during Burns's trip to southern Utah in 2012 that initiated *Negative Space: Untitled (grain)*, 2012. C-print, 30 × 44 inches (76.2 × 111.8 cm)

Back cover: Photo taken during Burns's trip to southern Utah in 2012 that initiated *Negative Space: Untitled (grain)*, 2012. C-print, 30 × 44 inches (76.2 × 111.8 cm). Text excerpted from Cole Graham, *A.K. Burns: Of space we are…*, exhibition brochure (Columbus, OH: Wexner Center for the Arts, 2023).

Interior cover, pages 20–21, 24, 32–53: Stills from *A Smeary Spot (NS0)*, 2015. Four-channel HD video (color, sound, 53 min.)

Pages 54, 88, 124, 160: *Research Palette (Internet Search)*, 2014–22. Digital collage designed for this publication

Pages 58–59, 68 (top), 72–73: Production stills from *Living Room (NS00)*, 2017. Photo: Eden Batki

Pages 62, 68 (bottom), 69, 70–71, 74–85, 86 (inset): Stills from *Living Room (NS00)*, 2017. Two-channel HD video (color, sound); 36 min.

Pages 86–87: Production stills from *Living Room (NS00)*, 2017. Photo: Lauryn Seigel

Pages 92–93: Production stills from *Leave No Trace (NS000)*, 2019. Photo: Mick Bello

Pages 98, 104–23: Stills from *Leave No Trace (NS000)*, 2019. Five-channel HD video (color, sound, 28 min.)

Page 128–29, 134, 140–59: Stills from *What is Perverse is Liquid (NS0000)*, 2023. Three-channel HD video (color, 5.1 sound, 35 min.)

Additional Photo Credits

Pages 26, 28–29, 65, 101, 102–3: Photo by Alwin Lay, courtesy the artist and Julia Stoschek Foundation, Düsseldorf, Germany

Page 30, 31 (top): Photo by Evan La Londe, courtesy the artist and Portland Institute of Contemporary Art, Portland, Oregon

Page 31 (bottom left and right): Photo by Chris Austin, courtesy the artist and Participant Inc, New York

Pages 55, 56, 57, 89, 90, 91, 125, 126, 127: Photo by Sean Fader. Courtesy the artist and Callicoon Fine Arts, New York

Page 64 (left and right): Photo by Maris Hutchinson/EPW Studio, courtesy the artist and New Museum, New York

Pages 66–67: Photo by Constance Mensh, courtesy the artist and Institute of Contemporary Art, Philadelphia, 2018

Page 100: Photo by A.K. Burns, courtesy the artist

Page 137, 138–39: Photo by Stephen Takacs, courtesy of the artist and Wexner Center for the Arts, Columbus, Ohio

Printed in Belgium